TREASON IN THE TWENTIETH CENTURY

CONTENTS

CONTENTS

Pun. Purch, 2-14-'63

APR 8 1963

FIRST AMERICAN EDITION 1963

© 1961 by Macdonald & Co. (Publishers) Ltd.

Originally published in Germany under the title *Der Verrat im XX Jahrhundert.*

Library of Congress Catalog
Card Number: 62-10962

MANUFACTURED IN THE UNITED STATES OF AMERICA

TREASON IN
THE TWENTIETH
CENTURY

MARGRET BOVERI

Translated by Jonathan Steinberg

G. P. Putnam's Sons   *New York*

Other Works by the Same Author

Sir Edward Grey and the Foreign Office, Series of Political Science, Rothschild, Berlin, 1933.

Mediterranean Cross Currents, Atlantis-Verlag, Berlin-Zurich, 1936, Oxford University Press, 1938.

From Minaret to Pipeline, Atlantis-Verlag, Berlin-Zurich, 1938, Oxford University Press, 1939.

An American Primer for Grown-up Germans, Minerva Verlag, Berlin, Badischer Verlag, Freiburg, 1946.

The Diplomat Before the Court, Minerva Verlag, Berlin. 1948.

Articles in monthlies and periodicals, especially on politics, during the Second World War and the Cold War.

ILLUSTRATIONS

following page 178

INTRODUCTION

We are living in confusing times and the word treason plays an important role in the confusion. Whole nations are divided by doubts, mistrust and open hostility. The human reaction to this state of affairs is very similar all over the world, but the different conflicts peculiar to different countries are so dissimilar that the parallels are often overlooked. Different generations living in our century experienced the manifestations of this confusion at different times and in different forms. There are Frenchmen living even today who went through the furious controversies of the Dreyfus Case, whereas the present French generation is divided over the OAS. The British, although much less subject to extreme emotions in politics, were so upset and divided about the Suez affair that for some families it proved impossible to spend the following Christmas holidays in peace together. The Americans, in the twenties, were up in arms against each other over the Sacco and Vanzetti case, in the fifties over Hiss, Chambers and McCarthy. All these cases live on in a kind of national subconsciousness after they seem to be ended. They crop up when nobody thinks of them and may connect an old man turned conservative with the deeds of his youth when he was a radical.

My own first encounter with this confusion occurred a few years after the end of the First World War. I was walking with a friend and was shocked about the news that Walter Rathenau, the German Foreign Minister, had just been murdered. My friend said: "A bullet was much too good for this swine [Schweinehund]." It was only years later that I was able to understand clearly what took place on that sunny day between two girls not long out of school, unable really to judge political events and therefore reacting as it was natural to react in their respective homes.

Rathenau, a Jew, was one of the men who took over after the German defeat and the breakdown of the imperial government. He was one of the so-called "Erfüllungspolitiker," the men who agreed to sign the Treaty of Versailles although they knew that it would not be possible to fulfill its financial stipulations, and though they believed its war-guilt clause to be wrong. They took over in the midst of civil war and anarchy, tried to save what they could of the old substance and make the best of a desperate situation.

I was in favor of our new republican form of government and aghast at the murder of one of its chief representatives. My friend, who later risked imprisonment by hiding a Jew in her house, came from a different sphere of life. Her father, a very fine old gentleman, reactivated as an officer during the war, had been attacked by a group of returning soldiers from the defeated army. They had torn off his uniform and beaten him to the ground. For him and his family these soldiers were a revolutionary rabble and the people who swept into government on the wave of the socialist mob were trampling the honor of the country in the mud just as the uniform of the white-haired old colonel had been trampled on. For them Rathenau was evil-incarnate, for me he was an intelligent and courageous man of the modern age. At the time I was quite sure I was right, and my friend entirely wrong. It took years of Hitler and war and defeat for her to learn that there was much to be said for the democratic, bourgeois Weimar Republic which she had despised during the twenties, as it did for me to understand that the men who refused to sign the Versailles Treaty were not merely obtuse reactionaries, but knew that there is a line beyond which submitting to the so-called inevitable in order to alleviate momentary hardship and suffering may entail giving up an inner core of self-esteem without which neither a person nor a country can exist.

The divisions of my own country under Hitler and the conflicts I observed in other parts of the world—from Sweden, during the first Finnish war and the German invasion of Denmark and Norway; in the United States, while public opinion was divided between the proponents of aid for the Allies and the "America Firsters"—enabled me personally to observe the reasons for such internal conflicts. But though I had written some essays on individual treason cases, it was only after I was asked to write a book on the theme as a whole that the enormity of the problem became apparent to me. Would I be able to find a common denominator in the motivation of personalities utterly dissimilar in character and in their individual actions? Would it be possible to arrive at a principle by which to judge the verdicts meted out during the last decades?

I set out on my task in an entirely empirical way, and without forming a theory in advance. I took the cases as they presented themselves, whether I personally believed the individual persons accused and condemned to have been traitors or not, whether they seemed to be driven only by external circumstances, even by opportunism, or by their living conscience, whether they operated from inside or from outside their home-country. Some critics have taken me to task for lumping together the major and the minor, the good and the bad, regardless of their place in what is morally, intellectually and psychologically a hierarchy of human beings. They believe that it tends to augment the confusion mentioned above. However, I believe that it serves to bring the confusion into full consciousness as a first step in overcoming it.

Thus the title of the book is not of my own making. It is the word which may in future times be seen to characterize an era that brought it into mass use as well as misuse. It has not only its political and juridical aspects, but belongs in the domain of psychologists, sociologists, theologists. To them and their deliberations I offer a mass of source material. What I myself learned while studying the implications of so many human histories was the possible existence of opposite truths. The rediscovery of the *coincidentia oppositorum,* a philosophical problem known in the Middle Ages and forgotten for centuries, poses in my opinion one of the important tasks of our time: to find the hidden relationships between the opposites in various fields of human endeavor. By showing some of the currents which influence our communal and political life of today and tomorrow, my book may have its use in strengthening an awareness for the urgency of this task.

ACKNOWLEDGMENTS

Several quotations are made in the text and the publishers wish to thank the following for permission to use them: Cassell & Co. Ltd. and McClelland & Stewart Ltd. of Toronto for permission to quote from *Speeches* by Sir Winston Churchill, and Cassell & Co. Ltd. for permission to quote from *The Second World War* by Sir Winston Churchill; the Thomas Y. Crowell Company of New York for permission to quote from Nathaniel Weyl's *The Battle Against Disloyalty;* Macmillan & Co. Ltd. for permission to quote from *The Meaning of Treason* by Rebecca West; Don Cook for permission to quote from an article in the New York *Herald Tribune* (European Edition); and the Navy League for permission to quote from *The Navy.*

The publishers also wish to thank Mosaik Verlag of Frankfurt for permission to reproduce illustrations 9–17.

PART I

The Landscape of Treason

1. TREASON—A DAILY OCCURRENCE

IN NORWAY, in the year 1945, an almost deaf old man entered a hospital under police protection. No one spoke to him. The three nurses attending him spilled his coffee and his soup intentionally. He tried to explain. He tried to make them understand that he had not killed anybody nor stolen anything nor set a house on fire. They did not listen to him and refused to answer his questions. A year later, in a psychiatric clinic, he had learned a little more.

"I came here with the police. I am a prisoner. I am a traitor to my country, you see." Asked by the senior Sister how he had become involved in such a disgrace, he said, "It doesn't matter."

"It doesn't matter." Knut Hamsun, the famous Norwegian poet, was eighty-five years old when he said that. For him, crimes had always meant definite acts such as murder, theft or arson In using the defiant words, "I am a traitor to my country, you see," he resembled a child who has just discovered something he thinks the adults do not yet know. Did he really know what he was saying? Could Knut Hamsun conceivably not know what he had done and yet be the author of many books in which he expressed such insight into the potentialities of human character? Was he merely pretending? In any event, his behavior revealed that something unheard of had happened to him. The very man who once wept bitterly because he was so homesick as an immigrant in America had now, it was claimed, betrayed his country. The same Knut Hamsun who believed that through his work as a writer he had demonstrated his love for Norway, had indeed exalted it above all other countries, was now a traitor.

Unlike Knut Hamsun, we can no longer say, "It doesn't matter"; for us treason has become a concept which permeates

5

every day of our lives. Treason embraces our lives, as if it had formed its own terrible and secret realm on a plane which does not fit the older categories: peoples, nations, constitutions and communities of belief. Treason somehow interpenetrates them all, destroying or transforming them. The meaning of treason changes as the wheel of history turns. Men, hanged yesterday as traitors, are today's heroes and martyrs. Though the interpretation changes, treason stays with us, as if it were a shadow cast by the flickering lights of our era. We meet it in our daily newspapers, in the courtrooms, and at all levels of public administration. It has become part of the vocabulary of the politician. The first chancellor of the West German Federal Republic brands as fools or traitors those who advocate a policy other than his own. Kurt Schumacher, the first leader of the Opposition, when he called Adenauer the Chancellor of the Allies, was implying a form of treason. In the American election campaign of 1952, a group in the Republican party called the Democratic party "The Party of Treason," and made the charge that the two decades of Democratic administrations had been "twenty years of treason."

Treason's threatening shadow falls on the universities, the schools, the families and even the refugee camps. A West Berlin schoolboy may not exchange letters with an old school friend if the latter lives in the East Zone. An atomic physicist working for the government dare not discuss certain topics with his colleagues at a scientific colloquium, even if his fellow scientists know the subjects quite as well as he does, because he might color his presentation ever so slightly as a result of his secret research. His colleagues might be able to guess from the way in which he discussed the subjects what sort of secret matters were being developed.

Once the traitor was just an individual, a solitary figure. Today, though individual traitors still exist, the group has replaced the single man in importance. Behind the individual, in the shadows near him, in front of him acting as his cover, there is the group, the cell or the fifth column. In 1946 *Time* magazine

6

spoke of the millions all over the world whose aim it was to destroy the institutions under which they lived. "In the twentieth century," *Time* wrote, "treason has become a profession, and its modern form is the betrayal of ideas."

To speak of millions is not the exaggeration it may seem. In 1946, as part of the purge of collaborators in France, of more than 500,000 men and women arrested on suspicion of treason, 160,000 were brought to trial. According to an American estimate, 100,000 Frenchmen fell as victims of the Liberation—considerably more dead than France had suffered on the battlefields and in prison camps. In Belgium there were 60,000 cases and investigations; in Holland, 130,000. "Security" laws have now replaced such purges as the Western world's major prophylactic measures, but the scale of operations has not shrunk. In the United States during the Truman Administration, 570 civil servants were dismissed and 2,478 were forced to resign. In the first two years of the Eisenhower Administration over 8,000 more civil servants left the government. In England the number of persons in responsible positions about whose reliability "legitimate doubt" was said to exist increased from an original 3,000 to over 10,000 in 1954.

The American security system reaches beyond the millions of civil servants. All employees and workers in industries engaged in Army, Navy or Air Force projects must be "cleared." University professors, recipients of state grants for research, primary schoolteachers and countless others must undergo clearance examinations at various points in their careers. In "sensitive" jobs the individual can be made responsible for his family or be found "guilty by association." Mothers, husbands, wives, mothers-in-law or aunts can be the cause of dismissal for someone under scrutiny. Relatives who have the misfortune to live behind the Iron Curtain have spoiled many a promising career.

Today the traitor or potential traitor suffers more than punishment. He faces possible exclusion from the community to which he belongs. The present time has seen a revival of the ancient practices of ostracism and banishment, with one new feature unknown to the ancients. The ancient peoples banished the man, or at most, the clique of plotters or political opponents. Modern states deport or exterminate groups just because they are who they are. The great landowner in East Prussia simply loses the right to exist under a Communist regime. Under the Nazis, Jews as Jews were exterminated. An American civil servant may lose his job because his father-in-law once published a radical newspaper or because he supported the Left in the Spanish Civil War. The significant feature of the contemporary form of banishment en masse is that some relative standard of values has been set up and given the status of an absolute, according to which certain classes of people lose all rights and can be disposed of summarily. Under the Eisenhower Administration, for example, a proposal was debated to make all American Communists stateless.

America, more than any other Western country, has suffered a profound crisis of confidence in the last four decades. The pendulum has swung from unsuspecting confidence to hysterical suspicion with remarkable violence and speed. During the 1920's, Communists and Socialists (apart from the famous "Red Scare" of the Wilson Administration) enjoyed a period of benevolent toleration. During the 1930's, it became "chic" in the expensive flats of New York millionaires to sympathize demonstratively with the Reds. It was the era of the so-called "Parlor Pinks." In colleges and universities it was almost a matter of intellectual honor to be Left Wing. The student generation of the 1930's to which Alger Hiss belonged had been young during the self-satisfied, reactionary 1920's. Appalled by the destructive effects of the economic collapse, it saw in Roosevelt and his New Deal the opening phase of a gigantic social revolution. For the first time in American history, scholars and intellectuals enjoyed the favor of those in high places and found positive responses to their schemes and ideas almost everywhere. Without disagreeable detours through political apprenticeships, they went directly to Washington. Many of them came from the Harvard Law School, where reigned the unconditional liberalism of Justices

8

Holmes, Brandeis and Frankfurter—men who had fought for freedom of speech, even unpleasantly radical speech.

How could Roosevelt be expected to believe the disturbing reports which reached him about his "bright young men"? They were his admirers, his solid supporters, and some were high officials in his administration. Could such young men, his friends and disciples, be capable of committing treason? In 1939, Undersecretary of State Adolf A. Berle handed him a list of names of important civil servants under suspicion of disloyalty. After reading through the names, Roosevelt laughed.

Whether one considers Roosevelt's attitude harmless, frivolous or dangerously irresponsible, one must concede that it contributed materially to the development of a fierce reaction, which culminated in "McCarthyism." McCarthy and his supporters genuinely saw every "Egghead" as a potential traitor. It was through their persistence that the co-creator of the atomic bomb was excluded from the subsequent developments in nuclear technique and publicly branded as disloyal. Americans, once convinced of the reality of some evil, can be implacable in their attempts to root out that evil. They set out to purify their society from the evils of Communism and subversion by sifting everyone through a mesh of objective tests, which would presumably separate the unconditionally loyal from the doubtful. The mesh of the sieve was at first so fine that grotesque situations arose and some true patriots found themselves among the security risks—a state of affairs with which the second part of this inquiry will deal.

There are many different regions and neighborhoods in what we are calling the Landscape of Treason. To chart and label them accurately it is necessary to point out that the French scarcely know the security phobia in its contemporary guise.* Possibly the anti-Vichy purges exhausted the French spirit. There are, after all, a great many French Communists. Some

---

*In fact, since these words were written, they have become acquainted with it in another, even more fantastic form, that of the Right-Wing extremists of the neo-Fascist, militarist or "*Algérie Française*" movements.

are prominent; some are highly honored and respected figures. Their Communism is certainly no secret. It may well be that their very numbers and prominence make it difficult for anyone to doubt their "Frenchness," at least for the moment. The English, on the other hand, know the problem well, although in a less virulent subspecies than the American, and they handle it in a calmer manner. Since Communism in England during the 1920's and 1930's was permeated with humor and good temper and often took the form of an intellectual game, they can easily afford to regard the few who still remain Communists after the great disillusion of the last decades with a benevolence impossible to the Americans. To the English they are often just harmless "cranks." Moreover, the English are prepared to permit an occasional scandal to arise, because they are deeply convinced that free discussion, together with a fundamental respect for authority in the mass of the people, will combine to prevent the spread of the virus and an epidemic of individual cases.

Once, however, there was real fear in England. It was the fear of a British form of National Socialism. Rebecca West has described it as she watched two supporters of the accused William Joyce leaving the courtroom for lunch during the noon interval at his trial: "Two young men among thousands. That is the real horror in the international war of ideologies, that a city does not know whom it houses."

The city does not know. The state does not know. Sometimes the individual himself does not know when he ceases to be identified with his own country or from which point of time he became a part of a new movement represented by another country. The transition period is perhaps the most uncanny aspect of the whole problem. There is an intermediate stage of indecision, a hanging back "here," although "there" has already begun to suck the individual across. With one man there may be forces and emotions of which he seems scarcely aware, pulling him in one direction or another. In some cases the motive stems from some ancient wound of the spirit, from the resentment of the unsuccessful, rejected or revengeful. With another type, objective fac-

10

tors play the major role. The critical intellect which he turns on his own government's policies or the considered approval with which he regards the aims of some other government constitutes the ultimately decisive factor.

The latter group contains commonly most of those who have many flirtations with the same cause. The intellectual rarely remains a convert once and for all. He begins to train the same restless, critical faculty which had led him to find fault with his own country and its political beliefs onto the adopted country or the new ideology. Often the individual's defection from the cause may reflect his reactions, equal and opposite, to the course of world events. The "zig" of the individual or small group merely corresponds to the preceding "zag" which world history has just completed. Thus a kind of attraction-repulsion pattern forms between the individual and his cause. A good example of such a pattern can be seen in the behavior of the liberal Left in Western countries vis-à-vis Moscow in the last several decades. Back and forth it went from one side to the other, as if through a revolutionary "no man's land" lying between the Communist and the bourgeois ways of life. Some switched sides with the precision of marionettes, responding predictably to each stimulus; others found the strength of spirit to stay on one of the two sides at some crucial point. Up to 1945, the most important turning points in the pattern were:

POSITIVE FOR MOSCOW

Hitler, National Socialism and the conviction that only Russia was a determined opponent.

The Spanish Civil War, in which the Loyalists and Republicans were supported by the Communists, while the Western governments behaved either hypocritically or indecisively.

The invasion of Russia by the German armies (and the violation of the 1939 pact) in June 1941.

The brave Russian Defense. The feeling of solidarity in the fight against Germany. Stalingrad. The failure of the Western Allies to form a second front.

11

NEGATIVE FOR MOSCOW

The Soviet purges and liquidations.

The pact between Stalin and Hitler in August 1939; the overrunning of Finland in November 1939 and the dictated peace in March 1940.

The growing Soviet mistrust of the Allies, made visible on the individual questions of the alliances.

The Russian treatment of the Polish question.

While the individual is engaged in tracing his own path, caused by his reactions to external events, he may not be aware that he had reached or passed some point at which he becomes dangerous or disloyal to his country. Governments also pursue such zigzag courses, with one difference. A government cannot be tried or punished for the same changes of policy for which an individual can be accused of treason. In the years 1936 to 1945, for example, the term "Loyalist" to most people in England, France, Scandinavia and America meant self-evidently republicans of all shades, including the Communists, who fought against Franco in the Spanish Civil War. As late as 1945, at the prompting of the American Government, all the Western countries withdrew their ambassadors from Madrid. In December 1947, *Time* magazine could still speak of the famous Fifth Column of Franco's General Mola as "the column of Mass Treason." By 1954 all had changed. Treaties of alliance, agreements of military aid and economic assistance had been made with Franco, who had become a defender of the free way of life. The Western view of Franco had changed so completely in the Cold War atmosphere that one of the "crimes" for which Robert Oppenheimer was cited was that between 1937 and 1939 he had given money to various Left-Wing Spanish-aid committees. In the same year an American, well known for the accuracy of his observations on foreign affairs, used the same term "Loyalist" to describe the followers of Franco, as if the expression had always been so employed. Another example of such governmental tergiversation can be seen in the case of Finland. From the autumn of 1939 to the spring of 1940, Finland was "good" and "heroic."

12

From 1941 to 1944, Finland was "bad," or at best, "misguided."
In 1947, Ernest Bevin, British Foreign Secretary, was a tough,
stubborn and successful opponent of the Soviet Union. Yet in
1920, the same Ernie Bevin had personally helped to prevent an
important, perhaps a decisive, victory of the Polish Army over
the Soviets by urging the London dockers to refuse to load any
ship with munitions bound for Warsaw.

Different peoples move at different rates and often in opposite
directions as the wheel of history turns. The same event may
have equal and opposite significance for two peoples, whose historical positions have shifted. In October 1939, many German
opponents of Hitler found the rejection by Chamberlain of Hitler's peace proposal "wonderful." For them, Chamberlain had
forced the peace from Hitler one year before, whereas for England he had become the man who had brought peace at any
price and who had to fall from power as soon as the war became
serious. In 1941, Charles Lindbergh was forced to withdraw
from American public life under strong suspicion of treason at
the very moment when men in Europe like Saint-Exupéry and
Carrel saw in him the only hope for America. To many Americans, Lindbergh had come to symbolize a kind of native American Fascism. Yet thirteen years later the same Lindbergh was
promoted by Act of Congress to the rank of general in the United
States Air Force Reserve in recognition of his services to his
country. For some men the turn of the wheel of history after the
Second World War meant political rehabilitation and renewed
influence, as in the case of Lindbergh, but for others it had exactly the opposite effect.

When Secretary of State Byrnes, said to be under the influence of Winston Churchill and in full agreement with President
Truman, switched the course of American foreign policy from
the alliance with Moscow to the Cold War, Harry Dexter White,
Julian Wadleigh, Lawrence Duggan, Alger Hiss and Laughlin
Currie resigned or were forced to resign from their high posts in
the American Civil Service. It is not too difficult to reconstruct

the situation after the event. During the era of cooperation with the Russians, these men, with their pro-Russian leanings, had not been conspicuous, but in the merciless glare of Cold-War politics they simply stood out too sharply to continue holding prominent government posts. Hiss and Duggan moved to chairmanships of international organizations. Today all of them are said to have been traitors.

The Oppenheimer case reveals the same sort of elliptical thinking which projects today's criteria onto yesterday's acts. For example, according to the rules of procedure which the Gray Committee had to use in the Oppenheimer investigation, a security clearance could be revoked, even though it had once been granted, if "national or international developments" demanded it. This remarkable point of view led *The Reporter* magazine to observe: "If the 'agonizing reappraisal' which Dulles threatened during the crisis over the European Defense Community had led us to give up our alliances with Britain and France, then all the American diplomats and soldiers who for years have been collaborating with their British and French colleagues would suddenly find themselves transformed into security risks." Simularly, Oppenheimer could never have been accused of lack of enthusiasm for the construction of the H-bomb if an alternative strategic plan in the Pentagon had been adopted. Had the alternate strategy—which called for greater balance between offensive and defensive weapons—prevailed, the H-bomb program would not have been begun. It is a curious "disloyalty" which can only occur under certain circumstances.

It is perfectly reasonable to expect a thoughtful individual who wants to remain true to himself, or to a set of principles, to change his mind from time to time. First of all, it is not always apparent which of several courses of action is most consistent with his principles, even if the principles are unusually clear. A simple "yes" or "no" rarely suffices to define the proper attitude to an issue, so that a man with clear principles may find himself forced to temporize or vacillate. Finally the external factors themselves shift constantly, as history unfolds, and these very changes compel the prudent man to reconsider, possibly abandon, an old or adopt a new position.

The great Winston Churchill's political career illustrates these difficulties perfectly. He could and did occasionally simultaneously contain within himself a "yes" and a "no" to the same question: before 1911, supporting a policy of cooperation with Germany, but later one of the chief advocates of war; from 1940 to 1945, undergoing numerous changes of mind about the proper policy toward France—once writing Pétain a deferential letter, later branding him a criminal—once again basing new hopes on Pétain and Weygand; in the spring of 1944, acquiescing in the decision to deprive Germany of her eastern provinces—dismayed a year later when it actually happened; in March of 1946, in the famous Fulton speech, urging the Americans to beware of Moscow; in May 1953, introducing a reconciliation with the Soviets against the wishes of the Americans.

History will ascertain how often Churchill's judgment was correct and how often not, but surely no one would accuse him of treason for making mistakes. Precisely that, however, happened to several State Department Far Eastern experts who were discharged in the 1950's for their written opinions of the 1940's. It was never shown that the diplomats in question were wrong, merely that ten years later their views on China were no longer terribly popular in some Congressional circles. In some regions of the landscape of treason, a mistake in judgment has become a punishable offense. It is important to see here that the American diplomats were condemned for expressing judgments about matters of fact, as if a man's assessment of an objective situation and his feelings about it were or should be one and the same thing.

Another example of this questionable kind of thinking was a questionnaire devised by a group of German journalists in 1945, long before the Allies began their de-Nazification campaign. The journalists tried to construct a standard of integrity by which to assess former colleagues. To do this, they asked a rather peculiar question: Had the individual under questioning believed

15

at some specified point of time in the possibility of a German victory? They were doing the same thing, in effect, that the State Department did with its China experts. They did not inquire whether the man had hoped for, or worked for, a German victory, by which question they might have uncovered his convictions; they asked only whether he had considered it possible. They examined the man's power of analysis of a given factual situation, not his beliefs, which were what they still had to assess. James Burnham's proposed distinctions between "conscious" and "unconscious" traitors and between "subjective" and "objective" treason rests on the same confusion between judgments and convictions.

After all, we are still left with the uncomfortable questions: Where does treason begin? By a movement of the heart? By merely thinking about treason? The problem of definition arises in all attempted distinctions, such as Mr. Burnham's. It perplexed the German journalists and plagued the security investigators in America. Does treason begin first in the deed itself?

The German resistance movement offers impressive examples of the difference between treason of thought and treason of act, as well as the presence of both points of view in the same man. As an example of one extreme, Helmuth James von Moltke's attitude stands out sharply. Von Moltke, together with Pastors Delp and Gerstenmaier, believed in nonviolent resistance and opposed the use of force or revolutionary violence against Hitler. During his trial before Roland Freisler, Hitler's infamous "hanging judge," von Moltke observed with evident pride that Freisler had recognized what sort of treason he and the pastors had, in fact, committed. "We are to be hanged," he said, "because we have thought together." This is a case of unusual clarity and precision. For other men of the *Widerstand,* the problems of treason were less clear cut. They loved their country. Hitler had that country in his hands. There was a war raging. To destroy Hitler might be the salvation of the Fatherland. On the other hand, it might so endanger the fabric of the state that the actual salvation could no longer be carried out, because the object of their efforts, that is, Germany, might no longer exist.

16

2. THE PATH FROM FEUDALISM
TO THE NATION-STATE

FOR the longest part of European history the head of state was indistinguishable from the people he ruled. Treason and loyalty were affairs which depended on a certain personal relationship to the head of the state, and could indeed only be understood in this way. The old Germanic word *Rat* (advice, counsel, or the body or person giving advice, i.e., the council or senate or ruler) stood for the central activity of the ruler, and the corresponding verb *raten* had as many meanings as the chief had functions: protection, defense of the *Volk,* leadership, judging, planning and directing. *Verraten,* to betray, originally meant simply to break out of the chief's demesne in the sense of "mislead," "give false support or advice," "give over to," "deliver into the hands of." In its original meaning, *verraten* makes it quite clear that the relationship is a reciprocal one. The ruler can as easily betray the *Volk,* by misleading them, as the traitor can, a truism forgotten until Hitler's day. In the Germanic tribe the circle of men enclosed in the *Rat* was visible to the eye. The heads of families, leaders of groups, chiefs of tribes or the king and councillors were the so-called *Schutzherren,* the protecting lords. Later, in the feudal age, the vassals ruled their allotments with the same fullness of power with which the king ruled over them. The political structure of society resembled a house of building blocks cemented together by the loyalty of vassal to lord.

As long as Europe had only one God and one Church, as long as all secular power was derived through the grace of God, there were no traitors—only heretics. In the year 1105, Pope Pascalis II felt himself powerful enough as God's representative on earth to grant a German prince forgiveness up to and including the Day of Judgment for having disobeyed his father. But when the spread of heresy prepared the way for one of the great

17

European revolutions, the authority of the church began to weaken. Emperor Sigismund, in his role of protector of the Council of Constance, still allowed himself to be talked into breaking his oath of safe conduct to Jan Hus—an action justified on the grounds that the word of an emperor need not be kept toward a heretic. The consequences of this treachery from above and the ensuing burning of Hus have made themselves felt in European politics up to this day: in the Sudeten crisis of 1938 and the expulsion of all Germans from Bohemia in 1945.

A new era began when heretics achieved recognition politically and began to enjoy equality. The great stained-glass window of European Christianity splintered into a million shiny fragments. Erasmus of Rotterdam, who took part in the new thinking, but as a conservative hated all revolutionary changes, was—as Ernst Jünger points out—one of the last representatives of the seamless, unified Europe of the Middle Ages. He had known the Fatherland as a unity, "moving between Paris and London, Oxford, Orléans, Lyon, Cambridge, Basel, Freiburg and Warsaw, where he stayed as long as he pleased, weeks or, perhaps, years; always continuing his own work and sometimes here or there holding an office of state."

In England and France the approach to the religious schism was entirely logical and consequential. In England everything Catholic, and in France everything Protestant, was simply liquidated. English jurists were able to prove that it offended against the Constitution to consider forgiving the Irish their Papism. Eugen Rosenstock-Huessy writes: "What we consider a perfectly self-evident duty of the King was reckoned high treason in James II." In Germany there arose the local principality based on the *cuius regio, ejus religio* principle. In the jigsaw puzzle of political boundaries which resulted, the sense of cleavage and mistrust was bound to remain alive. Erlangen and Bayreuth were Protestant; Bamberg and Würzburg Catholic; Schweinfurt and Meiningen Protestant; Aschaffenburg Catholic; Frankfurt predominantly Protestant; and Mainz Catholic.

The Protestant branch of the Wirsing family, banned from

18

Würzburg by Julius von Echterdingen, moved to Schweinfurt all of twenty-five miles away, and remained irreconcilable at the "iniquity." It never forgave the great counterreformer for that.

Yet even in the chaos of the sixteenth century, loyalty and treason remained polarized around the figure of the Prince. It never occurred to anyone that there was anything improper in the conduct of Prince Eugen of Savoy, born in France, educated in France, of entirely French blood, who fought against France in the service of the Emperor of Austria. Trenck's betrayal involved Frederick the Great and Maria Theresa, not Austria and Prussia. The major part of the eighteenth century understood loyalty in this personal sense, and indeed the attitude of the officers in the Napoleonic campaigns was very much the same as that which had prevailed in the fifteenth and sixteenth centuries. As late as 1831, the Prussian soldier's oath began: "I swear that I shall serve his Majesty, the King of Prussia, my most gracious Lord, in peace and war, wherever it may be, truly and loyally and I swear to fight for the sole advantage and good of His Highness." And in his controversy with Wilhelm II, even the aged Bismarck considered the feudal relationship as the basis of their mutual obligation of loyalty and reacted to the breach of trust by the emperor by calling it a "felony." However, this was no more than an anachronism in the solid structure of the Prussian State, which could never be wholly shaken by the French Revolution, perhaps because it was one of the first absolute governments that was tolerant as to religious matters, and just as to social differences.

However, the French Revolution, which abolished God as well as the monarch, created a new focal point for the concepts of loyalty and treachery: the Will of the People. It was bound constitutionally by the nation and represented by Parliament and public opinion. Talleyrand, the first great figure of the new age, remarked: *"La trahison—c'est une question du temps."* He betrayed what still seemed valid in favor of what was to come only when it was really already obsolete, and he differed from his contemporaries by being quicker than others to see when the abso-

19

lute monarchy, or when Napoleon or when the Restoration, were "finished." Then he helped on the future by giving them each a last blow. He knew no loyalty—or only loyalty to a power whose dictatorial quality was not yet realized during his time. In the words of Eugen Rosenstock-Huessy:

Talleyrand was the first to recognize public opinion. He believed in it from 1789 to 1838. In changing his convictions at least ten times, this most successful weather vane of his period became the speculator of the great power which was—even in Bismarck's view—to reign supremely over the nineteenth century: public opinion. Talleyrand was the most successful priest [minister] of the new cult. Public opinion moved from one sensation to the next, like the notations of the stock exchange. Cabinet crises are therefore nothing but public opinion in eternity, because this opinion knows no loyalty. *"Plus ça change, plus c'est la même chose."*

A new era had dawned. It differs in the nations just as the words *treue, vertrauen, verrat,* loyalty, disloyalty, confidence, faith—treason, *trahison*—sound different and have different meanings in the minds of various peoples. Not all countries believe treason to be the worst of crimes.

But in this new landscape, with the exception of England, one thing is common to all. André Thérive describes what is meant, in saying: "The crime against society replaced the crime against the Crown. There was one great difference. Whereas the person of the sovereign had been easily recognizable and simple to remove from the range of fire, the new 'society' is a Moloch of uncertain shape and unpredictable moods and gloomy rage." And he adds that, whereas the king could afford to give pardon, toward society there is only one choice: obey or betray, believe or betray, agree or betray.

The transition from Fatherland to Nation as a consequence of the French Revolution may have happened overnight as far as political systems were concerned. But in the living people the process of change was much slower. In some it has not taken place even today. It was the change-over from a consciousness of belonging that did not depend on the political system, but had its roots in the land, in its soil, its traditions and language and familiar surroundings, and was more a matter of the heart than the head. Whereas the new revolutionary patriotism, the belief in the *volonté générale,* was intellectual in its essence. It identified the nation with a political idea, and therein lie the seeds of the explosive forces in our present landscape of treason. The individual now had to commit himself to an idea or set of ideas. It is one of the minor ironies of history that the making of the nation as a political reality was also its undoing; the idea of the nation contains in it the germs of its own dissolution. A nation is, in the last analysis, just an idea and not really a terribly concrete one at that. No one has ever seen the General Will and few the Constitution. It has not involved very much imagination to perceive that one could substitute some other idea without great difficulty for the idea of the nation and thereby train loyalty onto the new focal point, for example, the working class. Such realigning of the sights cannot be done with a Fatherland. It is physically there already. The famous French editor and author, Raymond Aron, has pointed out that: "The moment the Fatherland is no longer defined in concrete terms, but instead in terms of ideology, it ceases to be the highest good in political life. It turns into a football of party politics."

German Sociologist Hans Naumann takes the idea a step further:

When the new element enters, the age of the national state comes to an end, because the hierarchy of duty and obedience has been made equivocal and uncertain. Each citizen can decide for himself. Each may choose his own secular religion and transfer in spirit to his new ideological Fatherland, as in the case of Klaus Fuchs. Nowadays treachery is rarely committed against the Fatherland. The traitors betray a group or an ideological clique. One can find oneself in the embarrassing predicament of having unwittingly betrayed an imperialist state, if in the meantime the ideological bloc in question has gained power.

Let us return from Naumann's description of our present stage of transition, which may develop in different directions, to the time of transition during the French Revolution, the consequences of which have become a matter of history. The chief object of the revolution of 1789 was to rub out all differences. The king and the peasant, the nobleman and the laborer, the burgher and the beggar, they were all to become the "Everyman," "Mr. Egalité," the citizen whose equality of merit and rank was so great that he became an interchangeable dot in the crowd. Just as the Church (which had shown itself so fallible and so corruptible) had ceased under the force of the heretics and the Reformation to be the mediator and interpreter of God— because now every individual was to understand and to proclaim on his own what God wished him to do—so the heresies of the period of enlightenment and the revolution had given every individual the right to know and to decide what was good for him.

This right of self-determination took different forms in different countries. In France, the heads of those who had been too unegalitarian had to roll. In America, which had turned its back on the way of life and the sovereigns of the old Fatherlands and which had been settled in the name of radical religious beliefs, the revolution was against the British Crown as a symbol of colonial power. What happened in America at the time is very useful in throwing light on the present situation, because many forms of warfare and propaganda were used in the new continent which Europe was to learn only in the twentieth century. The War of Independence was the first modern war which introduced the weapon of psychological influence. The pamphlets with which the rebels sought to lure the British troops over to their side showed how much further advanced the Americans were in this field, even then.

Hermann Weyl, in his study, *The Battle Against Disloyalty*, describes at great length the intellectual and political situation during the War of Independence. He writes:

The American conception was that man was endowed by his Creator with certain inalienable rights, that governments were established to protect them, and that when any government failed, it was the duty of the

22

people to overthrow it. This theory—at one blow—made loyalty to the Crown treason and treason to the king patriotism. . . . Patriot committees drew up eloquent declarations of principles, and each American was given the free choice between subscribing to them or being mauled, pilloried, jailed, deported, or deprived of his property.

Treason had a certain modern ring to it in the 1770's and 1780's in America. Not for more than a century were treachery and accusations of treachery to be so common in Europe. Another contemporary feature was the application of treason to whole groups. Benedict Arnold and Aaron Burr were examples of individuals accused of treachery, but in addition, families— whole social groups—were accused and suffered for the accusations. In the United States, the idea that treasonable groups were curled within the body politic like tapeworms gnawing away at the flesh has always been strong. There are always "un-Americans" lurking in a shadow. Lincoln fought bitter battles with the "Copperheads," who were Northerners with Southern sympathies during the Civil War. In 1941, Roosevelt was able to silence the opposition of Charles Lindbergh by calling him a "Copperhead." The tradition of uncontrolled accusation and counteraccusation has never died out in the American consciousness. During the Civil War, a typical American investigating committee "investigated" the loyalty of all Federal employees. It soon became known by the title of "the office of secret accusations." Its effect was that government clerks were terrified of losing their jobs and spied on their colleagues, and that the loyalty of employers at the navy yards, in the arsenals and in the White House were under suspicion. The years after the First World War were marked by another, rather similar, outburst of treason hysteria, called by an American historian the "epoch of fear." A wave of deportation hysteria tore families apart. Immigrants were herded together and bundled off to Europe as if they had plague or typhus. In such actions a nation, built up by succeeding waves of immigrants of different races and different creeds, paid its price of fear and anxiety. Foremost was the instinctive fear, recurring in every new crisis, that the unity achieved in the "melting pot" might be in danger.

On the other hand, it was just the continuation of this stream of immigrants in the 1930's and 1940's which contributed in strengthening the American ideology of the late eighteenth century. For now it was not the Irish and the Poles, the Germans, Russians, Italians, Lithuanians and Scandinavians, who came so often in search of good money and easy living. But from Hitler's Germany, from Franco's Spain, from annexed Austria and all the countries then occupied, there came a different type of immigrant—one who somewhat resembled the first colonists: lawyers, doctors, journalists, musicians, professors, poets, conservatives, liberals, Communists, Social Democrats. Of course, they too wanted to live, but their daily bread was not the dollar. It was the thought of what was happening without them—against them—in Europe. What influence they may have had served to strengthen the inborn American crusading zeal and the tendency to consider, as true representatives of a nation, people who had left their native soil, and to regard as traitors those who took the opposite view.

England, by contrast to America, has remained remarkably free of the infection of ideologies. The monarchy, though a constitutional one, has nevertheless remained the symbol of the unity of the nation and the empire. The oath of loyalty refers to the monarch personally. The queen remains the central symbol of unity of the entire social organism. Neither of the two parties, governing or opposing, can ever really become the "party of treason." Queen Elizabeth II speaks quite naturally of "My Peoples," even when she refers to the Negroes in Nigeria. It would, however, be illusory to imagine that England could have passed through the twentieth century's crises of confidence without suffering injury to its social fiber. The spy cases since the end of the Second World War, and the trials of traitors, have revealed to the English just how fictitious the oath of allegiance has proven to be, if it rests on weak emotional ties to the land and its traditional heritage. What good did Klaus Fuchs' oath

24

do? If he had become a Communist before his arrival in England, could a purely formal act of allegiance to George VI turn him into a loyal Englishman? Fuchs swore allegiance after a period of internment in Canada. He was removed from the camp because the British Government required the remarkable abilities of the young physicist for the war effort. It is not astonishing that an oath, the contents of which can hardly have had much emotional meaning to Fuchs, was in the end such a feeble tie. He himself felt no sense of allegiance to the British state, though he confessed to feeling that he had let down his colleagues, with whom for the first time in his life he genuinely had been at peace.

The oath of allegiance has lost its pull slowly, almost imperceptibly, during the passage of the century. One need not cite only the example of refugees, however, to illumine the change in the spirit of English life. There are native-born examples of far more dramatic impact. T. E. Lawrence, who cannot be accused of lacking national awareness, described in *The Mint* the effect that the oath of allegiance had on his fellow recruits in 1922. "The oath simply did not catch fire. It babbled on about the King. With all due respect, the common soldier of today is no royalist in the old sense that the army of George III felt that it belonged to the King. Yes, we are loyal in a way, not expressed in words. But our ideal does not have two legs and a hat. It has grown in us darkly as we wandered the streets and country roads of our homeland and felt that it was ours." Lawrence was a new phenomenon in English social history. His words and his life pointed to a break in the continuity of the English national consciousness, which was to become more pronounced in the 1930's. The first cracks appeared in the First World War. It was not a revolution but a slow evolution. We are still in the midst of it, and it is correspondingly difficult to give it a name or define it precisely. One thing is clear. There is a strain of treason in it.

In the course of this study we shall often have occasion to mark the sharp contrast between the older generation—those who experienced, however briefly, the stable, unquestioned so-

25

ciety of pre-1914 Europe—and the two younger generations—those who came to maturity in and shortly after the First World War and those who came to maturity during and after the Second. T. E. Lawrence belonged to the middle generation, the one which called itself "lost." In Europe, the members of the youth movements belonged to it as well. They had been caught up, as unsuspecting boys, in the fire and torment of the trenches, and returned determined to revolt against everything, especially against the artificial barriers which they viewed as one of the prime causes of the great disaster. At first, many thought that they had found the answer in communal life, in wandering, in the flickering twilight of the campfire. Their searing and terrible war experiences, which they had in common, would conquer all boundaries between nations and individuals and bring about a truly international movement for peace. Abetz, Rahn and Epting represented the nationalists of this genre. Sorge, Massing, Niekisch were Socialists. Rauschning and Strasser were national revolutionaries. Whatever political persuasions they professed nominally, they all shared the same strengths and weaknesses. The sheer intensity of their goodwill was a positive element, but also led to their complete lack of political realism. They succeeded in creating contacts across boundaries which had seemed insuperable, but they failed to influence the course of events in the long run, because they never saw these events in their real perspective.

T. E. Lawrence was a kind of model for his generation. His legendary revolt against society, God knows to what end, stirred their imaginations. Young people admired his rejection of his natural role in society and of his honors and perquisites. He took on the burden of the common soldier, looking for his true home among the poor and the battered. Sir Harold Nicolson, who was one of his admirers, wrote of him that he was, after all, neither loyal nor sympathetic, truthful, modest nor sincere. England was somehow strong and healthy enough to accept him in the end and include him among her great ones.

On the continent of Europe the representatives of the "lost" generation, in so far as they came back from the trenches at all, were of lesser stature. They faced a chaos on their return which the island kingdom had never known. They were caught up in the maelstrom of a society convulsed, and few escaped without severe injuries. The novelist Ernst Jünger, who belonged to their number, was one of the few who withdrew from the entangling bonds of the society in which he found himself. One wonders at what cost to himself and the influence of his writing this extreme nonparticipation was purchased. Of his contemporaries, few have managed as well, and there are not many who escaped the tribulations before or after 1945 without spending time in prisons or concentration camps.

The older generation, self-appointed guardians of order against the onslaughts of Socialism, Bolshevism, Fascism and Nazism, took no part in this wandering through the landscape of treason. The in-between generation went only part of the way. It was often chance which pulled them up short a step or two before the final act of treachery. Oxford undergraduates who took part in the famous Union debate of the 1930's, in which a resolution was adopted that the house "would not fight for King and Country," fought bravely, and died when "the chips were down." The outbreak of the Second World War proved to most of them that, despite what they had said, in the last analysis they were strongly loyal. They had a homeland which they loved, even if they had behaved all along as if it meant nothing. The dark feeling which Lawrence described in *The Mint* rose in them, as in him. One of the best examples of this type of person, a man of the same generation as Burgess and MacLean, was Esmond Romilly, Churchill's nephew. At the age of fifteen he ran away from Wellington and founded a newspaper which preached the overthrow of the public schools. He then proceeded to escape from the reform school in which he had been placed, and took part in the Spanish Civil War on the side of the Communists. He abducted one of the Mitford girls and disappeared with her, appearing later on the Continent as an exponent of revolutionary Communism. The party, tired of his juvenilia, threw him out, and for

27

a long time nothing further was heard of him, until he arrived as a Canadian air force officer at the beginning of the Second World War. While carrying out a bombing mission over Germany, he lost his life "for King and Country."

The postwar youngster, the generation of the juvenile delinquents and the *Halbstarken,* seems to have lost all trace of traditional loyalty. These boys have returned to a thoroughly primitive form of social organization, a kind of contemporary tribalism. The youthful gangsters of New York, London and Stockholm terrorize their teachers, break into shops, and steal cars, but the "Black Knights" or "The Golden Raiders" have a code of personal loyalty which the Western world has not experienced since the days of feudal chivalry. John Steinbeck, speculating on the phenomenon, suggests that it may have very profound consequences for the social order in the democracies:

> The kids are loyal to nothing outside of the gang. They never denounce one another. It may well be that the cause lies deeper than the feelings of the children themselves. In the feudal system each man was responsible for something. Each family member was responsible for every other member. The same held for the village. Today we consider such mutual responsibility as a sign of a relatively primitive social order, but what have we put in its place? Perhaps we all yearn for the old ways, and this explains the particular form of criminality practiced in the kid gangs. The youngsters, who have no chance at home, but seem to need to be responsible, leave the home and form street gangs. The gangs evoke and command all their capacity for loyalty and courage. They fight for one another, lie and even kill for one another. Is it not because the gang is all they have? . . . There is a terrible driving need within men to be responsible. Units in the army occasionally turn into whole platoons of heroes in which every private is a passionate and active member of the whole. The gangs are quite similar. They protect all those who belong to them, and each individual protects the gang in return. The family was once like that but it is no longer. The gangs may do awful things, but things which demand courage, self-sacrifice and much devotion. In a different setting the same attitudes would be heroic. The boy who refuses to "rat" to the police is a criminal. The boy who refuses to tell what he knows to the enemy is a hero.

Are these youngsters returning to the *Schützherr* and the ancient tribal *Rat?* Are they closing the circle of Western history and returning to the point where it all began? We can answer this question no better than the public-school masters who taught Romilly, Burgess and Maclean could have predicted which of the three would die heroically and which would end up as a traitor.

3. THE STATE—OATHS—OBEDIENCE

THE oath symbolizes, by a visible act, the relationship which is betrayed by a broken oath. Nowadays the oath is not sworn to a monarch, but to a republic, a constitution, the president of a parliamentary democracy. In all these cases it is ultimately the state which is meant. The state is to be served loyally; the state is to be defended courageously; and it is the state which can be betrayed.

But what is the state in our time? We present two answers to this question—the first by a statesman, the second by a theologian.

Theodor Heuss once made the attempt to honor the deed of resistance by the men who conspired against Hitler on July 20, 1944, and at the same time to uphold the authority of the German Federal Republic, a state created pro tempore, whose first president he had become. He said:

A state is no proclamation of sentimentalists, no league of well-meaning visionaries who have never heard of original sin, but a practical arrangement resting on the power to command and the claim to obedience. It is a secondary consideration from whence the state draws these powers, whether from God or from the idea of the nation. Despite all the historical vicissitudes and the unavoidable, almost banal opportunism of its supporters, the modern state has managed to weather most crises as a logical and reasonable system for ordering the lives of men. Throughout the several millennia of human history the power to command and the claim to obedience have always been the socially constant factors in political organization.

Romano Guardini, on the other hand, attempted to show that we had come to end of what is called modern time; that is—to the last phase of enlightened, progressive and secularized existence, and that we are now in need of something more:

The religious accent which used to rest on the state, and the characteristic of sublimeness which formerly emanated from some sort of divine consecration, are disappearing. The modern state draws all authority from the people. At the beginning of the nineteenth century, in the movements of romanticism, nationalism and early democracy, the attempt was even made to invest the people themselves with sublimity. But soon this idea became void, and since then it has meant only that the people—that is the multitude which comprises the state—are responsible for the executive will, provided that there is not in reality some powerful group which really runs the show.

The state must have an oath. It is the most binding form in which the individual can make a definite commitment or undertake an obligation. The adhesive power of oaths rests entirely on the connection by the swearer of his undertaking to the witness, the Almighty. If, however, and it is surely the modern trend, the oath no longer contains any reference to God, what then? It merely means that the man who breaks the oath will be punished with imprisonment, if caught. It is nothing but an empty formula with little meaning and less effectiveness. Everything that exists is more than itself. Everything that happens has more meaning than the externals of what happens. Everything is related to something that is beyond or behind it. Only from there does it become complete. If this transcendent reality vanishes, the things, as well as the order of things, become empty. They lose their meaning and their power to convince. The law of the state must be more than a structure of rules of publicly approved behavior. Behind it there stands something intangible, which makes itself felt in the individual's conscience when the law is broken.

The two statements, Heuss' and Guardini's, contradict each other on two crucial points, namely, the purpose and the inner justification of the state. Heuss places all the emphasis on the external *ad-hoc* order and tries to hurry by the question of meaning. Guardini has no use for the external order as such, declaring it meaningless without the transcending divine content, which he seems to imply is the inner significance. Though it may seem something of a digression to the reader, we must pause here to examine the two statements and to make an excursion into the role of the state in our time. Treason in the twentieth century only becomes intelligible when set against the background of the modern state.

America serves our purpose best, for it alone of the modern great powers has a short history. America has never had to shed a past. It strikingly demonstrates which features of the modern state seem moribund and which lively, because it is the purely legal state, the ideal state, constituted by a rational act. Loyalty of the citizenry is directed to the chief of state, not as a ruler sancified by God nor as a father of his country, but simply as the constitutionally appointed executor of the popular will. He is, moreover, the chosen protector of the legal order as such. He may occasionally be called upon to defend the legal order, even against the popular sovereignty which legitimizes that order, as in the recent case of Senator McCarthy. McCarthy, clearly the spokesman of a sizeable section of the people, called on 2,000,-000 civil servants to deliver to him all evidence concerning Communism in the government. In effect, he called on them to disobey the legally defined superior power of the executive. The answer to this was clear and was ultimately acknowledged, even by those who thought McCarthy right. No individual may exalt himself above the constitution of the land. The executive alone bears the responsibility for carrying out the law.

The parliamentary democratic constitutions on the continent of Europe have the same general aim. Unlike the organic development of the English Constitution, most of the constitutions on the Continent owe their existence to some sort of revolution. In all of them the borderline between the permitted and the forbidden has been drawn on the basis of a civil or military code. Whoever transgressed the line was a traitor. Thus it was society which defined the borderline between treason and loyalty. "As long as the hierarchy of values and responsibilities remained intact, as long as the state could maintain its claim to be the last resort, the final arbiter, or the dominating entity," argues Hans Naumann, "there was such a thing as 'classical treason,' for which the corpus of law could claim absolute validity. On the whole that was the state of affairs in the nineteenth century and up to the end of the First World War."

The Weimar Republic was the first state in German history which was not accepted unquestioningly by its citizens as the highest authority under God. The entire old regime had been abolished, not just the monarchy and the principalities, but all traces of the older forms of loyalty, even the flag itself. The new flag was never popular. Broad classes of the population simply rejected it, and some of them held high authority in the new state. The new oath was taken on the dead letter of the constitution.

Yet despite the doubts, hesitancies and conflicts, the citizenry somehow kept on obeying as it had always done. The habit of unquestioning loyalty to the state was so deeply ingrained that nothing seemed able to shake it. A political organism which survived the strike of the munition workers, the sailors' mutiny, the abdication and flight of the Kaiser, the Spartacus Rebellion and the Kapp Putsch, had a certain admirable doggedness, and it withstood a series of shattering crises with extraordinary stability. Which particular government happened to be in power was of secondary importance. It never occurred to the civil servants in the Foreign Office to quit their posts when the radical socialist Dr. Karl Kautsky was placed over them. They despised him, with the professional contempt of the civil servant for ministerial masters, but they knew that they would outlast him and his ilk. They considered themselves trustees of an area of the state, a private domain, for which they had to answer. Their main aim was to keep as much of the domain as possible out of Kautsky's hands, which they managed to do very effectively. The enormous imperial bureaucracy was a priceless inheritance from the previous state; a self-generating mechanism for preserving order and assuring the continuity of the daily tasks of the state.

It had a life of its own and for political decisions a certain instinct so refined that it bordered on intelligence. It could run along without a head and somehow kept the state going. All this came to an end when Hitler came to power and put Ribbentrop in office. This time neither they nor the minister nor the Foreign Office nor the very Reich itself, survived the debacle. It was an impossible situation for the civil servant when his tested method of dealing with political problems simply failed. The old tricks were useless, and genuine action was the only remaining alternative. They failed to notice how the state's orderly spirit which they embodied had become a shell, a sounding brass. The inherited loyalty, which was more of a patterned reflex than a commitment of the heart, was no longer sufficient.

All things considered, the Weimar Republic had its agreeable side. Life rolled on, relatively undisturbed. Crises came and went and the years passed. Somehow even those who cursed it managed to live to curse another day. Things grew perilous after Hitler's seizure of power in 1933. Each of us had his own experience. All of us active writers and journalists received a form one day, which concerned among other things the daily directives from the censors to the press. We were all ordered to sign an agreement stating that we would not divulge anything about these directives. Most people were still so guileless that many signed the document without realizing that they had signed their own verdicts of guilt, but they did not stop telling their friends all the things that should have remained top secret. Thus even in the nonmilitary sector many skidded into what afterward was called treason, without being aware of how it had happened.

The military loyalty oath had always had the deepest roots. Even before the flight of the Kaiser, it had been violently shaken by the dangerous situation in the retreating army of 1918. General Wilhelm Groener realized fairly early in 1918 that the time for traditional Prussian military loyalty was past, and when the problem arose of clearing the bridges across the Rhine for the retreating troops, an action which meant firing on mutineers. Groener appeared at the Kaiser's H.Q. as the representative of

33

the Army. In the course of a very lively scene, the general remarked that in times of upheavel and revolution one could hardly expect traditional concepts like oaths of loyalty to the Kaiser to be more than fictions of another era. There were and still are officers of the old school who have never forgiven Groener for that remark. After all the broken and discredited oaths of the intervening years, the fact that such men still exist shows that since 1918 no agreement about the content and the meaning of the oath has been possible in Germany. The *Reichswehr* had split on the issue of the new state, and the inner fissure exploded in the Kapp Putsch. Groener and General Kurt von Schleicher, who from the first had collaborated with Social Democratic President Ebert, were both strongly disliked. General Hans von Seeckt, who forced through the idea of the complete withdrawal of the soldier from politics (which was ultimately to prove so disastrous for the Republic), often toyed with the idea of simply taking over the government by a painless Putsch. What characterizes the history of the Weimar military story is the fact that there were many different tendencies in the officer corps toward the Republic, not all of them disloyal. Colonel Hans Oster who had to leave the Army under the Second and under the Third Reich, felt himself bound by his oath to the Kaiser until the day he died, a member of the anti-Hitler resistance. His chief in the Abwehr,* Admiral Wilhelm Canaris, felt that his oath had expired with the flight of the Kaiser.

The most curious example of oath interpretation by a professional soldier is the case of Paul Borchardt, a General Staff officer of considerable distinction, who had worked on the plans for the African Campaign. In 1938 he was dismissed from the General Staff and forced to leave the Army and the country, because he was half Jewish. When questioned by American Intelligence in 1942, he preferred a prison sentence of forty years to revealing what he knew about Germany's plans and thereby breaking

---

*German Military Counterintelligence—core of anti-Nazi movement in the forces.

the oath he had sworn to the republic. In its turn, this loyalty to the fatherland which had treated him so badly was necessarily a betrayal in the eyes of the large community of Jews and half Jews whom Hitler had expelled.

The question of the oath had been difficult in 1918. By 1933 a far more serious problem had arisen: the nature and significance of obedience under the Nazis. The day of Hindenburg's death Hitler took the place of the old soldier as the head of state and the recipient of the oath. Colonel General Ludwig Beck called it the blackest day of his life. In place of simple obedience, which had satisfied all Hitler's predecessors, the new sovereign demanded "unconditional obedience . . . before God" in a holy oath. During the Weimar period those who had not been believers had at least the right to strike out the religious phrases. This last freedom was taken away by Hitler. It is unnecessary for me to begin to recite the deeds justified by this oath of "unconditional obedience."

The student of treason who pursues the problem of the German military oath a little further comes upon the most curious collection of phrases ever to be proclaimed in German history as an oath—the new oath of the West German Army. For, though the West Germans have an army, they have no state, always assuming that the Federal Republic is merely a provisional solution to a split Germany. In view of this, what ought the new German NATO soldier to swear when called to the colors? One suggestion for the reform of the military oath would have permitted an officer to refuse to carry out a lawful order twice, if he felt that it would lead to an inhumane act. The third time he received the order he must then carry out, under protest, the command given. The two refusals to obey would be entered in his personal file. "No doubt," remarked a critic, "to be of use at a future Nürnberg Trial." The solution finally hit upon simply left the problem of obedience unanswered by not mentioning it in the oath. Instead there is a relevant passage in the law which states: "An order may be ignored when, through carrying it out, a crime or misdeed would be committed. If the subordinate car-

35

ries out the order, his guilt is only excusable if it can be shown that he obeyed the order unaware of the crime or misdeed which might result." The text is then supplemented by the following considerations. Where the soldier feels a doubt which he cannot allay, this constitutes a "mitigating circumstance." In other words, a reasonable doubt clears the undecided individual, which relieves him of examining the validity of a given order.

How the framers of this proposal planned to operate it during a war with a real army is not entirely clear. There are indeed some who clamor for further restrictions on the power to command. They demand that the mere existence of strong suspicion, *not* knowledge, that a crime will be committed, must be sufficient grounds for refusing to obey an order. If this idea, stripped to its essential, were ever to filter down to the ranks, it would produce chaos—a compound of indecision, opportunism and confusion. In case of war the Federal German NATO soldier would find himself in a never-ending conflict of conscience, since he could be ordered to kill soldiers who might be his cousins or even his own brothers.

To whom then is he to turn? To the state? To the executive? The state and its chief do not appear in the text of the oath at all. "To preserve the constitution of the Federal Republic of Germany, to serve loyally and to defend bravely, even at the risk of losing my life, the Fatherland and freedom," is the way it reads. What the Fatherland is supposed to mean, no contemporary German could say. Whom one is to serve loyally is never mentioned. This represents the final stage of the depersonalization of the oath. The person or body to whom one swore allegiance, the very essence of the oath in the traditional form, has disappeared without a trace. As a result the question of treason is befogged, for it is now no longer clear just exactly who or what can be betrayed if the oath is broken. Those who believe in God may close their oaths with the words, "So help me God." Those who prefer not to may omit the phrase. Until recently it had not been settled whether both voluntary and conscripted soldiers would have to swear the same oath. There might conceivably have been three classes of soldiers: those who swore by God; those who swore without God; and those, the conscripts, who had not sworn at all. On March 6, 1956, the Bundestag decided that professional soldiers, volunteers and men entering for longer periods of service would swear an oath, while conscripts would merely have to "affirm solemnly."*

The demolition of symbolism in society and the loosening of the individual's ties to it could hardly go much further. How many soldiers can be expected to understand what the conflict is all about? At the time of the debate on the oath, Dolf Sternberger wrote an impassioned article for the *Gegenwart,* the conclusion of which is worth quoting:

> One often hears the complaint that the West lacks faith. As opposed to the totalitarian states we are supposed not to know what we are defending. On the contrary I should say we know very well what we are defending, freedom and justice. In these two words, the minimum is laid down for the existence of a liberal, constitutional state. These words represent the last stand beyond which we dare not retreat. If we are to take upon ourselves the burden of German Armed Forces again, we must be quite clear about the unconditional principles which must fill the spirits of the soldiers and justify their existence.

It is questionable whether the soldiers possess the faculty of abstract thinking which would enable them to follow Sternberger's considerations. In all probability they will simply feel that

---

*The oath, in which the words "So help me God" may be omitted, reads as follows: "I swear to serve the Federal Republic of Germany truly and to defend bravely the rights and freedom of the German people." In the affirmation, the words "I swear" are replaced by "I affirm." In the meantime a furious discussion has raged on the question of the validity of the refusal to serve or to obey, if it involves firing on one's relatives or home neighborhood. The referent of the legal department of the Ministry of Defense, Dr. Georg Flor, has denied the existence of a legal right of the individual soldier to claim that his conscience forbids him to act in such circumstances. Walter Dirks, in a recent issue of the *Frankfurter Heft* in an article entitled "The Fatherland, The Oath and The Law," argues that we must turn from the idea of the fatherland to the reality of the "neighborhood fatherland." He develops an argument rather similar to that of Guardini by emphasizing the difference between the religious and the secularized oaths.

37

something, somewhere, has gone wrong and that an indefinable missing factor disturbs them.

However, these problems concern the future—and our task is to examine the historical factors which helped to shape the landscape of treason in its present form. With all due respect to the importance of an oath, to the imprint and meaning of the *Kaiserreich,* the Weimar Republic, the Third Reich or the Federal Republic—one could argue that under all these changes there remained intact a certain basic feeling toward the state which gives us its protection and to which we give our confidence, even if in many instances we should wish it to adopt different forms. After all, such a basic confidence, such a mutuality of confidence, has been a matter of course since the dawn of our history, so much so, that most Germans were not even conscious of its existence. In this region of the conscious and subconscious, the most dangerous damage was dealt to the self-confidence of the national community from 1933 on. At the beginning of Hitler's reign, when these feelings were still intact, people looked at one another in awe and said: "Why, he can't do that." The fact is that he could and did. He dissolved the parties, broke treaties, murdered Jews, crushed the trade unions. It was the same with the Berlin charwoman in the summer and fall of 1945 who said, first of the Russians, later of the Americans and British: "They can't do that"—namely: "Let us starve, turn us out of our houses, arrest us without cause, let us freeze to death." They, too, could and did, but they fell far short of Hitler. We have entered a time in which the readiness "to do" what had always been supposed to be "impossible" has spread from some isolated few individuals to many. In their way of reaction to this novel state of affairs, the young again showed how far they differed from the older generation. On the whole the younger generation was quick in recognizing that Hitler could do what seemed impossible. Whereas an internationally respected member of the older generation, the historian Hermann Oncken, in a heated discussion, held it to be impossible that Hitler could overrun a neutral country, and Baron Ernst von Weizsäcker, a secretary of state in the Foreign Office and an anti-Nazi, never grasped what Hitler really intended, though he fought him in a cautious and hesitant way.

Weizsäcker and Oncken could only have understood Hitler as a phenomenon if their faith in an orderly, stable and sane society had been completely destroyed. The older men still believed in the existence of such a world. The younger generation, born into a collapsing social order, brought up in defeat, hunger, inflation, depression and civil disorder, was better able to divine what Hitler was planning. Lacking any faith in the well-meaning utterances of elderly statesmen, already partially brutalized, the young men and women were ready for the "impossible." The older generation was crushed by the news of the Hitler-Stalin pact, while the shrewdest among the younger men, in principle prepared for what was "out of the question," had sniffed the new direction of the wind as early as Hitler's speech on April 28th and had become certain that something of the sort was brewing after the fall of Litvinov on May 6, 1939.

The younger generation and the one which has grown to maturity since the war have always been aware of the "double" identification with causes. Since 1918 in Germany there have always been at least two causes struggling for supremacy at any given time. First it was the *Kaiserreich* versus the Republic; then it was the Republic versus the Nazis; the Nazi ideology versus the rising tide of democratic pacifism; and finally in the last few years the struggle which still rages between democratic and pacifist neutralism and the rising wave of the new militarism. The result has been to suck the last drop of meaning from the concept of the Fatherland and to accustom the youngsters of today to a complete political indifference. In 1953, the sixth-graders of a South German school in reply to the question: "Do you believe that there is anything worth the sacrifice of your life?" declared unanimously that, if there were, it was certainly not the Fatherland. One wrote: "The Fatherland is for me a dead letter." Another: "In case of war I should fight solely to preserve my own life." In the summer of 1954 at the Evangelical

Student Congress at Heidelberg, students from both the Federal Republic and the *Deutsche Demokratische Republik* found themselves in passionate agreement in rejecting the assertions of a famous historian who had addressed the congress on the Fatherland as ideal. "There is no Fatherland as long as Germany is divided."

The seed here growing to maturity is ominous and too often ignored by adults. It is in the long run far more dangerous and incalculable than the state of mind in the generation of Burgess and Maclean. For the roots of these young Germans are not in the soil of a state which, like Great Britain, has known centuries of stability and possesses emblems and symbols that may seem archaic and obsolete in times of well-being, but which, in moments of danger and of "sweat, blood and tears," unite the hearts in a deep-welling loyalty.

4. THE "DIVIDED" MEN AND THE "TWO-FACED"

EUGEN ROSENSTOCK-HUESSY puts forward the view that the appearance of a special sort of deceitful person is the necessary preliminary and accompanying symptom of all great revolutionary changes in the life of politics:

Unbearable as it may be, all of us must suffer an inner schism. Let no one imagine that this internal conflict is just a chance manifestation of our times. It is, on the contrary, a condition of total revolution and has always been so. When men leave one group and join another, the act of changing allegiance demonstrates in itself that, prior to the formal conversion, they had become acquainted with, and often fluent in, the ideological jargon of the new group. The possibility of such conversions would not exist if men were not secretly listening to the words of the new faith while paying lip service to the old. If men spoke only one such jargon, they would be eternally bound and delivered up to the original social or

national group into which pure chance had placed them. We belong
where our language in the symbolic sense is spoken and where we are
understood. Those who have only one such language in their hearts have
no means of intercourse with others. The two groups face one another
and speak to each other, but are not heard or understood. Just as two
trees are contained in the acorn, the one from which the acorn came and
the one which will grow from it, so man stems from the polis, and bears
within himself the towers and ramparts of the future polis. The political
man, which is all of us, has a terrible power to deceive himself and to be
treacherous, transforming his ideas in the secret recesses of his heart.
Revolutions are merely the large-scale projections of the individual's
capacity for inner duplicity, and express in clamorous tones the way
language and ways of thought have been roughly torn asunder.

Today we live in just such an era, an era of discord, division
and duplicity. The scale of contemporary mass schizophrenia is
surely unique in world history. Richard Sorge, for example, not
only lived the double life of a foreign correspondent of the Third
Reich and spy for the Soviet Army, but grew into two different
men through a kind of Yoga-like double consciousness. Admiral
Canaris, the chief of the Abwehr, was mortally afraid of Reinhard Heydrich.* Yet he maintained an outer friendship with this
man, who was Canaris' mortal enemy, as each well knew. Six
days a week Canaris engaged in espionage against the Gestapo,
and on the seventh he played croquet with the Gestapo's most
dangerous figure. An American atom spy, Harry Gold, worked
out a system of "compartmentalized" thinking, in order to prevent his various personalities from exploding the shell of his
identity. Indeed, he had more than two lives; he had also a
dream life of family bliss with a wife and children, details of
which he used to relate to his friends, although in reality he was
a bachelor and a model son and brother. In the daytime he
worked in a factory as a chemist—during the night he returned
to a laboratory of the same factory in the service of the Soviet
Union.

Not only the people about whose treason there can be no

---

*Chief of Gestapo's *Sicherheitsdienst,* the gruesome S.D.

41

doubt, either from the old legalistic or from the present-day political point of view, have accustomed themselves to divided thinking. Klaus Fuchs caused astonishment and incredulity when, in his confession, he spoke of "controlled schizophrenia." But the same could be said of perfectly respectable and honored men in various societies whose lives are lived under "controlled schizophrenia," and indeed with the growth of the "top-secret" mentality in all the Western countries, their number continues to grow. A prominent American scientist, holder of every conceivable security clearance and the soul of loyalty and trustworthiness, spends each summer at Los Alamos engaged in top-secret research. His life has been irrevocably committed to schizophrenia under control, and he finds it natural to declare: "When I leave Los Alamos, I turn off that part of my brain which was concerned with the work there, as if I were turning off a water faucet."

Martin Buber has identified a kind of distrust which he calls "existentialist," which he maintains is different in quality and in kind from the ancient distrust and fear of the strange or the new:

> In our day something essentially new has been added, almost ideally conceived to undermine the entire basis of human relations. One no longer fears that one's neighbor dissembles wilfully or maliciously. One takes it for granted that he does and in fact has no choice but to do so. The perceived difference between his inner feelings and his statements and between his statements and his actions is no longer attributed to bad will or evil intent but is considered to be a necessary aspect of his nature. For example, my friend may communicate certain information which he has won from an object. I scarcely acknowledge his words. It is not a contribution to my knowledge of the objective world which I am obliged to take seriously. What use is it to move my neighbor to speak, when from the outset I am not prepared to believe him?

A perfect example of Buber's assertion is the exchange of diplomatic notes in the Cold War. Statesmen on one side send lengthy diplomatic notes to those on the other, knowing in advance that the other side will condemn them as worthless. One wonders whether they are ever read, despite statements by the various foreign ministries that experts are studying the texts.

A far more noxious form of split consciousness in the modern world is the refusal to see the existence of the next man. This curious manifestation borders on the land of the fairy tale. The high point in mutual "you-don't-exist" politics was reached in the Berlin strike of railway workers in 1949. It was as if the two halves of the city had each been struck blind. It made no difference whether a statement was issued by the East or West Berlin city magistrates or the West Berlin trade unions, or the East Berlin *Freier Deutscher Gewerkschaftsbund*. In theory the opposing organization was simply not there, because one or the other occupation power had not recognized it. Neither had the Western commandants recognized the East German mark currency, nor the East German commandant the West German mark. However, the question of how these two currencies should be exchanged was at the root of the strike. It was almost impossible at the time for a West Berlin reporter to persuade an editor in Stuttgart to print the word *Reichsbahn** in the text of his story. "It does not exist," the man in Stuttgart said. "The word is forbidden; it is now called *Bundesbahn*." But in the East Zone the railroad was and still is called *Reichsbahn*, and it was the workers of this *Reichsbahn*, which functioned in West and East Berlin, who were on strike. Thus there resulted a kind of intercourse between ghosts. Theoretically, negotiations between opponents who did not exist for one another were not possible. To listen to the other side was already treason, because it meant recognizing the other side. Only thanks to the fact that on the highest level protocol allowed the Western and the Eastern city commandants to know each other, and that on the lowest level the railroadmen themselves—whether they came from the East or the West—knew that they belonged together, could a late solution be found.

Anybody who followed these lunatic events at all closely knew

---

*The former German state railways and still the name of the East German railways.

that someday an Otto John case was bound to happen. The officers of the occupying powers began to grow nervous. They had to suspect every German civilian of being a double agent, and saw every German soldier as a future deserter. In the last analysis, it is the highest form of insanity when a man who happens to have been born in Leipzig is a traitor if he sympathizes with the capitalist system, and the man born in Heidelberg is a traitor if he spreads Communist ideas. Surely this is the quintessence of political schizophrenia.

We have now reached the no man's land which is the "homeland" of the men between the warring front lines. The countryside here looks very German, which is not coincidence, for the Germans have become the world's leading authorities on crossing the lines and on living conditions between the fronts. The man who has the strength to refuse to join either side becomes, to use Ernst Jünger's phrase, a *Waldgänger*.*

He may or may not be recognized by the world, but he remains whole. Few have such strength. Karl Heinz Schaeffer, born in 1927, is one. His experiences have been recorded by Heinrich Frankel. At the age of sixteen Schaeffer was a member of the Waffen-SS. From 1946 to 1952 he was a leading figure in the East German youth movement, and fled in 1952 to the West Sector of Berlin. On June 17, 1953, he crossed the border again to fight in the East German insurrection, and since then he has been working for an organization trying to strengthen resistance to the Communists in the East Zone. He lives and works in the West, but is by no means entirely happy there, as he openly confesses. The feeling of devotion is missing in West Germany, also the strong sense of comradeship and the waves of overwhelming enthusiasm which he knew in both Nazi and Communist youth movements. His type exists on both sides of the border, and it has become more or less of an established phenomenon. Such people move back and forth regularly, until they are caught by one of the two sides and condemned as

*A man "who walks alone in the woods."

THE "DIVIDED" MEN AND THE "TWO-FACED"

traitors. Wolfgang Schwarz, born in 1916, has written an extraordinary piece, called "The Lubjanka Ballade," which is the
epic poem of the dwellers in no man's land. The subject is, for
a change, not the German trapped between East and West, but
the European, drawn to Russia by its breadth and its primitive
power but repelled as an antitotalitarian by its Communism.
The hero, a former squadron leader in the Cossacks, joins the
doomed army of General Vlasov, the tragic Russian Army of
Liberation which Hitler created. The men in Vlasov's Army
were mostly Russian prisoners of war who had fallen into German hands. They hoped to liberate their fatherland from Communism, whereas Hitler wished to use them for his own purposes.
The Soviets, naturally enough, handled them as traitors, and
now those who managed to escape to the West work for the
Americans in counterespionage or propaganda. The men of
Vlasov's army are perfect examples of the unfortunates who in-
habited the no man's land in the Landscape of Treason.

The first citizens in the landscape of treason are the homeless,
the displaced persons, the people without families.* They dwell
in its most barren wastes and crevices. As Rosenstock-Huessy
remarks, it is they to whom the revolution appeals. They are
especially subject to what they believe to be the ideal of the
"other side," irrespective of where it may lie, either geographi-
cally or ideologically. In her chapter on the young British traitors who fought in Hitler's "British Free Corps," Rebecca West
reports that most came from broken or unhappy homes. The
American prisoners of war who remained in North Korea to
work with the Chinese Communists after the armistice in Korea
came from similar unhappy backgrounds. The problem of homelessness is subtler in its manifestations than the simple cases of
psychologically disturbed young men and women. One need
not lose one's home. Merely to alter its place in one's private
standard of values is enough, and involves the risk of commit-

---

*In a special way, homosexuals also belong among the homeless, because
according to present-day laws they live outside the law in most countries and
are therefore constantly subject to threats of blackmail.

ting treason. Several traitors learned to love two countries and were torn between their allegiances. The Japanese who worked in the Sorge spy ring had all made acquaintance with the outside world, which was different from and far more attractive than the picture the Tokyo war lords had painted of it. Julian Wadleigh, who alone of the suspected State Department executives confessd to having stolen documents for the Russians, had studied at Oxford. Ezra Pound was an American "expatriate." Noël Field, whose father was Swiss and mother English, was born in London and studied at Harvard. He married a German and came to resemble a cultivated European more than an average American. The fantastic complexity of William Joyce's nationality and allegiance will be discussed in Chapter 15. Sometimes retroactive feelings seep into the consciousness of immigrants. The American Jews of Russian descent cannot fail to feel an instinctive warmth for the regime which overthrew their hated enemy, the Tsar.

It is instructive at this point to recall that Italy has recorded none of the particular treason so marked in all other countries caught up by the calamity of the Second World War.* Catholicism as a unifying bond and the tightly knit family unit give each man his place in Italian society. And though the Italian vegetable dealer in one of New York's poor quarters would save his pennies all through his life for a trip to the "old country," his strong religious and communal ties never allowed him to betray the United States when war broke out between the two countries. Italians seem to be immune to the disease of internal homelessness.

The existence of such displaced persons is not always entirely negative. For some it has meant breaking out and starting anew. Each one must search out his own way and make a new life for himself, drawing only from his own resources. In the home country there is a certain pattern of behavior which continues

---

*The atomic physicist, Bruno Pontecorvo, does not disprove the statement, for he was an Italian Jew whom the Fascist anti-Semitic laws had forced into the kind of exile so often the prerequisite for later treachery.

to guide the individual mechanically, long after he has lost his inner direction. Once he has lost his home, this last prop is removed and he must face the world alone and unprotected. The magazine *Newsweek,* in an interview with Arthur Koestler, who has been through all the political and religious beliefs of our time in one way or another, found that of all the types of homelessness Koestler's brand was one of the most bitter. Koestler had wandered in and out of allegiance to so many ideologies that he had become a kind of virtuoso. In this way one can attain a certain stability, but as a rule it is accompanied by the loss of the kind of courage which springs from total insecurity. In the midst of inner disunity, falsehood and treachery, this courage to seek a new way and a new language is the blossom that can unfold in our landscape.

Walking on, we come upon the border peoples, who are not exactly homeless nor displaced in the ordinary sense but are torn between the two cultures which pull at them. The more often boundaries are pushed about arbitrarily in Europe, the more of them there are. Reinhold Schneider describes their plight superbly in his account of the Alsatian publisher, Joseph Rossé:

I have now to speak of a very controversial figure and a friend. The political twilight in which he was condemned to live cannot be dispelled, certainly not by me. I am not judging him but accepting him as he was. Just as the accent on his name—Rosse or Rossé—appeared and disappeared, so political estimations of him have varied. All that changes nothing in the relationship which held us together. Rossé may be a hero today and a traitor the day after tomorrow. That does not interest me, for I am determined to ignore the obsession with the political side of men's characters. On his fiftieth birthday, Rossé was awarded the gold medal of the Nazi party. Could he have refused it? On the street he always made a faint suggestion of raising his arm in the party salute, which quickly became the traditional French lifting of the hat. . . . In the crypt of the ancient church at Audlaw there stands a stone bear. Researchers into sagas and myths say that the bear is the beast of the border, shy, unsteady, always in lumbering flight. That was the way Rossé lived, powerful and timid. That was the way he crossed a street, hurriedly with his hands jammed deep into the pockets of his old trench coat and his eyes bent on the pavement. . . . I do not believe that time heals. If it does, it will have the blessing of the land and inheritance for which Joseph Rossé lived and for which in his third imprisonment, in bitter suffering and anguish, comforted by God like one of his chosen, he died.

5. THE IDEOLOGIES AND THE NATION

WE have seen how at the birth of the nation the feudal state was swept away and how ideology stepped into the gap left by the disavowal of the grace of God. We shall now look at the development by which ideologies came to be identified with specific political parties until each party could claim to be the only spokesman for the state. This union of ideologies with national political parties took place within the outer framework of the nation-state. When Pétain in Vichy, or de Gaulle in London, spoke of France, they both meant roughly the same thing and not a world state, a secularized religion or some general aim for humanity. As the parties and the ideologies became absolutes of their own, the moment moved inexorably nearer the time when they would force the bonds of the nation apart and break free of the connection with a given country or language. Raymond Aron outlined this situation in answering the question as to whether members of the L.V.F. (Hitler's Legion Volontaire Française) had been traitors. "If they were not traitors, who is a traitor? If they were traitors, why are the Frenchmen who collaborated with the Americans and the British not traitors? Why are the Communists, who may someday collaborate with a Russian army, not traitors? On the day on which each party has chosen its ideology, there is no longer a national entity, and with the same stroke of the clock there are no more traitors. There are just clusters of foreign parties accusing each other of treachery."

That grim hour has not yet been reached, but we are living in a period of striking transition, in which the individual's de-

48

cisions are taken now for—and later against—the state. The first great test case came in 1914. The Social Democrats in the Reichstag voted for the war credits, an act of loyalty to the Kaiser and the Reich, which betrayed the Socialist International. In those same heated days Jean Jaurès, the French Socialist, was shot by a nationalist who hated Jaurès for putting peace and Socialism above "patria." In another sense, the mute camaraderie of the trenches and the inconceivable stupidity of the slaughter broke down barriers between the nations which had formerly seemed impassable. Barbusse's *Le Feu* expressed the supranational feeling which grew up on the political Left Wing. The various "front" soldiers of the Right Wing, after the war, had a similar premise, despite their noisy nationalism. Reactionary veteran groups in all the European countries in the 1930's had much more in common with each other than with the Left-Wing pacifists or the Socialists in their own lands.

The decisive year in the progress from national to international civil war was the year 1917. From the West it brought the return of the emigrants embodied in a new military power, America; from the East it brought the Russian Revolution. Americans had claimed at the time of the founding of the republic, 140 years before, that they were the defenders of freedom and the rights of man. The fact that new citizens are "naturalized" and not "nationalized" speaks for the way in which Americans tend to see their form of political organization as the natural and given one, worthy of men. The Bolsheviks declared that they were fighting for the exploited. Both powers retreated from the European scene immediately after the war. America withdrew into "isolationism," disgusted with the treachery, ingratitude and corruption of the "Old World," and Russia recoiled to struggle with the colossal problems of internal civil war and upheaval. Because of this retreat, few political analysts saw what de Tocqueville had seen as early as 1835: "There are two great peoples on the earth who, starting from different points, seem aimed at the same goal, the Russians and the Anglo-Americans. Their histories are different and their routes to power as well,

49

but there seems to be a secret divine plan calling each to hold the fate of half the world in its hands."

In the period between the First World War, which had been a purely nationalist war, and the Second World War, which was a mixture of nationalist and ideological war, Fascism had spread as a kind of international movement. Wherever it had taken root, in Italy, in Germany, Spain, Portugal, Poland, it developed different forms peculiar to each country, so that the national differences always remained more pronounced than the ideological conformity. Therefore it was not astonishing that in the following war, only two of the Fascist countries fought side by side —Germany and Italy; the latter much against its will. Where Fascism remained nothing but a movement, as with Mosley in England, Degrelle in Belgium—or where it produced only isolated "leader" types like Major Kotzias in Athens—national goals were always in the foreground, and the "big brothers" in Berlin and Rome were hailed only when it was necessary to cover up weaknesses at home.

When Hitler seized power in Germany, the former arena in which a large part of the political and social problems of the day had been fought out was closed for the duration of his reign. Since Germany had been in the vanguard of developing moderate as well as radical Marxist thought for decades, the rise of a dictatorship there tended to push the struggle between Socialism and the liberal bourgeois and democratic way of life away from the center of Europe. Leading groups of opponents emigrated to the new centers of ideological warfare: New York and Moscow.

America returned to Europe and to the world scene in the Second World War. This time the missionary zeal of the crusaders from the New World was even greater than the first. As early as the Atlantic Charter, before America had actually entered the war, Roosevelt had taken the ideological leadership from Churchill on behalf of the whole Western world. The trumpet calls were out from Right to Left. On the Right, Henry Luce proclaimed the "American Century." On the Left, Henry Wallace predicted the dawn of the "Century of the Common

Man." Clarence Streit cried "Union now," rallying the World Federalists to his banner. And the representative of all that was good and true on Wall Street, Wendell Willkie, beamed at the tired peoples and promised them "One World."

In the field of ideology, Hitler had managed to create a considerable confusion by his shifty foreign policy. His pact with Stalin caused wailing and gnashing of teeth among Communists who could think for themselves. His subsequent attack on Soviet Russia drove what were later to be the predestined archenemies into each others' arms, where they stayed in close embrace until the Third Reich was defeated. This wartime alliance, in retrospect to become one of the chief territories of treason, was facilitated by strong Left-Wing tendencies among Roosevelt's advisers.

Because of this alliance, the latent civil war, which is the dominant political factor of our time, could break out in its present form—the Cold War—only after the weakest ideological opponent, National Socialism, had been eliminated. In this new kind of war, nationalist aims and ideological fronts sometimes fall together and sometimes cross each other, and this crisscross pattern sets the stage of present-day treason. There is generally a conservative streak on the nationalist side of the opposing forces, and a revolutionary element on the internationalist side. For the conservatives, the idea of heritage is a fundamental value, as is the belief in a constant process of transformation and renewal of old values. Both produce a cyclical view of history. Whereas the progressives conceive of history as a logical and straight course, and believe that man, whatever his inherited constitution, can be modulated by a change in the conditions surrounding him and thereby contribute to the betterment of mankind as a whole. It is this belief that man can be improved which gives impetus to both American and Russian action.

The totalitarianism on one side corresponds exactly to that on the other. Where they differ is on the question of freedom. Freedom under one system reaches just to the point where it stops in the other. On both sides one prefers to discover, rather than the beam in one's own eye, the totalitarian mote in another eye.

Albert Camus, one of the most uncompromising and courageous members of the French Resistance, and no Communist himself, is a good example. In his struggle against the clemency advocated by François Mauriac as a Christian who was ready to accord pardon even to the former collaborators, Camus claimed Christianity to be totalitarian when he wrote: "The Greeks did not deny the existence of the gods, but they assigned them their due share. Christianity, which—to use a fashionable word—is a totalitarian religion, cannot accept such a pluralist mentality in which everybody receives his natural due." In his turn the Camus of the 1940's demanded a totalitarian kind of absolute justice which contained its own brand of inhuman elements.

The totalitarian features of international Communism have been too often cited and explored to require elaboration here. It is just as important, however, to recognize the totalitarian features in Western behavior and thought. The demand, for example, that the political views of a poultry specialist must be in harmony with those of the government before he can get a job with the ministry of agriculture, if not totalitarianism, is surely a step in that direction. The famous debate between Camus and Mauriac shows in its broad lines how the democrat Camus, in his quest for an absolute justice, displays the very features of the totalitarian society which he so fiercely condemns, and it is one of the reasons that the dialogue between the two men had such great significance in drawing the lines between the ideological fronts.

National treason differs from ideological treason in several ways which are important to note in tracing the development of the ideology loosened from its national basis. When the French executed Laval, it was a clear case of betrayal of the country, France. Whatever world public opinion may have thought of the justice of the sentence, it agreed that the condemnation of Laval was an entirely French affair for Frenchmen to judge. Ethel and Julius Rosenberg, on the other hand, were condemned to death under American law, but the issue involved went far beyond the national boundaries of the United States. One side saw the Rosenbergs as traitors to the cause of humanity and freedom, but others, not all admirers of Moscow—men like Einstein and the editors of the *Gegenwart*—asked themselves whether a crime against general human standards had not been committed when the Rosenbergs were condemned.

Justice, human rights, human dignity, humanity itself have ceased to be merely cherished ideals of the whole race and are now the subjects of ideological movements. Although these movements dwell in the shadows of the giant powers in the Cold War, they make a hesitant effort to lead an existence of their own. The plan to work the codex of war crimes into a general code of crimes against humanity is one manifestation of an internationalist ideology. The failures and confusions of the Nürnberg trials have rather dampened enthusiasm for an international code of law, but in other areas of activity much progress has been made. The UN and UNESCO have cultivated loyalty toward an international body, as distinct from loyalty toward one's own nation. The International Labor Organization, which burst full grown from the League of Nations as its idealistic offspring, has even gone so far as to introduce a little loyalty oath of its own: "I solemnly promise to carry out the tasks laid upon me as an employee of the ILO in complete loyalty, to keep the interests of the ILO in mind in the performance of my functions and in directing my activities, and neither to request nor accept instructions from any other authority or government outside of the international organization." David Bellow, in an article reflecting on his years as an international civil servant, points out the dilemma and the fate of the delegate who actually tried to place the interests of the ILO above his instructions from the home country. In practice, it is very difficult for delegates, especially those from small countries, to resist pressures from their home governments. There are several cases which concern the dismissal of UN staff that reveal another kind of conflict related to the Cold War.

The chief difficulty in the effort of creating a supranational loyalty toward mankind has so far always been the fact that every ideological organization could be turned into an instrument of politics by one or another great power or group of powers—whether it was the League of Nations or the United Nations, the "Spanish Committee" or the "Fighters Against Inhumanity"—and that this made it a given field for treasonable activities. On the whole, the UN has so far been able to withstand being misused by one power group, but it is still far from uniting its members to common consent.

The world does not yet know a "total" ideology which could be accepted by everyone, as for instance all the world agreeing that a thief must be punished—whether in Arabia or Africa, Communist Russia or free America. At present we have only ideologies at war with each other, fighting the Great Powers (with whom, at the same time, they are inextricably bound) and producing among themselves the landscape of treason.

6. METHOD AND GOAL OF THIS WORK

WE HAVE SEEN that there is a difference between treason committed in the service of the nation or against the nation, and treason which is motivated by belief in or resistance to an ideology. This difference is the basis for the division of my material into two main groups. The first part, contained in the present volume, deals with treason and the nation; the second part—still to be published in English—is concerned with treason and the ideologies. In both parts, I have chosen to ignore the "bought-and-sold" traitors. Mercenaries are nothing new. They have always been, and will always be, with us, as long as greed for gain dominates men's spirits. The professionals and the mercenaries are more often spies than traitors, a distinction which, though hard to draw in the event, is nevertheless a meaningful one. A Frenchman who sends secret information to the military intelligence in Paris is a spy to the English and a patriot to the

French. The Englishman who sends material to a foreign power from his government post is a traitor. Richard Sorge, the German journalist and intimate of the German ambassador in Tokyo, who transmitted important secret information on German and Japanese military activities to the Soviet Union, was a spy to the Japanese, but to the Germans a traitor, or rather both spy and traitor.

In the following pages I try not only to describe one kind of treason, but to give typical examples of the complicated phenomenon. My approach is quite empirical. I do not ask whether, according to contemporary opinion, a case was really treason. I have simply chosen cases in which a court, police proceedings, a state or parliamentary investigating committee or a political committee, has accused or convicted the man of treason, or has deprived him (on grounds of insufficient loyalty or "reasonable doubt") of his job or means of subsistence, or prevented him from further practice of his profession or ordered him to leave the country. The sense of the proceedings against the man rather than the words of the charge has been my guide in selecting the cases presented. In America, for example, as a result of the legal system, the charge is more often perjury than treason—as in the cases of Hiss, Remington and Lattimore—but the real meaning is clear to everyone.

What has been happening in the Communist part of the world has been excluded from this inquiry because we lack the necessary insight into the technical approach of the legal machinery, as well as into the thoughts and the inner metamorphosis of the accused. But we obviously cannot ignore the enormous influence of decisions and actions taken in Moscow, since they have been able to produce a frightening organization of subversion and an apparatus to counter this subversion which seems to be almost as frightening.

I have also excluded the Nürnberg trials, together with the other proceedings arising from the defeat of the Axis Powers, though they must be mentioned when we deal with ideologies, court proceedings or crusades which have to do with crimes against humanity. But the Nürnberg trials and the de-Nazification proceedings, in so far as straightforward crimes such as murder, arson, plundering and robbery were not in question, have raised such a fog of accusation, counteraccusation and resentment, that unbiased judgment is still impossible. Discussion of them here would merely thicken the poisonous miasma which already lies over them. There are resentments involved in the cases which I consider below, but in most they are beginning to ebb sufficiently to give the student a chance to speak a measured word.

Similar resentments are also involved in other spheres, some of them still very violent, others beginning to quiet down. For this reason it is best to emphasize at this point that, on the one hand, men as far apart as Laval, Canaris, Quisling or Goerdeler were motivated by a similar fear of Communism. Whereas, on the other hand, the conviction that the wartime alliance with Moscow was a necessity constituted a factor which united men as different in other respects as de Gaulle, Klaus Fuchs, Roosevelt and Harro Schulze-Boysen. Similarly we shall meet persons who were driven by their hatred of the Jews, and others who were primarily activated by their abhorrence of the persecution of the Jews.

First of all, therefore, it is necessary to try to understand the motives of the individual actors, as well as the trends which moved whole groups or organizations, before we can get to the bottom of the question: What does the word treason signify in our time?

PART II
Collaboration

7. THE QUESTION OF ALLEGIANCE

IT IS an oblique and wry comment on our times that the word collaboration has come to have an evil overtone. The word means simply to "work with"; in itself a positive and admirable idea, one of the ideas fundamental to all human society. In tracing the history of the phenomenon of collaboration in its present sense, one must return to that great drama which heralded the beginning of the modern era, the French Revolution. The young Goethe was ten years old when his native Frankfurt was occupied by French troops at the outbreak of the Seven Years' War. Goethe lived through the period of transition, and in his life and experiences, as he relates them, one can watch the tentative development of the modern conceptions of war, treachery and collaboration. Through reading Goethe's account of the various occupations through which he lived, we get a picture of the changing attitudes, leading from old ones to those partially gripped by new concepts.

Occupation is always uncomfortable, but one learns to live with it. The King's lieutenant, the French Count François Thorane, arrived in Frankfurt and commandeered the stately old Goethe family house as his headquarters. The old house on Hirschgraben was capacious and cheerful with plenty of room to accommodate the Count and the Goethe family, which suffered very little physical inconvenience. Count Thorane was a severe, unsmiling man of upright and honorable habits. He had considerable interest in the arts, and early in his residence in Frankfurt summoned the most prominent of the Frankfurt school of painters, Hirt, Schütz, Trautmann and Seekatz, to report to his headquarters, where he met with the painters and ordered a series of works to decorate his own château. The studio was set up in the sunny little dormer room in which the young Goethe

59

lived. The children ran in and out of the studio and played in the house without overly respecting the military character of their uninvited guest. Frau Goethe, who could speak a little Italian, learned enough French from the gossipy interpreters to be able to get along more amiably with the count. Grandfather Textor, Burgomaster of Frankfurt, had a permanent box seat at the Frankfurt French Theatre, and the young grandson was allowed to go almost every night. He grew familiar with the entire range and breadth of the classical French drama, and soon spoke perfect French, even essaying brief works on his own in Racine's Alexandrines. During the battle of Bergen the residents of Frankfurt were anxious lest a French defeat turn Frankfurt into a battleground, and Frau Goethe and the children placed all their hopes on their house guest. In *Dichtung und Wahrheit,* Goethe wrote:

> The King's lieutenant had been constantly on horse-back during those days, something very unusual for him. We had seen little of him, and by the time he returned his presence was much needed in our house. We ran out to meet him, kissed his hands and poured out our joy. It seemed to please him. "There, there," he said, and smiled in a much more friendly manner than was his wont. "I am happy to be back for your sakes, my dear children." He ordered sugar cakes, sweet wine and delicacies for us and then went to his room, surrounded by a crowd of gesticulating, pleading and beseeching people.

How different the reactions of the occupied are to the occupier in the twentieth century. In Vercor's *Silence de la Mer,* the beautiful and moving story is told of a young German officer who is quartered with a French family during the German occupation of France. The family remains completely mute in his presence and flatly refuses to say a word to the hated alien. It suspects and soon knows that he is a kind and gentle human being, but still refuses to speak to him. At night his steps echo in the corridor and the sound of his pacing up and down in the room above their heads disturbs their evening meal. When he enters the room to speak to them, they are mute. Soon they begin to know his habits, to listen for the familiar sounds of his footsteps, and they begin to love the lonely young man with whom they will not speak. On the day, the last day, when they realize that he is leaving them forever, they assemble to see him off, and as he takes leave of them he hears an almost inaudible *"au revoir,"* the first and last words ever exchanged between them. This stubborn silence has a spark of intense goodness in it, for the family is still capable of loving its enemy, the representative of the occupying army. They do not close their hearts to the spark and accept their feelings. The events in the occupied countries after the liberation lead one to wonder if even that last spark has been drowned in a wave of revenge.

Goethe saw the attitude toward the enemy change in the course of his own lifetime. The way is long from the pleasant civility of the relations between Count Thorane and the family Goethe to the punishment of French musicians for playing in a concert sponsored by the Wehrmacht during the Second World War. In the days of Count Thorane, steps had already been taken along this road. Not everyone felt moved to kiss the Frenchman's hands after the French victory at Bergen. Goethe's grandparents and Frau Goethe, like most of the Frankfurt *Bürger,* were strongly pro-Austrian. Frankfurt loved the gala coronations of the Hapsburg monarchs as Holy Roman Emperors which continued up to the beginning of the nineteenth century, and the citizenry felt an emotional tie to the Austrian emperors. Goethe's father was, on the other hand, *fritzisch,* a follower of the great "Fritz," and not in the least pleased about the presence of the French. Goethe bursts out at one point in his recollections: "What were the Prussians to us?" His father glared with impotent rage at the promenading French and disapproved of his son's Francophilia, though he was proud of the boy's dazzling linguistic accomplishments. On the day of the French victory at Bergen, the father threw the family into an agony of embarrassment by replying to the Count's friendly greeting on the stairs: "I wish to God they had chased you all to the devil, even if I were forced to go too." The attitude is no longer just *fritzisch,* but German, the expression of a German nationalism which could not bear to see Frenchmen in German cities.

As part of the entourage of the Duke of Weimar, Goethe entered Mainz as the French troops were streaming out and the victorious German armies pouring into the city. The streets became scenes of scuffles and flurries of fighting. The defeated French had been promised a safe conduct for their withdrawal, but the anger of the mob was so great that incidents occurred to break the truce. Typically, the fury of the mob concentrated itself less on the foreigner than on the *Klubisten,* the Germans who had collaborated with the French. "Wagons and coaches rattled through the streets and everywhere the citizens of Mainz had concealed themselves in the narrow drainage ditches. When the refugees escaped one ambush, they fell at once into another. The coaches were halted and the men and women inside examined. If they were French they were allowed to pass, but if they were well-known *Klubisten. . ."*

Goethe intervened at a dangerous moment as the mob was about to catch up with a fleeing couple, a man in an ill-fitting French uniform and at his side "a well-formed and beautiful woman in male clothes." The mob screamed: "Stop them, kill them," and Goethe stepped in front of them as they rushed forward, commanding them to halt. The area of the headquarters of the Duke of Weimar was not to be sullied with blood. The mob halted, undecided. On Weimar territory there was no place for crime or revenge. One dared not take the law into one's own hands, better leave things to the proper authorities. . . . After a tense moment, Goethe succeeded. The pair went on its way. "The mob had been distracted from their lust for revenge, just long enough. Had it surged thirty steps farther, no one could have stopped it."

As Goethe returned to the headquarters, his English friend Gore, who had watched the whole incident from the window, began to scold Goethe for having mixed himself in a bad business and for having risked his life for people who were in all probability criminals anyway. They argued back and forth for awhile. "I pointed laughing to the clean square in front of the headquarters and said, at last, rather impatiently, 'Well, it's part of my nature. I had rather commit an injustice than tolerate disorder.'"

Here we have two opposing principles which play a significant part in the regions of collaboration: Justice (Gore) versus Order (Goethe). Or: Order versus Law; Human Being versus Citizen; even Being True Blue *(Treue)* versus Loyalty, if one takes loyalty in its restricted meaning as derived from *léges-loi,* in the sense of allegiance to the law or constitution. In most cases those who collaborate are on the side of order, those who resist, on the side of justice. Camus emphasized the distinction with sharpness in his first reply to Mauriac in the famous exchange to which we have already referred. Mauriac had pleaded for *"charité"* in dealing with the collaborators, to which Camus answered: "As a human being I am compelled to admire Mauriac for his capacity to love, which extends even to traitors, but, as a citizen, I must protest. His approach would turn us into a nation of traitors and mediocrities in a society which all would condemn."

In the decade since Camus wrote those words, his judgments became milder. All over Europe the contempt for collaboration has lost some of its poisonous quality, because every European nation has become more or less collaborationist. We Germans, who might have been inclined to scorn the Quislings and Lavals in 1940, have learned through our experiences with four occupying powers just how many shades of gray there are between compulsion and voluntary collaboration. We have watched friends and acquaintances who set out upon the road to Bonn or Pankow become prisoners of their own original choice the farther they travel. Sometimes the initial compromise was unavoidable and the eventual consequences unforeseeable. With each step the individual became more of a prisoner of the picture which the public had drawn of him from his words or his silence.

8. THE QUISLING RIDDLE

VIDKUN ABRAHAM LAURITZ JONSSON QUISLING was born in 1887. He holds the dubious distinction of being the first man in the Second World War to be called a traitor, and his name has become the word for a special sort of treachery of which he was the first practitioner. Yet in a way Quisling was the least typical of all the quislings. He was a citizen of the last European country to acquire nationhood before the great upheaval of the First World War. For years Norway had been ruled by Denmark. In 1814, King Frederick of Denmark ceded the Norwegian provinces to Sweden, and when Quisling first began to go to school, his monarch was Oscar II of Sweden. When he was eighteen his sovereign became King Haakon VII of Norway, for Norway had dissolved its ties with Sweden and had declared itself independent. Bitterness against the former Swedish masters and raging patriotism overwhelmed the country, carrying young Quisling with it on a wave of jingoism and throwing him head over heels into an entirely unexpected career. He himself wrote of his choice of career: "As a small child I had determined that I would preach on Sundays and practice medicine on weekdays. Under the influence of an assiduous reading of Norwegian history and, perhaps, caught up in the mood of 1905, I chose a military career and entered the War Academy in the same year." One can read several essential characteristics so marked in Quisling's later life in that brief quote. The preaching returned again in the religio-philosophical aspect of his national renovation program. The drive to help his fellow men became a reality in his work in the famous Nansen relief and rescue action after the First World War. The patriotic mood turned into fanatical Nordic nationalism, directed principally against Denmark and Sweden.

Tyresdal, the valley in which Quisling was born, was at that time as wild and as remote from civilization as anything in a Knut Hamsun novel. Bears roamed the countryside. Life was simple and hard. Quisling's father was an archdeacon and a very stern man. About his school days, we have available two contradictory opinions. David Abrahamson, in his book *Men, Mind and Power,* traces all of Quisling's failings to an unhappy childhood, to insecurity, fear of the bears, anxieties and inferiority complexes. He declares, on the basis of sources which he does not disclose, that the boy from the backwoods was disliked by his fellows, laughed at because of his country dialect, and given bad marks by his teachers. For his part the boy hated school intensely and despised the other boys. The shame of his dialect may have contributed to his later passionate advocacy of the use of a separate Norwegian language. During the union with Denmark, the mixed Danish and Norwegian *Riksmaal* was the official language. The struggle to make the native peasant dialect, the *Landsmaal,* the official language is still going on.

Benjamin Vogt, who knew Quisling well, paints a pleasanter picture of Quisling's relations with his fellow students at the War Academy. Although he was considered gloomy and eccentric (and he was surely both), he was held in a kind of awe. The Norwegian schools place more worth on academic performance than almost any other schools in Europe, and Quisling was a remarkable student, compiling one of the most brilliant records ever achieved at the War Academy. The other students respected and revered the startling prowess of the man, and their praise may have twisted Quisling's own estimate of his capabilities. Vogt writes: "In other countries the eccentric individualist would never have been allowed to go his own way to that extent." Quisling's career after graduation from the academy began as brilliantly as his academic one. At the age of thirty he was a captain on the General Staff. From 1919 to 1921, he was military attaché and secretary to the Legation in Helsinki. From 1922 to 1926, he was a co-worker of Nansen in the great relief program in Russia and Southern Europe, and later he became joint representative of Great Britain and Norway for the timber concessions in Moscow. After Great Britain broke off diplomatic relations with the Soviet Union in 1927, Quisling became British representative on the commission, holding the position of a legation secretary at the Norwegian Embassy in Moscow.

The fact that the celebrated Fridtjof Nansen selected young Quisling to assist him in his famous relief project in Southern Russia brought Quisling a good deal of sympathy he would otherwise never have enjoyed. It was Nansen who revived the great Viking tradition of Norway, and who forced the major powers to accept the right of neutrals to deal with belligerents on equal terms. Nansen immediately used this right to formulate practical relief programs, and together with the League of Nations devised the "Nansen passport," which returned the right to exist to thousands of homeless refugees. This great and revered Norwegian selected Quisling to be one of his closest co-workers, though their relationship revealed a hint of Quisling's impending tragedy. Nansen seems to have appreciated Quisling's remarkable abilities and the superb job that he had done in the Ukraine. Quisling spoke Russian perfectly, made an imposing impression, and was deeply connected with the people whom he was helping through his Russian wife. In the foreword to his journal, *Through the Caucasus to the Volga,* an account of a joint trip, Nansen praised the "inexhaustible amiability" of his traveling companion. On the other hand, Western journalists, who were working in Moscow during the 1920's, found Quisling anything but amiable—they found him peevish, morose and proud. His sullen silence, combined with a growing dissatisfaction at his lack of promotion and progress in the Army, hardly made him a charming companion. Nansen, a sensitive and gifted man, must have perceived these traits in Quisling's character. When Norwegian Professor Olaf Brock, who was doing research in Russia at the time, approached Nansen with the suggestion to award Quisling a medal, Nansen remarked: "I can never get to the bottom of that man. He never says anything."

The medal was not awarded, the promotion never came

through, and Quisling's feeling of having been unjustly treated grew ominously. When the War Office refused his request for a prolongation of his foreign leave of absence beyond the agreed five years, he resigned in a rage and remained in Moscow. Quisling had for some time been scrambling to get out of the narrow limits imposed by a military career, and he busied himself with a mass of plans and activities which had little or nothing to do with his military position. Professor Bergerson described how Quisling worked on his system of ethics during the civil war in Russia instead of studying the tactics of the Red and White armies, as he was supposed to be doing. At school he learned higher mathematics; at the War Academy he learned Chinese. While working with Nansen he made plans for building up a "red guard"; and as Cabinet Minister in the parliamentary government of Norway, he aimed at overthrowing the parliamentary system.

These confused intellectual and political activities were no obstacles to sharp practice in business. What actually took place in the chaotic first years after the Russian Revolution will very likely never be cleared up satisfactorily. What is clear is that Quisling's close friend, Fredrik Prytz, and to some extent Quisling himself, seem to have engaged in dealings in the expropriated holdings and properties of the dispossessed nobility, apparently with considerable profit. Prytz was caught in an enormous foreign-exchange scandal and was forced to flee across the border by night. Despite his abrupt departure, he managed to get away with a good part of his liquid assets and reappeared in Norway a very rich man. He later became a disciple of Alfred Rosenberg, and supported Quisling's reactionary party as its main financial backer. How deeply involved in all this Quisling was is not clear. He collected a fine array of art works which later became the foundation of his own fortune. Most of the pieces arrived in Norway under the cover of Quisling's diplomatic immunity, the same immunity which saved him from the clutches of the GPU, which examined him for four hours on the subject of Prytz's activities.

It may have been the shock of meeting the Russian secret police which took away his taste for life in Soviet Russia. In 1928, Quisling had decided to live in Moscow. In 1930, he returned home. No longer was he the brilliant young General Staff officer, the prominent philanthropist and well-known figure in international circles in Moscow. He was just a pensioned captain with half salary, embittered and forgotten. He had changed from a reformer sympathetic to the great Communist experiment to a mortal enemy of Bolshevism in any form, and he began to try to alarm his fellow countrymen to the dangers lurking in international Communism, which was threatening to submerge the "Nordic Race." His book, *Russia and Norway,* was a failure.

In his search for political allies, he first approached the Workers' Party, but soon drifted into the Peasants' Party instead, finally accepting a portfolio as Minister of War in the Conservative government of Herr Kolsted. From this vantage point he launched a sensational attack on the Social Democrats, based on documents in the War Ministry through which Quisling tried to prove them traitors. Behind the scenes he maneuvered to bring down the Kolsted Goverment and make himself prime minister.

His fickleness and vacillation were intensely annoying to all the political parties. We shall see later in our discussion of ex-Communists that these very years when Quisling wandered around in aimless circles were the crucial years for them as well, during which they broke their former ties and floated about in the same confused way. The victory of *petit-bourgeois* narrowness, embodied in Stalin, over the international and intellectual wing of the party, drove away foreign Communists. The rise of the terror and the new cant, the show trials and the liquidations, destroyed the last shreds of their faith and sense of purpose. Like Quisling, they wandered in the thickets and copses, stumbling and falling. Despite his similarities to the ex-Communists of the 1930's, he differed from them in one vital way. Where they reverted to liberalism, he went all the way to the reactionary Right Wing. He had lived through the mass state in Russia and wanted no part of it. The parlimentary regime in Norway disgusted him. His new aim became the creation of a tightly organized political elite.

At the time of Quisling's return from Russia, three years before Hitler seized power, he wrote a brief *curriculum vitae* as is customary in Norway on the twenty-fifth anniversary of one's graduation from the gymnasium. It affords an interesting insight into the direction of Quisling's thought:

> In intellectual fields, I have continued to study, in addition to military science, history, languages, the natural sciences and mathematics which were always my favorite subjects at school. In recent years, all these splintered activities have begun to center on philosophy as a common denominator. My interest outside of my daily affairs has concentrated more and more on the search for a unified theory of existence, based on science and experience, which combines the two with religion. Disturbed living conditions and other unfavorable circumstances have prevented me, up to now, from becoming effective publicly in a literary or scientific way, but I hope still to be able to say my word before the final silence comes down.

Quisling's philosophy as a "common denominator" was essentially an attempt to bridge the gap between reason and faith. Today it would be called a drive toward "wholeness" in an atomized civilization. In our century numerous extraordinary men have been striving for the same things: Werner Heisenberg, Carl Jung, Ernst von Weizsäcker, Max Scheler and Martin Heidegger, Rilke, D. H. Lawrence, Ernst Jünger and Gottfried Benn. They have all approached different sides of the problem, often misunderstanding one another and rejecting the very elements which they had in common. Unfortunately Quisling was not a clear thinker. His thought, such as it was, suffered the further disadvantage that it took place in complete isolation from the developments in other countries. It is doubtful that he had any acquaintance with the works of men who might have helped ease his discomfort. It was another of Quisling's misfortunes that he tended to seek the solution to these questions, which are in essence personal ones, by altering the political forms of human society. It is probable that he had heard of the school of political thought known as the conservative revolution in Germany, and may genuinely have believed, along with many others, that the Nazis were in some vague way the political realization of the program. National Socialism was to bring the "wholeness" so ardently desired. He was fully aware that Europe was in ferment, and he was determined to make a contribution of some sort.

His detailed program can be seen in a speech he delivered to a workers' meeting in 1936:

The struggle of the Nasjonal Samling* against Bolshevism is not a struggle against the workers but for the workers. The Nasjonal Samling is a movement for the protection of freedom and peace in Norway. Its aim is to bring about a new political order in our society. This new order is the organization of a national state for the liberation of all Norwegians. The only thing able to combat international Marxism is a solidly constructed national state which satisfies the demands of the people for a just order of society and foments a sense of national solidarity and idealism opposed to all internationalism and materialism. The Nasjonal Samling is not copied from any foreign movement, whereas Marxism is both international and un-Norwegian. The first task of the Nasjonal Samling is to found a constitutional government, a truly national government, independent of the political parties. Trade unions must be based on a healthy cooperation and not on the class war.

Bjoernsen once wrote; "We are all socialists and I am one." What Bjoernsen meant is precisely the future Nordic Socialism for which the Nasjonal Samling is fighting, built on security of property, nationalism, the family, religion and all the spiritual values, a kind of Socialism for which we all yearn, a Socialism which will free the spiritual life of the people. . . . Norway must leave the present League of Nations. We shall never surrender the rights and honor of Norway to any international body. Greenland must be returned to Norway and opened to our fishermen.

The last sentence in Quisling's *curriculum vitae:* "But I hope still to be able to say my word," shows plainly that it was not just philosophy, patriotism and Nordic Socialism which drove

*Quisling's Right-Wing party.

70

him, but the devouring unfulfilled ambition of the rejected man. Everything he tried to do to satisfy this consuming ambition, to be heard, to be known, to be honored, failed miserably. His attack on the workers' party and his wild accusations of treason were the first of several sensational attempts to get into the limelight and to force his way into the popular consciousness. The details of the second attempt are still dark, as is so much in Quisling's life. He claimed that he had been attacked by an assassin in his office, a man who was armed with, of all things, pepper. The assassin had beaten him up, he said. Nobody ever seems to have found out whether the story was true or pure fantasy. The third attempt was his cocky undertaking to collect the elite of the country in his new party. The Norwegians expressed their interest in the scheme by giving the Nasjonal Samling exactly 1½ percent of the votes cast—not enough for one pitiful seat in the Storting. The major part of his supporters deserted the party and many of his financial backers left him. At the same time he had to stand aside, impotent and absurd, while Mussolini built an empire in Africa, Franco crushed both the Communists and the liberal, democratic parliamentarians, and Hitler surprised Europe with his *faits accomplis*.

According to some of my information, it took a long time before Quisling, in the depth of his misery and frustration, put out feelers to the Nazis. He ignored Prytz's repeated offers to arrange a meeting with Rosenberg. After the outbreak of war in September 1939, Quisling approached the German professor, Ulrich Noack, who was living in Oslo, with an elaborate plan for an anti-Soviet program. The Molotov-Ribbentrop pact had just been signed, but Quisling could not possibly believe that the Nazis thought of it as more than a piece of paper. At the beginning of the Russo-Finnish War he declared to the German professor that militarily Finland could hold out until Germany was able to mount a large-scale attack on Russia. It was important, he argued, to make it clear in Berlin that the Scandinavian states would have no option but to call for help from the Western powers, if they were exposed to the unrelenting pressure

71

of Soviet expansion. An immediate intervention seemed to him a self-evident necessity for Germany.

Although in the end it was via Rosenberg and not Noack that Quisling found his way to Hitler, he had a very different view of the proper policy toward Russia than did the fanatical Baltic German. Quisling was a genuine Russian expert. He knew Russia intimately, and though an enemy of the Bolsheviks, he was a friend of the Ukrainians, Caucasians and Tartars with whom he had lived. Quisling assumed that a German invasion, if properly staged, would bring about the immediate dissolution of the Soviet regime, and urged the Germans to come as liberators and not conquerors. It was essential that they occupy the heart of Great Russia, which they could use as the core for the construction of a new and stable order, but the non-Russian areas might well be left unoccupied and ought in any event to be treated with great care and friendliness. Later in Quisling's program they were to be granted self-determination and autonomy. All the minorities were to be encouraged to express their separatist tendencies, and the peasants were to be given back their lands. The program outlined by Quisling has certain similarities with the broadcast of Radio Free Europe today.

To his astonishment, Quisling was compelled to recognize that the Germans were actually serious about their nonaggression pact with the Soviet Union. He learned of this on his first trip to Berlin in the middle of December 1939. An anti-Soviet strategy was not in favor, it appeared. The speed with which he adapted himself was dazzling and speaks for a highly developed talent for political opportunism. Noack was placed on the shelf. The way to Rosenberg's office was free. What was actually discussed between the junketeering Norwegian and his Nazi friends, what promises exchanged, is not known. It may well be that Quisling was given a wink by a person or persons in high positions that, although unfortunately his plans were not feasible at the moment, neither were they uninteresting in the long run. It may be that Hitler was secretly pleased with Quisling's rabid anti-Bolshevism. Plans for the invasion of Denmark and Norway may have been discussed with a view to allotting Quisling his role in the operation.

According to Churchill's account, based on the notes of Admiral Raeder, Quisling and Raeder were invited to a conference with Hitler on the 14th of December. Raeder wished to convince Hitler of the urgency of beating the English to the occupation of Norway, and Quisling obviously had his reasons for desiring a German invasion. Quisling laid out a full plan for a Putsch in Norway. Hitler, apparently frantic lest the secret get out, announced that he could not consider undertaking any further military actions, and anyway preferred a neutral Scandinavia, despite the fact that on the same day he had given orders to the High Command to begin preparations for launching the attack on Norway. According to Ulrich von Hassell's account, Hitler later became furious at the unexpected bitterness of the Norwegian resistance and accused the German Ambassador Bräuer and the Gauleiter Habicht of having placed too much confidence in Quisling and his friends and of having failed to cultivate King Haakon.

Churchill's version sounds more convincing. Bräuer, like the German Minister in Copenhagen, was surprised by the invasion, although since Christmas there had been rumors in Berlin about what was going to happen. He did not steer a straight course. Hubatsch's description of Bräuer's conduct during the crisis is fascinating reading. On the morning of the rejection of the German ultimatum by Foreign Minister Koht, the King, the government and the Storting began to leave Oslo for the north. Quisling, acting apparently quite on his own, declared himself head of a new government. The ambassador spent the morning with the military attaché, Oberst Pohlmann, whose orders directed him to leave all political matters to the civilians. The telephone rang uninterruptedly. Angry Norwegians demanded to know what was going on. Bräuer, in the disagreeable position of not having the slightest idea, merely replied wearily that he had no instructions covering Quisling. The confusion grew. Suddenly, an S.A. *Standartenführer* appeared, brandishing an order from

73

Rosenberg. Before the speechless ambassador and Oberst Pohlmann, the *Standartenführer* declared that negotiations with Quisling had begun, that Quisling was to form a new government,
and that if anyone had any doubts there was the order from
Rosenberg to prove it.

The phone rang again for the hundredth time. General Engel-
brecht was on the line. He said that a certain Herr Quisling
had appeared with his bodyguard, had announced that he was
the new premier, and had proceeded to occupy the third floor of
the hotel which the Germans had seized for their headquarters.
The general asked the military attaché: "May I arrest the man?"
Oberst Pohlmann replied: "Five minutes ago I should have said,
without the slightest hesitation, 'Throw the man out on his ear,'
but now I really don't know. There's some sort of S.A. emissary
here from Rosenberg with an order. We must wait. Perhaps the
commander in chief will prove to be better informed." A few
minutes later word came through from a higher military command
post in Hamburg: "Hands off the Quisling business . . . Even the
commander in chief is unable to act."

In the short space of one hour a disastrous series of events had
taken place which were to bring tragedy to Norway. There might
even then have been some faint glimmer of hope had Bräuer not
persisted so obstinately that King Haakon accept Quisling as his
new premier. By the time Bräuer realized how foolish his demands
were, the Luftwaffe had slammed the door on all further chance
of negotiation by bombing the field headquarters of the king. A
compromise government, acceptable to the king, might have been
found if the Germans had been more agile, and this would have
saved many lives. Who was to blame? Hitler? Quisling? Raeder?
Rosenberg? Bräuer? The generals? History will have a difficult
task in apportioning the blame.

The Norwegians view the course of events differently. For
them, there is no question but that Quisling was twice guilty.
First, when as a former General Staff officer and captain he flatly
refused to obey the mobilization order of the commander in chief
on the 9th of April; and secondly, when he apparently directed his

followers to act as guides for the onrushing German panzer columns, showing them the way into the heart of the country. It is of course debatable whether he was correct in urging Norway to lay down arms and face the inevitable, as Denmark had done. At times the king, the government and Hambro, the president of the Storting, had inclined to the same view. What is beyond any question is that Quisling, by *assisting* the German invaders, had committed an act of flagrant treachery. The worst of his crimes, however, in human terms, surely lies in the fact that by his overhasty intervention and seizure of power he prevented a compromise solution: the formation of a government which would have been neither Quisling's nor Nygaardsvold's. Quisling's act cost many lives. By the time the Germans saw that it was no use trying to run the country through him, it was too late to negotiate; too much blood had been spilled and too much hate aroused. They threw Quisling out and tried to piece together a caretaker government, all useless and vain. They might just as well have left Quisling in office.

The "counterfigure" to Bräuer and Quisling during the long period when the king and his ministers were out of reach was Bishop Eivind Berggrav. Bishop Berggrav, as the highest prelate of the land, became automatically the senior official left in Oslo because of the special constitutional role of the Church in Norway. Ambassador Bräuer had several meetings with the bishop. During one he said: "We have not put Quisling in power. We were simply forced to work with Quisling because there was no other civil administration left in Oslo."

Bishop Berggrav replied: "There are only two authorities in Norway. One is the authority of his Majesty the King and the Constitution, to which I have sworn an oath and shall remain true. The other is your bayonets. Before the latter, a temporary authority, I bow only to the extent that the word of God and my conscience permit. Any other authority does not exist. The man Quisling is simply a traitor, Ambassador, no more and no less."

Berggrav spoke for all of Norway. The young men who might have been reluctant to answer the call to arms, in the hope that

everything would settle itself peacefully as in Denmark, reacted
to Quisling's proclamation at once. The usurpation of power by
Quisling was too much for them. They threw their packs over
their shoulders and set out for the north with skis and weapons,
to join their king. One man whose views carried weight with
Norwegians spoke out for Quisling—Odd Nansen, the son and
successor to his father as the director of the Nansen aid administration. Nansen soon had reason to change his mind after an
unfortunate dispute with the traitor. After the occupation the
Nansen organization had joined forces with the Red Cross and
had become, naturally enough, a center of resistance activities.
Nansen knew perfectly well what was going on, as he later
admitted, and was, as a result, summoned to an audience with
Quisling which proved to be exceedingly frosty. At the end of the
audience Nansen said: "One last thing. I should appreciate it
if you were not to use the name of my father quite so often in
your speeches. You know it is almost indecent." Quisling reacted
with rage and screamed at Nansen: "It is not I but you who misuse his name." The result was that Odd Nansen joined Bishop
Berggrav in a concentration camp where both remained until the
liberation. Again, we cannot be certain whether Quisling alone
was responsible for the waves of arrests, for his role in the whole
course of events evades exact analysis.

At the time of Quisling's trial, in view of the state of public
opinion as a whole, it was not surprising that the whole press
tended to regard him as the scum of humanity. *Time* magazine
published a report of the trial which typifies the state of mind
in September and October of 1945. It said that there was not a
scrap of worthiness in his entire defense, only a certain obstinacy.
He sat collapsed in the box. His thin, reddish hair was uncombed.
His collar was far too big and his eyes looked like buttons in his
pasty face. "What have you to say for yourself?" the presiding
judge asked. Quisling was shaken from his stupor. He looked
over the heads of the tense, silent crowd in the court. "I am a
martyr for Norway," he thundered. The court smiled. His voice
sank to a whisper and a shrewd glitter appeared in his eyes. He

had, he claimed, merely intended to save Norway from an invasion by the English. He was nervous and his restless eyes filled with tears. His plump chin trembled and his hands shook. He reddened when his eyes met the gaze of the judges.

This was undoubtedly the image which the world wanted of Quisling. In reality, things were different. Vogt, for example, who genuinely disliked Quisling, paints quite another scene. "It was incredible that his speech could have had such an effect on the hearers. There was no question of its efficacy. The only plausible explanation is that Quisling was speaking of the only thing in the world which genuinely interested him. He was transported to a state of profound eloquence. A second explanation is surely the skill with which he wove the Kingdom of God and the land of his birth together. In connection with his plainly visible faith, the words seemed superbly believable." In another passage Vogt declares that Quisling's defense was masterly. Neither the judges nor the crown attorneys were successful in crushing his arguments. The defendant was often at loggerheads with counsel for the defense, a further indication of the stubbornness of Quisling's faith in his own ideas and the rightness of them.

The famous Swedish barrister, Hemming Sjöberg, wrote: "There can be no doubt about Quisling's patriotism . . . Neither for profit nor for honor was he guilty of treachery. His treason had its roots in love of his native land." The nine justices, led by Chief Justice Annaeus Schjödt, thought otherwise, and the Norwegian people agreed with the judges. In contrast to the Swede, they knew only too well what five years of rule by Quisling had meant. On the night of October 24, 1945, Quisling was executed by a firing squad.

Norway and the world were satisfied. A few voices were raised against the sentence and the nature of the proceedings. Counsel for the defense, Berg Paal, met with a certain amount of agreement in his assertion that the court had not been impartial. Annaeus Schjödt was well known as a leading opponent of Quisling's. Vogt replied to the charge by Berg with the rather primitive counter: "Are not the guilty always judged by their opponents?" The legal argument used by the court was, to say the least, unusual. Quisling and his counsel had pleaded that he had done everything to spare his native land from unnecessary bloodshed. The justices found in their verdict that it was not a question of the future consequences of present acts but of the nature of the acts themselves:

If, therefore, accused is aware that he wilfully cooperated to surrender his country to the hands of its enemies, he acted in bad faith, even if he argues that it was for the good of the country. It may, indeed, be further remarked that even in the event that later happenings justify accused's assertion and prove his acts to have, in fact, been for the good of the country, he would not be free of the guilt for having committed treason. The person who surrenders a place or a fighting unit in time of war to the enemy is guilty of treason, even if he saves human lives through doing so. If the ideas and wishes of the individual are to be placed above the law, then every law concerning treachery becomes illusory.

Four prominent Norwegian subjects, including Colonel Ruge, the commanding officer whose mobilization order Quisling had refused to obey, testified during the trial to Quisling's good character. Friends of the condemned man spoke of the "Quisling riddle." It seemed to them that his personality had fallen into two radically different parts, the one he displayed as a young man and that which replaced it. Vogt writes that the court, concerned with the points of fact and law in the charges, could not stop to consider the subjective nature of his guilt. The court, therefore, contributed nothing to the solution of the Quisling riddle. Many Norwegians and foreigners, according to Vogt, simply could not believe that the philanthropist and savior of countless human beings could have been a traitor. Some foreign observers have argued that it was not Quisling but the political conditions in Norway which were really guilty: the lack of political personalities with clear aims, the inadequate defense preparedness, and the confusion of foreign policy. These people look on Quisling as a man crying in the wilderness, who, hearing no answer, takes his own route.

In the General Staff file of General Nikolaus von Falkenhorst on the eve of the invasion of Norway the following estimate of Quisling was entered: "Pro-German; of no importance, considered a dreamer." Vogt, who had no taste for Quisling's ethical universalism, saw nothing whatever of the dreamer in him. He was just another intriguer. Noack asserts that Quisling lacked the crucial capacity to make decisions at the decisive moment and the will to stick to them, once made. Chief Justice Schjödt referred to him as a "slinking Führer." Eight doctors examined Quisling, two of whom were present throughout the trial. Their medical opinion was unanimous: Quisling was not mentally ill.

None of the answers fully explains the complex nature of Quisling's character. One element which appears again and again in the accounts of his life and personality is the strong sense of being persecuted and the resulting mistrust associated with it. He always felt himself rejected, disregarded and neglected, and he reacted with exaggerated sensitivity to the slightest suggestion of an insult. In this ceaseless watchfulness, the constant fear of treachery, and in the persistent feeling of being followed, spied upon or persecuted, Quisling displayed many of the same symptoms and traits which are so striking in those returning after long stays in the Soviet Union. Such people, even if not Communists, seem to bring back a persecution complex as a souvenir. This pattern of behavior, which we have noted in Quisling, marks several of the foreign correspondents who have spent any length of time in Russia, and of those the most virulent cases are the ones who have married Russian women. Had Quisling, during his long years in the Soviet Union, been so "naturalized" that he never got free of the omnipresent fear of the terror? Was his hate of Bolshevism merely a projection of a consciousness aware of similar drives and impulses within itself? There is much to be said for seeing the Quisling riddle not as a Nazi phenomenon, but as an unusually eccentric manifestation of self-perverted Bolshevism.

9. *KING LEOPOLD OF BELGIUM*

FOUR kingdoms were overrun by Hitler in the spring of 1940. In the first few days after the invasions all four monarchs expressed the desire to remain with their peoples and were more or less forced into different behavior by circumstances. Only one of them has been condemned as a traitor by world public opinion and by a section of his own countrymen for his actions.

The situations of the four states were different. Belgium's neutrality had already been violated once before at the beginning of the First World War, and the shock of that first invasion and its aftermath had not been forgotten. Holland, from 1815, and Denmark, from 1864, had enjoyed periods of uninterrupted peace. Norway found itself in a situation equally as exposed as that of Belgium: on one side, as the neighbor of Soviet Russia and Finland, between whom in the winter of 1930–40 a bloody war had raged, and on the other side, because of the shipments of ore from northern Norway to Germany and because of British attempts, in violation of Norwegian territorial waters, to stop those shipments.

The astounding German ultimatum presented after the military offensive had actually begun—for the receipt of which the two Scandinavian foreign ministers were called from their beds—was answered differently in the different countries. King Christian of Denmark and his government protested, but submitted without an attempt to offer even token resistance, and remained in office. Aside from occasional incidents and privations which increased as German power declined, the regime of the occupation in Denmark was bearable on the whole. The king evoked Hitler's fury once by omitting the obligatory, flowery phraseology in a birthday message which he sent the Führer, but he remained free to come and go and took part in the life of the nation. There has never been any criticism of his behavior during the occupation.

In Norway there had been not only a double violation of

neutrality by both the Germans and the British, but also an outbreak of shooting before the German ultimatum had been handed over. In addition to these complications, the German Ambassador in Oslo, Dr. Curt Bräuer, had only recently arrived in Norway, unlike Cecil von Renthe-Fink at Copenhagen, who had formed (as a result of many years of diplomatic activity in Denmark) an intimate and friendly relationship with the country, government and opposition. Throughout the crisis Bräuer displayed a marked inner uncertainty in his dealings with the Norwegians. As soon as they had rejected the ultimatum, the government, king and the Storting moved to a secret place, in order to preserve freedom of action in the face of German pressure. In Elverum, near Hamar, where the legal government had come to rest, preparations began for talks in which a *modus vivendi* was to be worked out with the Germans. The president of the Storting, Carl Hambro, the same man who later became the most irreconcilable foe of all collaborators, expressed on behalf of the entire parliment his confidence in the select committee which, under the direction of Foreign Minister Dr. Halvdan Koht, was supposed to lay down guiding principles for the negotiations. Since, as Hambro declared, the Storting could not lead a wanderer's existence indefinitely, it ought to grant the government wide powers to negotiate a treaty. Two members of the Workers' Party, two from the Right, two from the Left and two from the Peasants' Party were elected, and were to be assembled immediately. The rest of the Storting was to return home. Hambro himself flew to London. En route, in Stockholm, he asserted that it was self-evident that Norway would have to conclude an agreement with Germany.

That no solution was found was neither the fault of King Haakon and his government nor to their credit. It was rather the consequence of the activities of Quisling and of the indecision of the Germans themselves, among whom the Foreign Office and the Army General Staff favored negotiations with the legal government, while Hitler, the Navy and Rosenberg preferred Quisling (the consequences of whose arbitrary intervention have been described in the previous chapter). Finally a series of accidents

81

and unfortunate events rendered all delayed second thoughts futile. King Haakon's actions and his crossing to London after the war had been lost in Norway were thus contrary to his original intentions and conditioned by external events.

A month later German troops faced Belgians and Dutch under arms and ready to fight. Then began the crisis of conscience of the two monarchs confronted with military defeat. Queen Wilhelmina of Holland, who was the first to be faced with a decision, resisted for two days the entreaties of Foreign Minister van Kleffens to go to London. She wanted to remain, but an unsuccessful German attempt to kidnap her convinced her that she should move her headquarters to another part of Holland. She begged the British Government for a plane for this purpose, instead of which it sent a destroyer. The queen's intention was to go to Vlissingen, and only when the ship was under way did she learn from the captain that they were going to England. Her withdrawal from her own country was thus quite involuntary. Harry Hopkins has described the event as he heard it pictured by the English queen: "She got to Buckingham Palace at five o'clock in the afternoon, wearing a tin hat given to her by the commander of the destroyer. The queen said she was a fine, courageous woman, and it was perfectly clear from this conversation that she arrived in England entirely by accident and not by intent on her own part."

These are the events which one must know in order to judge the decisions of King Leopold III. In addition, it must not be forgotten that his father, King Albert I, had flatly refused to follow the call of Prime Minister de Broqueville to leave the country during the First World War, and that king and government had remained in Belgium throughout the war, without, however, falling into German hands at any time. Leopold's great-grandfather, German by birth, was both a Russian general and a British prince before he became the first ruler of the kingdom, a nation suddenly fused as a result of European power politics. The consequence was that, whereas in the people themselves the preconditions for internal cleavages and conflicts were always present, in the monarch there was an inheritance of

Greater Europe views, which in the age of suspicion were to bear bitter fruit.

Virginia Woolf, the great English writer, who has always been supremely conscious of the finest nuances in her use of words, wrote in her diary on May 28, 1940: "And today at 8 P. M. the French broadcast the treachery of the Belgian King. The Belgians have capitulated." This sentence could be the motto under which the life of Leopold III has stood since that day—the odium from which he never recovered, although Reynaud's radio speech and everything connected with it was pure propaganda, psychologically conditioned by the war.

In his person the king united both the functions of head of state and supreme war lord. Several of his critics, including England's late King George VI, have taken the view that he completely confused his two functions; that there could be no objections to his actions as a commander in chief, but that as a king he should have left his country to establish his government elsewhere.

Popular criticism, on the other hand, which found its way into Virginia Woolf's view, has seen his crime precisely in his action as commander in chief of the Belgian Armed Forces. And this, despite the fact that the military situation had been depressingly clear from the very beginning, and the only surprise was the speed with which the Germans, employing new methods of attack, came on. On May 20th, a mere ten days after the invasion, a joint British-French-Belgian staff conference was due to be held in Ypres, but so complete was the dissolution of the lines of communication that British Commander in Chief Lord Gort could not get to it. The breakthrough on both sides of the Courtrai followed on the 24th, and the Germans moved up to within thirty miles of Dunkirk. From that moment on Churchill had one aim and one aim only—to get the British forces safely out of the mess. On May 27th he telegraphed Gort: SENDING FOLLOWING TELEGRAM TO KEYES [British personal representative to King Leopold], BUT YOUR PERSONAL CONTACT WITH THE KING IS DESIRABLE. KEYES WILL HELP. WE ARE ASKING THEM [the Belgians] THAT THEY SACRIFICE THEMSELVES FOR US.

The telegram reached Keyes only after he had flown back to London on the 28th. The confusion had become so great and news communication so chaotic that King Leopold's communiqué to General Gort, saying that he was forced to lay down his arms, never arrived. He had, however, already informed Keyes and the British and French military missions at his headquarters on the afternoon of May 27th, as the situation steadily deteriorated, that he would have to beg for an armistice at midnight. The news reached London at 5:45 A.M. and the headquarters of the French High Command of General Weygand at 7 A.M. This did not keep Prime Minister Reynaud from declaring to the Belgian Prime Minister, in the presence of Pétain and Weygand— who knew the truth but preferred to keep silent—that King Leopold had sent a truce delegation to the Germans without previously informing his allies. As a result, Reynaud had the means of exerting strong political pressure on the Belgian Cabinet during the following days.

Keyes, who had been on the scene, tried to set him straight. While still in Belgium he had reported that the Belgian Army would capitulate far more quickly if robbed of the king's leadership. After his return to London, he asserted firmly that the king's resistance had allowed thousands of British soldiers to reach Dunkirk, and commented: "No one was in a better position to judge this than I. Had the king deserted his army during the exhausting retreats from the Thaye to the Lys, the consequences would have been far more disastrous."

With these telegrams, Keyes attempted to counter Churchill's determination to try, by every means in his power, to get the king to England. A telegram to Keyes read: TRUST YOU WILL MAKE SURE HE [Leopold] LEAVES WITH YOU BY AEROPLANE BEFORE TOO LATE . . . VITALLY IMPORTANT BELGIUM SHOULD CONTINUE IN WAR, AND SAFETY OF KING'S PERSON ESSENTIAL. On the afternoon of May 27th, Churchill telephoned the Belgian Prime Minister in France that all efforts must be made to ensure that the king and his mother come to England.

Churchill's position is easily understood. For him, who

throughout the winter had been urging the neutrals of Europe to join the war on the side of the Allies, it seemed vital that, in the rear of the victorious Germans and under cover of the occupation regimes, a resistance should remain active and that no general stabilization take place—as in Denmark. The war must be carried on. In this way it would not be just England alone, but a great part of Continental Europe, too, which waged war on Hitler. Besides, he had to try to intimidate the "capitulators," since the military situation, especially that of France, had become catastrophic. Churchill was too magnanimous to use the same kind of falsifications as Reynaud, and in a temporary statement in the House of Commons, refused to pass judgment on the actions of the king, in his capacity as C.I.C., and added a special word of praise for the Belgian Army. Nevertheless, on June 4th, after conditions in France had further worsened, he publicly associated himself with Reynaud's accusations.

Before things had gone that far, a fierce controversy had taken place in Belgium between the king and his ministers. It reached its peak when the ministers sought out the king in Castle Wynendaele to persuade him to leave the country with them. On the same day the retreat lines were cut, the French Army was fleeing westward, and the entire Belgian populace was in flight, pouring along the highways on foot, in cars, baby carriages and bicycles. The atmosphere in which this confrontation took place, two and a half days before the capitulation, has been described by Alfred Fabre-Luce:

> The men, who find themselves at the highest point of command, who must preserve their complete cold-bloodedness in order to meet a ceaselessly changing situation, can no longer rest. . . . They have become sleepless men, who begin slowly to lose their memories, to see things and hear imaginary noises. In their spirits well-known faces transform themselves into frightening ghosts. Outside the pale of reality, between the distorting mirrors of this enchanted cabinet, they form their opinions and make their decisions. Later during the years of exile, loneliness and reflection they will exhaust themselves to justify on the basis of later events and constructed excuses the over-hasty interpretations which sheer exhaustion forced on them. . . .
> On the other side, the king, surrounded by half-packed suitcases. . . .

85

But even when the niceties of etiquette begin to crumble, the king remains more tranquil than his ministers. He alone feels less oppressed by time, for he does not even consider flight. He does not fear falling into the hands of the enemy, for in spirit he has already made this sacrifice. Military duty is always simpler than civil. Nevertheless, his ministers take pains to work on his conscience. A question of principle separates them from the king. They are of the opinion that since the appeal of the 10th of May, if not a firm alliance, surely a strong tie exists between Belgium and its guarantors. Leopold asserts that the exact obligations of Belgium are restricted to the defense of her territory and he does not want to take on himself any additional obligations. We shall see that these differences of opinion are purely theoretical. To explain the violence of speech we must add other elements. Henri Spaak, a sensitive, impressionable man, dominated by a series of sincere, if everchanging, convictions, is in the grips of the raging epidemic Treasonitis. For several days now the French troops, who on May 10th marched in under triumphal arches, have been pouring back through hostile, silent villages, where an occasional shot is fired.

The arguments flew back and forth. Each side found that the other had left it in the dark. The ministers threatened to break with him when the king, with obvious contempt, chided them with their "ludicrous haste to flee." They declared that—and it was probably their best argument—if the king remained, the capitulation would be turned from a military act into a political one, and in any event he would either become another Hácha or be deported. The king replied that he must share the fate of his people, whatever it might be. If he remained, he would be better able to protect them from the dangers of hunger and forced labor. There appeared moments in this fierce grappling when each side could realize the justice of the other's arguments, and it almost seemed as if the king and his cabinet would share the terrible task: Leopold, by remaining and attempting to shelter the people; and the cabinet, by continuing the war from the outside, so that during the years of separation those who remained and those who left, the sufferers and the fighters, would together in mutual understanding create and preserve the unity of the fatherland.

But this did not happen. In the course of the ensuing four years the convictions of the ministers who had left suffered many changes. They, together with the 400,000 soldiers of the Belgian Army cut off from their homeland on March 28, 1941, became dependent on the goodwill of the French Government. Just how dependent was dramatized for them when Reynaud, at two o'clock in the morning, summoned Pierlot from his bed to inform him that as the Premier of France it was his duty to announce the capitulation of the Belgians. Reynaud added that this news would incite the people of France against all Belgians, and he therefore could no longer guaranty the safety of the refugees, whether in uniform or not, whether common civilians or cabinet ministers. Come what might, however, Reynaud demanded that Pierlot, as the head of the Belgian Government in Exile, publicly declare King Leopold as deposed and call the Belgian people to rebellion.

The machinery of propaganda was set in motion. French Minister of Information Frossard pleaded with Churchill to prevent Admiral Keyes from defending King Leopold. Reynaud deplored Churchill's moderation when speaking of the capitulation. The word "treason" filled the air. This is not the place to recount all the calumnies that the Belgian ministers and parliamentarians uttered about their king—Spaak, for instance, called the king's arguments crazy, stupid and even criminal—but it was not long before most of them retracted what they had said. There was a time during the French collapse when the Belgians wanted to negotiate with Hitler. Later they had the wish to return home. It was not conscience which held them back, but Hitler. Vichy cut their food supply, the Bank of France refused to honor their checks. In August, when the danger to England was greatest, Pierlot and Spaak intended to go to America. In September, during the Blitz on London, Spaak declared that the government in exile would resign as soon as the fate of the prisoners of war and refugees in France had been settled. In October —the danger of the invasion of England being past—Premier Pierlot appeared in London, the new headquarters of the governments in exile. "From there on," wrote Fabre-Luce, "the sovereign and his ministers find themselves in different worlds, between them is the firing line. They do not speak to the same Belgians. They must consider the effect of what they say on all sorts of strangers. The reserve forced on the head of the state in Belgium is incomprehensible in Paris and London."

The propaganda of the Germans, which the king had to battle even before the capitulation had actually taken place, showed just how different these two worlds had become. The German psychological-warfare campaign, launched parallel to the military invasion, had attempted to lame the fighting spirit of the Belgians by proclaiming that the government was about to desert the people. Leopold's counterproclamation began with these words: "Officers, Soldiers, whatever may come, my lot will be yours. I call upon you all for strength, discipline and confidence.

The slogan "My lot will be yours" was a good one, and many a Belgian heart may have beaten more proudly on that day. To carry out what has been promised in a moment of danger and high elation is not so easy in the gray monotony of day-to-day, passive endurance. The beginning corresponded to the intention. "What is to be the fate of my officers and men?" Leopold asked the German agent, Colonel von Tschuler, on May 29th. The colonel replied: "They will for the time being be considered prisoners." "In that case I declare myself a prisoner in your hands," said the king. He was not allowed to fulfill this pledge. Hitler directed him to remain in his palace, Laeken, and though he may have felt himself a prisoner there, he was nevertheless at home, surrounded by all his comforts, servants and family. This separated him from the people with whom he had vowed to remain. The exile regime released the troops from their oath to the king, because he had fallen into the power of the Germans.

Until he himself was finally deported to Germany, Leopold made several quiet attempts to soften the lot of the Belgians, to free the prisoners, and to halt the deportations. He received the president of the German Red Cross and offered him a cup of malt, which later appeared on the list of his treasonable offenses. The fact remains, however, that this quiet discussion brought the inmates of the prison camps a warm meal a day. One time only did he break his confinement to visit Berchtesgaden for an interview which his sister, the Crown Princess of Italy, had arranged. Later this visit was interpreted to mean that he believed in a German victory; this alone in the atmosphere of 1945 was an act of treason.

The king was thinking of other things. He had heard how the Gestapo operated in those conquered countries, Holland and Poland, which were left without leadership, and Leopold was convinced, in view of Hitler's sense of inferiority, that readiness to meet Hitler could lighten the burden for the Belgians. In fact a comparison with Holland does show that it had far more to suffer than did Belgium. However, the meeting during which the king refused to be involved in political talk was a failure. "Just another king whom I shall have to get rid of after the war," Hitler said, visibly irritated by the interview.

Leopold, however, had done one thing more which could not be set on the official list of accusations with which a committee of jurists and university professors concerned themselves in 1946: he had married. Not in terms of paragraphs of the constitution or principles of the civil law, not because of the capitulation which all thought reasonable, not because he remained in Belgium, which most were ready to understand, not even in the meeting with Hitler which remained just an episode, but in his marriage, Leopold condemned himself in the eyes of his people.

Although his wife was a commoner, that fact was not decisive. The destruction of the romantic image of the eternal mourning for his beloved Astrid, the princess from the land of ice and snow, whom he had brought home and for whose unhappy death he had been partly responsible, weighed less heavily than the fact that in a time of Belgian national agony he had thought of his own personal happiness. He had voluntarily assumed the role of prisoner and taken on the fate which befell his Army. Now he had abandoned that role, and into the place of his confinement he had brought the joys of a young bride. On the morning after the wedding there stood chalked on the walls of his palace this sentence: GIVE OUR PRISONERS GIRLS. In that sentence the people had condemned their king.

It is a prerogative of kings—rarely exercised by the heads of state in republics—to keep the larger lines of what is happening in perspective when their countries are overwhelmed by passions. King George V, during the First World War, had recognized this duty and brought to the notice of his government a warning that England's undertaking in Greece violated Greek neutrality as much as Germany had violated Belgium's. Despite a personal antipathy to Kaiser Wilhelm II, George V turned the force of his personality against the agitation to "Hang the Kaiser." King Leopold attempted a somewhat similar thing on the domestic political scene when he declared in his political testament of January 1944: "It is to be feared that the end of hostilities will be accompanied by a public thirst for revenge and by countless cases in which vent will be given to public and private resentments." At the same time he demanded that "the provisional holders of authority must contain expressions of opinion within legal bounds." He was trying to counteract in advance what later became a great purge.

Since he himself was out of the country and had earlier refused to follow the advice of Pierlot to dissociate himself from those who gave the appearance of doubting the eventual Allied victory, since mistrust had grown so great that many suspected his very deportation as a prearranged affair, he had no real influence. By refusing to rule, he had given his countrymen the example of passive resistance, as even de Gaulle and Eden admitted. But he had resigned himself to a role of passivity which was forced on him once more after the liberation—this time by his own subjects, who negotiated over him rather than with him. The controversy as to whether he should mount the throne again dragged on for years. Ideological influences from abroad played a considerable role, as did the internal conflicts between the Socialists and the Catholics—between the Flemish and the Walloons. Although Leopold was recalled after a popular referendum, the decision eventually went against him.

It was not only the events of 1940 to 1945 which worked against Leopold, although he had been cleared of all charges by the Servais Legal Commission. Domestically, the king was accused of having led from the very beginning far too personal a regime and of having given his confidence to Socialist Hendrik de Man, who like Leopold was convinced that certain basic, political weaknesses in the parliamentary system must be overcome, and who was prepared to fit selected Fascist elements into the Western pattern.

As to foreign policy, Leopold was accused of returning to neutrality. After the First World War, Belgium abandoned its ninety years of neutrality and allied itself with France through joint General Staff consultations, but when, in 1936, it became clear that England and France were not going to react to the German occupation of the Rhineland, that the Locarno Pact was a washout, that France was no longer able to help her allies, Leopold suggested that Belgium ought to arm herself and withdraw from her alliances.

The Belgian Government of the day agreed. The motive which moved the king at that time became gradually discredited, just as what had moved the English and French governments for a time fell into disrepute after Munich and the march into Prague. Leopold was one of those statesmen of the thirties who wanted to try coexistence with Fascism and National Socialism and who believed that the overflowing energies and land hunger of the Germans and Italians could be canalized into Eastern Europe and Africa. His conviction that Bolshevism was far more dangerous than National Socialism and that Hitler Germany formed the only barrier against Communism was a decisive factor. It would be most advantageous if both these menacing behemoths would destroy one another—something often thought but rarely publicly stated.

Leopold knew then what every child in the Western world of today learns in school—that Communist workers' groups are directed from Moscow. He had hurried ahead of his time and yet fallen behind, for he fought a two-front war: internally and

91

ideologically against the French Revolution; externally against the Bolshevist Revolution. In the world political constellation in which he found himself, he was inevitably crushed between the two.

10. MARSHAL PÉTAIN—SAVIOR OR TRAITOR?

MARSHAL PÉTAIN became a controversial figure for the first time during the course of the First World War and has never ceased to be one since. The irony of his controversial status is that with a slightly different turn of events he might well have been retired with the rank of colonel and never have been heard of by history. To some Frenchmen, on the other hand, he was France's greatest hero in the First World War, the peerless victor of Verdun and inspired leader of men. To others he represented the soul of incompetent defeatism and an archetype of the general who succeeds in nearly losing a war for all practical purposes already won. His controversial nature had been purely strategic and military in the First World War, but by 1945 it had become moral in the broadest sense of that badly abused word.

The son of well-to-do Picardy peasants, his career in the Army had been essentially both uneventful and uninspired, and seemed headed straight for the oblivion of retired officers when the freakish fates intervened by catching him up in the tornado of the First World War. There are those who contest the assertion that Pétain ever displayed any capacity for military leadership, and can indeed cite the evidence of reports from his military record, in one of which a commanding officer wrote that above all Pétain ought never to be made a general. Others, especially students of the Great War, endow him with above-average ability, nerves of steel, a sovereign calm and very great gifts for moving and inspiring masses of men. Pétain's year was 1917.

92

A crisis tore the battered French armies and mutiny spread through the sodden trenches and among the filthy and battered *poilus*. Pétain got them back into line, though no one quite knows how. He required no special discipline save the effect which his own still and confident personality seemed to have on the front-line troops. Léon Blum, whom the marshal put on trial in the Second World War, had remarked, during the First World War: "He is the wisest and most human of our generals." Foch, Pétain's great rival, said during the crisis of 1918: "Pétain is perfect in carrying out orders, but afraid of carrying responsibility and unable to command."

Elements of what was to happen in 1940 were already contained in the bitter inter-Allied controversies of March 1918. Ludendorff's offensive had thrown back the British Army. There was the danger of a wedge coming between the British and French armies while the British were rolled back toward the channel ports. Pétain, in his role of commander in chief, saw that the Allies were losing huge amounts of materiel and many prisoners. To his way of thinking, it was imperative to prevent the French reserves from being cut off, his own materiel from getting lost, and Paris from being threatened directly. Subject to assuring the success of these aims, he was ready to keep in contact with the British as far as possible. When Clemenceau covered him with reproaches because of his pessimism, Pétain said: "If we are defeated, we have the English to thank for it." A day later the fateful conference of the Allied commanders was held at Doullens and a unified Allied Supreme Command was created. Foch, not Pétain, was given command of it.

In the atmosphere of treachery and mutual suspicion which had poisoned Anglo-French relations by August of 1940, Field Marshal Sir Archibald Montgomery-Massingberd, G.C.B., K.C.M.G., writing at this time in the magazine *The Navy*, recalled that March of 1918 to memory:

At the Doullens Conference on March 26, 1918, at which Foch was appointed generalissimo, Pétain tried to let us down in a very similar manner, and wished the French Army to retire to a position covering Paris, leaving us to face the German onslaught alone and allowing the Germans to separate the British and French armies. I have seldom heard a senior general "told off" in public as was Pétain by Foch on that occasion! But Foch was a great gentleman, and treachery was completely foreign to his nature. Weygand's part in this sad affair is more difficult to understand.

Pétain, too, remembered what had happened on that day at Doullens. The recollection was to influence his decisions during the crisis of June 1940. The decisions of that summer are not the only points on the list of accusations against Pétain. Some of his opponents claim, in retrospect, to trace in his attitude a straight line which led to the defeat of 1940. In military affairs, they find that he cultivated the Maginot spirit, but failed to develop the line of fortress defenses to the north; that he rejected tank warfare, although its proponent, de Gaulle, was his favorite pupil; and that in 1934, as minister of war in the Doumergue Government, he allowed the arms budget to be cut. Curiously, it was Churchill who later defended the Maginot-line policy, saying that it took into consideration the difference in population numbers between Germany and France, presented a long succession of invaluable strong points and blocked off large sections of the front as a means of accumulating general reserves or "mass of maneuver." He added also that: "The offensive conceptions of the Maginot line were explained to me by General Giraud when I visited Metz in 1937. They were, however, not carried into effect."

In the field of foreign policy, Pétain was accused of showing sympathies for the authoritarian systems during the period between the wars. These sympathies were less for Hitler and Mussolini, whose approaches, personalities and methods were completely foreign to the elderly marshal, than for his neighbors on the Iberian Peninsula. Pétain made his first contact with the Spanish officer corps in the years 1925 and 1926, in the course of the joint Franco-Spanish military operations in Morocco to crush the revolution of Abd-el-Krim. It seemed the natural thing to send him as ambassador to Spain after Franco's triumph. All the normal diplomatic activities of an ambassador, friendly contact with the head of the state, good relations with the leading ministers, soldiers and industrialists, contact with the diplomatic corps (including in Pétain's case contact with the German Ambassador von Stohrer) have been held up by his critics to prove the old gentleman a Fascist. Exceedingly damaging in the eyes of his detractors were two meetings in the 1930's with prominent figures in the Third Reich. In 1935, at the funeral of Pilsudski, he met Göring, and in 1937 he met Colonel General Ludwig Beck. It is well here to recall that among the early followers of Hitler, Göring belonged to the conservative and relatively pacific wing. Despite the shady role he played in the Reichstag fire in 1933, Göring still enjoyed a glittering reputation as a dashing young flying ace of the First World War. Colonel General Beck was not a Nazi. A philosophically inclined, highly cultured gentleman of the old school, he met death after the bomb plot against Hitler in 1944. It is not surprising that Marshal Pétain received the impression from his conversations with Göring and Beck that the Germans, despite the noise and the violation of treaties, were essentially sane and moderate and that there was no serious intention of mounting an attack on France.

André Schwob has been Pétain's bitterest and most relentless critic. He goes furthest in imputing disloyal contacts between the marshal and the enemy. As an example he cites a note in Anatole de Monzies' diary from March 30, 1940, according to which Pétain said: "In the second half of May, they will need me." And from this deduces that Pétain had learned the date for the German offensive in the West in advance, through his Spanish contacts.

Since Pétain was a very taciturn man, his accusers found it difficult to prove that he took steps in the direction of conspiracy or treachery in the field of internal policy. His first real statement of opinion appeared in the *Revue des Deux Mondes* in 1940. "Liberalism, capitalism and collectivism are imports, which a France left to its own devices would certainly reject."

André Schwob's great indictment of Pétain appeared in his book *l'Affaire Pétain*. In it the year 1933 is selected as the beginning of the "conspiracy," because it was the year in which—in a reversal of their former attitudes—the reactionaries, instead of the Left, favored an understanding with the Germans. Even more disastrous, according to Schwob's indictment, was 1936, the year of the German reoccupation of the Rhineland. Premier Flandin hurried to London but came back empty-handed. At home the existence of the Popular Front offered new material for the Right against Communism. In those days a document—claimed to be from quarters close to Pétain—in which countermeasures were proposed in case of a Communist Putsch, went the rounds in high Army circles. In 1944, when the alliance with Moscow dominated Allied thinking, such a document could only be viewed as evidence of treason. The fact that Pétain never protested the use of his name in pro-Fascist articles by Gustave Hervé was taken as another sign of Pétain's participation in the "preparatory conspiracy."

Sympathy for authoritarianism, of which Pétain is accused, was at the time neither an isolated nor especially unusual attitude in France. Things were at boiling point. Radicalism was increasing on both the Right and the Left. The yearning for strong leadership grew as the fiber of the state was weakened, a yearning which has never been absent from the French mentality. It is one of the ironical twists of the Pétain story that of all people, de Gaulle, once Pétain's prized disciple, and under whose government the marshal was condemned, should become his first successor in the struggle against anarchy and party rivalries.

We have already outlined the chaotic events in the early stages of the war by describing the case of King Leopold. The story continues from there as the top British generals, together with Churchill and Attlee, arrived in Paris on May 31, 1940, for a supreme council of war. The British proposed a general evacuation of all fighting units from Dunkirk. Darlan countered by offering the British first claim on the ships. Churchill, in one of his splendidly magnanimous gestures, announced that the evacuation of the troops would take place on a basis of perfect equality between the two countries. Behind the flourish, Churchill was doubtless calculating that if the French Army, or a sizeable chunk of it, could be spirited off the Continent intact, the French would be psychologically prepared to continue the war from their overseas possessions. In May he had declared that the Belgian Army must be sacrificed. On June 11, in another meeting of the Supreme War Council, he made a similar demand of the French.

I emphasized the enormous absorbing power of the house-to-house defence of a great city upon an invading army. I recalled to Marshal Pétain the nights we had spent together in his train at Beauvais after the British 5th Army disaster in 1918, and how he, as I put it, not mentioning Marshal Foch, had restored the situation. I also reminded him how Clemenceau had said, "I will fight in front of Paris, in Paris, and behind Paris." The Marshal replied very quietly and with dignity that in those days he had a mass of manœuvre, of upwards of sixty divisions. Now there was none. He mentioned that there were then sixty British divisions in the line. Making Paris into a ruin would not affect the final event.

In the Second World War more than divisions were at stake. If the English considered France's withdrawal from the war as treason, the French considered the British attitude to the war in the air equally perfidious. General Sir Edward Spears has described the arguments on the question. General Weygand put pressure on Reynaud, Reynaud on Spears, Spears on Churchill, and Churchill on the staff of the Royal Air Force. At each stage the pressure weakened and the reservations grew, leading to the final British "No" to the whole business. Churchill justified the refusal by arguing that ultimately the battle for Britain, not the battle for France, would be decisive. "If we maintain control of the air and keep the sea open," he promised the French, "we shall win everything back for you." He kept his promise, but in June 1940, the French wanted something else. To them the British seemed to be saying that the fight for their country was a point of secondary importance.

Discord was the only constant factor in those dark and turbulent days. No one knew what was to be done. Churchill's opinion that France must continue the war from overseas had many supporters. At the end of the meeting on May 31st, while the participants were still clustered in murmuring groups, Roland de Margerie spoke openly of the possibility of waging war from Africa. "But Marshal Pétain's attitude," Churchill reports, "detached and sombre, gave me the feeling that he would face a separate peace. The influence of his personality, his reputation, his serene acceptance of the march of adverse events, apart from any words he used, was almost overpowering to those under his spell." The very question of North Africa shows how views change when the wheel of history turns. In the spring of 1940 it was a sign of their will to hold out that the French brought troops back from Africa. By the time Pétain was tried, recalling the troops had become a treacherous act, weakening the potential defense of North Africa. Reynaud himself later disavowed everything he did in May and June 1940, when he wrote: "On considering how the situation looked on May 19th when I took over the War Ministry, one reaches the following conclusion: both Gamelin and Georges should have presented me with the following alternative when I visited them together with Marshal Pétain: 'Either ask for a truce immediately, or prepare the continuation of war in North Africa.' "

In his reply to de Gaulle's attacks, General Weygand later offered a whole series of reasons for not having continued the war in Africa: the available troops were badly equipped and unprepared for battle; there was a shortage of transport ships to carry them; there were no supplies for their support; reinforcements could be carried by planes alone, and there were neither bombs nor spare parts at hand. His most cogent argument was that, had the French Government been moved to North Africa, Africa itself would have become a worthwhile goal of German operations. The Germans would have had no trouble, under the then prevailing conditions, in launching a major operation through Tripoli and Spanish Morocco, with the net result that

98

the Mediterranean would have become a German pond. In retrospect, Churchill expressed similar thoughts, when he asked if it really would have been in the Allied interest to move the French Government to North Africa. For then Hitler could have struck his opponents decisively in Africa and would not have needed to attack England or Russia to register progress in the war.

Be that as it may, after Reynaud's resignation on June 17th, the question was again raised for discussion. Pétain remained neutral. Weygand refused to consider it, fearing the effects of such an equivocal action on the armistice negotiations then just beginning. Laval was in favor of it. The attitude among the deputies was uncertain and hesitant. A majority had been initially for withdrawal and a minority for staying in Metropolitan France. One of the first decisions of the Council of Ministers was that the government should divide like an amoeba and one part should depart at once for Africa to avoid falling into German hands. Minister of the Navy Admiral Darlan placed the light cruiser *Massilia* at the disposal of any of those deputies who wished to leave France.

The adventures of the deputies who made the journey show that the atmosphere had already been thoroughly poisoned by fears of treachery and mutual suspicion. Herriot and Jeanneney feared a trap in Darlan's offer and took the land route via Spain. Twenty-four deputies—Mandel, Campinchi, Daladier and Mendès-France among them—stepped on board. The news of the signing of the armistice reached them while still at sea. Campinchi, who a week before had been minister of the navy, demanded that the captain change his course and sail for England. The captain refused to disobey Darlan and held his course, dropping anchor in Casablanca the following day. Mandel at once composed a declaration forming a government in exile and naming himself premier of the new cabinet. The manifesto, instead of going out to the world over the radio, landed on the desk of Governor General Noguès, who at once wired the contents to Pétain and Darlan. They, in the meantime, had abandoned the idea of two governments, and Noguès was ordered to place Mandel under temporary arrest. The dream of carrying on the war from Africa was unrealized, and with it the first of various possibilities of carrying on a consciously double-barreled policy from within and without, which would have worked in mutual, though necessarily secret, agreement.

A one-way policy of the opposite sort had been proposed by Churchill a few days earlier at the high point of the crisis. The immediate constitutional union between Great Britain and France which he proposed is probably one of the most unrealistic improvizations produced by his imaginative mind. It was the last attempt to tie the defeated ally to the British side in continuing the war. The French were not tempted. Churchill, who even in later years always had a soft spot for the plan, wrote of it: "Seldom has such a magnanimous offer met with such a pusillanimous response."

Suspicion was aroused, and the French began to murmur that the English were trying to place them under a guardianship. From that point on, relations between France and England deteriorated until they were no more than the expression of the changing fortunes of the war and time-serving maneuvers on both sides. Churchill himself registered, in his own attitude to France and to the French leaders, virtually every one of the changes in circumstances. At one point he was busily working on Roosevelt to get the President to exert full pressure on Vichy. At another point he turned back to France with flattering letters addressed to the "illustrious marshal." Next the rulers in Vichy were to be taught a lesson—that the British lion had teeth as sharp as Hitler's. Seven weeks later he wrote to General Ismay: "We shall support them [Pétain and General Weygand] with a minimum of six divisions, considerable air striking power and the necessary naval force, just as soon as they see themselves in a position to take that step for which we all yearn." Weygand was addressed as the "famous general" during his viceregency in Africa, and in the next moment as "a lame, pro-German defeatist," and finally, when Hitler demanded his recall, as the best friend of the Allies.

Pétain had certainly gone through his own moments of indecision, but since his tactics had always consisted of careful tacking in changing winds, his alterations remained nearly imperceptible. In contrast to Laval, who from the very beginning had opted for Germany, Pétain rejected any steps which might bring about a permanent break with England. In the period before his meeting with Hitler at Montoire, he was most active in this double game, perhaps merely as a balance to Laval's intense efforts to tie France to a collaboration with Germany. Two examples cited by Robert Aron, the historian of the Vichy regime, demonstrate how far Pétain went in this respect. For in the event that negotiations with Hitler broke down and the Germans began to march into the unoccupied zone, he had determined that Darlan, and not Laval, was to receive plenipotentiary powers to form a government in North Africa, while he, Pétain, would remain in France to do what he could to prevent excessive suffering by the population. This was all arranged, according to Baudouin, by word of mouth. "I want nothing on paper," Pétain told his intimates, "but you are to consider this order as final and absolutely binding nonetheless." More striking is the fact that during the very meeting with Hitler himself at Montoire, Pétain's agent in London, Louis Rougier, was negotiating with Sir Alexander Cadogan over a perfectly ordinary Anglo-French agreement. Rougier's account of these discussions contradicts Churchill's in several essential points, but they undeniably took place

In contrast to Darlan, who was a man of action, Pétain kept his thoughts to himself and abhorred definite commitments. Therefore nothing concrete ever resulted from his agreements, whether with the British or the Germans. Flandin's attempt to nail the Germans down to strict adherence to the terms of the armistice, which at the marshal's instigation the premier undertook, has the same airy and unsubstantial quality, although it threatened to break the agreement with the Germans or move them to break it. His similar attempt to prevent the German plenipotentiary Abetz from meddling, also undertaken during the period when Laval was out of power, melted away into nothing.

Pétain's attitude on domestic questions was by contrast quite unequivocal. Unlike Hitler, Mussolini and Franco, Pétain came to power without using force. The previous governmental system had simply caved in before the external threat. The marshal was responsible neither for the invading army nor for the collapse of the system, and had taken power as the legally elected plenipotentiary of the chamber of deputies. The vote in the chamber had been 569 for, 80 against him, with 13 abstentions. An entry in Anatole de Monzie's diary describes the mood in the country at the time: "All France prays for peace. Marshal Pétain appears as the priest in a monstrous mass of desperation. No man in the world has ever before, so suddenly, so perfectly, caught up in himself a people in its entirety, a nation in its semi-godlike nature." Pétain's claim to legitimacy was thus based on Parliament. Therefore the treason charge against Pétain does not rest on the way he came to power, but on the use he made of it. After the resignation of President Lebrun, Pétain did not name himself president, but *"chef d'Etat"*—for many, this in itself constituted an act of treason. In place of the traditional French motto *Liberté, Egalité, Fraternité,* he put a new and extremely suggestive one of his own, *Travail, Famille, Patrie.* The motto was admittedly authoritarian, but not in the sense of Fascism or National Socialism. It was rather the summing up of deeply rooted patriarchal tendencies in the French spirit along the lines of the Iberian paternal dictatorships of Dr. Salazar or General Franco.

Life under the thumb of the Germans was not easy for the stern old warrior, and in time he began to fret about it, calling his condition one of "semi-liberty." The sense of confinement grew until at one point it became unbearable for him and he decided to recall the chamber to dump the whole mess back into its lap. Berlin vetoed the move. It was, of course, no sudden revelation of the glories of parliamentary rule which moved him, but very probably the shrewd, tactical consideration that a solid demonstration of popular will might force the Germans to stop pushing him quite so hard and so incessantly. Pétain, in his way, was true to the people and the land, but his way had its special characteristics and limitations, best seen in the contrast drawn by Fabre-Luce between the marshal and the parliamentarian, Mandel: "The former thinks of the Fatherland before all else as a community of living beings, erected on a certain soil, whereas the other sees it as an instrument of an ideology, which goes beyond and, indeed, can outlive the instrument itself."

Pétain had few intimates among the men of Vichy, and of those most were the soldiers of his personal staff, none of whom appeared in public. There was Alibert, whom a critic called a "typical survival of the ancient regime," Baudouin, an opponent of Laval, and for a brief period foreign secretary, and others whose names are less important. He did not dislike Darlan as much as he did Laval, toward whom he felt an instinctive antipathy. When he dismissed him on December 13, 1940, he did so in a humiliating manner. The group of "young ministers," Pucheu, Barnaud, Bichelonne, Lehideux, Benoist-Mechin and Marion, were completely alien to him, and the "social revolutionaries," who during the years of occupation slowly turned into Nazis, like insects emerging from the larvae, were to the marshal quite incomprehensible. Pétain drew his support from the front-line soldiers' organizations, the peasantry and the archconservative middle class. These veteran organizations offered the old man a widespread network of cells and local bodies through which he could operate. Their journals constituted no visible part of public opinion, but had an invisible kind of influence, especially since the great and moving meeting of German and French veterans at Verdun in 1936, when the idea of reconciliation with the hereditary enemy was propagated by the same men who had once fought most bravely and had been wounded most severely. After the self-elimination of the parliament, a situation had been created in which a general of the

103

highest renown had to encounter the catastrophic defeat of his country with a cabinet of politicians, businessmen and writers who were strangers to him and his way of thinking. At the same time, he really was in contact less with the man in the street than with the man in the peasant farm and in the workshop. This state of affairs was subject to constant change, because many of those who had first recognized the government, later—especially since the winter of 1942–1943—turned away and joined the resistance movement. Despite this, Pétain continued to persevere in his efforts to preserve the substance of French life intact. His efforts in this respect had two facets, a domestic and an international, and it was in the effort to preserve the territorial integrity of France that he achieved things which even his bitterest enemies concede were successes. His aim was to protect France overseas, and in the European and African Mediterranean he succeeded remarkably. Good relations with Franco helped enormously. Robert Aron reports that Pétain had learned of the German plan to take over Africa by passing through Spain and Gibraltar, four weeks before his meeting with Hitler, from the Japanese Ambassador to Vichy, Renzo Sawada. He immediately summoned Spanish Ambassador de Lequerica to him and entrusted him with the mission of informing Franco. Four days later de Lequerica was back from Madrid. "In the name of the Caudillo," writes Aron, "he thanked the French *chef d'Etat* and assured him that Spain would refuse the right of passage to the Germans, or, better put, would handle the whole affair evasively." This quotation should correct some of the misapprehensions concerning the meetings in San Sebastian and Montoire. Franco kept his promise and withdrew from a position of active alliance with the Germans, thereby closing the road to Gibraltar. The preconditions were created for the eventual Allied landing in North Africa and the subsequent attack on the "soft underside of Europe," which marked the beginning of the end for Hitler. On other foreign political fronts Pétain was notably less successful. His attempt to defend Syria against the attacking English failed, because the German undertaking in Iraq was handled with irresponsible dilettantism. There was no chance of defending Indo-China against the Japanese, but it cannot be denied that the African possessions were held long enough for them to be passed into the hands of the Free French.

On the domestic side, German pressure waxed as its real power waned. The people were furious at the spreading hunger, the black markets for which one needed a great deal of money, and the formation of a new privileged class (which had it). The legally inclined were outraged at the cavalier disrespect for the rights of asylum and for the sanctity of French law. Pétain delivered refugees and Jews to the Germans with seeming liberality. He initiated proceedings against prominent politicians and seemed to allow the Germans carte blanche to arrest and deport whom they chose. The whole nation, peasants and intellectuals, Left- and Right-Wingers, were embittered because Pétain's cabinets always seem to fall all over themselves in doing the bidding of the Germans and continually showed themselves more German than the Germans. This resentment is a general phenomenon of all systems of occupation and collaboration. The reason is simple. Often a direct appeal to the representative of the alien occupying power seems to reveal the foreigner as moderate, civilized and sensible and more open to argument than the native collaborator. Besides, those who lead a government with only divided liberty of action are not free to proclaim publicly what they really think or plan, nor are they able to relate in what form they succeeded in circumventing the orders of the occupying power. Neither the marshal nor any of his ministers ever protested in public against the annexation of Alsace-Loraine. In what way they may have found it possible to resist it and other arbitrary moves, either by way of negotiation or by passive resistance, remained unknown to the public.

Pétain's shrewdest and most effective critics accuse him, not so much of taking power, since he was the last pillar of the social order during the collapse of 1940, but of staying in power later when he ought to have resigned. The first critical moment, cited by such critics, was November 11, 1942, when the Germans marched into the unoccupied zone. The second was August 19, 1944, when General Neubronn presented the marshal with Hitler's orders to leave Vichy. The proper course would have been, according to the critics, flight to Algeria in 1942, and flat refusal in 1944. If the Germans, in the latter instance, had attempted to remove the marshal by force, he should have summoned his bodyguard and met an honorable fighting man's death. Both times, though old and unhappy and oppressed by his role, he stayed on for fear of exposing the French to terrible reprisals. What such reprisals were likely to have been is clear from Hitler's mass slaughter of hostages. Fabre-Luce, an advocate of the view that on the whole Pétain did right to remain in office, argues in this respect that:

France had restored her administrative unity, attained the repatriation of 600,000 prisoners of war, and had made no essential concessions to the Germans. If the consulate of Marshal Pétain had ended in November of 1942 it would have been possible to see in this two-year period of French history one of the few complete successes in a foreign policy which had known nothing but failures since 1918. When Pétain saw himself placed in a kind of vassalage, like Leopold III, he refused to recognize the facts openly and, by clinging to the appearance of power, let himself be compromised by traitors who claimed to rule in his name.

Raymond Aron, representing the resistance, spoke for the other side. One can conceivably be of different mind about the success or lack of it of Pétain's policy up to November, 1942. "After that date, there is not a shadow of doubt left. It would surely have been better if the two policies about which good Frenchmen may legitimately differ had not become embodied in two rival groups, who hurt one another constantly and in the midst of a foreign war carried on a secret civil one." The accusations of fact and opinion on both sides have now been roughly cited. What happened before the court was necessarily of another substance. There the questions were legal ones, and both arguments and answers had to be drawn from the corpus of the law. The trial was long and the verdict voluminous. The essential points in the verdict were: that Pétain had overstepped the powers granted him by the chamber of deputies; that he worked actively with the enemy; that he voluntarily delivered men and materials to the enemy, thereby actively assisting the enemy's war effort; that he had created the anti-Bolshevik legion, the LVF, and had sent it to the Russian front for the enemy's sake; and that he resisted the Allies in Syria, Indo-China and North Africa.

Before he sank into the stubborn silence of his old age, Pétain spoke once in his own defense, pointing out that he had, in a way, been the first member of the resistance movement on French soil. He asserted that he had never so much as spoken a hard word against the resistance, and indeed had carried on negotiations in secret with England. Pétain called upon Admiral Leahy, whom Washington had sent as special envoy to Vichy, to testify on his behalf. Leahy, whose testimony itself, in view of the inflamed state of world public opinion, required a good deal of civil courage, wrote:

During that period I held your personal friendship and your devotion to the welfare of the French people in very high regard. You often expressed to me a fervent hope that the Nazi invaders would be destroyed. During that period you did on occasions, at my request, take action that was in opposition to the desires of the Axis and favorable to the Allied cause. In every instance where you failed to accept my recommendation to oppose the Axis Powers by refusing their demands, your stated reason was that such positive action by you would result in additional oppression of your people by the invaders. I had then, and I have now, a conviction that your principal concern was the welfare and protection of the helpless people of France. It was impossible for me to believe that you had any other concern. However, I must, in all honesty, repeat my opinion expressed to you at the time that positive refusal to make concessions to Axis demands, while it might have brought immediately increased hardships to your people, would, in the long view, have been advantageous to France.

The French reaction to the verdict was discordant and extended from frenetic cries for the death sentence to Bernanos's remark, "France is disgusted." As the years passed, the judgments of Pétain and his actions grew milder. Colonel Rémy, one of the earliest supporters of General de Gaulle, asserted: "De Gaulle was the sword and Pétain the shield." De Gaulle himself spoke a word of grace for Pétain in an appeal for amnesty of the 50,000 political prisoners: "It was necessary to condemn him, because his person symbolized the capitulation. But now there is just an old man in a fortress, who once did great things for France. Is he to die without ever seeing a tree again, a flower or a friend?"

Even after ten years the nation was split on the amnesty question. The quarrel over Pétain's wish to be buried in the cemetery of Douaumont broke out with renewed bitterness. The lasting dissension over Pétain is comparable only to the smoldering resentment aroused by the Dreyfus case. In that case, too, there had been a question of treason. Dreyfus had allegedly betrayed French military secrets to the potential enemy of France. From the other point of view in the case, the French officer corps had betrayed the honor of the Army and of France, in order to protect an image of its own infallibility and to serve unworthy anti-Semitic prejudices. The Dreyfus case, however, like the Pétain affair, went deeper than the mere facts. The military caste, the aristocracy, the militant Catholics, and a sizeable portion of the population staged a revolt under cover of the charges against Dreyfus, against the Enlightenment, against the principles of the French Revolution and the total claims of reason to rule in men's affairs. It is possible to see the same emotional forces bursting out of the ruined hulk of the Third Republic in 1940. Had it not been the same groups which tore the inner substance of the Third Republic to shreds— the Monarchists versus the Socialists? The Anticlericals versus the Catholics? When Dreyfus was condemned, Pétain was thirty-eight years old, and he was fifty when Dreyfus was rehabilitated. Surely the poison spread by the Dreyfus case had not left him unaffected. After Pétain himself was amnestied, he did very little to heal the wound to the spirit of the French nation which his own actions had caused. He sat morosely silent and insulted in his quiet retreat, without a kind or friendly word for his friends or a curse for his opponents. He disappeared as stubbornly silent as he had lived.

11. ADMIRAL DARLAN—DUPLICITY

ADMIRAL DARLAN was of decisive importance to the Allied war effort on three distinct occasions: in the days of the defeat in 1940, as the entire French fleet awaited his commands; in the fifteen months of his premiership, when he tried to steer a course between the growing pressure from Berlin and the waxing impatience in Washington and London; and finally, after the Allied landing in North Africa in 1942, when it was up to him to say whether the French soldiers and officials in Morocco, Tunisia, Algeria and French West Africa would fight with or against the Allies.

During the first phase Churchill was his great antagonist. In those days Churchill was far more concerned with the effect of the defeat on the French Navy, which was intact and formidable, than on the French Army, which had proven itself ineffective against Germany. It was vital for England to get control of the Navy, or at least prevent it from falling into the hands of the Germans. Churchill, though he had considerable respect for Darlan as a seaman, knew that the job would not be easy because the Admiral was a rabid Anglophobe. The Anglo-French Entente of 1903, which delineated the spheres of influence for the two navies, had never been popular among French naval officers, and Churchill was well aware of French jealousy and rivalry in naval affairs. Looking back, he has painted an attractive picture of the role which Admiral Darlan might have played—a far more dramatic one than that of de Gaulle, had he taken his fully effective and perfectly loyal fleet to England or Canada. Churchill saw nothing but egoism and ambition in Darlan's attitude. Darlan justified his decision to leave the fleet in French ports with the argument that if he had ordered it to set sail and put in at a British or Canadian harbor the German reprisals in Metropolitan France would have been terrible. He had obtained a solemn promise from the Germans that the fleet would not be touched, and had in turn promised Churchill at their last meeting that the fleet would never fall into German hands. This engagement was respected to the last minute detail by Darlan and his subordinates. Churchill distrusted the Frenchman profoundly, and events seemed to support his misgivings. His order to attack the injured *Dunquerque* on its way into Toulon harbor for repairs was never carried out, but English ships did shell French warships at Mers-el-Kebir. The bitterness aroused in the French population was considerable and only extinguished by the far more brutal indignities committed by the Germans. As long as the feeling persisted that France had been left in the lurch by her ally, and far worse, had been attacked and humiliated by that ally, Darlan could count on the support of wide segments of the population. English planes began to bomb French factories, and there was a famous raid on the Renault works. Popular rumor had it that only French targets had been chosen by the British, while German factories had been spared. In such an atmosphere Darlan was a free agent and knew it.

He was a man of explosive temperament and easily excited. After the raid on the Renault works, during which 500 people were killed and 1,200 wounded, Darlan fell into a foaming rage and dispatched this remarkable letter to American Ambassador Leahy: "I said to you some months ago that the British had piled mistake upon mistake. They have now committed an even greater blunder for which we shall never forgive them. To murder innocent women, children and old people for purely political reasons is a methodology filled with the Soviet spirit! Has England already been 'Bolshevized'? Anxiety is a poor counselor. Mers-el-Kebir and Boulogne-Billancourt have already demonstrated that." Leahy was forced to confirm Darlan's assertion that all France was filled with helpless rage and bitterness

110

against Great Britain. It helped to make matters worse that those were the days of the renowned German "correctness" in dealings with the population. The Army was in control and the Gestapo had not yet made its appearance. It did not seem entirely vain to many Frenchmen to hope for a genuine entente with Berlin.

During this phase of Anglo-French relations, Darlan began to pass information on British naval movements to the admiralty in Berlin. This was but the first of a long series of what the English have regarded as distinctly unfriendly acts. For example, in retaliation for British bombing raids in the spring of 1942, Darlan decreed that all British subjects in the overseas French territories were to be immediately interned and transferred to "dwelling camps." He permitted German tanks and munitions to be transported through Syrian territory, to support the revolution of Raschid Ali, and finally, when the Germans and Iraqui revolutionaries were completely beaten, he ordered his units to defend Syria against the English and the Gaullists who were marching in. General Dentz, then the commanding officer in Syria, was condemned to death in 1945 for having carried out Darlan's orders, but the sentence was later commuted to life imprisonment. Darlan would undoubtedly have suffered a similar fate. The murder of Darlan on Christmas Eve in 1942, prevented him from ever standing before a court, and in a way, by cutting off his career cleanly and at an early stage, made the case of Darlan's treason a perfect model of clarity, far less involved than the cases of the other two famous collaborators, Pétain and Laval. Only in Darlan's case can the student of collaboration take evidence, as it were, in the midst of the events as they occurred. The evidence comes from the reports of the men who participated in the events, without the embroidery of hindsight or the bitterness of a treason trial. In contrast to the cases of Laval and Pétain, the facts of the story of Darlan stand out in stark relief.

Although Darlan was forced to surrender the premiership to Laval, he still maintained complete control of all the armed forces. He was much closer to Pétain personally than was Laval. On November 6, 1942, two days before the Allied landing, Admiral Darlan traveled to Algiers to visit his son, who was very ill with polio. In Roosevelt, so terribly maimed by the same disease, feelings of human warmth were aroused, and according to Leahy, the President urged him to write a "nice" letter to Darlan, offering to help the young man with medical care. Leahy feels that this gallant gesture influenced Darlan's attitude at the decisive moment. It is more likely that Darlan was merely following the consequential course that he had had in mind from the very beginning. We have seen how, as early as 1940, Darlan had prepared the ground for a policy of complete duplicity— externally with England and internally with Germany. The attempt to play both sides off against one another was clear from his handling of the escape of the twenty-four deputies. The overpowering strength of Germany, the apparently hopeless situation of England, and the fear of possible reprisals, worked simultaneously on him and compelled him to join Laval and Pétain. Darlan was far too shrewd to leave any possibility of retreat unexplored. As a result, he suggested to Ambassador Leahy that he would of course view the situation in a different light if the Americans appeared with 500,000 men. He would be only too pleased to assist the Americans, if he were certain of a good possibility of defending the North African colonies.

In reality the Americans arrived with far fewer than the proposed 500,000 troops, and Robert Murphy, the President's special envoy and trouble-shooter, was forced to puff up the numbers just a bit in his first meeting with the admiral. The Americans, however, had never reckoned with the need to use Darlan. Up to that point they had consulted anti-Vichy Frenchmen only, and were stunned to find that French North Africa was more or less solidly loyal to Vichy. They had unearthed a brave and capable officer in General Giraud, who had been persecuted by Hitler, and had assumed that their appearance and the notes of the trumpet blown by the good Giraud would rally all right-thinking Frenchmen to the cause and that the bad men like Darlan would simply fall.

Darlan's coincidental presence in Algiers saved the day for the

Allies. He was, after all, the second highest-ranking military figure in the French state and embodied Vichy legality, the authorized representative and designated successor of Marshal Pétain. In the meantime the confusion had become colossal. While Murphy and Pendar for the Americans, and Admiral Darlan and General Juin for the French, began negotiations, the villa in which they sat was surrounded by an armed anti-Vichy band. These Free French were dispersed by the regular police, who were entirely loyal to Vichy. The police in their turn proceeded to seal off the villa, awaiting orders from God knows whom. At the conference table inside, the situation was no clearer, for General Juin had already cast his lot with de Gaulle, while Darlan was still the delegate of Pétain. Since Darlan realized that he was without authority other than the instructions of Vichy, there ensued his exchange of cables with Admiral Auphan. One of these messages was referred to later as a defense in the trial of Pétain, but was not admitted, since the actual text could not be found at the time. Since then it has been stated officially that, apart from Pétain's telegram which reflected the wishes of the Germans, he had sent another in a special code that gave Admiral Darlan a completely free hand.

English public opinion, which had been fed for a long time on propaganda against the traitors, was outraged. Once again the might of well-used ideological propaganda was demonstrated. American crusaders thundered against the pact with the devil, in support of the British attitude. De Gaulle joined the general outcry of injured virtue, probably because he had been left out of the negotiations. The result was that Darlan's trial, which never came before a court of law, took place in reality in the public prints of the day. Churchill, who could hardly be numbered among the more prominent appeasers in the Tory party, found himself in an embarrassing cross fire in the Commons. Some of his most intimate associates made wild and ferocious attacks on him. In a closed session of the House, Churchill defended the agreement with Darlan by means of a short lecture on the nature of the French mind, which closed with the following words:

113

All this may seem very absurd to our minds. But there is one point about it which is important to us. It is in accordance with orders and authority transmitted or declared to be transmitted by Marshal Pétain that the troops in North-West Africa have pointed and fired their rifles against the Germans and Italians instead of . . . against the British and Americans. I am sorry to have to mention a point like that, but it makes a lot of difference to a soldier whether a man fires his gun at him or at his enemy; and even a soldier's wife or father might have a feeling about it, too."

This was, however, not his last word on the question. In a letter to Roosevelt, he expressed misgivings which he had concealed before the House. "The more I reflect upon it the more convinced I become that it can only be a temporary expedient justified notably by the stress of battle. We must meet the serious political injury which may be done to our cause, not only in France but throughout Europe, by the feeling that we are ready to make terms with the local Quislings. Darlan has an odious record. It is he who has inculcated in the French Navy its malignant disposition by promoting his creatures to command." Roosevelt and Hull had themselves been under heavy critical fire. The alliance with a "reactionary Fascist" like Darlan evoked waves of protest from Roosevelt's ideological supporters. The uproar caused Roosevelt to state that the alliance was only temporary and conditional.

The withdrawal or semiwithdrawal of Roosevelt's support had unpleasant aftereffects in French North Africa. French readiness to cooperate with the British and the Americans slackened markedly. South African Premier Jan Christian Smuts described his impressions of the French state of mind in a letter to Churchill after a visit to Algiers:

Nogues has threatened to resign, and as he controls the Morocco population the results of such a step might be far reaching. From the point of view of securing French cooperation and stabilizing the situation, nothing could be worse than the impression that we were merely using leaders to discard them as soon as they have served our purpose. There can be no doubt that Darlan and his friends have burned their boats, and are doing their best to fight the Axis and consolidate the French behind us in this fight. . . . Darlan was not Eisenhower's choice, but that of other French leaders, some of whom were his enemies and our strong supporters, and who all argued that his leadership in cooperation was essential for our operations. It would be a great mistake to create the impression he is to be discarded at an early date. Military situation may call for his retention for a fairly long period.

It is interesting to speculate how this odd tug of war between strategic and political necessities and the dictatorship of public opinion would have ended. Fortunately or unfortunately, Darlan was assassinated on Christmas Eve, 1942, by a young man called Bonnier de la Chapelle. Churchill wrote: "Darlan's murder, however criminal, relieved the Allies of their embarrassment . . . and at the same time left them with all the advantages he had been able to bestow during the vital hours of the Allied landings."

What of the net result? Churchill and Leahy, in their estimates of Darlan, both agree that he hated England. There is less agreement about his attitude toward Germany. Churchill thought it decisive that Darlan's grandfather lost his life fighting the English in the Battle of Trafalgar. Leahy is probably nearer the truth when he argues that Darlan's actions were motivated by a deep suspicion of the English intentions in the Mediterranean. He suggests that the English intended to take advantage of France's defeat to strengthen their position in North Africa. Darlan was a far more serious obstacle to the realization of such plans than de Gaulle. A shrewd observer like Darlan could not have been blind to these various possibilities, and apart from the occasional outbursts of spleen, the practical needs of the moment were always dominant in Darlan's calculations.

The admiral defended his actions in three very instructive letters—one to Churchill, one to Leahy, and one to General Mark Clark, all three written shortly before his death. In the letter to Churchill he wrote:

115

On June 12, 1940, in Briare, at the headquarters of General Weygand, you took me aside and said to me: "Darlan, I hope that you are not going to turn over the fleet." I replied, "Out of the question. It would be against all the traditions of our navy to do so." If I could not at that time agree to order my commanders to move their squadrons to British harbors, it was because such a decision would have led irrevocably to the complete occupation of the unoccupied parts of Metropolitan France and the African territories as well. I confess that I was filled with rage and bitterness against England as a result of the painful events that followed. They moved me as a seaman deeply. Moreover, I always had the impression that you did not believe my words. Later Lord Halifax let me know through M. Dupuy that, though you had no reason to doubt my word of honor, you were dubious of my ability to carry it out. The scuttling of the fleet in Toulon proved that I had been right all along. Although I was no longer its commanding officer, the fleet carried out an order of mine, which I had given months before, without hesitation or demur and in direct contradiction of the wishes of the Laval Government. From January 1941, until April 1942, by order of my chief, Marshal Pétain, I carried out policies without the implementation of which France and her colonies would have been crushed. These policies were unfortunately diametrically opposed to yours. What else could I have done? You were in no position to offer the slightest help and any gesture in your direction would have brought disaster to my country.

[After a review of his moves during the Allied landing, Darlan continues] Supported by the highest authorities in French Africa and by public opinion, acting as deputy for the *chef d'Etat,* I formed the High Commissariat in Africa and ordered the French Armed Forces to fight on the side of the Allies. Since then West Africa has recognized my authority as well. This success would have been entirely impossible had I not acted under the aegis of the Marshal. Without his authority, I should have been just another renegade. I am convinced that the French, who are fighting the Germans today, will each in his own way eventually find a reconciliation with all his fellow countrymen in the homeland. For the time being, all of us must act separately.

In his letter to Leahy, Darlan writes: "If we had not promised to defend our territories against anyone who came to affect them, the Axis people would have occupied northern Africa long ago. We have kept our word. As I was in Africa, I ordered to cease fighting so that a ditch should not be dug to separate America and France."

A letter to General Clark makes reference to Roosevelt's remark, mentioned earlier, in which the President began to disown the deal with Darlan:

Information from various sources tends to substantiate the view that I am "only a lemon which the Americans will drop after they have squeezed it dry."

In the line of conduct which I have adopted out of true French patriotic feeling, in spite of the serious disadvantages which it entails for me, at the moment when it was extremely easy for me to let events take their course without my intervention, my own personal motive does not come into consideration. I acted only because the American Government has solemnly undertaken to restore the integrity of French sovereignty as it existed in 1939, and because the armistice between France and the Axis powers was broken by the total occupation of Metropolitan France, against which the Marshal has solemnly protested. I did not act through pride, ambition, or calculation, but because the position which I occupied in my country made it my duty to act. . . .

The letter to General Clark has a distinctly apologetic and self-justifying tone, while those to Churchill and Leahy have a sort of "man-to-man" frankness. This is already the tone of a man who has begun to suspect that he will face a trial after the war and wishes to begin to build a case.

12. LAVAL—IN THE VISE

PÉTAIN worked in silence. His political effectiveness was due to a combination of dignified old age and the authority of a military commander. Laval worked in and through words—the words of the parliamentarian, the rhetorician, the man of the people, who combined logical thought with emotional appeal. Up to the very end, he believed in the power of his own words. *"S'ils me laissent parler,"* he said to his defense counsel. If they would just let him speak, he would win them all over, state prosecutor, judge and jury. No doubt he felt the bitter hatred and icy reflection that was to prevent a fair trial. Yet he still managed to win over his jailers with his persuasive words, discussed his defense with them, and held them spellbound with his words. The written word was less his weapon, although his written defense, *"Laval parle,"* contains much sparkling argumentation. A manuscript cannot, however, be tried out on a conversation partner. It cannot be warmed, cooled or shaped by the mood in the chamber. It is dead and fixed. Pétain complained constantly that Laval never kept him informed of his activities and never submitted any reports. Laval laughed. "Af if I had nothing better to do than fabricate reports. Besides, as a matter of principle I never write anything at all."

There were other reasons as well for the lack of understanding between the two men. Their differences extended from their personal feelings to every aspect of method in politics and approach to problems. Among the collaborators especially close to both of them was Ferdinand de Brinon, a passionate Nazi. It was not easy for the Germans to understand the antipathy with which Pétain regarded Laval, and de Brinon, a Germanophile and thus an emotional collaborator, tried to make it clear in one of his letters to Goebbels. He described Pétain, the old soldier who despised politicians, and set up the archpolitician Laval as the perfect contrast:

The Marshal desires a sort of conservative revolution, which horrifies Laval, though that does not mean that Laval wants a National Socialist one. From the beginning of his political career as a young Socialist, Laval has always flirted with a realistic pacifism which fills the old soldier with disgust. The Marshal in his heart has absolutely no use for the parliamentarians and politicians who benefited by the old system, whom he considers jackals and profiteers. M. Laval protects his old cronies far too often, in the Marshal's opinion. Laval has slipped many Freemasons into important positions, which offends the Marshal's devout conscience.

Brinon's contrast gives the reader an idea of the difficulty of catching anything of Laval's elusive essence. The genuine collaborators and the Nazis saw in him the irredeemable politician of the old regime who was always shielding his pals and cronies, even if they were his enemies politically. Laval sabotaged the transport of French workers to Germany. He received the representatives of the Jews. To the Nazis Laval seemed a slippery negotiator who always promised and never performed, who was always making apologies for the fact that so and so many Jews, Alsatians or Communists seemed somehow to have inexplicably slipped away. They went so far as to suspect him of permitting the growth of the resistance and underground movements. The resistance, for its part, accused Laval of having betrayed the parliamentary system, of having delivered up Jews, French workers and Alsatians to the Gestapo, and of having attempted to crush the resistance movement. To the Maquis, Laval embodies every hateful quality of collaboration and is regarded as the most treacherous of all the Vichy traitors.

Both sides are in a way correct, for Laval was a man in a vise. Gripped in the iron pinch of his tool, he was always struggling to wriggle free or trying to push the grips of the tool apart. He resorted to a dazzling array of evasions, postponements, and delays, and if the worst occurred and he was actually pinned down, to apologies. He always threw up a cloud of obfuscating argumentation, like a frightened squid, and was an expert at filing things in his desk drawer. Once, upon returning from a particularly long and exhausting session with the Germans, he himself used the image of a vise:

You see, every day I try to attain a certain goal, which is that we suffer a minimum of unpleasantness from the Germans. When evening comes, I have often the feeling that I am caught in the clamps of a giant vise. Sometimes I ask myself sadly: Which side, the German or the French, has been worse to me in the course of the day? But I never lose my nerve. I have but one goal toward which I stumble, as if I were a kind of sleepwalker, the attempt to save everything I can for France. I try to relieve her daily suffering and strive to assure that the land which belonged to our fathers will continue to belong to our children and will be called France.

119

A kind of "sleepwalker," he called himself, but he was more than that. His was a unique fusion of passionate, burning ambition and a certain somnambulist instinct for the right direction, which carried him to the pinnacle of political power. It carried him, however, one step too far and ended his career before the firing squad. "That one—well, he'll end up either a minister or on the gallows." These eerily prophetic words were spoken by a schoolteacher, when she found the ingenious little Pierre busily engaged in lighting a fire under a recalcitrant mule. "The teacher," said Laval years later, "knew that I was not dumb, but she thought I was a sort of demon." His demon drove him to seek money, power, honor. The one was the prerequisite for the others. As a sixteen-year-old, he hit a master at his school and was taken before the juvenile magistrate. The chief of the county legal department, who had been present, led him aside afterward and said: "Study the law, young man. You have the stuff for it." Indeed he did. The young barrister went on to join the Socialist party and began to make a name for himself defending the poor from whose midst he had come. The party's narrowness began to oppress him after awhile, and he struck out on his own as a political lone wolf. Soon he had cultivated a circle of wealthy patrons and clients, and went on to marry the daughter of the richest man in his town of Chateldon, later purchasing the castle near the village as his residence.

Despite his social climbing, he remained true to the habits of his peasant boyhood. "All my life, I have risen early and gone to bed early. I am not a drinker and do not chase petticoats. I have never traveled for pleasure. I do not go to the theatre and have probably been to the cinema less than ten times in my whole life." The little man, who, although a sleepwalker, was in reality full of the peasant's realism and clarity, must have been astonished when he met the real somnambulists of modern history, the Nazi leaders, whose demons were stronger than his and far less predictable. He could barely believe the strange tales he heard of Hitler's nocturnal habits, of the Führer's inspirational sessions in the wee hours to a background of crashing Wagnerian noise.

120

Laval, the practical peasant, had no room for such "romanti-cism." But he was superstitious in the way all tillers of the soil are. His logic moved him to laugh at astrology, but he did believe in his star. He was afraid of the number thirteen and Friday the 13th, and saw his worst fears realized on that fateful Friday, December 13, 1940, when Marshal Pétain sacked and interned him for a short time. He always studied his horoscope with painstaking exactness, "to protect himself against an evil fate," reports Jaffré, his defense counsel. "He only believed it halfway, but with that half he took no chances."

His personal appearance was not especially attractive. His face was the color of a quince, the sallowness of which contrasetd sharply with the white necktie which he always wore. He seemed, as if the result of an ironic joke of the Mendelian laws, to be the living representative of the painted figures in the grottoes of his native Auvergne. Leahy describes him: "Small, dark, with a fascinating way of speaking and a clearly fanatical devotion to his country." Göring said of him at the Nürnberg trials: "At the bottom of his heart, he was as indifferent to us as he was to the English or the Khirghiz tribesmen. He was French to his very marrow, as only a French peasant can be." Ciano portrays him, arriving at a big conference of all the Axis governments, shortly after the Allied landings in North Africa. He had traveled day and night to reach Berchtesgaden in time. "Laval, with his badly cut suit, so typically French middle class, and his white tie, looked forlorn among all the glittering uniforms. He tried to chat fami-liarly about his journey, his long sleep in the train, but the words echoed in the huge, palatial hall. Hitler greeted him with icy politeness." Once again we meet Laval, the man who wants to operate with words. He was proud of his verbal talents, his capacity to negotiate, to make deals and arrangements and to confuse his opponents. He reveled in his casuistic capacity to twist, wring and stretch a document to suit his own ends. He boasted that he could pull anything he chose out of any text. As a lawyer he once remarked: "There are thirty-six different ways to interpret a treaty." But when commenting on his country's surrender, he was dealing with a fact and said: "In the light of certain situations, there are, when one thinks about it, not thirty-six ways to act; sometimes there is only one."

His love of his homeland, his social ambitions, his greed for money and power and his realism, were all jumbled together in his nature. His wish to serve France was undoubtedly sincere. His sense of dignity, his own, the marshal's, the *dignité* of the French state and French law, knew no bounds. Even in prison on a treason charge, he saw himself as a historic figure and the bearer of state secrets which might be useful to his successor. One point in his story, a hotly debated one, has never been satisfactorily cleared up: the source of his fortune. His remarks to counsel were most illuminating. He apparently earned considerable sums from his legal practice which he then used to purchase the *Moniteur,* a half-bankrupt provincial paper. By dint of his own efforts, involving working in each of the departments personally, he succeeded in multiplying the circulation five times. Next he bought out Radio Lyons and soon had it turning out good cash profits. As he put it: "There was a time when the French state encouraged its citizens to get rich . . . It wasn't bad advice. You know, it really is an amazing thing that no one will believe that my personal fortune was the very best possible guarantee that nothing which I have done was done for profit. Do you really imagine that Hitler or Mussolini slipped the Premier of France a paper envelope?"

Booty need not always take the form of little, unmarked envelopes. Murmuring never ceased during Laval's premiership. Things were not in order. General Doyen wrote in his report to General Otto von Stülpnagel that one reason for Laval's dismissal had been that, in addition to his unpopularity, he awakened the impression that his ministrial activities were contributing to his personal enrichment. Leahy ends his portrait of Laval with the following words: "It is reported that he uses his political office to enlarge his personal fortune." Any observer of administrative practice in the former French colonies between the wars will be hard put to consider such personal enrichment a rare phenome-

non. The question is anyway rather beside the point, for if Laval
had done nothing between 1940 and 1944 but enlarge his personal fortune, there would never have arisen the frantic hate
which overwhelmed the little man after the war. France hated
Laval so much that it would not let him die his own way. The
night before his execution he took poison and lay nearly dead
on the floor of his cell. The authorities ordered stomach pumps
and medical aid, just to ensure that the wretched man, reeling
and unable to stand, could be propped on a stool before the
firing squad.

Those who hated him hated his convictions and methods. He
was an opportunist of the most flagrant sort. He believed only
what he could see, taste, smell or touch. He distrusted ideas and
ideologies, although in a way he remained true to his own idea
of protecting France from a new war and of promoting peace at
any price. The preservation of peace was his leitmotiv from the
time of the Stockholm Peace Conference in 1918, through his
time as Briand's foreign secretary in 1931, in his treaty with
Mussolini, and in his opposition to France's entering the war.
Churchill and Leahy thought mistakenly that Laval hated
England. The truth was, as Göring pointed out, that Laval was
totally indifferent to all foreign countries. In the light of the
momentary grouping of forces, he was quite prepared to play
ball with the one or the other. "I can only laugh at them," he
said once, "or better said, feel sorry for them, the poor yokels
who are ridden by their ideologies, who swear by Russia, or
England, Poland or Germany. In foreign affairs, there are no
loyalties, only circumstances.

During his first premiership in the 1930's, he made two important political visits, one to Moscow and one to Rome. Odd as
it may sound, the trip to Moscow was undertaken to enable
France to strengthen her defenses. Two years' military service
in France could not be enacted in the Chamber against the
opposition of the Communists, and Laval knew perfectly well
that if Moscow gave the word, the opposition could be stopped.
The trip to Rome was determined by the Ethiopian crisis. Laval

took the view, as did the majority of the senior officials at the British Foreign Office, including Foreign Secretary Sir Samuel Hoare, that Mussolini must at all costs be kept from the arms of Hitler. The military convention which Laval concluded with Mussolini enabled France to remove eighteen divisions from the Italian frontier and place them on the German border. Liberal world opinion was furious. The English especially were aggrieved, though they had just concluded a naval agreement with the other dictator. As Churchill recalls, they led fifty nations in the League against Italy in a glorious "flow of martial, moral and world sentiment." They were prepared however, in the event of war, to send exactly two divisions to France at the outset. "If Britain," he continues, "had used her naval power, closed the Suez Canal, and defeated the Italian Navy, she might have had the right to call the tune in Europe."

The compromise which Laval worked out in the so-called Hoare-Laval Plan was revealed prematurely by a calculated indiscretion, and was smashed by enraged public opinion in England. Laval's reaction was very characteristic. "What earthly difference can it make to the English if the Italians sit in Addis Ababa, as long as they also sit, well armed, on the Brenner Pass?" The Rome-Berlin Axis was the direct result of the failure of Laval's efforts. "When I visited Moscow, people wanted to weave laurel crowns for me. When I visited Rome, they screamed their heads off. What for? What rhyme or reason is there in that? Was I not working in both cases in exactly the same way for exactly the same reasons? If a peasant back home sells a cow or buys a horse, does he worry whether his partner in the deal is a radical or a Communist? He tries to make the best possible deal."

What drove this realist to sheer frenzy was the fact that at the same time as the raging crusade against Fascism a wave of strikes broke out. The same groups, loudest in denouncing Fascism, were the ones which crippled the war effort and prevented France's rearmament. This is a nearly perfect example of the double thinking described in the first chapter. No tanks or planes were produced, and everywhere in the affairs and in the spirits of men chaos ruled. Yet the nation charged into a war against a fanatical opponent who was armed to the teeth and perfectly organized. "If there has been crime committed in the last ten years, that was it," Laval wrote. "Our country has been led straight into a disaster. The average Frenchman could not know it all, but I, a parliamentarian, I knew all about it. I attended the regular committee meetings and learned of the condition of our defenses and the incapacity of our diplomacy. I knew it all. The war which was permitted to develop, and into which we were thrown, was a crime against France."

Bolshevism was one of the few things which genuinely frightened Laval. He was compelled to make a pact with Moscow, because there were so many French Communists at home. It must not be forgotten that Pierre Laval was at heart a peasant, deeply rooted in his native soil, and filled with love for his country. Here one can find the beginnings of Laval's interest in National Socialism. The menace of the Soviet Union grew steadily after the annexation of Poland's eastern provinces and the occupation by the Red Army of the coast of the Baltic. After Hitler's attack on Russia, the French Communists suddenly became the most active and dangerous fighters in the resistance movement, and Laval became obsessed by fears of a civil war. Count de Chambron, Laval's son-in-law, who was working at the time in the French Embassy in Washington, declared that Laval believed that the Germans would either win the war or conclude a separate peace with Russia. In the event that German troops were removed from France, he expected a Communist uprising. A striking example of how positions change with the turning wheel of history is Chancellor Adenauer's startlingly similar statement in an interview with the International News Service, which he granted in 1955. Adenauer spoke out against the withdrawal of American forces from West Germany. "If the American troops are withdrawn, Europe can be written off. The Soviet Union is afraid of only one power on earth and that is the United States of America." Laval could easily have spoken the same words, substituting German for American, and Germany for the United States. It was his fear of the Bolshevik Revolution which led to the fatal words later so damaging at his trial: "I pray for a German victory." Interestingly enough, the rest of the sentence is rarely quoted but is of great significance. It runs as follows: "because without Germany, Bolshevism will gain control of all of Europe."

As Laval sat in his cell, awaiting the day of his execution, half of his fears had already been realized. The Russians were in Bucharest, Budapest, Vienna and Berlin. Laval added another sentence to the above: "I do not believe that England and America will be able to prevent the spread of Communism in Europe."

We have now examined the general foreign political position of the man who in 1940 decided to remain in France and co-operate with the Germans. His aim was to help his country "to live with misfortune." The example of Poland, where Hitler had attempted to root out the entire intelligentsia and ruling class, had convinced Laval that everything possible must be done to save France from a similar fate. His imagination was vivid enough for him to be able to conceive the sort of reprisal Hitler might inflict if he were thwarted or angered, whereas few of his contemporaries in either France or Germany had any idea of the bestiality which the following years were to show. Laval suspected, or seems to have suspected, that Hitler was capable of virtually anything. Passive resistance in Laval's sense required a basis of mutual agreement before it could be practiced. His initial approaches to the Germans were tentative and exploratory. He watched their every move and was much relieved by the words of recognition and respect which Hitler used in speaking of the French fighting men at the time of the signing of the armistice. Laval was not the only Frenchman who thought that things might not work out so badly after all. Hitler did not seem bent on revenge or humiliation, which was consoling. There were, as Laval so neatly put it, "possibilities for maneuver."

A policy of one step forward and two steps backward requires agility in more ways than one. On the top level all was to be cooperation and harmony. On the lower levels of administration the real resistance was to take place. A bureaucracy is ideally made for passive resistance. Even in normal times, one is never certain whether the maddening ponderousness is malicious or not. The two meetings at Montoire in October 1940, the first between Hitler and Laval alone and the second between Hitler, Laval and Pétain, marked the high-water mark of the policy of "going along" with the Germans. French hopes of German reasonableness seemed justified. Hitler, at the dizzy peak of his power, was inclined, in so far as his cramped, hysterical nature permitted, to a certain generosity. Italy's surprise attack on Greece had not yet begun. The attack on and the running aground in Russia still lay in the distant future. It seemed possible that Laval's policy would bear fruit.

Laval presented his requests with firmness and uttered the threat of the vanquished: "You may suppress us. You are the stronger. We are forced to let everything happen to us and can only suffer in silence. But because it is a law of nature, we shall one day revolt. You have defeated us this time, but we have defeated you on occasions in the past. If you choose to humiliate us now, then at some, as yet unforeseeable point in the future, the whole drama will begin anew." It was this "drama" that Laval wanted to bury forever. Even in his last hours, just before the execution, Laval remarked softly: "France and Germany must get together if they are to survive."

Evidently Laval made no impression at all on Hitler, who later called him "a dirty little democratic politician." What Hitler really wanted was the participation of France in the war against England, and this he could never get the French to do. This was more a result of Pétain's firmness, according to Robert Aron, than Laval's. "The great gamble," wrote Hitler's official interpreter Schmidt in his memoirs, "which Hitler had in mind was lost because of the reserve and caution of Laval and Pétain. Marshal Pétain gave us the cold shoulder at this meeting with his monosyllabic answers and his imperturbable silence. Laval was not much more helpful. I thought then and think now that

France had no cause to be ashamed of her two representatives at Montoire."

At the time of the Montoire meetings, Laval and Pétain worked together in reasonable harmony. They were both agreed in their strong aversion to Communism, but this alone was not enough to bridge the enormous gap between the two personalities. The first disagreement followed hard upon the Montoire conference. Laval had accepted Hitler's gesture to return the ashes of the *"Aiglon"* to Paris in a solemn ceremony, symbolizing the newly established understanding between the two former enemies. Pétain was unhappy about the fuss and about the ceremony. It made him suspicious, a state of mind to which several of his intimates contributed materially. At first agreeing, he suddenly decided not to come to Paris for the ceremonies. Laval was unexpectedly deposed and arrested. The German legate Abetz announced the other concessions which Laval's persuasion had won from the Germans and which were now to be revoked: release of 150,000 prisoners of war; return of the administration of the Departement du Nord and the Departement du Pas de Calais from Brussels Military District to the French Government; relaxation of the border controls between the occupied and unoccupied zones; and a general reduction of the occupation costs from four hundred to eighty million francs a day. Ambassador von Hassell, who as an opponent of the collaborators makes a good witness in the affair, wrote at the time: "The fall of Laval has effectively destroyed all possibilities of a permanent understanding. According to unanimous French opinion, Laval would have achieved real success, which would have meant winning the backing of all France, if he had not returned empty-handed. If one had only granted him a few hundred thousand prisoners and a relaxation of the border as originally planned, instead of deporting the inhabitants of Lorraine, he would have been hailed as a savior."

Far more difficult to explain than Laval's first collaborationist efforts is the fact that he allowed himself to be named premier again in April 1942. The first term of office can be justified in larger terms, but the second seems merely to have been the result of the simple urge to be the boss again. There was no doubt an additional impetus in his desire to get even with his rival Darlan as well. There may have been more honorable motives in his action, for he had heard from Göring that Hitler, enraged by the French attitude, was planning drastic measures. Laval's fears were quite justified, as a memorandum by Admiral Raeder after a high-level meeting shows. According to Raeder, Hitler shouted furiously: "If France becomes a disruptive factor, it must be crushed completely!"

The vise in which Laval now found himself made the earlier one seem a toy. It was no longer simply a question of wending his crooked way between the Germans and the French. He was caught between the parliamentarians and the passionate collaborators, between the secularists and the clericals, between the French administration—which sought order, regardless of whose iron fist protected that order—and the growing resistance movement, which was willing to bring about complete anarchy in order to destroy an order which it condemned as evil. He had to fight off daily demands in ever more urgent tones for the deportation of forced labor battalions, for fiercer persecution of the Jews, for the transfer of French industry—especially heavy-machine building and aircraft factories—and finally for sterner repressive measures against the Maquis. Every day brought further new executions of hostages, new threats and new reprisals. There was also the unnerving struggle for control of North Africa.

The case of the forced labor deportation offers a chance to examine Laval's methods of dealing with the Germans. He was never entirely successful but never entirely unsuccessful either. The French population saw only the deportation of thousands and the broken promises of the reunion of families. Anyone who studies the files must recognize what Laval actually accomplished. Fritz Sauckel demanded 2,000,000 men by June 1944. He got 490,000. At the same time 110,000 prisoners of war were repatriated, of whom nearly 100,000 were peasants—despite the fact that Hitler, in a frenzy over General Giraud's spectacular escape, had sworn that not one more Frenchman would be returned. In all the difficult negotiations, Laval always created the impression of "going along," though Sauckel knew, but could not prove it, that Laval was thwarting him in secret. "As a result of full and balanced consideration," he wrote to Hitler in 1943, "I see myself compelled to inform you that I have lost all faith in the goodwill of the French Premier, Laval. His refusal to cooperate means unequivocally an act of sabotage at a time when Germany is engaged in life-and-death struggle against Bolshevism." In January 1944, the German representative to the mixed armistice commission reported to Berlin: "It has been demonstrated beyond any doubt that Laval has not done a thing in the new recruiting program. On the contrary, the opinion has been spread that no new deportations need be feared. In addition, Laval's reorganization of his Cabinet, which we demanded of him in December, has not been carried out. Despite all our efforts and the assistance of the Embassy, he has somehow managed to avoid naming a Minister of Labor."

A fine example of Laval's technique of dodging and twisting out of situations is his handling of Ribbentrop's demand that the Vichy Government take steps to halt the activities of American agents in Morocco. The first step for Laval was always to play dead. The letter of May 1942 was simply not answered for months. The Germans kept on pressing for action, and Laval kept on avoiding taking any. After vigorous flapping through all the available files, Laval came up with a stunning reply: In September 1942, Premier Laval had the "honor" to inform the Government of the Führer in Berlin that America had never recognized the Morocco agreement of 1912, and that, unfortunately, America's relations with Morocco rested on the agreement with the sharif from 1836, which granted free entry to all American citizens. The premier "regretted" that in view of the terms of the agreements he would be unable to take any action on the matter. The consequence was that the way was opened for Robert Murphy and his agents to prepare the terrain for the American landings.

Laval was least successful on the Jewish question. To begin with, he could at best only protect French Jews, and there he ran into strong anti-Semitism in the circles close to Marshal Pétain. He promulgated a decree governing the treatment of the Jews, which prevented the Germans from introducing their own far more drastic laws. He gave orders to the police in the unoccupied zone that under no circumstances were they to follow any directives in this respect from the Gestapo. His temperament reacted more intensely to individual cases than to principles. He was never more cunning than in his efforts to save Herriot from the clutches of the Gestapo. His protests were never more passionate than after the murder of Mandel, especially so since people tried to blame him. "Mandel was my friend," he cried when he heard the news. S.S. Standartenführer Helmut Knochen and Embassy First Secretary Bargen confirmed the remarkable energy with which he tried to prevent a similar fate befalling Reynaud and Léon Blum, two of his bitterest political opponents.

Laval once defined the sort of collaboration he advocated in the following way: "When one begins to carry on an interesting conversation with someone, one is collaborating. In my opinion, it is always a good thing to make contact and talk things out if there are problems to settle, but especially if one is forced to play the petitioner." In this sort of collaboration Laval soon became expert and knew exactly which of the Germans were susceptible to his methods and how they could best be handled. Dealing with the S.S., "more gruesome and stupid than the most brutal army commander," was out of the question. With Abetz and with Hemmen, the representative of the mixed armistice commission, he could talk. "Abetz was not brutal and no fool. Besides he knew France well and understood more than the others. Believe me, it was not always easy to get around him. I often had to work really hard before I could get him around to my point of view, and even when I had convinced him, things were still not settled. I used to watch him thinking out how he could possibly present my suggestions to his Fuehrer."

Laval got along well with several of the Army commanders

and once said to one of them: "If Paris is not a mass of rubble, as it would have been without question had we given in to the Communists and the glory-seeking tin soldiers, we owe it all to a General of the Wehrmacht." His own assessment of his work was characteristic of the man. "I collaborated differently with Abetz and with Sauckel. If one had all the documents, one could see just how differently I worked. I collaborated again in another way with Oberg, the Commanding General of the S.S., and again differently with Hemmen of the armistice commission. I snatched French lives from Oberg, and money, property and goods from Hemmen."

The collaboration of the so-called hundred percenters was of quite a different kind. There were those who sought profit and nothing else; there were others who strove earnestly for a genuine understanding with Germany. Most of these men hated the constant tacking of Laval and his inexplicable shifts in policy. He always liked to leave the doors open ever so slightly. On the other side the activists were of various sorts. There was Darnand, who formed a militia which he placed at Hitler's disposal. Laval remarked: "A fine soldier but about as much political intelligence as a curbstone. When I heard that he had sworn an oath to Hitler, after having sworn one to the old man, I asked him if that did not bother him just a bit. Not in the slightest. The Germans thought he was superb. But I, good God, what rubbish of every sort I had to put up with from him, and the worst of it was, I had no choice but to endure him." There was Déat, who, although a leader of a right-wing group, had come out in 1939 against the war. He wrote a famous antiwar article in his magazine *Oeuvre,* entitled "Die for Danzig?" which evoked much comment. The same was true of Doriot, who, as an ex-Communist, was literally possessed by the fight against Bolshevism. He, too, had a Fascist organization with a sizeable following among the workers of St. Dennis. Doriot was killed fighting on the Russian front.

Such were the other collaborators with whom Laval had to deal. The more he withdrew into a policy of neutrality, the more

132

these activists pressed for greater cooperation and assistance to the Germans. Broken German pledges seemed merly to encourage them. They were deadly serious in their aims. The state of France seemed unbearable to them. They had seen enough of the corruption of the administration and the intrigues of the parliamentarian Laval. They wanted to do, voluntarily and eagerly, what the politicians of Vichy at best did halfheartedly, and when possible, not at all.

The explosion between the activists and Laval took place after the Allied landings in Normandy. Laval ordered all citizens to take no part in the military operations. The activists had once before been angered by a similar instruction of Laval's to the local prefects to the effect that, in the event of an Allied invasion, the local authorities were to assist neither the Germans nor the Allies, but were to concern themselves solely with the control and protection of the civilian population. The new order was the last straw for the hundred percenters. A manifesto was written and sent to Hitler, signed by four ministers (Bonnard, Bichelonne, de Brinon and Déat) and twenty-eight prominent collaborators. The five conditions listed sought to ensure that: "The Reich would find a France at her side able to travel the last stretch of the road, which will lead Europe to ultimate victory."

The protocol of the Cabinet meeting of July 12, 1944, was only discovered several years after Laval's death. It demonstrates once again, with great force, the remarkable verbal power of this curious little man. Laval confronted his opponents one by one, and each shrank from admitting his role in the composition of the manifesto. Some claimed not to have known the text, and others to have signed only with reservations. Déat simply failed to appear at the meeting. Laval's speech was addressed to the absent minister, as well as to the ones who were present. "You all want France to join the war on the side of Germany. With what weapons? M. Déat wants to fight. Fine, let him fight. He also, it would appear, wishes to see the LVF [Légion Volontaire Française] fighting side by side with the Waffen S.S. I have refused to permit that. I have made it clear to the Germans that,

133

when thousands of French soldiers are fighting on the other side and a few hundred in the ranks of the Germans, the true French feelings are likely to burst out with force." With this argument Laval had won the agreement of Abetz, who knew only too well what the true French feelings were. It was not long after that the reins were removed from his hands.

As the session continued Laval closed in on his opponents. He demanded the resignation of Déat. He then went on to what at first seemed a change of topic:

Now, I should like to say a word or two about the general psychological state of the French administration and, in particular, of the prefects. They come, when they can, to visit me. They remain at their posts out of a certain loyalty to their jobs and because they know that I embody the legal authority. But I have great difficulty in holding onto them. Their psychological state is easily explained. As a result of the repressive measures and the reprisals which the Germans have carried out in many departments, the prefects find themselves in a moral position, vis-à-vis the civil population, which is not enviable. If we were suddenly to get a government under Déat, we should experience without doubt and almost at once the complete dissolution of French administration.

Laval speaks as the man of order who is determined to maintain the peace internally at any price. In this respect he was on the side of Pétain. On the one side were the hundred percenters, and on the other the Maquis, both equally unconcerned about Laval's precious civil order. He was a man who could only be at peace "if things are in place." Even in his prison cell, which he kept painfully neat, the few pitiful objects were always returned to their proper places. "If disorder settles in things, it is not long before it settles in the mind as well." The vital question, however, is whether this sense of order remains frozen in external things. He who always searches for the proper place for things sees the world from without, as a structure of subdivisions. He who seeks law and justice insists on seeing the world from within, in terms of essential significance. If the legal order and the sense of justice harmonize, the internal and the external reflect one another without distortion. In France that harmony no longer existed. The fanatics in search of pure justice saw only half the truth. Laval, the realist and champion of order, was at least capable of seeing the validity of the arguments of his opponents. German Vice-Consul Aschenbach wrote: "To Laval it seemed important, in view of the situation in which his country found itself, that there be someone on the spot to defend the interests of France against the Germans and someone abroad in the person of General de Gaulle to defend those interests against the Allies."

Laval's great failing, despite his realism, was his blindness to one reality which he could never grasp, the power of ideas. His incapacity to understand the pull of ideas lulled him into a fantasy world. While the Allies rolled in from the coast, and cities and towns were turned into piles of rubble, Laval in Paris turned over in his mind his basically visionary plans for the legal assumption of power by General de Gaulle. He considered calling the national assembly into session. "Peace could only be maintained and order assured if the continuity of government were unbroken. That was only possible by recalling the National Assembly." Presumably Laval imagined that, as parliament had legally transferred power from Reynaud to Marshal Pétain in 1940, it could now similarly pass the authority of the state from himself to General de Gaulle."

Only the pure "realist" is capable of such self-deception. He never realized that his "order" was a flimsy fabric, which his opponents realized instinctively. Although Laval saw behind the masks of ideologies, Communist, National Socialist or Western democratic, he never saw the reality of the emotions, needs and driving force which make people willing to fight for, and even die for, such ideologies. Sometimes convictions, and not conditions, are decisive. Sometimes the social order of society has been so profoundly shaken that only bloodletting will restore it. Laval became an almost tragic figure through this flaw in his nature. The man of a thousand tricks fell victim to his own fundamental inability to recognize what was really happening around him. In his desire to avoid a civil war, he became its most prominent victim.

13. CONCLUDING REMARKS ON TREASON IN FRANCE

IN THE preceding sections an attempt has been made to portray the behavior, motivation and actions of Pétain, Darlan and Laval. Such an attempt, after the event and by a foreigner, can never be entirely successful. In this case, however, by a fortunate chance, Churchill, who both fought and knew all three, has come up with the most plausible summary of the phenomenon of French collaboration: the more brilliant because it was written at the very hottest moment of the struggle and not years later in mellow reflection.

In the aforementioned secret session of the House of Commons, Churchill had to defend his policy of alliance with Darlan before an outraged House. It is from that remarkable speech that I have selected this brilliant passage:

I now turn to examine a peculiar form of French mentality, or rather of the mentality of a large proportion of Frenchmen in the terrible defeat and ruin which has overtaken their country. I am not at all defending, still less eulogising, this French mentality. But it would be very foolish not to try to understand what is passing in other people's minds, and what are the secret springs of action to which they respond. The Almighty in His infinite wisdom did not see fit to create Frenchmen in the image of Englishmen. In a State like France, which has experienced so many convulsions—Monarchy, Convention, Directory, Consulate, Empire, Monarchy, Empire and finally Republic—there has grown up a principle founded on the *droit administratif* which undoubtedly governs the actions of many French officers and officials in times of revolution and change. It is a highly legalistic habit of mind, and it arises from a subconscious sense of national self-preservation against the dangers of sheer anarchy. For instance, any officer who obeys the command of his lawful superior

136

or of one whom he believes to be his lawful superior is absolutely immune from subsequent punishment. Much therefore turns in the minds of French officers upon whether there is a direct, unbroken chain of lawful command, and this is held by many Frenchmen to be more important than moral, national or international considerations. From this point of view many Frenchmen who admire General de Gaulle and envy him in his rôle nevertheless regard him as a man who has rebelled against the authority of the French State, which in their prostration they conceive to be vested in the person of the antique defeatist who to them is the illustrious and venerable Marshal Pétain, the hero of Verdun and the sole hope of France.

Another point of view has been expressed by Albert Camus, who in several works has grappled with the problem of order versus justice in the French state. He refuses to hear of *Staatsräson* or *Realpolitik*. He accuses Vichy only indirectly at first, and recalls that as early as the 1930's the totalitarian evil had begun to infect the French state. He reminds his readers that the left-wing Spanish poet, Antonio Machado Ruiz, was interned by a French government in the late 1930's and that as the decade passed, strong tendencies toward Fascism and authoritarianism began to appear in French intellectual and political life. It was not Hitler who imported it into France. In reply to Mauriac and his plea for clemency, Camus writes:

I should like to say to him that I see two ways to death for our country. . . . These two ways are hate and forgiveness. The one seems to me as fatal as the other. I have no capacity for hate. The mere idea of having enemies seems to me to be the most exhausting thing I can imagine. My comrades and I in the Maquis had to make considerable efforts to accept the fact that we ourselves had begun to hate. But forgiveness is not better. Today it would be an insult. In any case I am convinced that it is not open to us. If I am horrified by the type of verdicts arrived at in some of the recent purges of collaboraltors, that is my personal affair. I shall, jointly with M. Mauriac, forgive all, if the parents of Velin or the wife of Leynaud grant me permission to do so. But not before they do, no, never before. I honor and revere the quality of loyalty in man too much to betray it just so that I may enjoy the luxury of an outpouring of the heart.

The other France speaks through these words. We are back at the argument between Goethe and his English friend Gore— justice or order, citizen or human being? In Goethe's day a bit of good humor and some friendly discussion and the matter was dropped. One hundred and fifty years later it was deadly poison to all who touched it.

PART III

Propaganda

14. THE INSIDIOUS INFLUENCE

As LONG AS there has been warfare, propaganda has been employed as a means of warfare. Propaganda uses a truth or a half-truth, and by exaggerating or even distorting its meaning it seeks to influence the minds of people according to the needs of the war being waged. Different times knew different kinds of propaganda. It has been used as:

A means of intimidation
A means of waging war for a new faith or crusading for an old faith
A means of blackening the enemy in the eyes of the rest of the world and thereby winning fresh allies
A means of turning the enemy's own people against their government

Treason is possible wherever a war is being waged. And it is exactly in the area of propaganda outside the enemy that treason by words has its most fertile field.

In olden times we have a good example of the two first kinds of propaganda in a war between the mighty heathen Empire of the Persians and the Christian Byzantine Empire, only a few years before a third militant power was to set out on a series of conquests to propagate the new faith of Islam. In 611, Chusro Parvez, the thirty-six-year-old King of Persia, tried his hand at insult and intimidation when he addressed the following message to the Byzantine Emperor Heraclius: "Chusro, the greatest of the gods and lord of all the earth to his base and foolish slave Heraclius: You say you put your trust in your God. Why has he not freed [liberated?] Jerusalem from my power? Do not delude yourself in vain hopes of help from your Christ. He could not even save his own person from the Jews who killed him by nailing him to a cross." Heraclius was a courageous man, but he

141

would hardly have succeeded in winning back all the provinces the Greeks had lost since the days of Justinian had he not had the services of a great propagandist. This was the patriarch Sergius, who roused the people far and near to a crusading fervor with the cry that the Cross which had fallen into the hands of the Persians must be re-erected in Jerusalem.

During the Middle Ages and up to the twentieth century, all propaganda was directed to God and the world, and the outcome of a war was taken as the verdict of God. The world was immense. Wars occurred only here and there, and there was never more than a tiny fraction of all living people engaged, but since wars have become "global," the "world" to which the warring nations can appeal has diminished to a few neutrals. What is more, the warring parties do everything they can to eliminate even these by drawing them into their war, be it hot or cold.

The First World War marked the transition of the old pluralist world to the "One World" later hailed by Wendell Willkie. The British atrocity propaganda initiated and led by Lord Northcliff was still directed at "the world," and especially at the greatest neutral power, the United States, which was to be drawn into the war. The Germans were not capable of organizing an effective counterpropaganda, because they had not yet realized that what had once figured as "the world" was being replaced by "public opinion." Thus the First World War shows obsolete forms of propaganda side by side with forms that were just coming into being and being experimented with. At the time few people were able to recognize what was happening.

Public opinion was the new manifestation of a universal force (power). Its laws are not founded on the word of God, but on the principles of the French Revolution. Thus Germany's defeat in the First World War was not a verdict of God in the old sense of the word, but the verdict of the new secularized goddess: democracy. At all times it was possible to interpret the word of God in different ways—the dogmatic and papal conflicts of the Middle Ages have demonstrated this most clearly. But whatever the interpretation—God always remained the One, the Unchanging and Unchangeable. The demos, on the other hand, is subject to waves of emotion. Its opinions are unstable, fluctuating, easily influenced and therefore at the same time calculable and unpredictable. Accordingly, the field of activity open to propaganda becomes ever larger, its potentialities ever more effective.

In the era of public opinion, the most successful propaganda will have to fulfill two conditions. First, its creators must have an instinctive sense, rather like that of the great Paris couturiers, for what is going to be the trend of the near future. Long before there exists a common public awareness, they must feel the hidden movements of their time, which are interrelated all over the world in a strange and as yet unexplained fashion. If the coming landslides of opinion from transcendence to materialism, from Socialism to reaction, from belief in the supreme rule of reason to rebellion against this rule, are recognized in advance, they can be adapted and used in the service of the aims for which the propagandist works in a way which will instill in the majority of people the belief that the cause which they themselves have at heart, and in their subconscious wishes, is identical with the cause of the propagandist. Secondly, the propagandists must have such high degrees of intelligence and of persuasive powers, that the creators of the propaganda themselves become persuaded of the truth of what they have invented. Among the Germans, there was probably only Goebbels who had both of these gifts, whereas master propagandists are rarer among the Anglo-Saxons.

What is new in our days is that the propaganda penetrates beyond the fighting lines and there tries to gather supporters, to organize Fifth Columns, and to work explosively against the enemy from his interior. These new methods were possible only after the French Revolution had prepared the soil and nationl armies had replaced the mercenary armies of old. The will of the people, or what could be presented as being the will of the people, became a deciding force in the direction of wars. We find early examples of these two methods—the émigrés speaking to the people of the country they had left as well as appeals to minority groups in the enemy country—in the nineteenth century. Madame de Staël, who had fled to Germany and there engaged in propaganda activities against Napoleon and his form of ruling, is an early example of how to work on public opinion in the civilized world and at the same time influence the domestic scene from the outside.

The handling of the Armenian question by the British, before and during the First World War, is an example of the second. As the policy of the Ottoman Empire under the influence of German experts—with the building of the famous Baghdad Railroad and large concessions to the Deutsche Bank—moved nearer to Germany than England found tolerable. British propaganda used the suffering of the Armenian people for a propaganda campaign which attacked the Supreme Porte from within as well as from the outside. From within, by assuming the role of protector toward the tormented Armenians and inciting them to open and secret rebellion against the Sultan; from without, by denunciation in the face of world opinion. Again it was the late and explosive appearance of nationalism within the structure of the Ottoman Empire, where all religious and racial minorities had once enjoyed special freedoms, which sparked the whole chain of events. The awakening nationalism of the Armenians had provoked repressive measures by the Turks, and these in turn provided material for the atrocity propaganda. While the American reaction was genuinely humane and disinterested, the British reaction was also directed by ulterior motives and could not but evoke further Turkish repression.

The development of wireless broadcasting was a technical revolution in the field of propaganda, equivalent to the cotton gin or steam engine in industry. The radio really made propaganda, in its modern sense, possible. Waves of words could be transmitted undetected over national frontiers and into the homes and hearts of the enemy. During the Second World War this special form of contemporary poison was tested and perfected. In Europe and in Great Britain one could turn on the radio and hear the news in English or German, French or Russian. All the broadcasts contained a hard core of fact, but the listener needed a sharp ear for the underlying political tendencies so as to decide whether the Austrian voice was broadcasting English propaganda, whether the modulated English voice was speaking for Hitler, or the French voice talking from Moscow. The job was not easy, because none of the speakers had foreign accents. The announcers were speaking their native tongues, a bit colored perhaps by local dialect, rich in the everyday slang of the mother tongue, and full of an intimate, instinctive knowledge of the country concerned. These people were addressing their homes. Or were they?

All the invisible speakers had left their homelands for new ones, and in varying degrees had been converted to its ways of life and ideals. Thus brother spoke to brother as enemy to enemy. Collaborators cling to their native soil, preferring collaboration, with all its perils, to exile. Those who spoke for the Axis Powers were caught by the Allies after the end of the war and tried. Those who spoke from London, Moscow and Washington would have been caught and condemned by Hitler, if he had been victorious, in precisely the same way. His defeat was the judgment of God in modern dress. The propagandists in Washington, London, Calais and Moscow contributed as much as he did to make the judgment total and unconditional.

Since the propagandists in most cases had not yet become citizens of the new countries for which they were broadcasting, one might be tempted to call them mercenaries in the pay of the enemy. Obviously they were paid by the power for which they worked, but that fact becomes incidental when one notes that all of them had accepted the new ideology, with varying degrees of intensity, before the outbreak of war. These people were more than mercenaries, though there were the purely venal among them. They were "ideological traitors," and therefore have a place in this study. At any rate, the question of who paid them is of secondary importance and of moment only in a legalistic sense. Important are the motives which result in the switch to a new fatherland, and the attempt to stir revolution in the old fatherland in the key of the new ideology.

15. WILLIAM JOYCE—THE IRRESISTIBLE VOICE

FIFTEEN days after the outbreak of the Second World War, English radio listeners began to hear a voice speaking perfect English. But the voice came from Germany. It said things which no Englishman could have said. It described with jubilation the staggering series of German victories. As the war went on it reacted ecstatically to each further setback for the British. It went into rhapsodies over the power of the Stukas and prophesied total doom for the enemies of the Reich. Nobody in England was especially eager to be reminded of such things in the dark days after Dunkirk, but many could not turn off the radio. The voice had a hynotic fascination. It became a popular guessing game to name the man himself. Fairly soon the invisible speaker had a name for himself—"Lord Haw Haw." People chatted about him in the endless lines outside the grocers' shops. What he said was occasionally true and always irritating. And there was a touch of mesmerism in the very sneers themselves.

After the Allied victory, the unknown man was returned to England and placed on trial for treason. A drama of such remarkable complexity unfolded during the course of these strange proceedings that even today no one can piece the whole story together.

To the general astonishment of the public, it turned out that William Joyce was not a British subject but an American. William Joyce, in so far as he was aware of the fact, had always done his best to conceal it. His father Michael Joyce, who knew the true facts perfectly, had lied about them on several occasions. In the form which Michael Joyce filled out as part of his son's application papers for a commission in the British Officers' Training Corps, he wrote: "Dear Sir, Your letter of 23rd October

146

received. Would have replied sooner, but have been away from home. With regard to my son William. He was born in America. I was born in Ireland. His mother was born in England. We are all British and not American citizens." That was a lie. It took a bit of doing, but the defense proved beyond question that both the father and the son were American citizens. The defense produced the naturalization papers declaring Michael Joyce an American citizen in the year 1894, and the birth certificate for William, isuued in 1906 in Brooklyn. Witnesses were called who testified to the actual nationality of the Joyces.

It is not regarded as a disgrace to be an American. Yet Quentin, William's brother, testified to having witnessed a scene in which his father burned his passport and all his American papers. Michael Joyce had repeatedly warned the boys never to mention their American citizenships to anyone. Why all the fuss? Why the urge to be English and not American or Irish? This strange masquerade becomes clear when one recalls the fact that Ireland was an English possession right into the first decades of this century. Unlike the majority of the Irish Catholics in southern Ireland, the Joyce family had always been fanatically Anglophile. And it was not in Ulster, but in the heart of southern Ireland, that the Joyce family lived. This in itself was a first step in the process of becoming homeless. The Joyce family and a tiny group of like-minded Irishmen were supporters of law and order. When the 1916 revolution broke out, they turned against their fellow countrymen and became "Anglo-Irish." The Anglo-Irish, like the Anglo-Indians, belonged to a special chapter of colonial history. Their most marked feature was that they were more English than the English. Their burning patriotism and aggressive Anglophilia were embarrassing and painfully theatrical.

Despite the excess emotionalism, there is no question that the feelings in the Joyce family were genuine. At the age of fifteen William Joyce was already a valuable agent for the "Black and Tans." Later in life he used to end each evening at home by singing the national anthem. The loyalty of the Joyces was but shabbily rewarded. In 1909, Michael Joyce returned from America a well-to-do man. He had been highly successful in Brooklyn as a building contractor and had purchased several houses in County Mayo and County Galway. For some years he ran the County Galway horse-drawn cars. When the Irish finally won their independence and the British soldiers and administrators left the country, the Irish who had remained true to England became the victims of violent persecution. Many were killed. It was an early example of dealing with "collaborators," though in this sense the word did not exist at the time. Joyce's house was burned down and he lost all his property. He moved to his beloved England, where he suffered the rejection of his claims to restitution, which many believe to have been justified.

The Joyce family had loved a dream England and had been true to its dream. Now it found a real England which treated it badly. In addition, there was a sort of medieval romanticism about its feelings for England, partly accounted for by the essentially medieval conditions in Ireland. William Joyce's attitudes, in several respects, belonged essentially to feudal times rather than to the twentieth century. When he was sixteen he decided to become an officer and wrote in his letter of application to the War Office of his "loyalty to the Crown," of his ". . . willingness to draw the sword in British interests. As a young man of pure British descent, some of whose forefathers have held high positions in the British Army, I have always been desirous of devoting what little capability and energy I may possess to the country I love so dearly." This love of a romanticized fatherland which never existed, but which he determined to create, lies at the root of all his later deeds.

The discovery that this dream fatherland did not exist was the first step in a painful process. Joyce was gifted with remarkable intelligence. He achieved one of the most brilliant records of his time at London University and won honors in both English and History. His professors thought highly of him, but he never seemed to belong in the academic world. He never looked like a learned or cultured man, and he was both. He was small and wiry and always appeared foreign and strange in a group of Englishmen. Among the professors he looked like a street fighter who had wandered into their midst by mistake. He suffered repeatedly the special penalty of the outsider, the man who never seemed to belong anywhere.

He was an outsider in the field to which he turned after a short time at the university, politics. He felt the call and never doubted his capacity to lead people and to inspire them with the same fanatical enthusiasm and allegiance to the throne which he had felt as a boyish informer for the Black and Tans. He knew that he was a born orator and could move crowds. Yet he had not been born into the ruling class. Those who succeeded in breaking down the social barriers were either flexible opportunists who adapted themselves perfectly, or robust individualists who simply trampled their way through the social barricades. An incident from Joyce's private life is typical of his political career. It happened while he was still Oswald Mosley's right-hand man in the British Union of Fascists. Joyce was invited to an aristocratic country house for a weekend. The host had a fine stable and allowed his guests to ride on all save the finest of his animals. Joyce, who had ridden throughout his boyhood in Galway, performed so brilliantly that he was given the finest of the owner's stable to ride. One of the ladies present shouted into the ear of the nearly deaf father of the host, "Doesn't Mr. Joyce ride beautifully?" "Yes," shouted the old man in reply, "but not like a gentleman."

A man for whom the gentleman was the highest ideal could only suffer such humiliations in silence. It was a kind of crushing condemnation for him, because exclusion from the circle of gentlemen meant the death sentence for his political hopes—at least, so it seemed to him. Along with these failings, if indeed they are failings, he possessed many delightful and charming characteristics. His was a sharp and sparkling wit. His intellectual interests were genuine and his conversation pointed and flashing. He had the Irish "gift of the gab" and told stories masterfully. He had been a fine instructor, for he loved teaching and the signs of receptivity to ideas in his young students as they began to catch fire in the blaze of his own enthusiasm. The family life of the Joyces was especially warm and loving. Mother Joyce, known as "Queenie" to friends and neighbors, had a fine sense of humor and a homely goodness. She was the sort of woman "who bakes the best cakes in the world," and was adored by all her neighbors, even after it came to be known that she was the mother of Lord Haw Haw. Joyce's younger brother Quentin, "with the soft eyes of a cow," as Rebecca West described him, hung lovingly on his big brother's every word, and William's wife stood by him to the last. Only the world of his choice, of extreme conservatism, wanted no part of him. The next best thing was Mosley's movement, but even here Joyce was unhappy and impatient at Mosley's incompetence. The ostensible cause of the split between Mosley and Joyce was a question of money, but the real cause lay deeper. As time passed, Mosely moved closer to Mussolini ideologically, while Joyce felt drawn to Hitler and the Germans. This conflict may have been an expression of the subterranean split in the English consciousness between Germanic and Latin heritages.

Joyce's career coincided with a period in which a wave of doubt and anxiety was spreading about the healthiness of British democracy and the English way of life. Everything seemed to cry for reform. There were endless strikes, and the various governments seemed powerless to meet them or to end the unrest. The dissolution of older social forms in the hectic postwar years accelerated the growth of national anxiety, while the blunders of British foreign policy added to the burden of government. Joyce felt the insecurity of the times, perhaps more sharply than the normal Englishman, serene in his hundreds of years of unbroken tradition, and had as a result none of the Englishman's temperate and good-humored confidence that the nation would "muddle through."

His teaching activities were interrupted more and more frequently by the call to action in the British Union of Fascists and later by the work for his own Nationalist Socialist League, which he founded after his split with Mosley. His daily bread became street fighting. His life turned into a series of summonses for disturbing the peace, long hours on the party journal, *The Helmsman,* and night meetings on street corners. In those days a great many people in the working-class districts listened, reserved but interested, when William Joyce spoke. They liked him, even though his ideas were rather odd. The unusual qualities about him and his queer, fascinating oratory drew them again and again to hear him speak. Curiously enough, the police respected him. Joyce kept his men under control, and when the police complained to him, he would call them off, knowing they would obey without a murmur. He kept his word, which impressed the police very much. According to a high officer in Scotland Yard, Joyce was far more capable than Mosley and far more dangerous. After all, Joyce and his family had always maintained cordial relations with the British constabulary in Ireland, and the Germany which Joyce chose as his new home, and to which he swore loyalty when he became a German citizen in 1940, was a police state.

Joyce renewed his British passport twice, once in September 1938, at the time of the Sudeten crisis and again on August 24, 1939, the day of the signing of the Molotov-Ribbentrop pact, the signal that war was inevitable. This passport was to play a vital role in Joyce's trial. Both dates suggest that he was preparing for the possibility that his passport would be seized by the home office. How he managed to escape from England in 1939, when every customs agent and port officer had orders to be on the watch for him, is just one of the many puzzling features of his strange story.

The Nazis in the propaganda ministry, who apparently had no ear for the nuances of a truly great propagandist, failed at the beginning to recognize Joyce's remarkable abilities. At first he was used purely as an announcer on the English-speaking service. After awhile they began to permit him to write his own scripts. Despite his faith in Hitler and his idealism, he can scarcely have been happy in the Nazis' service. The other Englishmen in the propaganda ministry were all third-rate characters. There was a Mr. Leonard Black, who later pathetically attempted to prove to the court that he had really been in the service of the German anti-Nazi resistance movement. There was an aristocratic lady and the daughter of a well-known colonel, both of whose names have been allowed to slip gently and unobtrusively out of the main stream of English history. There was a former Army officer, Baille-Stewart, who had already served a prison term for selling information to a foreign power.

Rebecca West describes the difference between these shabby mercenaries, who tried to escape their punishments with every available means, and the immovable Joyce: "All such men hated William Joyce, who did not split his mind, who desired to make England Fascist, and to procure that end, was ready to help Germany to conquer England, and never denied that desire or that readiness, either during the war or after it." In contrast to the dramatic figure of a William Joyce, it hardly seems worthwhile to name these petty traitors. One man, Thomas Haller Cooper, should, however, be mentioned, mainly because he, too, was a man without a country. His father was English and his mother German. He had a dream fatherland, just as Joyce had, a Germany embodying the virtues of his mother, her cleanliness, her *häuslichkeit* and her flower boxes, which always seemed to bloom better than any others in the street. England twice refused to permit him to follow the career of his choice. At college Haller Cooper read Chinese and Japanese, in the hope of getting a position in the Foreign Office. His application was rejected because of his German mother. He then tried the Home Office and was again rejected for the same reason. When war broke out, Haller Cooper, still in search of his lost home, joined the S.S.

It was a bitter day for Joyce when John Amery arrived in Berlin, to be wined and dined as the new white hope of the ministry of propaganda. It was almost as if the long arm of Joyce's failure to crack the social barriers was reaching out from Mayfair and the West End to deal him its final and most ironic blow, for John Amery, the bankrupt and degenerate son of a famous Tory family, was a "gentleman," a fact perceived even by the heavy-handed and unsubtle Nazi functionaries. The Italians and the Finns, to whom Amery had first offered his services, had refused to touch him, and even the Vichy French showed scruples about such a man. The Nazis, on the other hand, were dazzled by his name, by the fact that his father had a portfolio in Churchill's War Cabinet, and most important of all, by the fact that he was at last the real thing, an English gentleman. One could see it in the cut of his suits, in his manner and appearance. They treated him royally, paid him a good deal more than Joyce, and gave him more airtime. Although his corrupt and unscrupulous style of life had turned him into a worthless renegade, he was favored above Joyce with his perfectly conditioned body, his correctness, his wit and learning.

The final blow to a man so often disappointed must have been the Allied victory. Despite his prophetic utterances, the Allies broke through in the West and shattered the invincible *Festung Europä*. Joyce remained true, to the bitter end, to his vision of a Fascist Britain. In his last broadcast to England from Hamburg on April 30, 1945, he said: "We are nearing the end of one phase in Europe's history, but the next will be no happier. It will be grimmer, harder, and perhaps bloodier. And now I ask you earnestly, can Britain survive? I am profoundly convinced that without German help she cannot." That same day he and his wife went out into the woods, where during those May days of collapse and chaos they camped, bathed in the fresh brooks and kept one step ahead of the advancing British Army. They had virtually nothing to eat and insufficient clothing to fight off the sharp spring nights. Joyce, who had always cared for his appearance, allowed himself to grow wild. In this strange situation an even stranger thing occurred. His love for the British uniform betrayed him. One morning he chanced upon two British officers, who were looking for kindling wood, and he felt somehow an urgent need to talk to them. When they were unable to understand his French, Joyce told them, in English, where they could find some wood, and there it was, that voice which for five years had been a daily sound in thousands of English homes. Only Joyce himself did not know that his voice had become a household article. The two officers froze at the sound. "You wouldn't happen to be William Joyce, would you?" one of the two finally asked. Joyce reached into his pocket to pull out his German passport, and one of the officers shot him in the leg, apparently imagining that Joyce was reaching for a pistol.

In a hospital Joyce dictated a statement of his position to an interrogation officer sent from Army headquarters. It is worth quoting several passages:

In the period immediately before this war began I was profoundly discontented with the policies pursued by British governments, first, because I felt that they would lead to the eventual disruption of the British Empire, and, secondly, because I though the existing economic system entirely inadequate to the needs of the times. I was very greatly impressed by the constructive work which Hitler had done for Germany and was of the opinion that throughout Europe as also in Britain there must come a reform along the lines of National Socialist doctrine, although I did not suppose that every aspect of National Socialism as advocated in Germany would be accepted by the British people [There followed several sentences in which Joyce elaborates his idea that a war between Germany and England was a great catastrophe. He then went on to answer the treason charge before it was actually made] As by reason of my opinions I was not conscientiously disposed to fight for Britain against Germany, I decided to leave the country, since I did not wish to play the part of a conscientious objector, and since I supposed that in Germany I should have the opportunity to express and propagate views the expression of which would be forbidden in Britain during time of war. Realising, however, that at this critical juncture I had declined to serve Britain, I drew the logical conclusion that I should have no moral right to return to that country of my own free will and that it would be best to apply for German citizenship and make my permanent home in Germany. Nevertheless, it remained my undeviating purpose to attempt as best I could to bring about a reconciliation or at least an understanding between the two countries. After Russia and the United States had entered the war, such an agreement appeared to me no less desirable than before, for, although it seemed probable that with these powerful allies Britain would succeed in defeating Germany, I considered that the price which would ultimately have to be paid for this help would be far higher than the price involved in a settlement with Germany.

154

He was aware that he had been called a traitor. Although he was able to understand the "resentment" evoked by his broadcasts, he denied the charge of treason. He considered his behavior toward England to have been perfectly correct and straightforward. At no time had he betrayed anyone and at no time had he acted subversively or secretly. He chose as his ultimate judge the course of future events and closed his remarkable statement with the following words: "Whatever opinion may be formed at the present time with regard to my conduct, I submit that the final judgment cannot be properly passed until it is seen whether Britain can win the peace."

The prosecution at his trial was, of course, quite unconcerned with such historicopolitical arguments. As long as the prosecution was under the impression that Joyce was a British subject, it rested its case on the law of 1351, according to which: "If a man do levy war against our Lord the King in his realm or be adherent to the King's enemies in his realm, giving them aid and comfort in the realm or elsewhere, he is guilty of treason." When, however, the defense succeeded in proving beyond question that Joyce had never been a British subject—not for one instant—the prosecution's case collapsed. Obviously such a man was not obliged to be loyal to the king and could not be tried under the law of 1351.

The prosecution returned with an argument based on a precedent from the year 1608, according to which anyone, regardless of nationality, if standing under the king's protection, is obliged to be loyal to the crown. The holder of an ordinary British passport is under such protection. There was, however, no precedent for the assertion that the simple possession of a British passport constituted an act of allegiance. For a full day prosecution and defense tilted with one another on this point in a brilliant and complex legal struggle. On the following day the court gave its ruling. A man carrying a British passport is, in fact, under the protection of the crown and owes it loyalty, whether he is in the immediate territorial area falling under royal jurisdiction or not. This technical ruling was Joyce's death warrant.

Joyce took no part in his own defense. Perhaps his perverse love for England went so far that he preferred being hanged as a Briton who had committed treason to being acquitted as an American. He followed the proceedings with a detached, intellectual curiosity, as if it were all just a jolly, interesting conundrum. At one point he whispered to his guard, "It will be amusing to see whether they get away with it." "They" were the lawyers fighting for his life. He might have saved himself, or at least made things difficult for the prosecution by testifying that he had not used the passport in question to get out of England. In fact, he said nothing at all about how he managed to slip out of the country. "But he was not a perjurer," writes Rebecca West. "He had at least chosen to play out his drama in the real world. If sentence is to be passed on him, let it be based on the truth."

There were those who took a different view. "A miscarriage of justice," said the clerk in a government office, handing out a legal document concerning Joyce to an inquirer some months later. "That's what that verdict was. I hold no brief for the little man, though he was a wonderful speaker. I'm no Fascist but I always used to listen to him when he spoke up our way by the Great Northern Hospital; but it stands to reason that giving an American a British passport can't change him into an Englishman." Rebecca West, who followed the trial in great detail, continually attempts to refute this view. She is most convincing when she argues that this is a case in which the letter of the law cannot be separated from the spirit: "It was debated whether a man can live all his life among a tribe and eat their salt, and in the hour of their danger sharpen the sword that their enemies intend for their breasts and then go free because of something written in an old book which said that this man was not truly of that tribe."

At another juncture she tries to remove the case from its human perspective altogether and place it in the realm of heavenly justice: "So he went to his trial, which was not like most earthly trials but was the pattern of such trials that must happen in the hereafter. For we shall be judged at the end unjustly, according to the relation of our activities to a context whereof we, being human and confined to a small part of time and space, knew almost nothing." Joyce himself had said in his declaration, while lying wounded in the hospital, that a judgment of his actions could only be made when history had determined whether England had won the peace. In thinking of Joyce, the judgment of history coincided with the judgment of God, whereas Miss West places the case beyond human judgment entirely. Neither view bears any relation to the argument of the crown counsel, although Miss West approves and Joyce denies the legal verdict.

What was, in the last analysis, so terribly wrong with Joyce that despite so much of value in his nature he met such a tragic fate? Surely it was not just his peculiar politics. Can his sense of exclusion from the circles which attracted him so powerfully explain everything? Miss West argues that ultimately Joyce was a man whom one simply could not like. She certainly found him unappealing, and describes him with her own special sharpness, though she could not deny the elements of greatness and tragedy in his nature. The fairness of her estimate can only be judged by Englishmen who knew Joyce personally, without being his supporters. He was loved in his family. His students liked him enormously. His supporters at the trial, many of them with Irish blood and all in the trench-coat uniform of the "movement," left the courtroom with tears running down their cheeks when they heard that William Joyce was condemned to hang by the neck until dead.

16. LITTLE PEOPLE FROM THE UNITED STATES

THE drama and poignance of the story of William Joyce lead one to forget that for every William Joyce (and regardless of what one may think of him, one must concede that he was a remarkable person) there were a number of men and women of no stature. In this section I shall describe six who flit briefly across the stage of history like extras in a Wagnerian opera: Robert Best, Herbert John Burgmann, Douglas Chandler, Mildred Gillars, Frederick W. Kaltenbach and Max Otto Koischwitz. The last named died in Germany in 1944, and the accusation against Kaltenbach was stricken from the books, since the Russian Government informed Washington early in 1948 that Kaltenbach had died in a Russian prison camp in 1945. The other four were sent back to America at the end of the war, tried and condemned to prison terms as traitors—in the cases of Best and Chandler for life. None of them achieved the fame of Lord Haw Haw, for none of them had any real ability. The single woman, Mildred Gillars, became quite well known to American soldiers as "Axis Sally." Her broadcasts were originally intended to reach the home front in the United States, but the signal was too weak to reach across the Atlantic, so after a time her broadcasts were rewritten for G.I. consumption. Axis Sally was never more than a clumsy joke to her soldier listeners, who were amused and often entertained at the expense of Goebbels' Ministry of Propaganda.

Herbert Burgmann was a clerk at the American Embassy in Berlin who refused to leave when the diplomatic personnel was recalled. Burgmann was a clerk by nature, and his treachery was the petty sort of the very small man. When he began to broadcast for Goebbels he decided to use a less foreign-sounding name, calling himself "Joe Scanlon, the true friend of the boys in the Army and Navy. I only want to make sure that you boys don't get it in the neck." His attacks were directed against the military leaders: "The professionals have always proven themselves to be money mad. Now that war has come, they have no intention whatever of doing the actual fighting. . . . On the contrary, now that war has come and Army life is dangerous, they expect our boys to do the fighting, get killed, or be wounded and remain cripples for life."

In contrast to Burgmann, Best and Chandler were trained journalists. Best belonged to the old, comfortable school of foreign correspondents, who sat around in cafés and brewed their stories from a potpourri of facts and "atmosphere." With his two hundred and twenty pounds, his broad-brimmed brown hat, his high-laced boots and his soft, feminine face, Best cut quite a figure and had been well known in Vienna for years. An elderly White Russian woman called the "Countess" had exercised an extraordinary power over him and had taught him to hate the Bolsheviks and the Jews. Best came from a good, conservative Southern family and had been well educated. He first tasted the joys of life in Europe during the First World War. He returned home after the war, to study journalism at Columbia University. In 1923, he won a Pulitzer traveling scholarship for a year's study in Europe, left for the Old World, and never returned. In a way, this was his real treachery in the eyes of his fellow citizens. Expatriation, though not against the law, offends the deepest emotions of most Americans. Such feelings arise from the nearly mystical faith of the average American that the real significance of the great immigration of Europeans to America was a moral one. Immigration was an act of ideological commitment to the ideals of freedom and equality, and a radical conversion from European despotism and moral degeneration.

William Shirer, a colleague of Best's in both Vienna and Berlin, whose *Berlin Diary* stirred up American emotions about Germany and helped to prepare the climate for America's entering the war, wrote a book about Best called *Traitor*. In it Shirer argues that a foreign correspondent gradually begins to lose his "feel" of the home country if he remains abroad too long without a break. He begins to lose touch with public opinion at home and cannot report properly unless he returns home regularly to soak up the atmosphere. It is not irrelevant here to point out how subtly and effectively journalism, in Shirer's view, crosses imperceptibly that line between reporting and propaganda. One cannot report well unless one senses the mood of the public and knows instinctively what it wants to hear. The genius of the free Western journalists lies precisely in this ability to write ideological propaganda without realizing that they have done so. They fulfill the two essential conditions of good propaganda so perfectly that their effectiveness far surpasses anything which the totalitarian press has ever produced. If the reader will recall, we suggested the two essentials of successful propaganda as: first, the feeling for the great movements of the day; and second, the ability to believe in self-created propaganda. In both respects, Western journalists have been spectacularly successful.

Best's own motives for not returning home are not clear. Perhaps he was staging his own private war against the invisible pressure to "tell them what they want to hear." At any rate, he continued to evade the order to report to the New York office of the United Press, for which he had been working. The requests were numerous and Best's excuses feeble. Finally, in the summer of 1941, he was discharged from the United Press on grounds of "insufficient work and performance." He began to live the peculiar and uncertain existence of the free-lance journalist, which was the more difficult in his case, because for some time he had apparently misunderstood or ignored the changing winds of public opinion at home. His articles, written in the early days of the German military successes, had always been a little too positive and a little too pro-German to be printed with comfortable conscience. There even seems to have been a silent agreement with th Germans behind the scenes at this time. Later he was given special and unmistakably preferential treatment when all the American diplomats and journalists were interned at Nauheim after the outbreak of war. For no apparent reason, he remained behind when the internees were repatriated as a group in May 1942.

Shortly thereafter his propaganda began to be sent out from the mammoth Funkhaus in Berlin. He spoke of Adolf Hitler as the "crusader for civilization," and Roosevelt as "a tool of the Jews." In his mouth the New Deal became the "Jew Deal," and America was turned into a "slave plantation run by talmudic Christian-killers." Defending himself before the Federal Court in Boston in 1948, Best asserted that he had never intended to betray America but had only tried to warn his countrymen against the

Bolshevik peril and Roosevelt's warmongering. He based his anti-Communism on two papal encyclicals. It was on his fifty-second birthday that the court found him guilty. The thin, tight-lipped little man, a shadow of the old Best, heard the verdict defiantly. "If I had it to do again, I would."

His colleague Douglas Chandler also came from a very good family, but there the similarity ended. Chandler had always been much more of an aesthete than a journalist. He loved music and the fine arts, wrote poetry and prose for a Baltimore daily paper, and depressed himself over the lack of cultivation among his fellow citizens. A marriage with a wealthy woman enabled him to abandon journalism and become a stockbroker. The collapse of the New York Stock Exchange wiped him out, and in 1931 he and his wife and daughters sailed for Europe to get away from it all, but most of all from the "miasma hanging over America." The Chandlers traveled in Germany, Belgium, Scandinavia, Turkey and Yugoslavia. Chandler wrote articles for the respectable and remunerative *National Geographic Magazine.* Sometime shortly before the war he was put on the German Ministry of Propaganda payroll at the rate of $960 per month (Best received only $600). He made several propaganda journeys, in the pay of Germany, through England and Scotland.

Chandler was far more original and imaginative in his broadcasts than Best. At the beginning of each program "Yankee Doodle" was played and Chandler, calling himself Paul Revere, would begin by crying out: "Hello, from the heart of Hitler Germany. Your messenger Paul Revere calls to you, my fellow countrymen and foes." This time, however, Paul Revere had a message which would have shocked Longfellow. "America began the war and is going to lose it. . . . Down with the Jews." Like Best, Chandler, too, was unreconciled at his trial. "I am prepared to die for my convictions," he declared theatrically, "but my convictions will not die with me."

Whereas Best and Chandler had at least had sufficient vitality to make lives for themselves in Hitler's Germany, Mildred Gillars remained on the outskirts of things there, as everywhere. Her

life seems to have been an uninterrupted succession of failures—
as an actress, as a singer and as a radio announcer. At one
point she had been forced to live on crackers and apples for
months. Worldly brilliance and success, which she so ardently
sought, always lay just beyond her outstretched hands. When
she appeared in the courtroom in 1949, though her hands showed
the pallor of the long, weary months of imprisonment, her face
radiated painted good health. She wore her elegantly set hair in
long, silver-gray waves, had painted nails and wore expensive
lipstick. The *New Yorker* commented that the forty-eight-year-
old woman, with obvious determination which must have cost
her great effort, had preserved the figure of a twenty-four-year-
old girl. She came from Maine, the most conservative of the
New England states, which she abandoned in her early twenties
to seek a career on the stage. When her attempts to become an
actress proved unrewarding, she left for Europe, at the age of
twenty-eight, to study voice. In Germany her energy simply ran
out and she was stranded. When there was no more money left,
even for apples and crackers, she took a job on Radio Berlin.
In 1941, according to her account, her passport was taken away
by a very rude vice-consul at the American Embassy and she was
thrown entirely on the mercy of her German employers.

Her inspiration and comfort during this bad period was Professor Max Otto Koischwitz, who for many years had taught German literature at Hunter College for Women in New York.
Koischwitz apparently exercised an incredible power over the
female spirit. During the war former students of his would blush
with pleasure when his name was mentioned. Some even went
so far as to try to catch the faint sound of his voice during his
propaganda broadcasts from Berlin, and were blissful when, despite interference and jamming, the familiar voice could be
discerned. Although he had a wife and three children, he had
determined, during long walks in his beloved Silesian mountains,
that his relationship with Mildred Gillars was blessed. Whatever
opinions he poured into her ear, she repeated faithfully over the
air. Since he was anti-Semitic and hated Roosevelt and the Brit-

ish, Mildred Gillars merely reproduced, in a female voice, the same uninspired Nazi claptrap as Best and Chandler, but without their conviction that the propaganda had substance. Tokyo Rose was a force; Axis Sally was just a voice. Mildred Gillars had neither the conviction nor the intellect with which to defend her treachery before the court. She protested vainly that she had been patriotic, that she had wept when the Japanese bombed Pearl Harbor, and that hers was an unjust fate.

17. EZRA POUND—CLASSICIST AND REVOLUTIONARY

IN 1949 the newly established Bollingen Prize was awarded to an American poet for the best published lyric work of the preceding year. The members of the committee which made the award were among the most eminent figures in the Anglo-American literary world, Conrad Aiken, W. H. Auden, Robert Lowell, Katherine Anne Porter and the chairman, T. S. Eliot. The award caused an immediate uproar. Hundreds of letters were written to all sorts of journals and newspapers. The effect of the public outcry was so enormous that the Bollingen Prize was not awarded again. The *Saturday Review of Literature* printed a survey of the hundreds of letters for and against the award, and *The Nation* protested against the suppression of freedom of thought implied in the arguments of those who disapproved of the award. The committee declared that "objective consideration of values, which is at the root of every healthy, civilized society, will be lost, if other than aesthetic determinants be introduced into the judging of art and made decisive."

The man so honored and so attacked sat in a mental institution and until recently was still there. His name is Ezra Pound. Until Pound's release it was true to say that the day the doctors of St. Elizabeth's Hospital in Washington, D.C., declared Pound sane and opened the doors of the institution for him would be the day on which the high-treason proceedings against him would be reopened. The trial had been postponed indefinitely as a consequence of Pound's "illness." This confusing and paradoxical state of affairs lasted for years. The work for which the Bollingen Prize was awarded was the now famous "Pisan Cantos." Pound wrote the cantos in an American prison camp in Italy, where at first he had been placed in the death cell and later in a "gorilla cage," where he could be shown off to the mob. Finally he had been confined to a solitary cell for months, until, broken and ill, he was returned to the United States.

The first psychiatric examination determined that Pound's was "a psychopathic personality which had developed paranoid psychoses with manic coloration." This argument was advanced to show that Pound was not mentally fit enough to be made responsible for his acts. Later the argument was simplified and the doctors suggested that he was suffering from early senility brought on by his iniquitous treatment during his confinement. The German poet, Rudolf Hagelstange, who was allowed to visit Pound in the mid-1950's, describes his experience: "Pound was the first insane poet with whom I have ever held a conversation, and the only genuinely insane thing about that conversation was that Pound was not insane."

Ezra Pound was born in Hailey, Idaho, in 1885. He studied literature and then taught it, until he fell out with the authorities at his college. In 1908, he sailed for Europe on a cattle boat, and remained in Europe without interruption until 1945. At first he lived in London, where his influence was so great that one can meaningfully speak of the "Era of Ezra Pound" in English literature. In the 1920's, he moved to Paris, where he became the neighbor and friend of James Joyce, Ernest Hemingway and Gertrude Stein. He lived the typical existence of the expatriate colony in Paris, shunting between bistro, bordello and salon. In the early 1930's he settled in a run-down villa outside Genoa, from which perch he bombarded his friends and enemies with polemical letters and suggestions for improving the world.

Pound hated the era of money. He believed that Mussolini and his corporate state were on the right road toward eliminating the dominance of wealth. He concerned himself with the free-money theories of Silvio Gesell, with the withering away of money as preached by Wörgls, and finally developed his own social-credit theory, with which the world was to be purified. Among his pet schemes was one that poets should live in academies and that millionaires, as long as they existed, should be their "angels." His capacity to hate was not, however, confined to generalities or ideas. He had an outspoken contempt for the snobbish, ossified literary world of his homeland, and in this field he knew what he was about. The following sentences come from one of his early polemics: "It is well known that in the year of grace 1870 Jehovah appeared to Messrs. Harper and Co. and to the editors of the *Century,* the *Atlantic Monthly* and certain others, and spake thus: 'The style of 1870 is the final and divine revelation. Keep things always just as they are. . . . ' "

In England he became a pathfinder. Günter Blöcker writes about Pound's role as follows:

At the turn of the century, the Anglo-Saxon world's lyric poem had driven itself into such a dead end that only a violent rebel of the type of Ezra Pound could attain what Eliot has described as the "discovery of a contemporary expression for poetry." Pound solved the problem in a paradoxical way. He demolished poetry, but with great reverence for its heritage. On the one hand, Pound succeeded in developing a new sign language for reality, in creating an idiom suitable for the changed feelings, the changed facts and the changed vision of modern life. Pound created a modern cryptographic art of the highest sensitivity in which the images stand hard by one another in cold exuberance, tied only by the invisible bond of association of ideas. It is a sort of poetic shorthand which converts verse into ideograms and, even at the point at which the verse sweeps into hymn, the constructed units retain their mathematical and musical precision. On the other hand, Pound works with ancient coins from the world of classical forms. He dives into the oldest linguistic streams and digs in half-collapsed mines, long forgotten by the present, in order to unite the "once upon a time" with today. Pound is, thus, a classicist and revolutionary at the same time, welding the two together by the power of his commanding spirit.

Hemingway was one of the first to recognize Pound's greatness: "A poet, born in this century or in the ten years before, who can claim that he has not been influenced by Ezra Pound deserves pity rather than our criticism." T. S. Eliot sent the typescript of *The Waste Land* to Pound and received it back with at least half of it cut. This was the version that Eliot published in 1922 dedicated: "For Ezra Pound. *Il miglior fabbro.*"

Pound aimed at a restoration of the validity of the individual word. He busied himself with Confucius. From the ancient Chinese philosopher he derived one of his leitmotivs, that most of our troubles arise from the separation of the word from its meaning, which leads in turn to a lack of harmony in our conceptions. Pound wrote that: "Contemporary language serves merely to conceal meaning and to befog our thinking. It has produced the inferno of the past century. One thing alone will help, care for the language and the utmost precision. When people fail to care for language, their children and their children's children will find themselves impoverished, holding begging bowls." He determined to free the language of the lyric from all romanticism, all rhetoric and pathos—better bare, restrained and harsh than dithyrambic. He gave his disciples direction in their struggles to purify the language and their diction. They had to immerse themselves in foreign cadences and rhythms, the wild music of Anglo-Saxon magic and incantation, folk songs of the Hebrides and the verse forms of Dante and Shakespeare. His influence was not unlike that of Herder's on the poets of the Sturm und Drang period, with, however, one vital difference. Pound, like Herder, Mallarmé, George, Hofmannsthal and Eliot, had been trained in philology, but in contrast to Herder, Pound was more than a mentor and intellectual guide. He was a creative power of the first magnitude. The force of his archetypal memory images, the magic of his language and forms, override the purely academic in his methodology.

Pound was in a way a changeling. He loved metamorphosis and the flowing alteration of form and content. For the student of treason, this feature of Pound's nature has great significance and may well be the decisive factor in his curious career. Max Rychner writes: "The barriers fall. Essences change places and mix with one another as in a dream or fairy tale or in a chemical retort. The sea is a woman. Pound is Dante. Past and future are present and the dead become contemporaries of our great-grandchildren. Things move in and out of each other. The soul in Pound's world drives toward its own metamorphosis. Each existing form is both essential and godly and masklike at the same time."

How can judge and jury consider such a man? How can he be measured by paragraphs of law? What medical criteria are appropriate to determine whether Pound is normal? The accusation against him was in its way clear: he had not come home. He loved Italy and had become, like Gertrude Stein, Scott Fitzgerald and Henry James, an expatriate. In 1939, after the outbreak of the war, he began to make speeches on Radio Rome. Pound was a pacifist and spoke out often and vehemently for a negotiated peace. When America entered the war, he suddenly felt an urge to return and applied for the proper papers, but was ignored. He was furious, as only he could be, and attacked the warmongers and the Jews in a series of violent broadcasts which the prosecution described as obnoxiously Fascist and filthy. Though it mattered very little, for he would have been found anyway, Pound did surrender freely to the American forces as they rolled into Genoa. From 1943 on, Pound was lined up along with mercenary and second-class men like Best and Chandler and ultimately charged, as they were, with treason.

In the life of such a man, there are no coincidences. What may seem at first to be chance has in the long run some sort of significance. Nothing typifies this proposition more than the story of Pound's lost manuscript. In 1913 he submitted a book to a small Chicago publisher who proceeded to lose it in the chaos of a totally inefficient firm. During a cleaning of the Augean stables in 1950 it came to light and was immediately printed. The work was called *Patria Mia*. For the first time, Americans could read what the so-called "traitor" felt about his homeland. There were many bitter words, but many of profound love—a love grown strong in exile. Of Walt Whitman, for example, Pound wrote: "One may not need him at home. It is in the air, this tonic of his. But if one is abroad; if one is ever likely to forget one's birthright, to lose faith being surrounded by disparagers, one can find in Whitman reassurance. Whitman goes bail for the nation." At another point he reflects on New York: "A crowd pagan as ever imperial Rome was, eager, careless, with an animal vigor unlike that of any European crowd I have ever looked at. There is none of the melancholy, the sullenness, the unhealth of the London mass, none of the worn vivacity of Paris."

A single manuscript—*My Country*—was for years the only one he had sent home. And there it was mislaid. Pound did not try to publish it in Europe, as he did thirty-one other books and translations which found their public before the outbreak of the Second World War. However that may be, one of the terrible myths of our century, the world of the concentration camps, found its first expressive form as the fruit of Pound's suffering outside Pisa in the camp with its merciless watchtowers, staring out over the surrounding wasteland: the symbolic "four giants at the four corners."

When one looks at a picture of Pound in his early manhood, the energetic forehead crowned with thickly curled red hair, the closely cropped beard and the fierce, piercing stare, one is reminded of the curious figures of the Peasants' War, a Hermann Götz or a Florian Geyer. The pictures of Pound on trial show a man in a prison suit, a blasted face, tired and drooping features, trembling beard and watery eyes. But even in these pictures the eyes of a broken man are as penetrating as ever.

When Hemingway received the Nobel Prize in 1954 he thought again of his old friend, Ezra Pound, in the mental hospital. "Ezra Pound is a great poet and whatever he did he has been punished greatly. I believe he should be freed to go and write poems in Italy, where he is loved and understood. He was the master of T. S. Eliot. . . . I believe this would be a good year to release poets. There is a school of thought in America which, if encouraged far enough, could well believe that a man should be punished for the simple error against conformity of being a poet. Dante, by these standards, could well have spent his life in St. Elizabeth's Hospital for errors of judgment and pride." Hemingway was clearly condemning "McCarthyism," as were many Americans at that time. Yet even among those who opposed McCarthy as vehemently as Hemingway, there were other views about Pound and about the poet's place in society. In the same year, the German poet Hans Holthusen found himself in conversation with a prominent lady novelist who was also a great admirer of T. S. Eliot. At one point in the conversation the lady turned to Holthusen. "But tell me, what do you think of Eliot as a citizen?" "As a citizen?" echoed Holthusen, rather nonplussed by the question, which for him was essentially meaningless. "Why, he's a poet, that is all." The lady wrote later that she knew in that moment that a gulf separated them. Man or citizen was Camus' problem; poet or citizen was the American lady's. An abyss wide and deep enough to swallow a man whole. The next sign on this road reads POET OR FUNCTIONARY. The Russians passed it long ago.

18. TOKYO ROSE—THE WRONG RACE

DURING the late summer and autumn of 1945 a curious scene took place every evening outside of a large prison in Tokyo. Groups of American soldiers would gather outside the main gate to demand autographs from a woman whom they had never seen. A few would bring flowers or candy for her, though they, too, knew her only as a voice. It was a voice which spoke to them daily through the long, bitter years of the war in the Pacific. The voice belonged to a young woman whom none had seen but all knew well. They knew her as Tokyo Rose.

Her real name was Iva Toguri, a Japanese-American born in

169

Los Angeles on July 4, 1920. Iva Toguri had done remarkably well for the daughter of an immigrant family. She had studied at the University of California, and had taken a degree in zoology. She had done what all the members of her age group did. She had gone to football matches; she had been an ardent member of movie-star fan clubs; she knew all the slang expressions then current. In fact she belonged in every external respect, it would seem, to the same generation whose male members had become her regular listeners while serving in the Pacific. She was able to speak to the American troops more effectively than any other propagandist on the enemy side. She was one of them.

What went wrong? Why did Iva Toguri turn against her own country to serve Japan? The answer lies less in the details of her own life than in the historical background to it. To understand what happened to Iva Toguri one must know the significance of the words "Yellow Peril." The slogan Yellow Peril was first used in the Far Western states against the Chinese immigrants, who began to arrive in large numbers during the last decades of the nineteenth century. At first the relatively small number of Japanese immigrants were not included in the Yellow-Peril campaign. The Japanese were considered to be more flexible, civilized and obedient. Most important, there were not many of them. By the turn of the century, sentiment had begun to turn against the Japanese as well. The 1906 California School Law decreed that "Oriental children" must be instructed separately from white children. Granting citizenship to Japanese or Chinese immigrants was considered out of the question. In 1913 the Alien Land Law adopted in California made it impossible for "nonnatives" to purchase land. Pressure to extend the anti-Oriental laws, especially restrictions on further immigration, caused serious internal conflicts throughout the United States and occasioned considerable embarrassment in the Department of State which found itself facing an imminent war with Japan over the issue. In 1913, a Connecticut newspaper commented wryly that it would be far cheaper to wage war with California than with Japan. In the meantime Californians continued to apply themselves to the problems. They founded organizations to extend the Exclusion and to fight the growing numbers and influence of the Asians. There were the "Native Sons of The Golden West," and the corresponding "Daughters," "The League for the Exclusion of Orientals from California," with over 100,000 members, "The Southern California Committee of the Thousand," and countless others.

Morton Grodzins, from whose book, *Americans Betrayed*, the above facts have been taken, cites several of the appeals and declarations which such groups published in the years before Pearl Harbor, such as:

The proposed assimilation of the two races is unthinkable. It is morally indefensible and biologically impossible. American womanhood is by far too sacred to be subjected to such degeneracy. An American who would not die fighting rather than yield to that infamy does not deserve the name.

Wherever the Japanese have settled, their nests pollute the communities like the running sores of leprosy. They exist like the yellowed, smoldering, discarded butts in an over-full ashtray, vilifying the air with their loathsome smells, filling all who have the misfortune to look upon them with a wholesome disgust and a desire to wash.

In such an atmosphere, only slightly softened by other groups which felt differently, young Americans of Japanese extraction grew up: Iva Toguri, Tomyo Kawakita, who supported the Japanese in the interrogation and mishandling of American prisoners of war, and Miyagi Yotoku, a member of Sorge's spy ring.

The twenty-one-year-old Iva Toguri traveled to Japan in the summer of 1941, to visit a sick aunt, according to her testimony; to study medicine, according to the prosecution. There she was caught by the sudden and unexpected outbreak of hostilities between her homeland and the land of her forefathers. The news which she heard from America could hardly strengthen her loyalty toward the land of her birth. For the first time in the history of the United States, race, and race alone, was the reason for the arrest of American citizens and residents. Grodzins has described the events in the following words:

171

One hundred and ten thousand Americans of Japanese ancestry were evacuated. Aliens and citizens, children and adults, males and females, were moved on short notice from their lifetime homes to concentration centers. No charges were ever filed against these persons, and no guilt was ever attributed to them. The test was ancestry . . . evacuation swept into guarded camps orphans, foster-children in white homes, Japanese married to Caucasians, the offspring of such marriages, persons who were unaware of their Japanese ancestry, and American citizens with as little as one-sixteenth Japanese blood.

That was at the beginning of 1942. More than a year later, Iva Toguri began her broadcasts to American troops in the Pacific. "Hi, boys," she cried in the purest American slang, "this is your old friend. I've got some swell new recordings for you, just in from the States. You'd better enjoy them while you can, because tomorrow at 0600 you're hitting Saipan . . . and we're ready for you. So while you're alive let's listen to. . ." At the beginning she had no idea that the troops had given her the name of Tokyo Rose. She first called herself simply "Ann," and later on "your favorite enemy, Orphan Annie," suggesting that the war had made orphans of the whole lot—of her and the GI's at the same time.

At her trial in 1949 over ninety witnesses were called. Nineteen of them were flown from Japan especially for the hearings, which excited considerable public interest. The actual court process was complicated by the fact that Tokyo Rose had consisted of seven different women, though Iva Toguri was by far the most important and the only American citizen among them. Her defense pleaded that, since she had married Felipe D'Aquino, a Portuguese employee of the Domai agency, in 1945, she was no longer an American citizen and therefore outside the court's competence. The main group of broadcasts had, however, been made before 1945, when she was in fact an American citizen, so the court dismissed the argument. The second defense argument had more humane justification, though it was legally of less weight. American officers had declared repeatedly that Tokyo Rose had been of great assistance in raising the morale of their troops. Commanders of particularly nervous or untried units openly confessed their debt to her. The sound of her voice and the familiar music took the minds of the troops off their own anxieties and the heat and discomfort for a little while at least. This was certainly true. The abundance of the greetings and gifts which she received in prison was a visible demonstration of it. The military authorities were eventually forced to forbid categorically any further contact with her, to halt the flow of presents from her fans.

As she sat before the court, pale and still, she seemed to be little more than a frail doll. Her eyes were red rimmed from lack of sleep in the prison, where she had been confined with the common criminals and prostitutes, whose noisy arrivals, all during the night, kept her awake. Her weight fell from 130 to 98 pounds.

The twelve jurors, six men and six women, required four days after the completion of the hearings for their discussion, and were forced to report to the court that they were unable to agree on a verdict. They were directed by the judge to return for another attempt at agreement, and finally, after long consideration, returned a verdict of Not Guilty on the first five points of the charge and Guilty on the sixth. The sixth point stated that Iva Toguri had broadcast the following words after the Japanese had reported the sinking of a large number of American ships off the Gulf of Leyte: "Orphans of the Pacific, you really are orphans now. How will you get home now that all your ships are sunk?"

The public had expected an acquittal. The prosecution had not demanded a death sentence. The minimum punishment for treason amounted to five years. The sentence was read aloud— ten years. Iva Toguri was released in 1956.

19. KNUT HAMSUN—THE DEAF POET

KNUT HAMSUN is an exception. He never spoke over the radio from the capital of an enemy power. Indeed, he never spoke over the radio at all. He stayed at home, and as the Germans over-ran his beloved Norway he wrote articles in the newspapers in honor of the conquerors, in honor of Adolf Hitler. Simply a collaborator then? The word collaborator does not quite fit Hamsun's activities, because it implies working together or co-operation, whereas Hamsun remained in solitude on his remote estate. He never really had any contact with his epoch and very little with his fellow men, except of course for the occasional card party or glass of wine with a friend. He had even less in 1940, for he had grown old, deaf and lonely in his personal world.

The tool with which he became effective was the printed word. Just as it had used the spoken words of a Joyce, Best, or Chand-ler, the German Ministry of Propaganda intended to use the words of Knut Hamsun. Hamsun was to tell the English-speaking world what decent, right-thinking people the Germans of the Third Reich really were. Unfortunately the planners made a mistake. Famous as Hamsun may be, he was and still is rela-tively unknown in the Anglo-Saxon world. The English editions of his books have been infrequent and the sales tiny compared to the mass consumption of his works in the Scandinavian and Ger-man worlds. Hamsun's words had hardly any effect on the British and the Americans, but they turned the Norwegians against him. There is a story that every day the postman delivered scores of volumes of Hamsun's books—returned to the lonely farmhouse by his former readers and admirers. The pile grew, according to this probably apocryphal tale, until it was so large that there was no longer any room for the books in the house and Hamsun simply let them stand in heaps in his yard. Whether true or not, it satisfied many Norwegians, in their fury and shame, to circu-late the story, so that it came to symbolize what Norway felt.

Hamsun, the son of a country tailor, had himself been a post-man once, also a shoemaker, coal miner, traveling salesman, street-car conductor, farmhand, estate overseer, private tutor, dockhand and vagrant. He knew the world's width from the underside. He knew the world from the inside, too, the living natural world, wood, earth, thicket, the sublime indifference and amorality of nature, its timelessness, the old spirits and the ancient gods who haunt the souls of country people, seamen and peasants. This was the world which he resurrected in the middle of the modern era. He was not a Christian, though he believed in mercy and grace, for his grace and his mercy were the gifts of a mystical nature. He lived for forty years in the nineteenth century and fifty-two in the twentieth, but remained in a curious, eerie way a prehistoric manifestation of Nordic mysticism. Of the Nordic peasant Isak he once wrote: "One risen from the mists of prehistory, who points to the future, a man from the first age of agriculture, an ancient homestead, nine hundred years old and yet of today." One could easily use the very words to describe Hamsun himself.

But he was many other things as well: brusque, high-handed, arrogant, wide open, gay, bubbling with laughter and marked by sudden silences and inwardness. Basically he only wanted to be a peasant. The name "Hamsund," which he chose as a pseudonym for his first book of verse, was the name of the farm which his family had lost. A careless printer omitted the "d" in the first edition, and peasant superstition held Hamsun back from changing it in the following ones. After the success of his first great novel, *Hunger,* Hamsun, whose surname was actually Pedersen, bought himself a beautiful, big farm. At last he was a farmer and well off at that. Yet something in him continually drove him out of his comfortable, prosperous homestead into a bare, cold workhouse, to feel again the atmosphere of hunger, thirst and weariness so deeply embedded in his poetry. To be independent from everything was his highest wish, free of the city, of his fellow men and even of his own desires. As a very old man, during his trial, when he had been "interned" in a hospital and had no more tobacco, he wrote in his diary: "Fair enough. I shall stop smoking. I shall simply stop. I have done it three times, each time for exactly one year by the calendar. I shall master myself and stop. Good. But if I begin again? What use is it all then? I shall be strong, strong enough to begin again."

During the trial, the endless examinations and the arbitrary decisions, he remained aloof and unmoved by the vagaries of his fate. One day, while he was being examined by a doctor in the hospital to which he had been confined, the doctor suddenly looked up and asked, "Would you like to go home?" Hamsun replied, immovable, "I want what the police want. I have no will of my own." It is impossible to get a hold on such a man, even with a charge of treason.

He had no head for politics. He returned from a life of starvation in America with the conviction that America was a land without culture, filled with "prudish, self-satisfied ignorance" and "patriotism sounded a tinhorn." He hated the English long before there was a National Socialist movement. It could be read in his works, and nobody objected before Hitler came to power. He hated big cities, parliamentarians and Anglo-Saxon tourists. He fumed over the growing "Switzerlandizing" of his homeland and over industrialism which destroyed the good and simple way of life of the Norwegian peasant. He loved the Germans, whom he considered healthier and fresher than the English. He believed that every great name in Norwegian culture had to pass through and be approved by German culture before fame and world recognition could follow.

When the National Socialists took power in Norway, he was over eighty, hard of hearing, and cut off from the world in his lonesome retreat. He sat in his kitchen on the farm and read the papers as the world became convulsed. The program of the Nazis, their land laws for agricultural inheritance, their cry of *"Blut und Boden,"* could not fail to please him. Later Quisling began to make promises: the Russians were to be driven from Spitsbergen; Greenland was to be taken from Denmark; Norway was to have a special place of honor in the Greater German Bund. The days passed and Hamsun sat alone, reading the *Aftenposten* and *Fritt Folk,* nodding in agreement. Eventually he felt dissatisfied with simple agreement and began to agree aloud in public, in articles for that same press which he hated and condemned as a perversion. Was it not in this pact with one of the modern age's mightiest instruments, bent on the destruction of everything Hamsun believed in, that he committed his real treason?

His son Tore has described his father's deep disappointment after a visit to Hitler. Hamsun had attempted to have the hated Gauleiter Terboven removed, and to do so had appealed directly to Hitler. The conversation began politely and grew cooler and stiffer. Hitler declaimed, as if from a platform, according to Hamsun's description, and in every sentence there was an "I." He looked like an itinerant laborer, with his squat figure, whereas Hamsun, even in his days as a vagrant, had always looked the complete aristocrat. The old man's nerves began to give way and suddenly he burst into tears; according to Tore Hamsun, they were of frustration at the failure of his mission. The tears could just as easily have been shed for the collapse of his mythical world at the sight of Hitler. Hamsun never recanted. He was too proud to admit an error. Unlike André Gide, whose books contain a minute, step-by-step account of his disillusionment with, and estrangement from, Communism, Hamsun remained true to his words to the bitter end, for among other things he was a very stubborn old man. Admittedly, it was a bit impractical, in a country under German rule, to retract in public. Still, after his disappointment, he could have held his peace, which would have been a tacit concession of his misjudgment of the Nazis. Not Hamsun. He continued to pour out praise of the Germans with his peasant doggedness, even after the Thousand Year Reich collapsed around his head. After Hitler's death he wrote a eulogy.

In *The Overgrown Paths,* his last book, Hamsun describes a pair of rubber-soled shoes which had split and how he tried to sew them together with heavy thread. While working, he thought about the shoes: "They were good shoes. This split seam and I have been together in many countries. They accompanied me to Vienna and one famous time to Hitler. Now I would throw them who knows how far if only I did not need heavy shoes so badly."

It can hardly have been agreeable for the Norwegians to have to confiscate the fortune of, and confine, their famous poet. It may have been just the sight of his venerable figure being led away which caused the sloppy and inept handling of his case, or it may have been a lukewarm willingness to do justice to his great old age. He was first brought before a county court and then before the Riksadvocat, but was not put in jail, whereas his wife was condemned to three years of hard labor. Hamsun was placed in a public institution for the aged and needy, mainly housing penniless, dying old men. The first of these old men's homes in which he was confined was in a remote country district, high on a mountain. Later he was moved to another, from there to an "examination" in a psychiatric clinic, and from the clinic, completely exhausted and broken, he was allowed to go home. Even under such conditions of dependence, Hamsun, although penniless and with holes in his shoes, was able to lead his own life. He took long walks in the woods. "I no longer hear the whispering of the forest, but I see the branches sway, enough cause for joy." He developed a tender feeling for a tiny pine tree which he began to cultivate. He had a few books, pieces of newspaper gleaned from wrapping paper, and his writing. The things he wrote while living this life are poetry.

He even disagreed with the courts, not so much during the proceedings, where his hearing was poor, his sight impaired, and his understanding limited—altogether confused. This of course might have been innate shrewdness. But he wrote a long letter to the prosecutor. In it he said that he was not a member of Quisling's Nasjonal Samling; he had never done anything against the Jews. He had written to Terboven, even to Hitler himself, and had telegraphed in an effort to help people under arrest.

I could have tried to steal across to Sweden. I believed I was serving my country best by remaining where I was. I sought to understand National Socialism, to become familiar with it, to interpret it. It all came to nothing. It is quite possible that now and then I wrote in the spirit of National Socialism. I don't know, for I do not know what the spirit of National Socialism is. Perhaps some of the things I read in the newspapers filtered in. Anyway my articles are there for all to see. I don't seek to make them milder or less significant than they are, which is bad enough. On the contrary I stand responsible for them, as I always have.

178

ILLUSTRATIONS

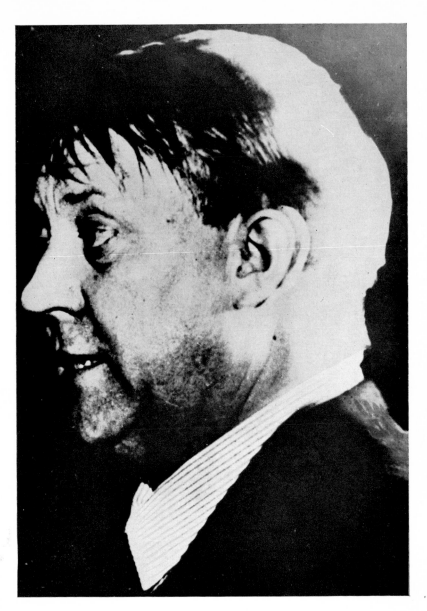

Quisling at his trial.

Admiral Darlan (*fourth from left*) in North Africa with General Mark Clark, Admiral Sir Andrew Cunningham and General Anderson.

Pierre Laval with M. Flandin in 1935.

Laval with Anthony Eden in Paris, 1935.

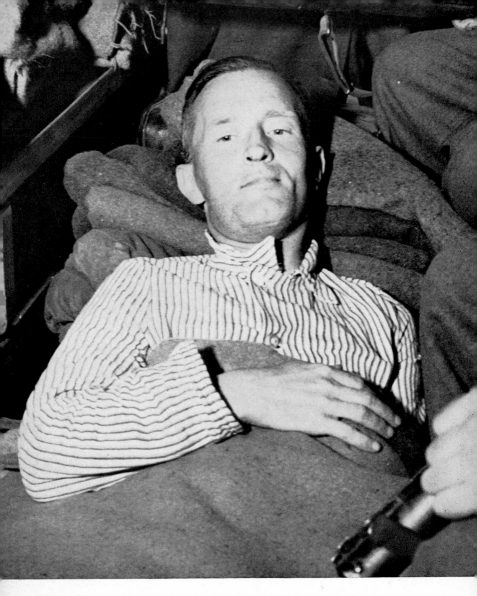

William Joyce after his capture.

Ezra Pound
before and after
his confinement.

Tokyo Rose in 1956.

Karl Friedrich Goerdeler, former Mayor of Leipzig and professional politician, the proposed Chancellor of the Revolutionary Cabinet.

Ulrich von Hassell before his judges.

Hans Oster, officer, gentleman, horseman of distinction.

Helmuth James Count von Moltke, great landowner, member of the English Bar, main source of spiritual vigor in the German Resistance.

Peter Count Yorck von Wartenburg, Prussian aristocrat, before the People's Court.

Adam von Trott zu Solz, a man of great intellect and integrity, whose execution deprived postwar Germany of a great foreign minister.

Popitz, archconspirator, Nazi minister, the Resistance "link" with the Gestapo.

Father Alfred Delp, S.J., priest, historian and resolute social reformer.

Klaus Schenk Count von Stauffenberg, aristocratic revolutionary, the real "man of action" in the Resistance.

He refused the "mercy" of being declared insane, in order to remain free from punishment. What he could not bear was the time spent in a psychiatric clinic. His description of this clean, orderly institution, with "its psychology in lines and columns," with the incessantly stubborn, questioning doctor, the countless questionnaires he had to fill out in the badly lighted rooms, is more depressing than the ghastliest scenes from *The Snake Pit*.

Letters which he had written more than fifty years before were shown to him. His beliefs were questioned. All the secrets of his stormy but happy married life were probed. Did he still think the Germans were great *"Kulturvolk"?* Did he know that a great majority of his fellow countrymen considered Quisling a traitor? Hamsun's answers were typical in their blending of cunning and childlike naïveté. "We never read anything about that in the newspapers." "Not one of the 'majority of the Norwegian people' told us about that." It was devilishly hard to catch the old man. The object was to penetrate to his soul, spirit and conscience. The doctors asked him questions about his assessment of his own character, his aggressions, his sensitivity and jealousy. He answered:

I have never analyzed my own nature in any other way than through the creation of hundreds of people in my books, all spun from my own being, with faults and virtues, as poetic figures have them. During the so-called "Naturalist" period of Zola and his contemporaries, human beings were portrayed with one dominating feature which determined their actions. I do not believe that in all of my works from the very beginning of my career as a writer there has been one such single-dimensional figure. My people are all without what is erroneously called "Character." They all show splits and tears in their fabric. They are never good or bad, but both. . . . So, without a doubt, am I.

Peter de Mendelssohn has described the lack of communication between the court on its level and this old man on his. Where was the common ground on which court and accused, community and private conscience, could meet? How could they convince one another? Where was the land which the poet could betray?

179

. . . His homeland had not been betrayed, for it was not the Norway of the daily press and the Second World War. Wherever Hamsun's Norway may have been, it was unreachable by the normal methods of travel. It lay somewhere in the remote, swirling northern mists. In the land in which Hamsun had been charged with treason, he had never been at home. The court was unable to deal with the poet Knut Hamsun, who was, so to speak, not there at all.

Erwin Jäckle saw the problem differently: "Hamsun's creativeness lies in the everchanging, not in the establishment of values. His earth knows no decisions, but bears the good as well as the bad, and goodness as well as evil. He was a master of abandonment to life, but not a master of fulfilled consciousness . . . Hamsun was and is human, all embracing and not exclusive. The error lies in his concession, and his concession can even be an error . . . But both make up the truth, his truth, the truth of life as such." This feeling about Hamsun has prevailed in Norway with the passing of time. Unlike Ezra Pound, who until recently sat confined in a mental hospital, Hamsun was allowed to return to his lonely farm. Norway was, after all, proud of the man who had won the Nobel Prize in 1920 and had given away the money. When he died a Norwegian flag covered his coffin.

At the beginning of this chapter we said that the loss of the homeland lay at the root of this type of treason, the treason of the propagandists. Loss of one's home can mean different things. Best, Chandler and Gillars seem hardly to have been aware that they had lost anything, and perhaps Tokyo Rose belongs in this group. They were far too hollow as human beings to suffer very greatly. In Joyce, Pound and Hamsun, there burned a homesickness which was nearly physical pain. For Joyce, the Irish-American who had settled on the southern, "nonimperial" side of London, it was a homesickness for an England of the time of Elizabeth I or the Tory Empire of Disraeli—an England long gone, which would never have accepted a "nongentleman" anyway. We have already seen what Pound wrote about the danger of losing one's home. Hamsun had experienced violent nostalgia in America, where he had wandered from job to job among strange people who did not cling to the soil, who sold a farm from one day to the next and took off for Florida. "We never forgot," he wrote of those days, "that we just wanted to go home. . . . When we were alone, we cried and were filled with self-pity." He makes fun of these tears, but such tears of bitter homelessness create the oversized archaic patriotism which we saw in Joyce. It is then that the dream homelands arise, having no contact with the real countries or real people.

Joyce, Pound and Hamsun had one other nostalgia which went beyond the bounds of countries and peoples. All three found the self-satisfied world of the "technocratic" citizen unbearable. They rejected the class struggle and the Marxist revolt against this world. They sought a new image of man by seeking him in the past or in archaic forms. Their errors were those of misplaced confidence. Each thought that he had found the first signs of a rejuvenation in parties and men who were in reality the incarnation of the very world they hated. They had, as they believed, discovered the first new traces of what they longed for in other lands, and in men who had intuitively understood this yearning of their time, but who very soon misused it for their own ends.

PART IV

Resistance

20. THE LIVING CONSCIENCE

THROUGHOUT Europe there was resistance against Hitler, but only in Germany could this resistance be construed as treason. For here the target was not an occupying power but the national government. It is not easy for a German to ask whether the men of the German *Widerstand* were traitors or not. Reverence for the death of so many thousands who were the victims of this *Widerstand*—reverence for their persons and gratitude for their stand—have made it almost impossible for all those who were on their side to face the question whether, and in what degrees, their actions were treasonable or on the borderline of treason. Fear of the dreaded word paralyzes their supporters and provokes their opponents. But history cannot be written under this sort of hide-and-seek. Therefore one reads with relief the account of an artillery officer of his first meeting with Count Stauffenberg. "As the talks drew to a close, he [Stauffenberg] turned to me suddenly and said, 'Look, let's get to the heart of the matter. I am engaged by every available means in the active practice of high treason.'"

The "stab-in-the-back" legend evokes the same nervous anxiety. General Beck believed it in 1918, and Hindenburg contributed to its spread. This may be one of the reasons why the anxiety caused by the "stab-in-the-back" myth affected the thoughts and deeds of the older men of the 20th of July profoundly, so often to the detriment of their resistance work. The friends of the resistance always find themselves on the defensive about this undeniable fact. However, it is impossible to adopt an attitude of defensiveness in two directions at the same time; to state that the thoughts, and often the deeds, of many Germans were directed against Hitler by day and by night, while also claiming

185

that these same men were working for final victory with heart and soul.

Modern total war demands more of the individual than mere performance of duty. Ultimate victory requires flair, initiative and willingness to give that extra something which only faith in one's cause can evoke. It was precisely that faith which was so glaringly lacking during the war when one met men in high positions. There was dismay over the unfortunate foreign policy, anger about the Jewish persecution, and despair about the barbarism of the policies being pursued in the occupied countries. These people were not saboteurs. Many worked to the very limits of their physical endurance. Yet it was the energy of bitter resignation which robbed their efforts of hope and their work of its fruits. Some openly confessed that their only hope for destruction of the Nazi regime lay in the complete military defeat of Germany. Others were torn between the fear of a defeat whose aftermath they could well imagine and the horror of a further extension of National Socialism. Others, especially those at the front, fought desperately for a victory in which they could hardly believe and for which they scarcely dared wish. A different attitude in these men, of whom the Gestapo caught only a small percentage, would not have brought about a victory or a negotiated peace. Hitler himself was the real obstacle: in failing to show the slightest sign of generosity toward France; in the fanaticism with which he ordered the enslavement and eradication of what he called Eastern subhumanity; and in the obstinacy with which he denied military facts and necessities. The lack of inner consent played its part nevertheless. Hitler had an uncanny "feel" for concealed opposition. He fought with even greater bitterness because of the prevailing air of enmity which he felt but could not grasp. Gösta von Uexküll uses the legend of Siegfried and the Dragon to describe the schism in German thinking about the *Dolchstoss*:

The dragon was, at least partly, Germany itself. The dragon was made up of the soldiers at the front and the people at home in the rain of bombs.

THE GERMAN RESISTANCE MOVEMENT

The Groups and their Relations

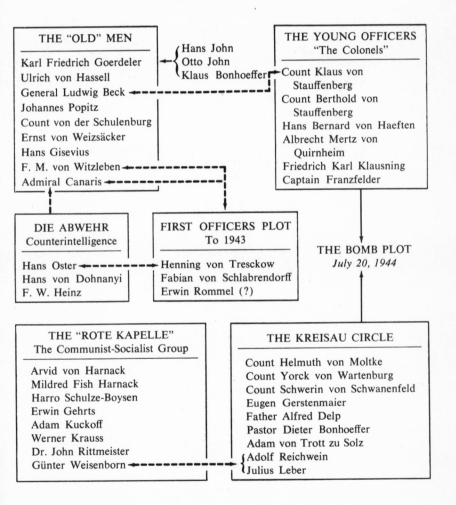

THE "OLD" MEN

Karl Friedrich Goerdeler
Ulrich von Hassell
General Ludwig Beck
Johannes Popitz
Count von der Schulenburg
Ernst von Weizsäcker
Hans Gisevius
F. M. von Witzleben
Admiral Canaris

Hans John
Otto John
Klaus Bonhoeffer

THE YOUNG OFFICERS
"The Colonels"

Count Klaus von
  Stauffenberg
Count Berthold von
  Stauffenberg
Hans Bernard von Haeften
Albrecht Mertz von
  Quirnheim
Friedrich Karl Klausning
Captain Franzfelder

DIE ABWEHR
Counterintelligence

Hans Oster
Hans von Dohnanyi
F. W. Heinz

FIRST OFFICERS PLOT
To 1943

Henning von Tresckow
Fabian von Schlabrendorff
Erwin Rommel (?)

THE BOMB PLOT
July 20, 1944

THE "ROTE KAPELLE"
The Communist-Socialist Group

Arvid von Harnack
Mildred Fish Harnack
Harro Schulze-Boysen
Erwin Gehrts
Adam Kuckoff
Werner Krauss
Dr. John Rittmeister
Günter Weisenborn

THE KREISAU CIRCLE

Count Helmuth von Moltke
Count Yorck von Wartenburg
Count Schwerin von Schwanenfeld
Eugen Gerstenmaier
Father Alfred Delp
Pastor Dieter Bonhoeffer
Adam von Trott zu Solz
Adolf Reichwein
Julius Leber

Siegfried could not strike at the dragon without slaying himself. Like a monstrous Siamese twin, both had the same body and in a sense, where Hitlerism and basic features of the German spirit had fused into one, the same heart. To have halted the fusion and driven the dragon back to his cave would have been an act of the greatest historical significance. Ten years are not sufficient to assess its magnitude. Though Siegfried failed to do this, he showed at the very least that the two were not identical.

The struggle between the "monstrous Siamese twins" had as many settings as the protean dragon had forms. The Iron Curtain is due in a way to the internal struggles within the German resistance movement. There are, for example, two separate and almost mutually exclusive literatures about the resistance. They completely ignore one another. The one is proletarian and Communist oriented, and the other is bourgeois and Western oriented. During the days of the resistance, all the antipathies and fears which bedevil European politics were at work on the very men who needed unity of thought and action most. General Beck and Admiral Canaris feared the Marxists. Otto John hated the military. Ernst Niekisch saw the real danger in the bourgeoisie, Arvid Harnack in the abuses of capitalism. Former members of the Reichsbanner found difficulty in cooperating with the nationalists. Ex-members of the Free Corps hated the parliamentarians. Ten years of Hitlerite *Gleichschaltung,* or leveling, could cover but not eradicate the profound differences of conviction and temperament in the members of the resistance.

The men of the 20th of July were fully aware of the danger of the divisions within their country. The appeal which they intended to make to the German people after a successful coup shows this. Instead of falling into the pitfalls which beset the denazification program, with its bureaucratic stubbornness, they proposed that only a crime actually committed should be prosecuted. Mere party membership was not to be the criterion of guilt. "We want to avoid division in the country. We know that there were many who joined the party for idealistic reasons, in bitterness at what they considered the injustice of the Versailles settlement or in shame at the state of the nation. Some joined under political

189

or economic pressure. Let us, therefore, not divide on this issue."
There were countless members of the party who were later condemned by Hitler for defeatism, treason or undercover opposition. In some professions, party membership was the necessary
prerequisite. Others saw the only possibly effective opposition
as working from within. Professor Jens Jensen, for example,
sent his best students to the S.S., because he was convinced that
there the decisive struggle would take place. Giselher Wirsing is
supposed to have done the same thing.

Paul Scheffer (former foreign correspondent, later editor in
chief of the *Berliner Tageblatt,* now living in the United States)
wrote a description of Adam von Trott's basic position which
could be used to sum up all the men of the resistance:

> The problem was this. The Leviathan, the monster of the state appa-
> ratus, had assumed a particularly dreadful and evil form. If one were
> unwilling to allow it full freedom and unable to take pistol in hand, the
> only alternative was to attempt to gain control of one of its tentacles and
> use it against itself. . . . A people cannot live without certain institutions.
> These institutions have to be maintained, even if they have to be perverted.
> Opposition can only take place within the Leviathan itself. The whole
> thing is like a race: Am I doing more to *destroy* the Nazis by staying in
> my job than I am *assisting* them by helping to keep the machine running?
> This was Adam's basic dilemma, and it was on this point that we came to
> agree in New York. One could talk of staying in contact with the enemy.
> But this is not quite correct, since it was only possible to fight in his army
> whenever action was necessary. What it comes to is that the state is not
> an individual, but a monster. In this I agree less with Thomas Hobbes than
> with Lord Acton. The state is so overpowering that one is compelled to
> play according to its rules, even if one is out to destroy it.

Since the above was written the volume of the German Documents on Foreign Policy containing the time from March 13 to
August 8, 1939, has appeared (H. M. Stationery Office, London
1956). A report by Adam von Trott on his talks with Lord
Halifax, Lord Lothian and Prime Minister Chamberlain, and
the controversy which ensued in the British press are good examples of what it meant to take possession of and use an arm of

the Leviathan against the Leviathan, and how difficult it is for outsiders to understand this, even now when there should be no further doubts about Trott's true stand. An English commentator, who evidently had never heard of the opposition inside the German Foreign Office, saw Trott as an agent of Ribbentrop, the Nazi Foreign Minister. As a matter of fact, Weizsäcker, the Secretary of State, who was an opponent of Hitler's policy, had enabled Trott's unofficial visit to England. The first aim was to inform leading British personalities about the existence and the strength of the German opposition and the necessity of winning time. Trott did this in a manner which precluded the tenor of what he said in England from being brought to the knowledge of the National-Socialist Government, as had happened after a similar visit by Goerdeler, with ensuing difficulties for all persons concerned. Secondly, Trott wished that a strong public declaration by a member of the British Government would convince Hitler that he could not succeed in accomplishing a second Munich or a second Prague. Third, as a countereffect to Ribbentrop's frivolous assertion that the British would not march, this strong British determination was to be made known to Hitler. However, the Nazi leader could be influenced only if the language of Trott's report was adjusted for his consumption. The language adopted to "sell" the contents of the report to Hitler must be misunderstood by posterity, as long as people remain unable to understand what it means to deal with dictators. Thus is it not astonishing that some British interpreted it as being "Nazi." Trott's friend, David Astor, wrote in a rectification in the Manchester *Guardian* (June 4, 1956): "At the time that he visited London in June, 1939, he was endeavouring to gain the confidence of the German Foreign Office, to represent himself as a man with useful contacts to Britain; and to use the position thus created to transmit messages to Hitler which would influence him to delay making war. This Trott considered to be the most important objective to pursue." Christabel Bielenberg, who, together with her German husband, was a close friend of Trott's, stated in a letter to the Manchester *Guardian* (June 7, 1956)

191

that Trott later heard that his report never reached Hitler, but was suppressed by Herr von Ribbentrop.

In the light of this, the attempt of Rudolf Pechel (longtime editor of the *Deutsche Rundschen,* who spent the late war years in Sachsenhausen) to judge the members of the resistance by the degree of cooperation with the Nazis seems to me to be misleading. Ulrich von Hassell, for example, who as German Ambassador in Rome until 1938, obviously served the regime, gets bad marks from Pechel. Anyone who knew von Hassell can testify that he was a complete human being with all the strengths and weaknesses of a highly developed personality. He was undeniably ambitious and possessed a sufficient degree of adaptability to reach the rank of ambassador. He cooperated with the Nazis quite often, because he though they were doing the right thing. His experiences as a young diplomat in Spain after the First World War made him a supporter of the Franco revolution, and he used to talk gleefully of the success of German U-boats in Franco's cause. Lastly, it is undeniable that von Hassell had a pronounced fixation regarding power and its manifestations. He loved power and loved to be near it. Long after he had become deeply involved in the resistance, he was having tea one day with friends in the Kaiserhof when Hitler made an unexpected appearance. Von Hassell grew distraught, stopped talking, and could only worry about whether or not Hitler would greet him.

Von Hassell belonged to that group of patriots which, having failed to prevent the war in 1939, turned all its energies to the attempt to avoid a defeat or an unconditional surrender. Adam von Trott, on the other hand, considered complete military defeat inevitable as early as 1942, and was quite prepared to suffer the consequences. Here again the men of the resistance differed. There were two poles at the ends of which stood Moltke and Stauffenberg. Stauffenberg was first and last a German officer who passionately desired the victory of German arms. After the war had (to his horror) broken out, he tended to see it not primarily as Hitler's war but as affecting the entire fatherland. He rejoiced in the victory over France and recognized Hitler's role in it. He was, according to Zeller, "to the last day of his life, in all that rank and job demanded of him, entirely devoted." Moltke often said to German and foreign friends that he wanted Germany to lose the war. Only through defeat and suffering could the inner renewal for which he was working take place. A letter to an English friend closes with these words: "Please do not forget that we trust that you will stand it through without flinching, as we are prepared to do our bit. *And don't forget that for us a very bitter end is in sight when you have seen matters through. We hope that you will realize that we are ready to help you win war and peace.*"

Underneath these fundamental differences, which were put aside in the common struggle against Hitler, there remained a unifying factor: the political thinking and arms of these men were all in the context of the nation. Even Moltke saw in defeat a chance to purify Germany as a nation. The lawyer and officer, Fabian von Schlabrendorff, may have placed religion higher than his love of country, but he acknowledged no other human ideology. Greta Kuckhoff writes of Arvid Harnack and Harro Schulze-Boysen, the two spiritual and intellectual leaders of the "Rote Kapelle" resistance group, that "despite all the profound differences of temperament which divided them, a deep love of Germany was common to both. They wanted Germany to stop obstructing world progress and to begin to contribute to it. For nine years I was a witness at their discussions. Their thoughts grew from their deep love of their country—a critical love, to be sure—the love of convinced Socialists for their fatherland." Often they knew nothing of each other. Sometimes they were in close contact. The important thing is that, in spite of differences of opinion, their beliefs were rooted in common ground. Harold Poelchau, who as a prison chaplain accompanied and ministered to many of the victims of the Nazi regime, says that he saw three distinct groups inside the larger frame of the 20th-of-July plot: the civilian group, the officers and the Kreisau Circle members. Gerhard Ritter argues that there were actually four, the Socialists, the clerics, the civilians and the soldiers. It seemed to me that, even before July 20, 1944, and much more sharply after it, the most important distinction was between the older and younger men in the plot. In a short but impressive article in 1946, Sebastian Haffner divided the resistance movement into men of rank who had known the old Germany of the pre-1914 days and who yearned to return to it, and the young officers, noblemen and Socialists who really wanted to make something new out of their revolution. The turning point came in the years 1942–43 when it became clear that the older men had failed and the younger men assumed the leadership.

Like all general distinctions, this one does not always apply. We shall meet younger men who were genuine revolutionaries and some who thought much more in terms of spiritual renewal. The "Rote Kapelle," which included everything from Communists to Conservatives, was basically "progressive" in the inherited sense prevalent since the French Revolution. Even the Socialists in the Kreisau Circle were not "progressive" in that way. Their aim had religious overtones and their politics had distinctly conservative elements. Similarly, there are many who cannot be arbitrarily classified by the dates of their births. Some of the older men had more affinity intellectually to men thirty years their juniors. Fritzi Schulenburg, whose cousin Ambassador Schulenburg belonged indisputably among the "old" men, was a genuine revolutionary. He had been a Weimar civil servant in the provincial government of East Prussia, had had contact with the revolutionary Left of the Nazi Party, knew Gregor Strasser, and had been interested in Albrecht Haushofer's geopolitical theories. He had formed a circle of young people who plotted for a reform of the Reich from within. He could keep silent in a way that only the younger, tight-lipped men of the underground could. During the war his troops drew confidence from his aura of calm and self-possession. Another of the unclassifiables was Major-General Henning von Tresckow, who had been Stauffenberg's predecessor in the planning of the military side of the revolution. He was the only one of the plot who managed to commit suicide in such an unobtrusive manner that his death implicated no one, because it looked as if it had been part of the front-line fighting. Men like Popitz, Halem and Ernst von Harnack also managed to free themselves from the patterns of thought of their generation. Popitz had probably the best political mind of all the older men. It is unfortunate that his role has been so cursorily treated in the literature of the *Widerstand*. His activity would have been particularly suitable for inclusion in this study, because Popitz tried to use the mightiest tentacle of the Leviathan, the S.S. of Heinrich Himmler.

It is difficult to classify individuals, but almost as hard to keep the groups themselves apart. There was so much crossing of lines and comingling of thought that the outlines blur. The Kreisauers shared a common faith in Christianity with the men of the Goerdeler group, although the Christianity of Trott, Delp and Bonhoeffer had striking revolutionary features lacking in the stern orthodoxy of Beck, von Hassell and Goerdeler. The older Socialists and the younger men of the "Rote Kapelle" were one in placing the ideal of humanity above the individual human being.

There are of course no sharp borders, but one is fairly safe in reckoning all those born after 1900 to be the young men. To these must be added the men who went through the First World War as very young men and who were permanently seared by front-line experiences. This was true of Ernst Jünger, Jens Jensen and Julius Leber. The "old" men were by contrast fully developed personalities by 1914. They saw the defeat of 1918, the mutiny of the soldiers and sailors, the abdication of the Kaiser and his subsequent flight, and the political chaos and coups as bad luck, but as in no sense historically necessary developments. They were tied to a fixed concept of order all their lives. Their imaginations were not sufficiently great to grasp events in turbulent flux, springlike jumps in the process of history, illogical reactions or open deception. Even Hjalmar Schacht, one of the shrewdest and most flexible of the older men, said to a dinner partner in 1938: "We have fallen into the hands of criminals. How could I have imagined such a thing?" Undersecretary von

195

Weizsäcker, who could well have imagined such a thing and who was actively connected with several resistance groups, was still not able to understand to what lengths Hitler and his cronies could go. Admiral Canaris, the chief of the military counter-espionage, the Abwehr, came into contact with adventurers, spies and underworld types regularly. He had a dashing career in the secret service in the First World War. He knew everything that was planned. Yet he was constantly surprised by a new evidence of Nazi brutality or cunning. Canaris was puzzled when Heydrich, of the Gestapo's S.D., requested the signatures of Generals von Seeckt and Hammerstein. He could not imagine what on earth Heydrich could be up to. We now know that the signatures were affixed to forged documents which helped to bring about the fall of Marshal Tukhachevsky and the six other Russian generals in the 1937 purges. Thinking up something of that sort was beyond Canaris.

This helplessness in the face of everything dynamic is not unnatural in older men. Much more serious for men playing with life and death in a conspiracy was a certain exhaustion of nerves and accompanying weariness of the spirit. Such was the case with Field-Marshal von Witzleben and Colonel General Beck, who became more and more cautious in all their decisions. General Friedrich Olbricht prevented Stauffenberg from blowing up Hitler in Berchtesgaden, when the circumstances were much more favorable than they were later to be in the Wolf's Lair on July 20, 1944, because he was afraid of destroying Hitler without Himmler. These same older men, so cautious in deed, were incredibly imprudent in speech. One would be tempted to accuse them of irresponsibility were it not clear that they talked so carelessly not from a lack of responsibility, but of imagination. Hassell's diary is by no means "notorious." Beck demanded that all decisions made within the conspiracy be put on paper, in order to show the world how early the decision to fight Hitler had been made. The Gestapo was, of course, the only beneficiary of this bureaucratic thoroughness. Goerdeler forgot his briefcase in the Hotel Askanischer Hof after an air raid, and the Gestapo was immeasurably aided in its round-up of members of the conspiracy after the 20th of July. Even up to 1944, von Hassell had to be reminded repeatedly by Haeften, Kiep and Moltke to be more careful on the phone. I myself was often told things which ought never to have got beyond the very inner circle.

The younger men were never guilty of these lapses. I knew Adam von Trott zu Solz well, and we often talked about the kind of Germany we wished to see in the place of the Third Reich, but he never indicated that he was in the plot to remove Hitler. I recall once remarking that no conspiracy could ever be a success in Germany, because conspirators could not hold their tongues. Trott just laughed. Stauffenberg hated carelessness and would fly into a rage at what he called "conspiratorial innocents." I saw the differences perhaps more sharply than many Germans, because as a foreign correspondent between 1939 and 1943 I came to Germany only occasionally. Once in the winter of 1939–40, I had occasion to have a conversation with a high civil servant in the ministry of labor and two diplomats. Of the two diplomats, one had resigned in 1933 and the other had fallen out of favor a short time before our meeting. All three were well-informed and anti-Nazi. One had warned the Dutch of the impending attack, at the request of one of the generals. The second had known about the plans for the attack on Scandinavia to follow in the coming spring. The third talked of preparations for a seizure of power from Hitler as soon as the first serious military setback occurred, which he expected to be on the borders of France. The vision of what was to follow Hitler was for all three a return to what had been. The only dispute was over the type of return; that is, a return to the Weimar democracy or to the monarchy. They had drawn up prospective cabinets and were concerned with things like whether Bruening had enough "sex appeal" to become chancellor again. Their thoughts had a curious ephemeral, almost spooky quality. My meetings with Trott from 1942 on were of a very different kind. Trott spoke of the tasks facing a new Germany, the reestablishment of contact with a Nazified German youth, the development

of a social program which would not be a return to the bureaucratic sterility of the Weimar Social Democracy.

The young men were different, too, in another respect. Despite
their opposition to the regime, they associated with Nazis daily,
with no "Iron Curtain" in their minds. The older men too often
had little or no idea of the kind of men against whom they
fought. By contrast, the young men were a genuine threat to the
Nazis. They could imagine what was going on in the minds of
their foes and what plans were being hatched. They appreciated
those positive features in the Nazis which made the movement
so overwhelmingly effective politically—their intelligence, their
unbridled imaginations, their instinctive psychological cunning,
and their fanatical determination. Stauffenberg's "Operation
Valkyrie," the military operational plan to go into effect after the
assassination of Hitler, shows how much he had learned from the
Nazis. It contained the same kind of brilliant bluff and sleight
of hand which the Nazis had used so effectively for their bad
ends.

Count Stauffenberg and the Socialist Julius Leber were entirely agreed that they were not going to stage a "revolution of
the senile." Canaris, for his part, had distinct reservations about
the propriety of letting these young men meddle in domestic
politics. He really thought in terms of the limited Putsch of the
Kapp Putsch type in which he had participated in 1920. He had
a hunch that a few of the younger men harbored distressingly
radical ideas. Hassell's diaries reveal the same anxiety about anything Socialist. His principal objection to National Socialism was
essentially that it prepared the way for Bolshevism. Hassell, as
mediator between the Goerdeler group and the Kreisau Circle of
Count Moltke, could judge the differences between the groups
better than most men in the resistance. After a meeting with
Popitz and Trott, he wrote: "What is, after all, an unnecessary difficulty is all this business about Socialism, another of the
cuckoo's eggs which the Nazis have laid in the German nest."
The sentence is interesting when one recalls that there had been
an active Socialist movement in Germany since the time of Bis-

marck. What disturbed Hassell, Canaris and Goerdeler was the extension of Socialism beyond the proletariat. It threatened to make real inroads in the "better" classes, and worst of all, to penetrate the ruling elite.

Another point of tension between the older and younger men was the monarchy, to which the older men almost automatically gave allegiance. Despite their many reservations about the person of the crown prince, they were determined, virtually to a man, to return him to power. The conversations which Hassell had with the younger men are very revealing on this point. First with Trott, "who argued passionately that the slightest tint of re-action, militarism and 'Herrenclub,' must be avoided at home and abroad. Though he is a monarchist he is against any attempt to do anything whatsoever about the monarchy *now*. The monarchy would evoke no response in the people, and all confidence in the good intentions of the new government in Germany abroad would be destroyed. 'Converts,' by which he meant Socialists who had assumed Christian coloring, would never go along with such a plan, and he named a former member of the Reichstag as an example." In his next meeting at the home of Count Yorck von Wartenburg, Hassell was "thoroughly worked over by all four—Yorck, Moltke, Trott and Guttenberg." On the following day, at the home of Popitz, "Schulenburg continued in the same vein." Among the junior men he was the soberest and most politically adept, but at the same time the most antimonarchist. His father, in his fury at the behavior of the crown prince and the royal family in the critical days of 1918, had made his son swear to fight the monarchy.

Other differences were visible to outsiders. The Bishop of Chichester, who held talks in Stockholm with Pastors Schönfeld and Bonhoeffer, to see if there were any basis for negotiation in the event of a successful coup, came away with the impression that he had been talking to representatives of different groups with quite different objectives. And indeed this was correct. Bonhoeffer belonged to the circle around Beck and Goerdeler, while Schönfeld had come from the Geneva Ecumenical Council

199

and was close to members of the Kreisau Circle. Otto John belonged to the Canaris group and was a monarchist, though he supported Prince Louis Ferdinand instead of his father, the crown prince. John complained bitterly about all the disagreement and lack of centralized leadership. There were personal dislikes and antipathies as well, to add to the confusion. Popitz swore that he would have nothing to do with Goerdeler, whom he could not stand. Popitz was cordially disliked and intensely distrusted by many of the older and younger men, especially because of his curious relationship with Himmler. Stauffenberg refused to reveal anything of his plans to Gisevius and his friends, who were members of the Canaris-Beck group, because he was suspicious of their relations with Police Chief Count Helldorf and because he disliked them personally.

The most revealing comments on the members of the various wings of the resistance were made by Oberstürmbannführer Dr. Georg Kiesel, the Gestapo agent in charge of interrogating the men of the 20th of July. As a competent, and in an ironic way entirely impartial observer, he was in a position to see the cleavages and conflicts in the resistance better than any of its members. He, too, noted the split between the old and young. Several of the generals apparently tried to escape the rope by saying that they had innocently fallen into the hands of irresponsible elements. He remarks on the "manly stand of the idealists which brought a bit of light to the darkness." He contrasts the idealists with the opportunists, and saw in the younger officers, the Kreisauers, the older and younger Socialists, the good Catholics and Protestants, the Conservatives like Beck and Goerdeler:

. . . personalities whose opposition to Nazism rested on political, moral and religious foundations. It must be called genuine enmity. The slowly developing opposition of business circles was purely materialistic and does not deserve the title of an ethical opposition. German business had welcomed the increase in production and profits brought about by Hitler, without reservation. Their gains from the expropriation of the Jews had been considerable. As doubts began to grow during the war about the inevitability of final victory, the German business leaders noted such symptoms attentively and began to worry about their capital.

Although the older men grew increasingly tired, worn out and ineffective, there was little the younger men could do at first. It was only after the first few years of war that younger men reached positions in which they could not only observe events but to a certain extent become active in shaping them. The sharpening of the crisis after Stalingrad and the loss of Tunisia were decisive. On the military level the failures of the military leadership were glaring. On the political level the bitterness and implacability of the enemy countries increased. The "unconditional-surrender" slogan was its expression. In the ideological wake of America, the Allies began to be unable or unwilling to see any difference between German and German. Sebastian Haffner, as an exile in England, could see what was happening in a way denied to the Germans until after the war:

> The resistance had lost its credit. No one could believe in "another Germany" any more. Just at that moment the resistance came to life again and began to change its nature. Behind the indecisive faltering of the commanding generals, a clique of tough, decisive colonels formed. Entirely new conspiratorial nerve centers sprang up. In the new conspiracy, a much colder wind blew. These were able and active men in their late thirties and early forties, not aging marshals in their sixties. Anxieties about avoiding violence and disorder were forgotten. The young men saw clearly that the first and crucial step was to kill Hitler. The problem was simply how.

Although Haffner exaggerates somewhat, he is correct in saying that there was a great change. Formerly there had been a conspiratorial government in search of men to do the shooting. Now there were men, ready to shoot, in search of a government. The young men did not think much of the honorable men of the Goerdeler group and hoped that they would only function as a provisional government during the chaotic transition period. The young officers looked further, hence the first exploratory feelers between Count Stauffenberg and the Kreisau Circle. The political differences, the lack of new and constructive thinking among the older men, and the lack of political experience among the younger men, led to many of the mistakes which were to be made along the way. Himmler, to cite an unusual source, thought that the laws, proclamations and operational plans found in Fritzi Schulenburg's flat after the round-up were really quite good and could easily have been put into effect. What seems to have been missing were the necessary measures for the transition period. Kiesel, who of course saw the whole affair from the point of view of the Gestapo's security section—a very important point of view for those involved—felt that the conspirators had failed to capitalize on the fact that the two leading competitors of the Gestapo, the criminal police and the military counterintelligence, were both controlled by men in sympathy with the resistance, Arthur Nebe and Georg Hansen (Canaris' successor). He claims that, using the criminal police and the Abwehr, the conspirators could have easily checkmated S.S. Gruppenführer Mueller, their most dangerous adversary. He remarks on the "astounding paucity" of plans for domestic affairs. The men who were to have taken charge of key bureaus and offices were often lacking in any sort of administrative experience whatsoever. Others like Noske, Gessler and Lüningk were much too old to find the sort of energy and decisiveness demanded of them by revolutionary conditions. Split-second timing would be called for in a situation in which the rebels might have a few hours at the most to put their plan through. The generals designated to assume deputy command, who were mobilized on the 20th of July, reported for instructions to, of all people, the *Gauleiters,* the very men who were supposed to arrest them. K. A. von Wülckwitz, in an article in the *Tagesspiegel,* showed how the soldiers themselves had failed to secure one loyal regiment which they could count on or even a small shock troop of determined men to carry out the important military maneuvers. The reason was that the conspirators assumed firstly that the captains and lieutenants—that is, the next generation—were loyal to Hitler, and that secondly the formation of such a shock troop would have so widened the number of people in the know that secrecy would have been lost. It was obviously dangerous. In hindsight it is hard to say whether both assumptions were correct. General Halder initiated a private-opinion poll among the ranks, which his son-in-law carried out, to test the mood of the troops. He found that up to the time of Stalingrad the troops had faith in Hitler. General Friebe testified at the Remer trial that the high-ranking officers had been the only ones who regretted the failure of the assassination in 1944. The young officers had been against it.

The question of the general feeling toward Hitler in the Army and among the people was only one of the problems. The second and allied problem was how the conspirators ought to address themselves to the Army and people after Hitler had been dealt with. The older and younger men disagreed here as well. The order of the day, composed by Field Marshal von Witzleben for use on the day of the coup, began with the following sentences: "The Führer Adolf Hitler is dead. An unprincipled clique of party leaders remote from the shooting tried to betray our troops struggling for their lives on the many fronts." Witzleben was convinced that he must consider the state of mind of the soldiers and civilians still under the spell of Goebbels' propaganda. Wülckwitz remarked that "Witzleben's subtle caution merely nullified the effect of the appeal." Witzleben, like so many men of his generation, was completely ignorant of the laws of mass psychology. Stauffenberg ordered Captain Klausning to strike out the sentence, "The Führer Adolf Hitler is dead," when the order of the day was actually broadcast on July 20, 1944. Stauffenberg knew that, even if it were true that the mass of the people still believed Goebbels—which was far from certain—timidity was not the way to handle the problem. Stauffenberg understood instinctively that masses can be redirected instantly, if in a situation of exhaustion and hypertension an incendiary spark can be lit. A stirring appeal, saying the exact opposite of everything they had heard for years from Goebbels, could smash the whole edifice of lies the Nazis had built so painstakingly. He was anxious to make a new spirit felt from the very first moment; a spirit of reform and not of hate or bitterness. At the beginning everything difficult to understand would be left out, but under no circumstances were misleading or false statements to be permitted. There was to be no doubt about the convictions of the new government.

Convictions united the younger men as they looked to the time when Hitler should be no more. Everything else was secondary and beside the point when compared to the question of belief. The older men clung to the hope that talks with the enemy would be possible, to avoid the worst consequences of a total defeat. The young men were willing to give that a try, but had no great faith in the willingness of the Allies to negotiate in a world so thoroughly poisoned by hate. Stauffenberg and the Kreisauers foresaw with prophetic accuracy that the invasion of the Allies would produce areas of occupation in which different conditions were likely to prevail. It became all the more necessary that the unifying set of convictions be hammered out before the defeat and agreed upon, since the various individuals in the movement would in all probability be unable to communicate with one another after the country had been divided into occupied sectors, and might be forced outwardly to act in a way which friends in other sectors might misunderstand. There was no intent to organize a secret opposition or a "Werewolf," but simply to try to implement the program worked out in Kreisau by tacit co-operation. During the last days of his life Stauffenberg worked on an oath which he hoped would serve as a kind of pledge of allegiance to the new Germany.

We desire a new order, in which all Germans will participate in the responsibilities of the state and enjoy the guarantee of law and justice. We reject the doctrine of absolute equality and submit ourselves to the natural order of subordination and rank which emerges in any healthy society. We want to see our people close to the earth of their Fatherland and rooted in its natural succession of seasons. We want our people to find their happiness and fulfillment in the daily round of existence and to reject such incentives as envy and malice. Let our leaders grow organically from the various layers of society. Let them be bound by the divine

204

will and let them receive their right to lead through their magnanimity, breeding and self-sacrifice.

Anyone who is acquainted with the deep spiritual and physical division of Germany today is only too well aware of the need for just such a unifying code of belief. This one was devised even before the split which we see today could have been clear.

21. THE MEN OF RANK

KARL FRIEDRICH GOERDELER

(Born July 31, 1884, in Schneidemühl, West Prussia; executed February 2, 1945)

The history of Germany since the failure of the Putsch in 1944, and the defeat in 1945 seems to prove that the older men, after all, really embodied what the German people want. The carefree satisfaction with which the average German of today enjoys the benefits of the economic miracle and the restoration of the old forms is sufficient testimony. Gerhard Ritter, Goerdeler's biographer, finds this development entirely self-evident. Franz Böhm says that "the destruction of the National Socialist regime was a sufficient goal for the resistance." The construction of a *modus vivendi* in domestic and foreign affairs based on the *status quo ante* seems to him entirely adequate as an aim for the German resistance. He concedes that there were many areas in German life ripe for reform, but does not go into them in detail. The attitude just described belonged to the older men of high rank whom we meet in these pages. Foreign diplomats and political leaders could feel safe with them. In such men the Western democratic leaders saw, or thought they saw, the traditional ruling class of Germany returning to power after a period of mob madness. Haffner wrote:

The motives which drove such men to take unusual action were moral indignation and patriotic anxiety; in short, highly respectable motives. And what did they want, these white-haired conspirators? No revolution, just a restoration of order; no barricades, no shootings, no wild outbursts. No, none of that. At a given signal, the Army was to take power out of Hitler's hands in the way that a father removes a dangerous toy from the hands of his child, unemotionally, seriously and sternly. Hitler and his crew were to be arrested and later tried. From the very first moment, the German people were to have the feeling that the old authority was back, whose rule was moral, just, clean and irresistible.

Men of that type were bound to be surprised and dismayed by Hitler. Even those who were in a position to know—such as Admiral Canaris, because of the secret work in the Abwehr carried out by his assistant Colonel Oster; Secretary of State von Weizsäcker through the foreign office documents which passed through his hands—were stunned by Hitler's acts. They were surprised by the "Austrian Solution," the occupation of Czechoslovakia, the Hitler-Stalin pact and so on. They had been surprised by the occupation of the Rhineland in 1935, and by the general conscription law, and it was no wonder that they were never able to understand what Hitler was up to.

Equally typical of these men was their choice of indirect rather than direct countermeasures. By sending secret emissaries and warnings, they tried to get Paris and London to take a "strong" stand against Hitler. Their idea was that if Paris and London could be moved to take a hard line, Hitler would suddenly lose his nerve and pull back. If their attempts had been successful, it is most unlikely that Hitler, the master of bluff, would himself have been bluffed. He knew too well how pacific and inert the people were in France and England and how miserably inadequate the military preparations of those countries. They tried to do the same thing at home by painting the enemy as stronger than he really was. During the Sudeten crisis they asserted that it was doubtful that the German armies could break through the Czech "Maginot" line. Canaris, who alone among the higher officers in the admiralty knew England well, doubted whether the Scandinavian operation could succeed with the English fleet in the northern waters. General Hammerstein believed that the German invasion in the West would collapse on the walls of the French defenses.

Both approaches failed. The failure in turn made the situation for opponents of Hitler even more difficult, because the Führer now assumed the cloak of prophetic infallibility. The politicians, officers and businessmen had been wrong with their defeatist pessimism. Hitler had been right, and this undermined the confidence of his older opponents. In the meantime, Hitler had spread his own private network of informants over the world—young, enthusiastic Nazis, unburdened by much knowledge or manners, but alive and alert. They reported what they heard, not in the high-ceilinged offices in Whitehall or in the Quai d'Orsay, but in the bars, in the Underground, in the Métro, at the theatres and at the races. They paid no attention to what Lord Tyrell, Lord Vansittart, the Quai d'Orsay or Cordell Hull might say, but concentrated on what the barber and the taxi driver said.

The older men had to rely on their own experience. They had known the collapse of their world and social position during the chaos of 1918. They had lost a war which they expected to win. They had led armies which they confidently deemed to be the best in the world, and they had been defeated. They had seen Red mutineers in the streets of Berlin, a sight which they never wanted to see again. As a result, they became conservative nationalists. Ex-Ambassador Hassell's conversation with the Swiss historian and diplomat, Carl J. Burckhardt, in the summer of 1941, exemplifies their thinking. Hassell listed a series of points in a program for concluding the war. He rejected in advance any demands by the British for a change of government; that was a purely domestic affair of the Germans. He condemned with vehemence Point Eight of the Atlantic Charter, which demanded the disarmament of all militaristic nations. In his view this virtually destroyed any hope of arriving at a sensible peace.

Germany would make only very moderate claims, but these she would not abandon.

Although they agreed in general terms on the sort of Germany which they wanted to follow Hitler, they differed among themselves about personalities. In 1943 Hassell wrote in his diary:

> In our inner circle sharp disagreement about the all too weak leadership of Geibel [General Beck's pseudonym], also considerable reservation on several sides about Pfaff [Goerdeler], at least as political leaders. Geissler [Popitz] is accused of the way he acted under Göring—a general feeling that he made financial mistakes and worked too closely with the regime. Adlerheim [Falkenhausen] rejected for having taken too great a part in the terrorist system. I try my best to keep out of these personal squabbles, try to tighten Geibel's corset a bit and argue that the number of useful men is far too small and the qualities of the above-named far too valuable to let minor differences get in our way. Velsen [Gisevius] is drumming up support for Herz [Schacht]. The latest idea to which Geibel inclines is a directorium before the formation of a real cabinet. The members to be Beck, Schacht, Goerdeler, Hassell and a general.

In another entry Hassell expressed doubt as to whether the man who had made himself leader of the resistance, was capable of recognizing the extent of the job. "In the course of our conversation, Goerdeler showed himself quite often to be the prisoner of a whole set of very old-fashioned ideas. He seems not to have realized that the world really has, alas, changed and in a way that can at best be regulated but no longer halted."

Similar reservations about Goerdeler were often expressed. The former civil servant, the banker Schniewind, had originally accepted the Ministry of Economics in the proposed cabinet, but withdrew because of reservations about Goerdeler. Gisevius, who for years was an intimate of Goerdeler's, told Pechel that Field-Marshal von Witzleben had broken off all relations with Goerdeler because he was so furious at the absurdity and insubstantiality of Goerdeler's ideas. Goerdeler had urged von Witzleben to lead a regiment back from France to Germany, and upon crossing the Rhine, to proclaim à la Caesar the new executive power. Beck refused to let Goerdeler get to see Zeitzler, Chief of the Army General Staff, 1942–1944. Julius Leber, a leading member of the Social Democratic Party, said that Goerdeler was a visionary in foreign affairs and in domestic matters a spokesman for heavy industry. Even Goerdeler's devoted biographer is forced to shake his head wonderingly at the naïveté of Goerdeler's plans for a Hohenzollern restoration in 1943. In the Kreisau Circle, expressions like "Goerdeler, the con man," "or "Goerdeler rubbish" were common. Financial and economic experts who were not members of the resistance say that Goerdeler had been a failure even in his own field as price commissioner.

It was only after the publication of Gerhard Ritter's great biography that the public learned what the gentlemen of the Wednesday Club, gentlemen who met to read papers to one another, had recognized or at least suspected about their fellow member. Goerdeler could never have assumed the leadership in the catastrophic situation which would undoubtedly have followed a successful assassination of Hitler. Perhaps they should have drawn the natural conclusion at once. That they did not was due, one supposes, to their concern for unity at all costs. Besides, Goerdeler was a dynamo of constant, galvanic energy. He was the source of countless contacts, producer of hundreds of reports and memoranda, creator of many new ideas. From the evidence in Ritter's biography, one finds some difficulty in visualizing Goerdeler's full personality. He was a man possessed. Whether his motives were ambitious or disinterested, whether he was the sort of man who could only gain self-esteem through the approval of others, or whether profound anxieties permitted him no ease, are all questions the answers to which we simply do not know. Ritter's vast biography is peculiarly silent about the role of Goerdeler's wife. Indeed, one often gets the impression from the literature on the men of the 20th of July that all the participants were unmarried and unburdened by families, whereas the facts are quite different.

For me the most revealing view of Goerdeler was expressed by Bonn Professor Theodor Litt, who wrote:

Goerdeler was a clear-thinking, fair-judging and plain-dealing man. There was little, if anything, of the darker side of life, the unresolved or concealed, in his personality. He assumed that his fellow men, in so far as bad will and self-seeking could be excluded, merely required understandable enlightenment and good moral teaching to lead them back to the straight and narrow. The uncanny mixture of good and evil, the seductive power of many intellectual creeds, the force of unconfessed prejudice and repressed desires, the whole twilight world of the spirit, in which so many men lead their lives, did not exist for him and had no place in his picture of man.

Goerdeler's unconditional, virtually total, faith in reason fitted well into the character of his home, which was that of a West Prussian civil servant. A combination of Goerdeler's sort of enlightenment and the essence of Prussian bureaucracy seldom occurs in such complete purity. Politics and history had been the only acceptable topics of conversation at his father's table. Goerdeler's social class believed strongly that it was always right, and his own choice of the law as a profession certainly did little to shake this innate faith in his own rectitude. During the Weimar era he served as Oberbürgermeister of Königsberg and Leipzig, positions which afforded him unusually wide powers of decision. His talent for simplification helped him to sweep aside difficulties and obstacles, and gave his speeches a strong suggestive effect. The English bankers to whom, in 1938, Goerdeler revealed the names of the leading members of the underground opposition were most impressed and deeply moved when this Prussian broke into tears as they were parting, declaring that the meeting would undoubtedly be the last time that they would ever see each other. Goerdeler made an overpowering impression on General Kluge and Colonel Henning von Tresckow during his visit to the front in 1942. By that time courage had become something of a rarity, and courage was one quality which Goerdeler possessed to a high degree. Impatience was another. There was never enough being done to please him, and it was all too slow. His suggestions were to be carried out at once. Otherwise all was lost. This refrain ran through his whole life. "Inactive waiting was simply unbearable for him. His faith in the ultimate victory of good commonsense was unshakable," writes Ritter.

Goerdeler had been a German nationalist from his early youth, although he refused to join the extreme Hugenberg wing of the German National Party in the 1920's. His nationalism grew from his love of Germany east of the Elbe, where he had been born. At home, his father had talked constantly of the problem of the Poles. After the defeat of 1918, Goerdeler thought that a war with Poland was absolutely inevitable. In the chaos of 1919, his outrage at the soft line taken by the new regime on the question of the Polish border seriously led him to consider leading a separatist movement to withdraw the eastern provinces of Germany from the Reich. As late as 1935, Goerdeler, in a memo written for Hitler, took as his basic assumption the necessity and unavoidability of a war with Poland. His overseas contacts, which grew in frequency and intimacy during the 1930's, came to soften his own views a little. The morality underlying his plan for a "European Union of States," on which he worked in 1938 and 1939, had begun to display genuine features of an almost Wilsonian idealism. Ultimately, however, he always wanted to see Germany in the first place in the Western World. "We need only to get used to remaining silent about our primacy and holding ourselves in check so that we never misuse our position," he once said. In foreign affairs, therefore, he was not an unconditional opponent of Hitler. In domestic affairs, too, he often agreed with Hitler very closely, although he opposed the contemptible methods which the Nazis used and was a violent opponent of the plundering of Jewish stores.

What astonished anyone who lived in Berlin during the 1930's more than anything else was Goerdeler's ignorance of events. After all, the man already had ambitions to become Reich Chancellor during the Weimar Republic. He only learned of the fall of von Papen long after the event, and seems to have been unaware of the tortuous negotiations consequent upon that fall. He never learned of the bitter intrigues which led to the removal of General von Schleicher. He only heard of the extent of the

murders and slaughtering of June 30, 1934, the infamous Night
of the Long Knives, years afterward. And so it goes. He was
surprised at the Sudeten crisis and its resolution. The outbreak
of war caught him unprepared, and so did July 20, 1944,
about which he had been intentionally left in the dark for security reasons.

His reports to Krupp, Bosch, Göring, Schacht, Fritsch, Beck,
Halder and Thomas, on his trips abroad, have the same queer
naive quality. He often presented ideas as entirely new and facts
as just discovered which would have been long known to any
reasonably competent observer of the course of foreign affairs.
His optimism tended to play tricks on him. In the very year of
Roosevelt's famous "quarantine" speech, which publicly announced for the first time that the administration had changed
its attitude to Germany and Italy, Goerdeler was writing from
the United States that there was a definite willingness to compromise with Germany. He claimed to have found readiness to
concede on the colonies, the Polish Corridor, Sudetenland and
the *Anschluss*. His judgment on the relative military potential of
the Allied versus the Axis camp was colored by wishful thinking.
"What he completely missed," writes Ritter, "was the total in-
adequacy of Western military preparations and the radical decay
in fighting spirit in France. In this regard he was misled by his
military advisors, especially General Beck. On the other hand,
he himself always overestimated the importance of economic
bottle-necks and confusions in the German war machine."

In the area of economic thought Goerdeler was entirely the
prisoner of his old-fashioned ideas of the "hard work and belt-
tightening" sort. Under Bruening he made the unbelievably grotesque suggestion that the work week be lengthened when 6,000,-
000 people were unemployed. His fanatical opposition to all
forms of economic control led him to resist not only Nazi state
planning but even milder phenomena like the American New
Deal, the Kreisau Circle, and all the theorists of "Prussian Socialism." Many of his numerous memoranda are dedicated to
the "Red Peril." He was so confident of the support and sym-

pathy of the Conservatives in England that he could imagine England joining a new and reformed Germany in a crusade against Bolshevism in the winter of 1943–1944.

The tragedy inherent in his nature came out only in his behavior during his imprisonment. His drive for recognition remained untamed. He wanted to impress and make clear to Hitler that the 20th of July had not been an act of a clique of reactionaries, but that there was a grand and mighty movement behind it and him. He made out lists and named all the prominent persons, in the attempt to show how very important the movement had been. To the very end he continued to churn out memos, three for the Reich Security Office alone, and a last will and testament, which he had smuggled out of his cell. Near the end he reached a curious state of mind which his biographer describes as follows: "Bit by bit, the thoughts of the lonely man in the cell began to move in a circle. With endless monotony he repeated the same old ideas, the same long historical theories, the same appeals to posterity, the same warnings in letters to his family, to friends and the youth of the world." At the end his faith in God failed him. He had believed all his life that there was nothing one could not understand, and once understood, put in its proper place in a comprehensible world picture. He began to feel "that the sufferings of the innocent cannot be made clear to me. Yet I continue to seek through Christ the merciful God. I have not found him."

ULRICH VON HASSELL

(Born November 12, 1881, in Anklam, Pomerania; executed February 1945)

Hassell was made of very different stuff. It is perhaps a bit unfair to compare him so directly with Goerdeler. Yet what a contrast there was in their behavior after the failure of the plot in 1944! Goerdeler took flight, harassed, fearful, hiding at the home of friends. Finally throwing all caution to the winds, he decided to revisit the graves of his parents as a last homage. On

213

the way he suddenly changed his mind, because it occurred to him that he was very well known by sight in that area of West Prussia. Hassell, by contrast, remained completely calm and self-possessed. When the Gestapo burst in on Frau von Hassell in their country home in Bavaria, she first scolded them for their dreadful manners and then informed the astounded secret policemen that "every morning until seven thirty you will find Herr von Hassell in Potsdam at our flat, Seestrasse thirty-five. Then he goes riding, an activity of which you boors would naturally disapprove, and at nine thirty he goes to his office, Fasanenstrasse six, two flights up." There, sitting at his desk on July 28, 1944, Ulrich von Hassel received the agents of the secret police.

Hassell, too, was a nationalist. His entire life proved the strength of his convictions. It is most movingly expressed in an entry in his diary dated July 10, 1944, in which he describes a visit to the Bismarcks in Friedrichsruh. "Everything receded before the memory of the great man, in the house, in the mausoleum and in the little museum. Almost unbearable. I was near to tears when I thought of the ruined work. Germany, set in the middle of Europe, is her heart." Yet his nationalism was limited and modified by expert knowledge of the world. His Germany was more than a mere mixture of history, economics and civil order. Even before he entered the Foreign Office he had traveled widely, studied in Lausanne and London, and worked as a law clerk in Tsingtao in China. When he considered any German problem, he always saw it in terms of the wants and needs of the rest of of world. When he was assigned a post in a new country, he did more than familiarize himself with its government, press, political parties and administration. He tried to get to its essence. He listened to its music, read its literature, visited its art galleries and talked with its people. His Dante studies went far beyond the pure dillettante's interest.

Hassell was the son-in-law of Grand Admiral von Tirpitz and had, one imagines, approved the policy of unlimited U-boat warfare in the First World War, devised and implemented by his father-in-law. For him war was an entirely legitimate means of

214

attaining political ends, and service in the Army was the self-evident duty of every German. He always carried the French bullet which narrowly missed his heart in the battle of the Marne in 1914, and mentioned it in his farewell letter to his wife. Frau von Hassell was a "grande dame," the most open hearted and outspoken of all the wives in the diplomatic corps. Her remarks in Rome were legendary. She horrified some and delighted others of her hearers with the biting criticisms which she voiced on the Nazi regime. All her friends said that she was very "indiscreet," and she may have contributed to Hassell's dismissal from his Rome embassy post. Hassell himself was not silent either. As German Ambassador to Rome, he warned again and again against turning the Italian alliance into a military pact. Such a man soon became *persona non grata* with Hitler and his chief rival, Ambassador von Ribbentrop. He infuriated Mussolini, who had hitherto valued the polished, literate and Italianate wit of the German Ambassador. Hassell realized the weakening of the Italian Army, a fact soon to be made clear to the entire world during the ignominious Greek campaign. However, Mussolini could not tolerate the doubts of the German Ambassador, particularly after the victory in Abyssinia and the "triumph" in Spain.

After he had been "put on ice," Hassell continued the concealed double game described earlier, working for and against the regime simultaneously. He was undeniably ambitious and chafed at his dismissal. Ritter reports Hassell bought art works in Italy for Göring and congratulated him for the success in Austria, all in the hope of getting back into the diplomatic service. Ambition and a high estimate of his own not inconsiderable ability and cleverness were, however, not the sole motives. Like Jensen, Gisevius and Popitz, Hassell believed that the Hitlerite state could only be undone by boring from within. As Gisevius put it, all people without positions in the state lacked an Archimedean point and were therefore ineffective.

All his efforts were in vain. The most he achieved was the retention of his rank and the assignment to make several special

215

trips of a semiofficial nature. He traveled to Scandinavia on such a mission shortly after the outbreak of war. Much more important was his position on the board of the Central European Economic Conference, a small committee, barely known to the public, which like a finely spun spider's web had become an important source of confidential information and reports. Hassell remained a sharp observer and penetrating analyst of events until his death. Unlike Goerdeler, he labored under no illusions. He took every opportunity in political meetings, in lectures or articles, to discredit false views and to spread correct ones. In August of 1939, he tried, with the help of Undersecretary von Weizsäcker of the Foreign Office, to use his close personal friendship with British Ambassador Henderson and his Italian colleague in Berlin, Attolico, to prevent the outbreak of war. He tried to work on Hitler and Ribbentrop through Göring. He held other meetings, primarily to learn the views of the world outside Germany. His voice had more weight than other resistance leaders like Goerdeler, Bonhoeffer and Trott, because he was well known and genuinely liked in most of the major European capitals. His dismissal had undoubtedly raised his prestige in the eyes of the anti-Fascist world, especially in England.

Goerdeler became an opponent of Hitler's for a variety of reasons—personal dissatisfaction and an outrage of moral and legal sense among them. Canaris was sick of the ugly atrocities of the regime; the structure of lies and deception brought Popitz into opposition. Hassell's opposition was purely political. After a visit to Princess Herbert Bismarck, he wrote in his diary, dated Autumn 1938: "I agree with Princess Bismarck that a system which requires such immoral and brutal methods can never bring anything good. She, however, together with General Beck and thousands of others, concludes that, therefore, the system cannot last. I can only say that this prognosis is surely not, or not sufficiently, founded on the facts." Like Gisevius, he considered Goerdeler's declaration that "such a regime must fall" entirely unjustified by the facts. For his trial before the People's Court he wrote a peroration which expresses his political testament well, that of a clear-thinking nationalist: "A government which is forced to recognize that its policies are pulling the country down into the abyss of a general catastrophe is obliged to turn over the reins of rule promptly to others in order that they may strive to avert the onrushing doom. For there is no identity of people and government. The people are eternal and the government transient, yet responsible."

22. THE "BRASS HATS"

ONCE during the Hitler era there was a congress of philosophers in Berlin. All of the ministries which had their central offices in that city ignored it, save for one, the ministry of defense in the Bendlerstrasse, which sent a representative. When the story spread through Britain, those in the know laughed indulgently. A wag remarked that "the generals were obviously the only pacifists left in the Reich." How is this to be reconciled with the picture which the world had then, and to a large extent still has today, of the typical German general? The conflict between "pacifism" and "militarism" runs through the troubled history of the Army between the years of 1918 and 1945. The generals, as the oldest men in military service, had the closest contacts with the Kaiser, the royal family and the princely houses. They were most intimately tied in their hearts to the Bismarckian conception of the federalist monarchy. At best, they could summon dry feelings of duty to the Weimar Republic, but not much more. They distrusted intensely the two generals closest to the Weimar Government—General Groener and General von Schleicher. General von Seeckt wished the army to remain nonpolitical and stay aloof from party struggle, though despite this neutralist stand he himself was at times Weimar and was encouraged in this by Goerdeler. They had led the world's best army and had been defeated. They had no intention of being defeated again. Hitler was the man who was going to prevent

217

a second defeat. The shrewdest among them, however, quickly suspected that Hitler's war would be the kind which they as generals would never have chosen and could not win. As a result, they were, as a group, both supporters and opponents, and as the year 1939 drew near they became distinctly pacifist.

The generals were at a singular disadvantage in the new era of plotting and intrigue. Accustomed to the solitary existence of the barracks, where intrigue and conflict remained relatively clear, they were not very capable of holding their own in the ever-more-complicated circumstances. The impressive scene in the garrison church when Hitler, in civilian clothes and hatless, seemed humble and dwarfed by the massive, immobile figures of the field marshals, generals and colonels—Hitler standing in the shadow of that ancient relic of Prussia, Hindenburg. All this allayed their misgivings about the methods Hitler had used to seize power. The fear that Röhm and the S.A. might develop into a competitor to the Army was allayed, not without a measure of cooperation on the generals' part, by the sanguinary events of June 30, 1934, the Night of the Long Knives. That Generals Schleicher and von Bredow, two of their own men, were unfortunately also murdered that night showed for the first time the helplessness of the Army outside the military sphere.

The next incident stripped all pretensions from the Army's position; the crisis of Generals Blomberg and Fritsch. Canaris' biographer writes of this incident:

The dirt of the Blomberg affair had a powerful impact on Canaris. He had always stood for the utmost clarity and decency in his official activities and, despite all the guile and trickery of the counterintelligence work in which he engaged, had maintained a sharp distinction in his own person between good and evil. Canaris was not so much offended by the fact that the Minister of Defense, General von Blomberg, had married a woman of the people, a dreadful mésalliance about which most people could only speak in the most derisory of terms. It was rather the completely incomprehensible behavior of Field Marshal von Blomberg under the circumstances which troubled Canaris. The more he learned, the more disturbed he became. Blomberg had not, as Canaris had first assumed, stumbled

218

blindly into this unholy mess, but had acted in full consciousness of the awful impropriety of the affair. His good taste, considerations of family and position, but even more important, and to Canaris crucial, his sense of duty to the Wehrmacht, should have forbidden him from making such a blunder. He had to admit that Fritsch, whom he admired and whose integrity he never questioned, had cut a helpless and pathetic figure. It was deplorable for two reasons in Canaris' view. It damaged the position of Fritsch and gave aid and comfort to all the intriguers in the party and the S.S. who were seeking to undermine the Army.

Canaris would have done better to give more thought to the political and less to the moral implications of the affair. Still, through his contact with the Gestapo, he had a better idea of what was going on than most of the generals. One gets the impression that the generals, blind to the real motives on the other side, could only see the smudged honor of Field Marshal von Blomberg and the humiliation of the Commander in Chief of the Wehrmacht, Colonel General von Fritsch. How could men of such prejudices prove equal to a life-and-death struggle with the likes of Hitler, Göring and Himmler?

Hassell once said in a conversation with Oster that Halder, then Chief of the General Staff, and von Brauchitsch, Fritsch's successor, were no more than "technical stooges." This was surely a result of the political abstinence practiced by the Army for decades. The radical separation of the Army from political life had been accomplished by General von Seeckt. His success stemmed from the vivid recollection of the disastrous consequences of the intervention of Ludendorff in political events, and by the deeply imbedded professionalism of the Prussian military tradition.

On the other hand, when politics began to enter the Army, in the appointment of political commissars, for example, the generals did fight back. Unfortunately they rarely fought directly. They usually circumspectly tried to get around or undermine the orders once they had been given. Their outrage was undoubtedly genuine, but they seemed more eager to avoid a fuss than anything else. Fabian von Schlabrendorff writes that there were tears of rage in the eyes of the officers in the headquarters of General Bock when the atrocity orders were issued. Hassell found the officers in the Paris headquarters "desperate about the policies pursued in France." A completely nonpartisan witness, the Greek journalist J. Gaitanides, told of General Lenz, who simply refused to obey Hitler's order to shoot 6,000 Italians accused of mutiny, and of General Felmy, who managed to get an order revoked which commanded him to shoot all hostages taken.

Before the outbreak of war there had been no such orders, and it is just barely possible to argue that the generals failed because they did not see the true nature of the Nazi system. More plausible is the argument that to oppose Nazism meant taking a stand on matters of domestic and foreign politics. During the 1930's, they maintained that domestic politics were not the business of the soldier. They watched the tendency to stupefy and brutalize the German people grow, and they were alarmed. The most they could ever bring themselves to do was to allow Pintschovius, the Wehrmacht psychologist, to criticize Goebbels, by implication, in a book entitled *Spiritual Powers of Resistance in Modern War*! In foreign affairs, however, they only became active when they realized that Hitler's policies were leading straight to war. That was roughly about the time of the annexation of Austria. General Halder began to plan a Putsch at that time. It was his intention to take advantage of the high point of the Sudeten crisis, by which time he assumed that everyone would see that Hitler was going to unleash a war, to overthrow him. Due to a tragic paradox, the activity of the other wing of the resistance centered around the Foreign Office, and the visits of Chamberlain to Berchtesgaden and Bad Godesberg took the edge off the crisis and frustrated his plans. The plans of General Hammerstein before the beginning of the Polish campaign, and General Halder's second attempt after its conclusion, also came to nothing. The opportunity was never there. The prerequisites did not correspond to the needs, and the inner conflicts loomed too large. Sebastian Haffner described the whole episode in the following words: "On one side, Hitler ready for war, on the other, the plotters prepared for their coup, in the middle the German Army indispensable to both sides, acquainted with both plans and vacillating between war and Putsch. It could conquer Europe. It could arrest Hitler. The one thing it could not do for a year and a half was to make up its mind which to do."

Those are the words of an outside observer, spoken many years later. The reaction of the participants was far more bitter. Canaris said to Hassell that he had lost all confidence in the generals. Stackelberg accused Falkenhorst of being just another general, without will or civil courage. Gisevius said that there was nothing more to be done with the generals. They would be fattened up with decorations, promotions and Iron Crosses. Hassell wrote: "Anyone who can see the situation even moderately clearly begins to boil with rage over our military leadership; their fawning sycophancy knows no bounds." Popitz: "The High-ups think of nothing but their medals." People spoke this way "among themselves" in the Foreign Office. Only after the progress of events forced the generals to see that purely political and purely military questions are inseparable in a totalitarian state did the great mass of the generals begin to stir. They were most exercised by questions of military leadership. Gestapo investigator Kiesel listed their main complaints. The generals claimed that:

1. The exacting and professional work of the General Staff was ignored.

2. Hitler informed himself on military questions through unreliable and "irresponsible" channels.

3. False, politically colored estimates of the military situation were leading to false operational decisions.

4. Hitler's demand for an army of 400 divisions was megalomania, in view of the General Staff's estimate that only 300 could be properly mounted and trained. The unpracticed newcomers could not be absorbed into existing units. Unnecessary losses through inexperience would result.

5. Hitler's intense suspiciousness had led to an unfortunate division in the highest military organization, which allowed him to take vital decisions into his own hands.

It was the last fact which really hurt and which finally brought about action. Halder and Zeitzler repeatedly demanded a reorganization of the top command, which Hitler stubbornly refused to countenance. A plan called the "Action of the Field Marshals," was worked out. The top generals were to go to Hitler as a group, under the leadership of the respected General Kluge, and compel Hitler to accept their demands. After the proclamation of the law of 1942, this meant a step on the road to high treason. It meant putting illegal pressure on Hitler. Keitel got wind of the action and issued an order forbidding all further discussion of the topic. Kiesel reported that thereafter no further concrete discussions of the Action of the Field Marshals were carried on by the generals. Heusinger obeyed and others, Stieff for example, decided that the situation had become so catastrophic that it would be a higher form of treason to acquiesce than to disobey.

However, it took a series of crushing defeats before such a discussion began to take place. During the first few years of the war, Hitler scored one success after another, and that was enough for most of the generals. Admittedly, success is the ultimate test of a soldier, but few had the imagination to consider the long-run implications of the early successes. The unhappy scene in the Bendlerstrasse on July 20, 1944, was undoubtedly caused by the long imprisonment within the myth of success. Field Marshal von Witzleben arrived and learned that the attempt on Hitler's life had failed. Instead of thinking of the next step, von Witzleben flew into a rage, hurled criticism at the abashed officers, pounded the table and refused to listen to Beck's calming words. Stauffenberg and Schwerin stood like marble pillars. No attempt to salvage a situation not yet lost, no resourcefulness in adversity, just annoyance at a miscarried plan. As if he were a nonparticipant, Witzleben gave vent to his fury and then ordered his driver to take him home.

COLONEL GENERAL LUDWIG BECK

(Born June 29, 1880, in Biebrich-on-the-Rhine; committed suicide July 20, 1944, in Berlin)

Colonel General Beck, who was a historian and philosopher as well as a general, had considered the causes for success and failure in war at length. Gerstenmaier testifies that Beck consistently refused to support a Putsch attempt until he saw at least a slim chance of success. Unlike the others, Beck demonstrated that there were things which meant more to him than success; conscience, for one, and moral responsibility. Again in contrast to his colleagues, Beck began to oppose Hitler long before the war began and the imminence of defeat became clear. In 1935 he received an assignment as the Chief of the General Staff, to work out the operational plans for an attack on Czechoslovakia. He accepted the task, completed it in his brilliant, lucid way, and submitted it to Hitler with the warning that he considered the work as purely theoretical in nature. Should Hitler ever seriously consider such an operation, he would be forced to tender his resignation. One suspects that Beck's statement is unique in the long history of the General Staff. He meant it too. On the occasion of the invasion of Czechoslovakia, Beck resigned his post. An officer who was present has described the scene of Beck's last speech to the General Staff:

When we entered his office he was standing erect at the side of his desk. He moved slightly to acknowledge the greetings of those coming in. His hands were folded neatly, and the delicately chiseled face seemed worn, almost other-worldly. The gaze from his fine and startingly beautiful eyes was remote and far from us. Perfectly straight and poised, he delivered a short speech of, perhaps, fifteen minutes in length, standing at his desk— a speech which literally sparkled with the classical elegance of its structure and the wisdom of its content. The sense of it was to make clear to the assembled officers the significance of the struggle for an independent, creative and resourceful General Staff. Under the prevailing circumstances he could only claim to have been partially successful. His appeal to us to preserve our independence in judgment and character was very moving. I am certain that even the small minority among us who felt that Beck's retirement was necessary and right could not fail to have been deeply stirred by the evident seriousness, dignity and proud sense of moral responsibility of the slender, elegant man, who was to prove to be the last true chief of the German General Staff.

223

Not all those who welcomed Beck's departure were Nazis. Panzer General Heinz Guderian said that Beck had enclosed himself within a high wall of "reaction." Even his friend and admirer Hassell remarked in his diary, after hearing Beck's famous and brilliant lecture on Marshal Foch at the Wednesday Club: "He looked his old self again, but his 'old self' shows more and more signs that it is pure Clausewitz without the least dash of Blücher or Yorck."

It may have been that Beck's profound revulsion from the Nazi brutality merely strengthened unduly his innate love of the classical, the measured, the prudent and considered in thought and deed. His classicism determined, in a real sense, everything he did during his last years. In 1929, the forty-nine-year-old colonel in command of a regiment in Ulm had protected the two young Nazis, Ludin and Scheringer, who were spreading propaganda in the ranks. Again, in 1933, he welcomed the nomination of Hitler as Reich Chancellor, together with the majority of the German generals, mainly because Hitler had promised to give Germany equality of arms after the long years of fruitless disarmament negotiations which had so wearied the spirits. He was convinced that the Stresemann *Erfüllungspolitik* could never lead to anything. Extraordinarily early for a general, Beck began to have doubts. When the activists stormed ahead in 1934, Beck began to apply the brakes. He had military reservations as well as political ones. He denied the theses of men like Liddell Hart and Charles de Gaulle that the tank had revolutionized warfare and that consequently a new type of military leadership was called for. Beck never had a very clear idea of the probable outcome of the collision between the new theory of war, as practiced in the German Army most brilliantly by Rommel and Guderian, and the old theory as represented by the Polish and French armies.

In 1937, as the invasion of Austria was being planned, he argued that "Germany is not in a position to undertake a military operation of any proportions in Central Europe." He painted an exceedingly grim picture—fed to him partly by Goerdeler—

of the vulnerable economic situation of the country. In 1938, he went even further and argued that an attack on Czechoslovakia would automatically unleash the Western democracies which were bound by treaty obligation to come to the defense of Czechoslovakia. Defeat would be inevitable. While Beck was formulating his pessimistic thesis, everyone in the know in Berlin had heard the story going about that French Ambassador François-Poncet had informed Czech Ambassador Mastny, in no uncertain terms, that France would not "march." This rather undiplomatic sincerity could, had it been openly confessed in Paris and London, have spared the Czechs at least the form of betrayal which they were to suffer at Munich. The success of the new warfare with panzers and stukas in the Polish campaign failed to convince Beck. His successor, General Halder, warned him repeatedly that he was far too pessimistic.

"Much tactic and little will," said Popitz about Beck in the years of common conspiracy. Hassell often wrote in his diary that Beck had been too soft and reserved at the meetings and too weak as a leader, in view of the violence of the internal conflicts. In a comparison of Beck with Guderian, General Manstein remarked that Beck was "sober, thoughtful, and, I won't deny it, often hesitant." Kiesel distilled the following picture of Beck from the statements of the various imprisoned officers: "a procrastinator, a master of conspiracy, and yet a miserable revolutionary. Not one of the conspirators could recall so much as a single occasion on which Beck had discussed the affairs of the conspiracy with more than one person present at a time." August Winning recalls how adroitly Beck turned a restaurant conversation from the plot to horses, stag-hunting and animal breeding as soon as anyone even neared their table.

For Beck, everything had to be planned, considered and analyzed. His high degree of self-control always made an enormous impression on people. Paul Fechter writes that "everything in him was completely formed and molded. Intellect and will had fused into a perfect unity, which lent the features of the living man something of the grand harmony of a statue." The few instances when Beck actually lost his self-control must have been terribly distressing. Needless to say, they did not occur during or immediately after the 20th of July, but came suddenly and quite unexpectedly. Beck was once listening to a speech on the English radio by a British general who had served a brief tour of duty in his youth with a German guards regiment. He described in glowing terms the courtesy and breeding of the men he had met in the old imperial regiment before the First World War, and closed his talk by asking ruefully where those men could be today after Poland had been so brutally and rapaciously dismembered. The program ended with the playing of the famous old German soldier's song, *"Ich hatt'einen Kamerad,"* in memory of General von Fritsch who had recently died in the front lines. It was undoubtedly an effective piece of propaganda, but Colonel General Beck suddenly burst into tears.

Beck's greatest teacher had always been history itself; his dearest friend was Friedrich Meinecke, the historian. Objectivity was for Beck the self-evident prerequisite for any action. Such a world view, tempered by a concept of history in which there was recurrence and development but no genuine dynamism, could not fail to make him the opponent of all outbreaks, unexpected or radical departures from the norm, and perilous novelties. His views reached a kind of classical perfection of expression in the two memorable lectures which he delivered to the Wednesday Club on "Total War" and "Marshal Foch." In "Total War" he begins by rejecting the thesis of Ludendorff's that under contemporary conditions only total war is possible. Beck brilliantly demonstrates that Clausewitz had in his time already recognized, and indeed exhausted, the various possibilities of total war, and that therefore neither the idea nor its consequences are in any sense new. He goes on, and here a bit less convincingly, to argue that the First World War need not have turned into a total war, since England's entry could have been avoided. Beck fails to see, it seems to me, the uncanny mixture of civil war and crusade which crept into the thinking of the leaders on both sides after the German invasion of Belgium, which mixture came to dominate the Second World War and has become, since the outbreak of the Cold War, the self-evident nature of modern conflict. It is typical that Beck chooses to cite the courteous orders which Wilhelm I issued at the beginning of the Franco-Prussian War in 1870: "We are not waging war against peaceful dwellers of the country. Our war is with French soldiers and the French armies, not French citizens." Beck remarks with a sigh that such words were not heard in 1914. Here again he fails to see that such sentiments were no longer possible in a world in which people fought behind slogans like *"Gott strafe* England," "Make the world safe for Democracy," and "Hang the Kaiser." In such expressions the beginnings of totalitarian thinking manifest themselves. This same thinking brought about that fusion of politics and war which so dominates our times.

It was patently Beck's aim to prevent just such a fusion. Contrary to Ludendorff's theory and practice, Beck regarded politics and warfare as separate entities. As a result, he draws a sharp distinction between the armistice conditions of Marshal Foch and the stipulations of the Versailles treaty. Military leaders, according to Beck, are always obliged to take every precaution to secure their countries against renewed attack on the part of the defeated enemy, and thus are correct to press the most exacting terms for an armistice on the opposing army. Had he been in the position of Marshal Foch, he would not have acted differently. The statesman, on the other hand, has to act politically and must consider the long-term consequences of what he does. Beck again points out that total war is far from inevitable, and indeed its very existence is a danger that new total wars will follow upon it. He says that preparation for total war, with its sapping of the nation's strength and excessive organization, is in itself dangerous. "Far more serious," he wrote, "is the nervous tension among nations, which results from constant arms races and which not only threatens their relationship to each other, but also increases the danger that war will break out." He concluded the lecture by stating categorically that "each total war bears within it the succeeding one."

In considering Beck's thesis today, more than twenty years later, we are of course struck by the accuracy with which he characterized our era, but on the other hand, we can now see, perhaps more clearly than he could, that total war is not an exceptional experience. Beck felt that eliminating total war was more or less a question of goodwill, insight and moderation, whereas we today are inclined to see Hitler as merely an early example of a series, the end of which is by no means yet in sight. Politics and warfare have fused far more closely than Beck realized, and today we hardly know how to tell them apart.

Beck was certainly not just an academic theoretician. His aim was to use history to influence his listeners. In his lecture on Marshal Foch, he chose parallels to Hitler which are remarkably striking. From Foch's military philosophy, Beck selected passages referring to the fall of Napoleon and used them to illustrate Foch's basic military creed, while at the same time commenting indirectly on the Nazi regime. Naturally he used the facts cited by Foch to show that the very forces which felled Napoleon could bring Hitler down as well. He quoted this passage from Foch:

Laon [the next to last defeat of Napoleon] is the defeat which the revolt of Right wreaked on the genius. Therein lies the lesson for us soldiers. Justice always goes its own way in the implacable and eternal cycle of the ages, whatever we may or may not do. This battle is a repetition of Valmy and the events of 1792 and 1793, only now turned against us. Indeed at the end, after Europe had witnessed a rising of the peoples one after another to have their independence, Europe itself can be called the victor at Laon and Waterloo. They rose for the same reasons and used the same techniques as the most colossal military genius of all time had used with such brilliance against them. For he had been guilty of the unforgivable. He had attacked Europe's Rights.

One can almost see the distinguished members of the Wednesday Club, a good many of whom belonged to the inner circle of the resistance, nodding sagely in agreement as Beck read out the sentences of the famous French marshal. After all, their hearts' desire was just that, a repetition of Valmy, a turning back of the world political landslide. Beck quotes again from Foch the sentences in which the Marshal suggests the reasons for the fall of Napoleon: "The most crucial factor was the final identification which Napoleon made between the might of the nation and his own person. Strengthened by this madness, he dared to try to settle the fate of peoples by his own naked force of arms, as if it were not, in the last analysis, morality which ultimately determines the final victor in the struggle among the nations and is itself always stronger ultimately than power, be that power as brilliant or massive as it will." Was not that exactly it? Had not Hitler in his madness identified himself completely with "the power of the nation"? He ruled by, and believed in, power alone. Against him was arrayed the entire civilized world. The civilized world sat, as it were, in that comfortable room on a Wednesday evening, the guests of the distinguished surgeon Sauerbruch. How rousing to the dismayed spirits that lecture must have been in a time when all seemed irrevocably lost. The lecture was given on May 31, 1944; forty days later Ludwig Beck, Colonel General (Ret.), was dead. The genius of power had triumphed over the revolt of Right.

Beck acted perfectly in keeping with his nature on that last day. The failure of the Putsch was unfortunate from a political point of view but ethically of no consequence. He expressed this attitude in a radio speech dictated to Gisevius: "It is entirely irrelevant whether or not Hitler is dead. A leader in whose immediate surroundings conflicts rage so fiercely that a bomb plot can be conceived is morally dead anyway." General Kortzfleisch, who had been selected to take over the command of the Berlin military district, refused to do so, citing his oath of allegiance to Hitler as his grounds. This was the only occasion on the 20th of July when Beck lost his serenity. "You have the nerve to talk of oaths," he cried. "Hitler has broken his oath to the constitution and people a hundred times and you uphold oaths to such an oathbreaker."

Only a man of faith can be so secure in his moral convictions;

a man who is certain of how life was meant to be lived. Beck saw history in its entirety and its individual concreteness as a manifestation of the will of God. From his study of history he drew solace and conviction as to the purpose and direction of that will. Much earlier Beck had taken part in one of the many discussions then going on about the Nazi plans for greater economic spheres of influence and had remarked that "such formations ought not to ignore divinely willed factors tested through the long development of historical experience, namely, the various national identities." It was this "unconditional" outlook which so distinguished him from his military colleagues and made him so immutable in matters of conscience and morals and unfortunately hobbled him in matters of practical policy and technique. Listening to the dictates of conscience turned into over-conscientiousness and occasionally degenerated into pure pedantry. Everything had to be written down, properly arranged, and filed. Ritter says that: "It was Beck's pedantic insistence on documentation which was responsible for the complete papers of the conspiracy not being destroyed in time, as they should have been at the very latest after the arrest of Dohnanyi in 1943." Canaris' biographer noticed how much Oster and his associates had been influenced by Beck Every action, decision or event must be preserved in writing. Beck was convinced that at some future date the resistance would be called upon to show that its opposition to Hitler dated from a time when the great mass of the German people were still solidly loyal to him and still convinced of his infallibility and the ultimate victory. As a result, the former chief of staff became accustomed to making a memo on every single step he took.

On the 20th of July itself, Beck took great pains to record everything which happened, for the benefit of future historians. The only military command which he gave on that day was an order to withdraw the Army Group North from its perilous encirclement in Kurland. He called all those present in the Bendlerstrasse into his office and declared portentously that "one could not tell how things would develop in the coming few hours but there were certain things which would interest future historians." For this reason he had ordered the preparation of a memo which contained the full text of the important order he had just given. Gisevius, from whose account the above passage has been drawn, then continues: "Beck drew his watch from his pocket and announced that the exact time was 19 hours 21 minutes. We could feel that he was moved. What was going on inside him? Had he a suspicion that it was to be the only order that he would give on that day?"

It was not merely his only order. Except for the altercation with General Kortzfleisch and a desperate telephone call to General Kluge, who was unable to make up his mind which way to turn, it was General Beck's only act on the 20th of July. The Bendlerstrasse was a scene of unexampled chaos. Stauffenberg had returned from the Wolf's Lair in the late afternoon when he first heard of the failure of the bomb explosion which he had confidently assumed had killed Hitler. His dismay was even greater when he learned that Operation Valkyrie had not even begun. Contradictory reports streamed in. Nervousness grew. Waiting became unbearable. Stauffenberg threw himself down behind his desk and began to make telephone calls with demonic fury, speaking on three lines at once. Beck, the only soldier in the entire War Office in civilian clothes (he wanted to emphasize the civil character of the Putsch), sat perfectly still, almost lost, in a corner. Gisevius urged him wildly to do something. Beck replied, "Keep calm, keep calm," and remarked repeatedly that a good commander must know how to keep his nerves under control. A chief of the General Staff had no business intervening in the execution of the individual actions. Great as the strain of these hours might be for him, too, he had no intention of making the confusion even greater than it already appeared to be. "We dare not suffer ourselves to be infected by the general disorder," he said. "A good general knows how to wait." Gisevius continues resignedly: "He may have been right, but waging war and staging a successful *coup d'état* are two quite different things." Gisevius had never heard of the famous conversation between Beck and General Halder in 1938, when Halder had asked him what was to be done now that the plans for a Putsch had gone awry. With these words his chief had forbidden Halder to talk any further about the question. "Mutiny and rebellion are words which are not to be found in the lexicon of a good German officer." It is hardly surprising, therefore, that a man who thought in such categories had not turned into a brilliant and resourceful revolutionary, even after six years. His outer calm was, however, the fruit of extreme effort. According to Kiesel, Beck was in reality far too agitated to have been effective or "even to have uttered one sentence coherently. The younger General Staff officers, especially Bernardis and Klausning, were astonished when they saw the condition of the man who, they had been told, was to lead the Reich out of its dreadful peril. The entire burden of command fell on Stauffenberg."

A new group, which saw the world differently, had moved onto the scene. In a way it heightens the tragedy of the older generation that it even managed to fail to take its own lives successfully. At least Ludwig Beck was spared the anguish and humiliation of Gestapo torture and Freisler's People's Court by finding death in the Benderstrasse during the night of July 20th.

ADMIRAL WILHELM CANARIS

(Born January 1, 1887, in Aplerbeck, Westphalia; executed April 9, 1945)

Beck was a man of clarity. One knew where one stood with him. But even the closest associates of Canaris were certain that they could only catch a glimpse into a tiny fraction of his doings and personality. He never revealed himself fully to anyone. For Beck, calm was the first commandment. By contrast, Canaris united in himself a lust for adventure with an inner restlessness and impatience which reached feverish levels as the war raged on. No train could race quickly enough to suit him. He dashed from place to place and was constantly on the road in his speeding staff car. Relaxation was nonsense, and a free Sunday merely

232

made him uneasy. Vacations were annoying interruptions of the really important business at hand. On the rare occasions when he permitted his family to talk him into going away for a vacation, he found after a few days that he did not know what to do with his time. He was not a night owl. Indeed anyone who voluntarily stayed up later than ten o'clock was in his eyes a person of highly questionable morals. This alone was enough to condemn Hitler, who held midnight conclaves, in the eyes of Canaris.

Canaris possessed a delicate facility for languages and a sense of the right tone to use in each conversation. Even as a young officer he was given a variety of diplomatic assignments for the Navy. His talent as a negotiator was aided by sharp observation and a swift, free-wheeling intellect. He combined in unlikely union uncommonly quick reactions, vividness of imagination, and an almost impenetrable circumspection, which made him an elusive adversary.

It was not "moral indignation" which turned Canaris into an opponent of Hitler, nor was it Hassell's highly developed political sense, but the sheer physical nausea which overcame him every time he ran into further examples of Hitler's atrocities. He collapsed and was physically ill for several days after a visit to the smoking ruins of Warsaw, scarred forever by Hitler's destructive barbarism. Driving through Belgrade, in 1941, he was so shaken by the desolation, the human suffering and the evidences of Nazi brutality, that he asked to be taken back to his hotel room, where he was violently ill. Afterward he sank into a chair and burst into tears. "I simply can't go on," he said to his adjutant. "I've got to get out of here somehow." "Where to?" asked the stunned young officer. Canaris brightened. "To Spain," he replied.

Spain, Italy, Greece and the Mediterranean islands—he was always drawn to that warm world of bright colors and clarity, as if to some paradise. North of the Alps, he was always cold, even in summer. In the south he blossomed out, his restlessness eased, and he relaxed. On one occasion he had even managed to enjoy a vacation in complete harmony of self and environment on the island of Corfu. He thought seriously of resigning his commission and staying on the island. Perhaps it was the southern blood of distant ancestors which sought the light. His biographer makes much of the presumed Mediterranean ancestry in his attempt to portray and explain the strange chiaroscuro in Canaris' radiant personality, his bright and vivid imagination, his almost painful sense of reality, his submerged, bubbling, often scurrilous sense of humor, and his instinctive harmony with the mentality of the Latin peoples. Forced to live in the darkening gloom of Hitler's Germany, Canaris' life was a sort of personal hell. He found much comfort in his family and in his superb, highly strung dogs, which he loved passionately.

Canaris was in many respects a very strange man, a hypochondriac and a pill-eater. He was armed with a variety of irrational prejudices which he observed with almost superstitious awe. A small and delicate person, he had a profound loathing for those "muscular chaps," and an even greater one for the terribly polished military types. All robust and burly men were "kidnappers." Indeed one of those "muscular chaps" whom he loathed most, Vice-Consul von Bibra, did in fact turn into a kidnapper in Hitler's service. General Jodl he found quite insufferable. Often able men in the Abwehr were dismissed and replaced by lesser men or acknowledged mediocrities who got on Canaris' nerves less or whose outer habits pleased him better. He never mistook their limitations, but allowed himself a sort of luxury in choosing sympathetic personalities to fill out his immediate surroundings. His remarkable powers of assessing the possibilities in thought and deed in other men led him to believe that he could always calculate well in advance to what extent a given individual would be able to carry out a specific order. One of his staff described his extraordinary methodology in the following words: "If the orders were, in Canaris' view, beyond the mental abilities of the recipient, which unfortunately and unavoidably in time of war is all too often the case, he would combine the mistakes to be expected from the agent with cross or counteracting orders to third or fourth parties. Mistakes which would be made tomorrow were rectified by counteracting them today." Whether all this subtlety achieved the desired end is doubtful. Any foreign correspondent during the war years will surely recall the incredibly naïve blunders and *gaffes* of the German counterintelligence.

By far the strangest side of Canaris' character is revealed in his mysterious, ambivalent relationship to Reinhard Heydrich, chief of the Gestapo's Sicherheits-Dienst and the head thereby of the leading competing secret service. It is probable that this love-hate relationship kept Canaris in power until Heydrich was shot by Czech underground fighters in Prague in 1942. Heydrich had almost nothing in common with Canaris, though he, too, had been a naval officer until his dismissal by a military court of honor. Canaris first met Heydrich in 1935, when he arrived in Berlin to assume charge of the Abwehr, and from the very first they had seen a great deal of one another. Abshagen has described their friendship:

Canaris was frankly scared to death of Heydrich. Everything about the fellow was sinister and made Canaris uneasy. He was too big for comfort. His cold, penetrating eyes set deeply in his almost mongoloid features had the frozen glint of a snake. Canaris always felt in Heydrich's presence the reality of evil, that his personality had none of the usual human limitations and that he was an evildoer of the highest order. Yet he was fascinated, virtually mesmerized, by the high intelligence of his companion, whom he once called the "cleverest of the beasts."

In his diary he wrote of Heydrich as a "brutal fanatic with whom it would be difficult to cooperate on a basis of mutual confidence." His fear of Heydrich was never laid to rest until the Czechs murdered the chief of the Reich Sicherheits-Dienst in 1942. A telephone call from Heydrich could make Canaris nervous all day.

Yet despite the fact that Heydrich was literally everything in person which Canaris loathed and abominated, he was always at pains to maintain the heartiest of external relations between the families. It was perhaps only coincidence that when Canaris moved to Berlin in 1935, he took a house on the Döllestrasse on the very street where Heydrich and his family had lived for some time. Despite his profound revulsion, he assiduously cultivated the social life between the two families, and it was not an uncommon sight on a warm summer Sunday to see the Canaris family strolling up the Döllestrasse to play croquet with the Heydrichs. In 1936, Canaris bought a charming little house in Schlachtensee on the Dianastrasse. Was it purely chance that shortly thereafter Heydrich had a house built on the Augustastrasse, scarcely two minutes' walk from Dianastrasse? The total opacity of Canaris' personality makes it impossible to judge his behavior on hearing the news of the murder of Heydrich in 1942. In a voice heavy with emotion, Canaris said that he had valued Heydrich as a great man for whose high intelligence he had had the greatest respect and whose friendship he had been privileged to enjoy. All play-acting? Perhaps Canaris had been forced to recognize qualities which he knew to be in himself in the chief of the competing Secret Service.

Canaris had already demonstrated his innate mastery of the arts of duplicity in the First World War, when as a young naval officer he escaped from internment in South America and with forged papers passed effortlessly through the British passport station at Plymouth, where so many German agents had been caught. Later he found himself in a much more perilous position after his arrest in Italy. He had tried to return to Germany over enemy territory from Spain, where he had been engaged in espionage. After nearly being shot as a spy, he extricated himself by a series of ruses worked out in advance for that very eventuality, and managed to get on board a Spanish freighter for Barcelona. He was not, however, out of danger yet, for he would most certainly be arrested if the ship were to put in at Marseilles. His sure instinct for choosing the right moment to drop the mask came to his aid, and relying on the Spanish sense of chivalry, he reported to the captain and revealed that he was a German officer on a secret mission who would undoubtedly be shot were the

French to get hold of him. The Spaniard reacted as Canaris had guessed he would and hid the young man in his cabin during the twenty-four hours in Marseilles.

At all such moments the man's double nature came to light. He loved and was stimulated by the thrill of real danger, but no sooner had the threat passed than he began to tremble, grew pale and often collapsed in a fever. It was doubtless this shadowy complexity and mercurial change in the man which so unnerved his fellow sailors, accustomed to plain, open personalities. Doenitz distrusted Canaris intensely, and Raeder hesitated for a long time before naming such a man, whose intellectual flexibility was a bit uncanny, to be chief of the military counterintelligence, the Abwehr.

The leading Nazis, on the other hand, considered the little naval officer with the rosy complexion, snow-white hair and brilliant blue eyes, one of the "reliable" men. Originally they were not so very wrong. Canaris was born into a patriotic, Bismarckian family of Rhineland industrialists. The mutiny of the sailors in 1917 had outraged him and left him an abiding hatred of both Communsits and Social Democrats of every stamp. His reaction to the events after 1918 reflected his upbringing and the searing experience of the mutiny. In 1919, he organized the citizens' defense brigades. He served on the staff with unemployed sailors and peasants in the forming of the Löwenfeld Naval Brigade, took part in the trial of the murderers of Karl Liebknecht and Rosa Luxemburg, on behalf of the defendants. He fought in the Kapp Putsch in 1920, and spent several days in the jail on the Alexanderplatz. These are all typical episodes in the latent civil war which raged in postwar Germany at that time. After the normalization of conditions, Canaris was sent by the admiralty to work on the perfection of U-boat techniques in Finland, Holland and Spain, where the Allied Control Commission could not touch him or interfere. There, too, he worked in secret, though not in the Secret Service. Even his closest comrades at the Wilhelmshaven naval base never suspected that the busy and bustling little first officer of the *"Schlesien"* was actively engaged in circumventing the armaments clauses of the Versailles treaty. Of those who did know, several were not in agreement, but they could do nothing to stop him, since the admiralty spread its full protection over him.

It is obvious that a man who had worked so long and devotedly to destroy the Versailles treaty would welcome the rise to power of a politician whose aim so closely coincided with that of his own. From the beginning, however, Canaris was disturbed by the dominant role of "the street" in Nazi machinations and power, but was convinced that Hindenburg and the Wehrmacht would be strong enough to keep their dog on the leash. The deception and fraud of the "Reichstag Fire" appalled him, the brutality of the aftermath revolted him, and it was at this point that his real reservations began. The boycott of the Jews, the persecution of all non-Aryans, the blood-soaked night of June 30, 1934, and the docility with which it was suffered, brought Canaris to the view that Hitler was not likely to change for the better, and that consequently he would have to be fought and destroyed. The counterintelligence was the ideal instrument. In assuming the post, Canaris gained control of a far more lethal tentacle in the Hitlerite Leviathan than that available to the ordinary officer. The resulting question, whether he could serve the regime and yet operate against it, presented itself more sharply to Canaris than to his fellow officers. His biographer writes:

The problem never ceased to trouble Canaris. For seven years, until his fate caught up with him, he tortured himself with constant self-questioning. It robbed him of his peace of mind and inner poise. After a while it became quite impossible for him to sit still. His mounting anxiety and tension forced him to take ever more strenuous and extended business trips, rushing, like King Ahasuerus, from city to city and land to land, but finding peace nowhere. In 1937 he made up his mind to stick it out in office, rejecting the comfortable way out. This was in a way his last chance, because it would have been almost impossible to resign during the war itself, though Canaris' dexterity and adroitness were capable of doing wonders. There were, one supposes, several reasons for his staying at his post. Firstly, Canaris knew that only those in high position could hope to bring down the regime. Secondly, there was no assurance that his successor would be more effective at warding off and harassing the Gestapo than he was; probably less effective. Finally, he felt a deep sense of responsibility for maintaining a protective screen behind which Oster and the younger officers who relied on him engaged in constant and relentless sabotage against the Party and the Gestapo.

In contrast to Beck and the others, whom Hitler called "buoys wailing in the night," Canaris understood how to get along with the Führer, which made him a most useful figure in the resistance. His enormous ability and zest for playing with people in an intricate cat-and-mouse game must have challenged him to try his hand with Hitler. Apparently he was quite good at it. For one thing, he never lost his nerve during the legendary outbursts of maniacal rage which afflicted Hitler periodically. Keitel would turn ashen gray and the rest of the officers would stand in pained silence. The little admiral stood quietly, his icy blue eyes fixed on Hitler until the waves of rage began to subside. Then he would begin to talk, quietly and soothingly, and to the amazement of all would soon conjure up a smile on Hitler's face and the resurgence of good spirits. Abshagen writes:

> Hitler had had a special weakness for the dapper little sailor from the very beginning, and respected his flexible intelligence and wit. Canaris, master of men, knew how to bring the full force of his own very captivating charm to play on Hitler. . . . But as early as 1938 Canaris was complaining that he was not getting to Hitler often enough. "If that infernal Keitel would only let me get at Hitler," he once cried in frustration before his assembled department heads, "I'd be able to handle him." After the outbreak of the war, Canaris pressed less and less for interviews with Hitler, having seen the futility of trying to move a raging megalomaniac with his own brand of sober reality. Besides, with time, he got ever fewer opportunities to see Hitler alone. Keitel was always there.

Much more important than any sort of direct influence was the man's role in countering Hitler's orders. In doing this, he used certain techniques: he would often deal with something so slowly and hesitantly that the order would be pushed aside or buried by some new and dramatic turn of events. In addition to simple procrastination, he actually managed to prevail on Hitler to with-

239

draw orders by using arguments skillfully drawn from Hitler's own brand of thought, and finally he would conceal inactivity behind the most impressive show of hectic and purposeful activity conceivable. He was masterly at turning Hitler's words to the very opposite effect intended. A beautiful example is an occasion on which Hitler flew into a rage about a serious blunder in the Abwehr overseas. Canaris objected that the bunglers were not his agents but over-zealous young National Socialists who had been foisted on the Abwehr against Canaris' wishes. "What!" shrieked Hitler. "You would have done better to have used criminals or Jews." Canaris assented silently, and the audience ended with Hitler still raging. Canaris quietly turned those remarks into an "Order of the Führer" against the wishes of the Gestapo, which suddenly found all sorts of Jews leaving the country as Abwehr agents under the Führer's new order. Canaris saved many lives that way.

When something really went wrong in the Abwehr, or it seemed possible that the enemy had infiltrated its ranks, Canaris acted with a coolness and resourcefulness which sharply differs from that seen in any of the other older men whom we have studied so far. It had been reported to Berlin that Dr. Josef Mueller, General Delegate to the Vatican, had in all probability passed plans of the German offensive to the Dutch and the Belgians. This was quite true. Mueller, acting under orders from General Beck, had been doing just that. The moment Canaris got wind of the danger he coolly ordered the very man suspected to carry out a thorough investigation to determine the origin of the leaks. Mueller brilliantly and convincingly proved that the circle around Ribbentrop had, in fact, also leaked the news to friends of Count Ciano, who in turn had blabbed in several quarters. On another occasion Canaris was on the carpet and Hitler was beside himself with rage at the spectacular escape of General Giraud from the Königstein fortress. Instantly connecting the dates in his mind, Canaris calmly pointed out that there had been an agreement covering the respective areas of competence of the Abwehr and the Gestapo's Sicherheits-Dienst in respect to Giraud on a certain date. As Canaris well knew, Heydrich was unable to deny the allegation because he was already dead.

These were all small incidents in which Canaris countered Hitler in definite but limited ways. What did Canaris do on a large scale? The answer must be that, in keeping with his predilection for indirection and deviousness, he did very little. His great service to the resistance was to support the activists among the conspirators and to use the blanket of the Abwehr to cover them in moments of danger. This was true of his own assistants and co-workers, especially Hans Oster, but it also applied to all whom Canaris knew to be working against the Hitler regime in any capacity. He placed the priceless information network of the Abwehr at the disposal of the resistance, and Oster made extensive use of it to find out what was going on in the Gestapo. He managed to inform both Beck and Keitel, who were stunned, of the exact nature of the accusations which were going to be raised against Fritsch. He cooperated in a similar way with Undersecretary von Weizsäcker, for whom he had a genuine affection, and helped Weizsäcker's closest assistants, the Kordt brothers. He maintained a loose but friendly contact with Schacht, but he mistrusted the great mass of the generals and was very cautious in all his dealings with them.

The fog which he spread over his department and co-workers produced a community of spirit which held to the bitter end. Canaris always intervened to save any of his men from the Gestapo, even when he considered both ends and means of a given undertaking to be wrong. "No member of the Abwehr," writes Abshagen, "could have failed to see after awhile that Canaris was opposed to the regime. Occasionally he ventilated his bitterness openly. The majority knew furthermore that Oster's doings were, at least in terms of the Third Reich, high treason. Nonetheless all the conspirators felt entirely secure at all time that no denunciations ever need be feared from any quarter of the Abwehr. Anyone who lived through the police state under the Third Reich can judge what that means in human terms."

Canaris came nearest to direct action, at least in thought, when his department began to form a so-called "construction and training company," in which paratroops were to be trained. In this, their "own" company, the conspirators saw a golden opportunity to train a private shock force for the day of the Putsch, under cover of official approval. Heydrich watched the growth of the company with increasing suspicion and finally intervened to prevent its realization. Unfortunately, even if Heydrich had not intervened, the conspirators would have had problems enough, since heedless bravery and readiness to die—the qualities they sought in the paratroopers—were almost always coupled with fanatical loyalty to Hitler.

Canaris was, oddly enough, furthest from action in the fateful summer of 1944, when the plot nearly worked. He was not easy in his mind about the assassination. On the one hand, he saw the inevitability of defeat and knew that Hitler had to be destroyed if anything were to be salvaged from the ruins of Germany; on the other hand, he was a deeply religious man who simply could not find the inner toughness to accept assassination. Canaris was far from a pure man of reason. There was, deeply embedded in his personality, a mystical streak with strong fatalistic overtones. The wilder Hitler's extravagances became, the greater loomed the proportions of the disaster awaiting Germany, the more Canaris felt that it was somehow right and inevitable that the dark wave should engulf the country. "In Canaris' mind, the German people had loaded themselves with too much guilt," writes his biographer, "to prevent their suffering the scourge of God in the person of Adolf Hitler to the bitter end."

Here we find him in agreement with Moltke, with whom he otherwise had very little in common, but in disagreement with the group around Beck and Goerdeler, and of course Stauffenberg. The split was consciously accepted by all participants. External circumstances had changed to Canaris' disadvantage and his position had become very precarious. Councilor von Dohnanyi had been arrested and Oster had been dismissed, which led to the strong suspicion that the entire Abwehr was

242

"unreliable," and Canaris' dismissal. It was partly their own fault that the entire delicate and sensitive apparatus collapsed like a house of cards, as we shall see shortly. Hassell was prompted to write in his diary, in the middle of October 1943: "The front of the clear-seeing men crumbles. The whole Canaris stable has exposed itself pitiably and has failed to measure up to all that was expected of it. 'If the good be not wily as serpents and without falsehood as the doves' nothing will ever be accomplished."

The criticism was mutual. The "good" surrounding Canaris considered themselves indeed as wily as serpents and missed precisely that wiliness in the careless planning of Stauffenberg and the younger General Staff officers. In addition, Canaris disapproved of the undue emphasis on questions of domestic policy in the conspiracy, especially since the general trend of thinking was running counter to every fiber of his being. The words he spoke to an acquaintance two days after the failure of the bomb plot, in a chance meeting on the street, are typical of the man. "No, my friend." He smiled. "One just can't do things that way. Ring me up at my office in a few days." It is an unhappy comment on those dreadful days that these sarcastic, flippant words were unfortunately not to be his last, a debonair epilogue to the Canaris story. Instead of departing with a flourish, Canaris lived to see all his fears and anxieties about "the muscular chaps" confirmed in the most gruesome way during a long and ghastly imprisonment. Maimed and broken, death finally claimed the pitiful remains of Admiral Canaris in the grim camp of Flossenburg on April 9, 1945.

Major General Hans Oster

(Born August 9, 1888 in Dresden, Saxony; executed in Camp Flossenburg, April 9, 1945)

Canaris was a man who worked behind the scenes, spreading a fog of duplicity and cross-purposes about all his activities. Hans Oster was, by contrast, a man of initiative and direct action, despite the fact that his métier was the secret service. Though younger than his chief, Admiral Canaris, in his respect for tradition and in the uncomplicated clarity of his personality he was in some respects the elder of the two. He hated National Socialism with a hard, white heat. For him there were no reservations, no qualifications, no extenuating circumstances. During the Sudeten crisis he prayed passionately that it might lead to war, a war which would give the Wehrmacht the chance to wrest control from Hitler. Canaris worked equally zealously for peace during the same period. Tension developed between the two men at this and at many other points. Tension between them was unavoidable simply because they were so different. Despite the fact that Canaris disagreed both with Oster's methods and with his ultimate goal, he made sure that Oster advanced from major to colonel to general under his aegis. Their tacit agreement to disagree did credit to both.

Abshagen described Oster in these words:

He was a man of slender stature, elegant to a fault. His entire thinking derived from the period in which he had formed his ideas as a young officer before the First World War. Although he was too much the realist to consider a monarchist Putsch with any seriousness, he remained thoroughly and passionately convinced of the superiority of the monarchist form of government, especially for Germany. Throughout his life he felt himself bound by the oath which he had sworn to the Kaiser, and even though the Kaiser was in exile in Holland, his oath of allegiance remained as a personal tie. From childhood on he had been accustomed to enjoy the pleasures of life, his horses, his elegant circle of friends.

As a result of man-power cuts under the Weimar Government, Oster had been retired from regular service in 1930. In Abshagen's opinion this may have accounted for the fact that Oster never took on the peculiar characteristics of the typical Reichswehr officer and remained the exemplification of the old officer corps of the Imperial Army.

Oster's active nature, his "quick, almost light-headed delight in making decisions," early led him into close association with the adroit Gisevius, the equally quick-thinking police official. Both were determined to fight the regime, especially the power of Himmler, Heydrich and Göring. Both had a gift for uncovering state secrets and party plans and were masters of camouflaged maneuver. Both had wide circles of acquaintances and were constantly trying to move influential men like Schacht, Brauchitsch and Greutner, to take action. Oster never thought of himself as anything more important than a handyman, and he was willing to place the elaborate secret news service which he perfected at the disposal of anyone resolute enough to use it. He left military planning to Beck and political strategy to Goerdeler, concentrating on uncovering the secret intentions of the Gestapo and the party. Oster cared not at all that he was condemned to live his life in the dangerous jungle of intrigue which was the Abwehr. "He began each day cheerfully," wrote Gisevius. "No annoyance or frustration could disturb him, and no disappointment depress him. He stood firmly on his own two feet, drawing on his faith in God and personal good cheer."

Oster was the technician of resistance, the master of its tools and potentialities. Had there been a Putsch between the years 1939 and 1942, Oster's plans would have been the operational basis for it. They differed in one important respect from those of Henning von Tresckow and Stauffenberg—those that were put into effect on July 20, 1944—in that in Oster's plan Hitler was not to be killed, but seized and declared insane. The plan aimed at breaking the spell which Hitler had cast over the German people by showing up either the mendacity of his peace proclamations or the disastrous nature of his war policy. As a consequence, these plans, contrary to those relying on Hitler's death, could be put into effect only after a political situation had arisen in which even the gullible part of the German public became aware of Hitler's true role. Unfortunately these political events never occurred in the manner Oster and his friends had predicted. They ran roughly as follows: The Berlin Guard Regiment, later to play such an unhappy role in the course of events on July 20, was to be immobilized during the time needed for

245

the coup. Simultaneously all news services and communication nerve centers were to be seized. Hitler was to be taken prisoner in the Chancellery by a group of determined young officers.

The reader will recall Canaris' remark to his friend. "One just can't do things that way." The admiral's biographer takes the view that the blunders and unnecessary messes of July 20th would never have taken place had the technical side of the insurrection still been in Oster's hands. Canaris' biographer and the other subsequent critics tend, I think, to overlook how radically the situation had altered between 1942 and 1944. It grew increasingly difficult to get anywhere near Hitler's person. He had withdrawn to the East Prussian woods, and there, secured by triple electrified fences, lurked in what was only too aptly called the Wolf's Lair. Secondly, unlike the younger men, Oster and his immediate assistant, von Dohnanyi, committed a series of careless mistakes which eventually led to their own arrests and to conflicts within the resistance itself. Halder refused to receive any communications from Oster after a certain point, because he considered him just too rash and careless. Canaris was once so dismayed by one of Oster's indiscretions that he temporarily relieved him of all duties. An example of Oster's thoughtlessness occurred on a front inspection trip, during which he left an appeal which Beck had written—for the day of a successful coup—lying on a table in the headquarters of an Army group. The most serious crisis in the relationship between Canaris and Oster took place in 1940, when several Abwehr officers deduced from reports from tapped phones that Oster must have been the man who had leaked the news of the imminent German attack on the Low Countries to the Dutch military attaché. Pieckenbrock and Bürkner, who first uncovered the connection, remained silent in order not to damage their colleague's honor and the prestige of the department. Things got hot, however, when a zealous young officer in the *Abteilung* III of the Abwehr overheard a cocktail-party conversation which pointed directly to Oster as the man responsible for the leaks. The young man promptly reported his suspicion to his superiors, who passed it on to Canaris. The admiral saw at once that this could be serious trouble for Oster. Although he was furious and disapproved bitterly of what Oster was up to, he covered up for him and saved his life.

The files which Dohnanyi foolishly collected have already been mentioned. In addition to minute and painstaking records of every detail and name in the conspiracy, the files contained virtually complete documentation of all of Hitler's atrocities, which had been assembled at the orders of General Beck. Abshagen writes of the discovery by the Gestapo of the whole collection: "It is quite inconceivable to the outsider that Oster and Dohnanyi allowed themselves to be caught in this simple-minded way. They must have been aware for quite some time that the S.D. were on to them. Indeed, shortly after the Munich arrests, Arthur Nebe, Criminal Police Chief of the Reich, had warned them that there was real danger awaiting them. Once again, a day or two before Dohnanyi's arrest, Canaris warned Oster personally that he had got wind of something, the exact nature of which he had not yet uncovered, and begged Oster in God's name not to get caught with anything incriminating in his office." The worst part of all was that Oster lost his nerve for a split second in the presence of the Gestapo men, who were going through his files. Among the folders was one containing an application for the release from military service of Pastor Dieter Bonhoeffer, which had been initialed with the letter "O," General Beck's code symbol. Seeing the folder, Oster moved his hand to try to slide it aside and was caught doing so, which the Gestapo, of course, immediately interpreted to mean that "O" stood for Oster. He was arrested on the spot and forced to quit the Abwehr.

Until the day of his arrest, Oster's great trump card had been his close and easy contact with the central offices of the Gestapo and his cooperation with Arthur Nebe and Count Helldorf, the Berlin police chief. There were other contacts, never disclosed, with high officers in the S.S. and with the Reich Chancellery

247

itself. The atmosphere in Oster's office must have been remarkable. Zeller wrote of it:

One grew used to seeing the most extraordinary figures in a wild variety of dress and appearance, pushing through the beehive of activity. Anyone working in that uncanny hum had to have many faces or one quite impenetrable one. His right hand never dared know what his left was up to. His element was a game, the stakes were life and death, his more than engrossing daily task to catch without being caught. Oster, teetering often on the very edge of the abyss, worked for years in that surrealist atmosphere until an unguarded movement of his hand, as he tried to shove a paper aside, betrayed him. Anyone who ever saw Oster at work in his office trembled at the artistry involved in such a complicated game, especially if he knew that Oster was working for both sides at once. Oster had four secret telephone lines. It was a terrifying experience to watch him speaking to four unseen agents, giving different instructions, without batting an eyelid. All this took place in an atmosphere where treason and high treason were no longer distinguishable.

It was a fact that among the nationalist group Oster was closest to treason most often and not only as interpreted by the People's Court. He warned the Dutch regularly from November 1939 of every new development in the plans for the German invasion, and finally of May 9, 1940. The Scandinavian capitals received the same expert information about the attacks planned on Norway and Denmark. Gerhard Ritter has gone into great detail in his analysis of Oster's motives and his relationship to the question of treason. It is, I think, in our context, worth referring to Ritter at some length. According to him, there could be no question of mere "military espionage" or "misleading the enemy," as a few well-meaning defenders of Oster have asserted. What earthly use would such a game have been? A variety of motives might have moved Oster to act as he did, but about one thing his closest friends have never had any doubt. Oster was entirely conscious of what he was doing, and was moved by hate more than by anything else—a profound elemental hate for everything that Nazism stood for, born out of the genuine moral indignation which moved him. His straightforward, chivalrous

248

military spirit was aroused by the blatant criminality of an invasion of harmless, peaceful neighbors who had nothing whatever to do with the war. In Oster's view there was not a scrap of justification, not even the argument of military necessity used in 1914, to defend the invasions. The simple dictates of morality required a gentleman soldier to come to the aid of beleaguered victims of Nazi aggression and to separate himself and his friends from the bloody tyrant. All barriers of formal legality appeared to him quite irrelevant in the light of this overpowering moral call. He was entirely prepared in his spirit to become a criminal in the eyes of official Germany, and death in such a cause held no terrors for him. The question, however, remains for us and for posterity, whether the means Oster used to fight these crimes were themselves entirely justified. Treason, as emphasized in the Remer trial in Brunswick, implies evil intention to harm one's country. It is superfluous to say that Oster had no wish to harm Germany. Is it not true to argue that he harmed the German Army by exposing it to dangers of his own creation? Was not his first duty to his fellow soldiers and citizens one which took precedence over any duty to foreigners? Such, with the exception of the Communist groups, was the unanimous opinion of the active members of the resistance. Indeed, when the great majority of the members learned of the lengths to which Oster had actually gone, there were many who condemned him in the severest terms. Yet Oster's treason cannot be equated to that of the "Rote Kapelle" without some qualification. Oster was not striving to defeat Germany and to turn it over to a foreign rule, but merely to wreck an unjust offensive mounted by evil men against neutral and peaceful countries. So argues Ritter, and Oster himself would doubtless have agreed that his conclusions were entirely right.

23. THE "ROTE KAPELLE"

THE distinction which Ritter draws between morally permissible and impermissible treason is far too simple. The difficulty of drawing such distinctions leads us to a discussion of the "Rote Kapelle," a theme surrounded by deep darkness and confusion. The impenetrable camouflage covering the group was partly its own intention and partly the work of the Gestapo, which we have to thank, among other things, for the term "Rote Kapelle" itself, which the Gestapo coined to describe the miscellaneous persons rounded up and tried in the monster clean-up of the winter of 1942–43. Propagandist distortions of Eastern and Western origin have added their contribution to the difficulty of sorting out the various people included under a "blanket" designation. It is important to try to penetrate to the realities, since not all the participants were by any means Communists and not all belonged to the same cells within the larger movement. The Gestapo found it convenient to throw them all into one pot and condemn them wholesale as "Red conspirators." The verdict of the Reich court-martial states that "Oberregierungsrat von Harnack and Oberleutnant Schulze-Boysen had contrived to collect a group of persons in Berlin drawn from all social classes, who made no secret of their inimical attitude toward the state. These persons were in part former members of the prohibited K.P.D. (Communist Party of Germany). Others inclined to their own versions of Socialism. All had the same negative attitude toward National Socialism."

Karl O. Paetel, who calls himself a Conservative Socialist and who barely escaped the concentration camps by emigrating in the mid-thirties, knew Schulze-Boysen well in the days before the latter was converted to Communism. He writes that "even if it is true that the group later began to cooperate with the Russians

250

in espionage, the essential character of the group, that of a resistance movement to which Socialists and Conservatives, Right and Left, belonged, is in no way altered." Günter Weisenborn, the playwright and novelist, has described in detail the nature of the group and its activities, which as a member he knew well. One must, however, take his testimony with a grain of salt, especially where he calls persons "anti-Fascists" whom we, in contemporary terms, would call Communists. One must further assume that the "good contacts" to Polish, Belgian and French workers, which Weisenborn describes, were through Communist agents. He argues and can cite the Gestapo as evidence that there were two distinct groups: a "domestic or inner circle," which the Gestapo called the high treason group (*Hochverrat*); and an "external circle" (*Landesverrat*), which the Gestapo accused of betrayal of Germany to a foreign power. This "outer circle" broadcast news to Soviet agents from a small boat on the Wannsee from the time of the German surprise attack on Russia to its apprehension in 1942. Several parachutists were dropped into Germany with instructions and addresses, some of whom fell into Gestapo hands. Through the capture of the parachutists and through the alertness of an Army radar station, the whereabouts of the secret sender were uncovered and the group taken into custody. The "domestic" or "inner" group apparently knew nothing of the activities of the outer group. Schulze-Boysen, it would appear, was the only liaison between both.

Prison Chaplain Dr. Harold Poelchau, whom we have already met as the ministrant to so many victims of the Nazi reprisals, confirms the fact that from his vantage several distinct groups within groups were visible among the members of the "Rote Kapelle." "I never had the impression of one united and determined clique. They seemed to prove the rule which Jacob Burckhardt formulated in his chapter on the outbreak of world historical crises: 'A crisis breaking out for one reason will often be affected by other doctrines as well. As to which of the doctrines will ultimately win the day, none of the members has the slightest idea.' Only, if the action had succeeded, would an unambiguous political direction have revealed itself." Poelchau names Legation Secretary Rudolf von Schelila, an emphatically bourgeois, prematurely old and resigned man, as one of those executed under the banner of the "Rote Kapelle." He certainly did not share the political persuasions of von Harnack and Schulze-Boysen. Another was Lieutenant Colonel Erwin Gehrts of the Air Ministry, who had once belonged to the editorial staff of that arch-Conservative paper, *Die Kreuzzeitung.* He shared with Professor Otto Hoetzsch, Ambassador Nadolny and Arthur Just, the journalist, the conviction that an agreement with Russia, no matter how distasteful it might be, was the only solution to Germany's problems. For such Germans, Hitler's attack on the Soviet Union was the beginning of the end.

There is some evidence that members of the group maintained contact with the West as well. Louis Lochner, who until the attack on Pearl Harbor in 1941 had been chief of the Berlin office of the Associated Press, wrote in his memoirs that he had received the codes of two different resistance groups secretly before his departure from Germany. He was to have set up a liaison between the Washington Administration and the German underground. Nothing more was ever heard of this, because Lochner never managed to get to Roosevelt with his plans. If one puts two and two together, one arrives at the following conclusion. It is reasonable to assume that Lochner came into contact regularly—at the meetings of the German-American Chamber of Commerce, of which he was president—with Arvid von Harnack, who had the American desk at the Ministry of Economics and whose wife, Mildred Fish Harnack, was one of the most prominent American women in Berlin society. She had helped Martha Dodd organize those now legendary tea parties which were such social events in Berlin in the 1930's. The assumption that one of the codes which Lochner bore concealed on his person upon his return to the United States originated from the "Rote Kapelle" is far from fantastic, and would, if it could be proved, help to demonstrate that the "Rote Kapelle" was not entirely dominated by Soviet spies and agents.

The main activity of the group around Harnack and Schulze-Boysen related to the struggle on the domestic front against the National Socialist regime. Most of them, according to Poelchau, were thinking in terms of a mass popular uprising, instead of a Putsch, for which their work was to prepare the ground. Their aim was to win over the young, who were the least able to oppose Hitler's influence, the artists, scientists, soldiers and police, which groups seemed likeliest to oppose National Socialism by virtue of traditions long honored in their respective callings. How far their efforts met with success can be seen in one of Weisenborn's statistics: Of those executed as members of the "Rote Kapelle," 20 percent were soldiers, civil servants and government employees; 21 percent were artists, journalists and writers; 29 percent were academics and students of all sorts.

The illegal pamphlets which the group distributed contained articles of enlightened liberal and Communist nature: "The Development of the Nazi Movement," "What is the Meaning of the Majority Vote?" "Why War Was Inevitable," "The Life of Napoleon," "Freedom and Force," "An Appeal to the Workers of Hand and Brain Not to Fight Against Russia." Those are a few of the titles. Speeches of Roosevelt, Churchill, Stalin, Thomas Mann, Ernst Wiechert and Bishop Wurm, were also printed and distributed. One can see that many of these things were also passing from hand to hand in the bourgeois resistance group. Of course in those days the political fronts were not yet aligned as we see them today in terms of the Cold War.

The most active and passionate spirit in the "Rote Kapelle" was Harro Schulze-Boysen, a grand-nephew of Admiral von Tirpitz, and a nephew of Frau von Hassell. He was married to a granddaughter of the Princess Eulenberg, and destined by birth and ability to have a grand career in the Air Ministry. The traditions, social prestige and wide circle of acquaintanceship of his family, were the ideal covers for his secret work. He was only twenty-four when he was first arrested as a student in Kiel in 1933 and badly mishandled. It was this experience, an interesting parallel here to the similar one of another young Kiel student,

253

Klaus Fuchs, which turned the young aristocrat into a Socialist. Up to that point he had been in search of a political faith, but having found it, he never wavered again until his death. In the Air Ministry he had charge of the counterintelligence section, and like Oster gained a deep and frightening insight into the internal affairs of the Nazi party organization. He must have exercised a fascinating influence on those around him, with his bubbling enthusiasm, his Rilke and George quotes, his witty impatience and intolerance of the petty bureaucrats, patterned thinking and party officiousness. It was certainly his personal charm which enabled him to collect a group of forty or fifty deeply devoted young men during the 1930's, which he intended to build into the cadre of an armed resistance group.

In him the officer's tradition and revolutionary zeal fused. His farewell letter to his parents differs sharply from those of the men of the Kreisau Circle of the same age. For them, ideas, politics and society were important, but in the last hours the world of men receded, giving place to the great confrontation of the individual soul with God. Schulze-Boysen wrote: "This death suits me. As Rilke once said, it is my own death." But Poelchau thinks that, despite his external composure, deep in his spirit there was great bitterness about his fate. "Today there are so many vitally important things that one life extinguished matters very little. If you were here, invisibly present, you would find me laughing in the face of Death. For I conquered him long ago. In Europe, it is an iron law that intellectual seeds must be fertilized with human blood." During his imprisonment, Schulze-Boysen was martyred with thumbscrews, presses on his calves and ultraviolet rays.

It was the union of the impetuous clique around Schulze-Boysen with the more settled group of Arvid von Harnack which brought a new force into being—a force which the regime justifiably regarded as a serious threat. Arvid von Harnack was a striking contrast to the impulsive, highly strung young air-force officer. He was all that the sober, esteemed civil servant ought to be—measured, grave, prudent and not a little mistrusting.

Harnack has been accused of receiving money from the Russians, which seems most unlikely. He died penniless. His cousin Axel von Harnack, in an article in the *Gegenwart,* pointed out that the most excruciating Gestapo tortures could wring from Harnack only an admission that he had sought to make contact with the Russians by means of Swedish intermediaries. In other words, he tried to do with the Russians exactly what Dieter Bonhoeffer tried to do with the English. In those days the world had not yet been taught to differentiate so nicely between such contacts.

Arvid von Harnack, scion of the famous Harnack family of distinguished professors, was born in 1901. He received the decisive intellectual impulses of his life during a two-and-a-half-year residence in the United States, where he wrote a very good study on the pre-Marxist working-class movement in North America. He lived through Black Friday in 1929, and the subsequent depression in the United States, and he and his American wife were soon deeply engaged in systematic studies of that crisis of capitalism. They investigated the precepts of the planned economy of the Soviet Union. In 1932, Harnack took a long trip to Russia and began to work on a book about the U.S.S.R. When, after 1933, such plans became impossible of fulfillment in Germany, he could easily have migrated to America, where he would certainly have found a welcome, but he refused to do so, feeling that his place was at home.

His cousin describes him as a sharp-thinking, thoughtful person, practiced in debate, and not at all averse to using his flashing wit to demolish lesser adversaries. He was not without ambition or self-esteem. I had a chat with him during the summer of 1940 in the Ministry of Economics, when he recommended a series of articles on America by Giselher Wirsing. This seemed to me at the time to suggest that his ideas about free and planned economies were by no means orthodox Marxist ones, and the works which he completed during his long imprisonment tend to confirm that view. In his theory of the planned economy, the existence of a national "body," that is, the composite of historical and political factors which together define the identity of any

255

nation, is considered just as important as the economic laws. Harnack's debt to Friedrich List was fully as great as his debt to Marx.

He took Plato's *Apologia* with him to the death cell. During his last night he asked Poelchau to read him the Christmas story and the famous orphic poem of Goethe, *Die Sonne tönt in alter Weiser*. In his farewell letter to his family, he cites attachment to nature, love of his dear family and friends, and the faith in human progress as the roots of his inner strength. His wife Mildred was executed at the personal command of the Führer himself, a rather singular "honor." I knew her moderately well. With her fine blond hair, sternly brushed back at the temples, her clear, direct blue eyes with their level gaze, she embodied for me the very prototype of the American Puritan. She lived up to the motto "high thinking and plain living," a woman with a vocation, who believed both in progress and in human improvement. She was dedicated to reform and to action. She was ambitious not for herself but for her ideas. When Mildred Fish had been at the university, the Left was generally accepted as the bearer of enlightened progress. Intellectuals were Pink, if not Red, though in those days this was not necessarily equivalent to membership in the Communist Party. Mildred Fish Harnack may have been a member of the party or she may not, but she would certainly not have been a pure Stalinist. It would not have been her way.

The group around Schulze-Boysen united aristocratic, Conservative and Socialist elements with a sort of ebullient abandon. Harnack led the other group, which was mainly middle class and influenced fully as much by the Anglo-Saxon as by the Russian world of thought. The psychiatrist, Dr. John Rittmeister, who undoubtedly must have belonged to the Harnack wing (though these things have become hopelessly difficult to sort out), was concerned with the preservation of the old natural ingredients in European civilization through a Socialist rejuvenation of Germany. Werner Kraus probably belonged to the Harnack wing too. Kraus later became co-editor of one of the first postwar

256

literary magazines, *Die Wandlung,* in Heidelburg, which he ran jointly with Dolf Sternberger, under American auspices. Later Kraus was to take a professorship in Leipzig.

There were of course several undoubted Communists in the group, the toolmaker Walter Huseman, for example, the son of an old trade unionist from Berlin North, who wrote to his father in a farewell letter: "I die, as I have lived, a class fighter." He pleaded with his father: "Whatever happens, stay hard, hard, hard." Not all were indomitable or fierce men from the working classes. The sculptor Kurt Schumacher believed that "only the international Socialists can create a healthy Europe." He placed himself in the tradition of the heroes of the Peasants' War in the sixteenth century. A special figure among the Communists was the poet Adam Kuckhoff. Just before he was led away to his death, he wrote a tiny poem for his son:

> *Mein lieber Sohn, Du Grosses spätes Gülck,*
> *So lasse ich Dich vaterlos zurück?*
> *Ein ganzes Volk—nein das ist vielzu klein,*
> *Das Menschenvolk wird Dir Dein Vater sein!*

Two babies, born in prison, lived to be both fatherless and motherless a few months later. They remind us of all the young women—Liane Berkowitz, Maria Terwiel, Eva Maria Buch, Erika von Brockdorf, Oda Schott-Müller, Cathe Bontjes van Beek, Hilde Coppi and Ilse Stöbe (just a few)—who, having fought with their men in the "Rote Kapelle," died equally bravely with them. Were they traitors only in the Nazi usage? Or were they traitors in the sense in which we understood the word? The last word has not yet been spoken on this question. Judgments change with the passage of time, and reflect the varying constellations of political and ideological power. The two editions of Fabian von Schlabrendorff's book demonstrate how closely such opinions follow the political changes of the times. Although the editions are separated by only five years, the second edition has been altered to contain a condemnation of the "Rote Kapelle" in

root and branch, accusing the members of having been agents of
the Soviet Union, although it has been convincingly demonstrated
that the "domestic" circle knew nothing of the espionage work
of the "outer" circle.

Different as all these human beings were in origin, personality
and attitude, they shared a common faith in "progress," and an
optimism about the possibility of improving the world and mankind through politics, reason and scientific and economic measures. In that sense, to use an expression of Romano Guardini's,
they belong to the "end of the modern era," whereas the other
group of young men, the Kreisau Circle, gave evidence of a
search for a new picture of man and a new form of social organization. They mark the beginning of the postmodern era.
One way in which the profound difference between the two
groups expressed itself was in the role accorded to women. We
have noted the many young women who were members of the
inner circle of the "Rote Kapelle." There was not a single one in
the Kreisau Circle. It is important to remark this. The members
of the "Rote Kapelle" were the intellectual heirs of the French
Revolution, the bearers of its ideals of progress, democratic
egalitarianism, and of course the concomitant equality of the
sexes. The Kreisau Circle also had, in this connection, a progressive view of the role of women in society. The widows of
Yorck, Moltke, Trott and Haeften prove it in their daily lives.
All are active, some in the professions. However, their attitude
differs substantially from the ideals of the "emancipated" woman.
During their husbands' lives, they took part in what was felt and
thought in the general atmosphere of the opposition.

24. THE KREISAU CIRCLE

THE Gestapo's phrase the "Rote Kapelle" was a lucky hit, and
the term has gone into history as the overall designation of its
members. Its description of the Kreisau Circle as "baroque" is

less fortunate. The "baroque" calls to mind an untrammeled pleasure in life, spacious estates and gardens adorned with marble figures. Although some of the "Counts" in the Kreisau Circle (a few were barons) actually were of the landed aristocracy, there was a strong ascetic aspect to their lives. The group evolved from the workers' and students' summer camp at Löwenberg in Silesia, which was to have served as a model for a chain of regional camps, on the same voluntary work-study basis, to be propagated throughout Germany. Eugen Rosenstock-Huessy, the director, and three younger men, von Einsiedel, von Trotha and von Moltke, were the initiators. This cooperation between an older and younger generation, in sharp contrast to the uniformity in the age of the "youth movement" (later to become the "Hitler-Youth"), was a special feature of the experiment. In contrast to the practical common sense and slightly cynical weariness in the Goerdeler group, the men of Camp Löwenberg, later Kreisau Circle members, had a different spirit, old and at the same time fresh and new. It was, writes Haffner: ". . . an unusual aristocratic sort of Socialism, great names of Prussian history mingling with the best of the working classes. There was, perhaps, an element of inexperience and uncertainty, compensated for, however, by a sense that they were breaking new ground, entering an area of unlimited possibilities."

As time passed, Hitler's regime narrowed the unlimited to very limited possibilities indeed, and as a result, with the outbreak of war, the once loosely joined association was forced to become an even more tightly knit community. Yet the very expression "tightly knit" fails to convey the spirit of the Kreisau Circle. It was its intention to rebuild Europe on new, decentralized principles, beginning with tiny cells, small communities of realistic persons, forming naturally the larger associations from the basic cellular building blocks. A very immediate advantage of its thinking was the fact that, when arrested, members of one cell literally did not know the names of members of other cells. It was quite the most natural operating method to select for a resistance group in a police state, and in fact functioned far more effectively than the elaborate camouflage of the Beck group or the mathematical anonymity of the similar cells in the Communist groups. Each group in the Kreisau Circle was both in theory and practice a separate entity with its own significance, responsibility and area of competence, submitting voluntarily and informally to direction from the leadership. Significant, too, that there were no waves of arrests of members in the Kreisau Circle, as there were from time to time among the Communists, simply because spies could not creep into cells organized in such a way.

Special groups were formed and given "areas"—social, cultural and economic affairs or foreign policy. The special groups met usually in Munich and Berlin. The entire Kreisau Circle met only three times during the war years, at Moltke's castle, Kreisau, near Schweidnitz. Membership in the Kreisau Circle was diverse, East, North, West and South Germans, landowners, soldiers, priests, barristers, workers, students, teachers and diplomats. Many met for the first time as they arrived at the Moltke estate. All knew that the entrances and exits to the property were closely guarded and that no one not personally invited by the host was present. Under his generous protection, people could really talk for the first time in years about anything and everything. Zeller writes:

> They were little concerned about victory or defeat. The main preoccupation was the cause of the decline of humanism and the collapse of civilization which had made Hitler's rise to power possible. At the same time they sought the healing forces which might yet save man. Despite the fact that they were all constantly exposed to the acts of terrorism of the regime, complaint and accusations were tacitly forbidden. They did not regard the passionless violence and cold-blooded destructiveness of the Third Reich as the work of one man and his followers. Rather it was a crucial *"mene tekel"*—a disease which had its roots centuries back, and was now spreading from Germany to her neighbors.

It is clear that for such men politics could comprise only a limited section of a much larger pattern of historical development. Political means alone could not, there, suffice to combat the corrupting evil. As a result, they tended to think less in terms of a *coup d'état* than the other resistance groups. Poelchau, who was himself a member of one of the Kreisau groups, explains that: "We were preoccupied with the probable course of events on Day X, the day on which Hitler's rule would be over. This Day X was not necessarily to be the day of his assassination."

The Kreisau Circle shared the view of the younger officers that Day X would probably be the day of total military defeat. An order for that day, planned by the Kreisau leaders, assumed that German territory would be occupied by foreign troops, doubtless divided into zones, between which communications would be cut. There would, it was assumed, be no government of any sort other than the military administration of the victorious powers. "A compelling necessity of the day will be to ensure that responsible leadership in the various parts of an occupied and divided Germany act in uniformity according to certain previously settled principles, assuming the impossibility of any contact among them. Only in this way can the internal cohesion of the German states as one cultural unit be preserved." With their help, some of the blunders of the de-Nazification program might have been avoided, while at the same time carrying out a thorough purge. "To persecute anyone merely because of membership in the Hitlerite party is impermissible. Those guilty of crimes or misdemeanors are to be tried, wherever possible by German courts. If no such courts exist, international bodies, composed of three judges from the victorious powers, two from neutral states and one from Germany, are to be set up."

The task which the Kreisau Circle set itself during the conflagration of National Socialism had many facets. "The search for a synthesis of Conservative and Socialist values; the intention to make democracy again a reality through decentralization and creation of new political organs no longer remote and impersonal; the drive to return to the Christian Churches a measure of their political and social efficacy; finally, a double-edged reinterpretation of federalism, loosening, on the one hand, central government within Germany, and tightening, on the other, the bonds of

261

European unity." Thus, Haffner sums up the aims of the group. He is convinced that Stauffenberg intended to form a "Kreisau" Government at the first possible opportunity, with Julius Leber as chancellor and Adam von Trott zu Solz as foreign secretary. He goes too far, in my opinion, when he writes: "Such a government was to transform the initial *coup d'état* into a genuine revolution. German and foreign workers were to be united under the old banner 'Workers of the World Unite.' Governmental power was to be surrendered to the resistance groups, and the onrushing armies of the three great powers confronted with a Europe welded together into absolute unity by the blue-white flame of revolution." The facts would appear to contradict Haffner at every point. We know that Stauffenberg rejected the idea of following Gneisenau's example by unleashing a people's war, and that, as an officer, he disagreed with the Churchillian use of partisans in the military campaigns. "The English will live to regret the unleashing of such forces. Fighting power must always remain in responsible authoritative hands. On lower levels of the military hierarchy the only sensible requirement is order and obedience." Admittedly he tried, as Karl Michel writes with passionate sentimentality, to do something to alleviate the misery of the forced laborers by forming volunteer units of Russian prisoners, but most certainly not under the motto "Workers of the World Unite." He acted clearly from purely humanitarian motives while at the same time ensuring that the potential might of the collected workers passed into the control of responsible authority.

It is undeniable that the Kreisau Circle wanted no part of a return to the Weimar Republic. Nor, one supposes, would it have been delighted with Bonn, had it been able to conceive of anything quite as improbable. The only living Kreisau member still active politically, Eugen Gerstenmaier, President of the Bundestag, said, in drawing a comparison between the political climates of 1944 and 1952:

Today, characteristics other than those which made us ready to gamble in 1944 have become important. Today all has become a question of parliamentary routine, forensic ability, appearances in public, influence in parliament or in the local constituency. The Kreisauers had left not only Hitler's dictatorship but Weimar's democracy far behind them. They could not, of course, forsee that the old political parties and formulae would be presented to us again in 1945, nor that the Russians, curiously enough, would be the prime movers in a return to the old ways. They would no doubt maintain a polite and respectful silence about the achievements of German parliamentary practice since 1945, which does, after all, represent a commendable desire to abide by a constitution, but I hardly dare to think what some of my late friends would say to the horse-trading and lively barter which is also a feature of our party political activities.

Heinrich von Trott zu Solz, brother of Adam, comes closest to a compact summary of the intellectual position of the Kreisau Circle. He declared in an article in the *Frankfurter Allgemeine:* "Their tragedy and the negative source of their greatness was that they were left in the lurch by all the doctrines which control the world today and by the groups embodying them. Who dare say that the demonic power, against which they took arms and which finally swallowed them, is no longer around to trouble us, even if its National Socialist incarnation is not as obvious as before?" The doctrines to which von Trott refers are those of the French Revolution, which replaced the Grace of God with the "natural rule of justice and the infallibility of reason and, following from these two premises, with the infallibility of the new sovereign, the Popular Will." After an analysis of the kind of lies used by Hitler, as well as after Hitler, he continues by arguing that:

The old élite is frail and incompetent, its members prisoners of their national conditioning and class origins. The poison has eaten through the walls. Unobserved, a new generation of resistance fighters is growing, emissaries of a world already present but not yet seen as such. They are spreading over the entire globe. The 20th of July was just the overture. A new chivalric class expands slowly and secretly, following its own inward necessity. It will be firmer than the medieval religious orders and tougher to crush than the nineteenth-century bands of Russian nihilists. Certain isolated Frenchmen, Georges Bernanos, Albert Camus, Antoine de Saint-

Exupéry, knew this. So did the English colonel, T. E. Lawrence, and perhaps Ernst Jünger as well.

Each of the Kreisauers worked for this rejuvenation, concentrating each on his own field, and avoiding high-sounding generalities. Schwerin began to redistribute the land of his own ancestral estate among the peasants. Moltke ran Kreisau, not as a great landlord but as a modern manager—an appointed agent, as it were, of all the farm laborers. Julius Leber fought the bureaucracy of his own Social Democratic Party from within. Father Delp fought the bourgeois prejudices of his own church. Count Schulenburg decided to give up his title, and meant it as more than an idle gesture. Count Stauffenberg, in his silent rebellion not only against Hitler but also against the generals, sacrificed first his career and later his life. That is a "socialism" not to be found in any handbook. It asks of each not the same contribution, but his own personal, special, separate one. It does not confiscate, but solicits contributions. It does not level men, but raises them through a sense of solidarity not possible in a class-war atmosphere.

It is hardly surprising that the ideas and demands of the Kreisauers caused discomfort both in Eastern and Western Germany after 1945. Gerhard Ritter speaks of "the romantic features of a half-matured program." He argues that its members were less tied to the traditional Western concept of freedom than were the older men of the Goerdeler group, which conclusion he draws from their willingness to see Germany in the position of intermediary between the Russian and Western worlds, and from their often outspoken attacks on Western forms of government, especially "Western capitalism." Himmler at first considered them quite harmless, pure phantasts, German "Parlor Pinks," but his henchman, Obersturmbannführer Kiesel, saw at once that their opposition was exceedingly serious. During his investigation he recognized how uncompromising the Kreisau members were in their principles, how strictly they rejected all cooperation with men of dubious character or shady pasts, even if such men were absolutely opposed to the Nazi regime. There was no opportunist hedging or personal consideration involved. They refused, for example, to work with Count Helldorf and with respected men like General Thoma, because they felt that their opposition was not directed toward the regime as such, but to its policies, which were leading inexorably to defeat.

HELMUTH JAMES COUNT VON MOLTKE

(Born March 11, 1907, on the family estate, Kreisau, in Silesia; executed in Plötzensee, January 23, 1945)

Count Moltke was essentially less concerned with overthrowing Hitler than with the aftermath. He insisted on a complete separation of the sheep from the goats, which led him into bitter struggles with the older men, especially Goerdeler. Originally he wanted to have nothing to do with the officers either. He found it difficult to see anything constructive coming from such heterogeneous groups. It was his meeting with Count Stauffenberg, who was a cousin of Moltke's close friend, Yorck von Wartenburg, in 1942, which changed his mind. Although the two men were not always in agreement on details, they were kindred spirits and recognized the fact at once. Otherwise he had his fill of officers, working as he did in the foreign affairs department of the High Command of the Wehrmacht, a key position between the diplomats and the Army, which offered him special opportunities for effective action. Moltke used his position with great tact to help endangered people to safety. Poelchau relates that he often went to beg Moltke to intervene in special cases. "How well oriented he was. I was astounded to see how often he knew the story anyway long before I came to him, and had already begun to take steps on his own. It was always important to him to hear the human side of the story from me with a view to assessing the general political atmosphere. Peter Yorck von Wartenburg was usually present at these talks."

In addition to this quiet activity on behalf of individuals (which incidentally in the case of Minister Kiep led directly to Moltke's own arrest), he did what he could to win some respect from the Nazis for the ethics of International Law. Canaris used a memorandum prepared by Moltke for an official protest against the treatment of Russian prisoners. Moltke countered the Nazi argument that Russian prisoners were not entitled to the protection of the Geneva Convention because the Soviet Union had not been a signatory to the agreement by arguing that according to the principle of international law, as accepted since the eighteenth century, that imprisonment of enemy soldiers was neither a legal punishment nor an act of reprisal but purely a security measure.

Nothing could characterize better the man Moltke than his own words in a letter to his wife describing, in laconic but dramatic terms, the course of his trial before the People's Court in Berlin:

And now for the second day. That was where my turn came. We started off quite mildly but very fast, practically break-neck. Thank goodness I'm quick in the uptake and could take Freisler's pace in my stride; which, incidentally, obviously pleased us both. But if he carried on like that with someone not particularly quick-witted, the victim would have been condemned before he so much as noticed that Freisler had passed beyond the preliminary account of his career. Up to and including the conversation with Goerdeler and my position with regard to it, everything went quite smoothly and without much fuss.

At this point I objected that the police and the security authorities had known all about it. This gave Freisler paroxysm No. 1. Everything that Delp had previously experienced was mere child's play by comparison. A hurricane was let loose; he banged on the table, went the color of his robe, and roared out, "I won't stand that; I won't listen to that sort of thing." And so it went on the whole time. As I knew in any case how it would turn out, it all made no odds to me; I looked him icily straight in his eyes, which he obviously didn't care about, and all of a sudden could not keep myself from smiling. This spread to the officials sitting to the right of Freisler, and to Schulze. I wish you would have seen Schulze's expression. If a man were to jump off the bridge over the crocodiles' pond at the Zoo, I don't think the uproar could be greater. Well, anyhow that exhausted the subject.

Next, however, came Kreisau. . . . And who was present? A Jesuit father! Of all people, a Jesuit father! And a Protestant minister, and the three others who were later condemned to death for complicity in the July 20 plot! And not a single National Socialist! No, not one! Well, all I can say is, now the cat is out of the bag! A Jesuit father, and with him, of all people, you discuss the question of civil disobedience! And the Provincial Head of the Jesuits, you know him too! He even came to Kreisau once! A Provincial of the Jesuits, one of the highest officials of Germany's most dangerous enemies, he visits Graf Moltke in Kreisau! And you are not ashamed of it, even though no decent German would touch a Jesuit with a bargepole! People who have been excluded from all military service because of their attitude! If I know there's a Provincial of the Jesuits in a town, it's almost enough to keep me out of that town altogether! And the other reverend gentleman! What was he after there? Such people should confine their attentions to the hereafter, and leave us here in peace! And you went visiting Bishops! Looking for something you'd lost, I suppose! Where do you get your orders from? You get your orders from the Führer, and the National Socialist Party! That goes for you as much as for any other German, and anyone who takes his orders, no matter under what camouflage, from the guardian of the other world, is taking them from the enemy, and will be dealt with accordingly! And so it went on, but in a key which made the earlier paroxysms appear as the gentle rustling of a breeze.

The upshot of the examination "against me"—since it would be absurd to talk of "my examination"—the whole Kreisau meeting and all subsidiary discussions arising therefrom, constituted preparation for high treason. . . .

Taking it all in all, this emphasis on the religious aspect of the case corresponds with the real inwardness of the matter, and shows that Freisler is, after all, a good judge from the political angle. . . . The submissions we all made in our defense, that the police knew, that the whole thing arose out of official business, that Eugen didn't catch on, that Delp was never actually present, these must be brushed aside, as Freisler rightly brushed them aside. So then all that is left is a single idea: how Christianity can prove a sheet-anchor in time of chaos. And just for this idea five heads (and later it may well be Steltzer's, Haubach's and even possibly Husen's as well) look like being forfeited tomorrow. But for various reasons— because the emphasis during the trial lay on the trio Delp, Eugen, Moltke, and the others were only involved through having been "infected," because no member of any other faction was involved, no representative of the working class, no one having the care of any worldly interest—because he made it clear that I was opposed in principle to large estates, that I had no class interests at heart, no personal interest at all, not even those of my wartime job, but stood for the cause of all mankind—for all these reasons

Freisler has unwittingly done us great service, in so far as it may prove possible to spread this story and make full use of it. And, indeed, in my view, this should be done both at home and abroad.

How the letter breathes and bubbles with vitality. It is not hard to imagine the effect such a man must have had on his fellows. A man who in the moment of extreme danger and in the face of certain death disarmed cynicsm with impishness and smiled at the terror. His giant frame, nearly six feet six in height, radiated serene power and a big man's gentleness. While the waves of Freisler's insanity crashed around him, he stood like a fortress of goodwill and good sense. Both Moltke and his close friend, Peter Count Yorck von Wartenburg, counted great generals among their ancestors. An important clue to Moltke's nature, however, is his Anglo-Saxon heritage, which he got from his English mother. He spoke English as a mother tongue and was completely at home in both languages and cultural worlds, which gave him a certain breadth of perspective rare in his social class. He had been called to the Bar in London and felt quite as much at home in Chancery Lane as on the vast hazy expanses of his estate in Silesia.

PETER COUNT YORCK VON WARTENBURG

(Born November 13, 1904, in Klein-Oels, Silesia; executed August 8, 1944)

Yorck was withdrawn, less the world citizen than his cousin Moltke. He was more profoundly German, a slender, handsome man. Theology and philosophy shared equally with the military in his family's tradition. Count Paul Yorck von Wartenburg, a friend of the philosopher Wilhelm Dilthey's, had followed in the steps of Schleiermacher during the era of positivism and natural science in the nineteenth century. The little townhouse of the Yorcks in Berlin had a superb library of history and philosophy, including folio upon folio of the complete works of Martin Luther in fine and very rare editions. Yorck was moved far more by purely German considerations than Moltke, and he found it less easy than his friend to contemplate complete defeat and foreign occupation. As an active officer, he acted as liaison between the Kreisau Circle, the soldiers and the Socialists, and after Moltke's arrest assumed the leadership of all the Kreisau groups. At the beginning, Yorck assented to the policy of waiting to let National Socialism consume itself, but after Moltke's arrest he switched to Stauffenberg's view and took an active part in the events in the Bendlerstrasse on the 20th of July. He must have been impressed by Stauffenberg's almost superstitious determination to get Julius Leber, whom he needed desperately, out of jail, and he was undoubtedly as concerned about Moltke's safety. He came to realize, with great clarity and with mounting despair, that allowing National Socialism to burn itself out meant in effect offering helpless millions and most of Europe to the flames. He was one of the first of the conspirators to be executed.

ADAM VON TROTT ZU SOLZ

(Born August 9, 1909, in Potsdam; executed in Plötzensee, August 26, 1944)

Adam von Trott zu Solz resembled Moltke in many ways, especially in his ability to see things in terms of the world outside Germany. He, too, had English blood in his veins, from his mother's side of the family, and like Moltke, had lived and studied among the English as a Rhodes scholar. German ties pulled him more strongly than Moltke—love of his wooded Hessian homeland and a profound will to work for Germany. His Oxford friends felt that, though he lived their life to the fullest and partook of their existence in every way, he remained evidently and intentionally German. They marveled at the ease with which he glided across class barriers, making warm and genuine contact with people of every social group. The lanky young man left an indelible mark on his English contemporaries. David Astor, now editor of *The Observer,* wrote of him in a letter to his widow: "Adam was my teacher, a kind of elder brother and a deeply loved friend. He was the greatest man of my generation. I have never met anyone like him anywhere."

After the completion of his two years at Oxford, he returned to Germany to begin reading for the Bar. Hitler had been in power just six months, and from the start, the twenty-four-year-old Trott found himself forced to fight a political phenomenon which filled him with great disgust. In his dissertations he combined his love of philosophy with the law, writing on "Hegel's Theory of the State and International Law." In 1936, he began a lengthy period of study overseas, lived for six months in the United States, and for fourteen months in China. By the time he returned to Germany it had become clear that Munich and "Peace in our time" were merely steps along the road to war. Trott had been deeply affected both by his stay in the United States, with its high-pressure living, and by the Eastern wisdom and serenity he found in China, and he returned, nearly thirty years old, matured and ready to act. His goal was twofold: to find his way to a high post in the state which he hated, in order to help destroy it and to stop the outbreak of war. He was in London three times during 1939, and tried vainly, in conversations with Chamberlain, Lord Lothian, Lord Halifax and others, to get England to take a strong, threatening stand—which the opposition in Germany hoped would avoid the error of 1914 when it had been assumed that England would not intervene— and possibly thereby restrain Hitler.

With the tacit approval of the Foreign Office, Trott then set out on a trip to the United States in October 1939, via Gibraltar. Officially, he had been designated German observer at the general assembly of the Institute of Pacific Relations. In New York, his uncle, Schieffelin, gave him an opportunity to speak to a large gathering of prominent personalities, and in his speech Trott described the danger to the world from Germany and National Socialism, outlining at the same time the existence of a deep-rooted opposition. Although he had not received an assignment from the Beck group, his famous memorandum to Roosevelt was certainly in its vein. It was an improvisation. While in New

York, Trott visited Paul Scheffer, whom he had first known in Berlin. During their second meeting Scheffer showed Trott a memorandum which he had worked out, demanding that the German resistance be given freedom to act. Such freedom had, of course, been entirely eliminated by the outbreak of the war. At the same time it demanded from the Allied governments a guarantee that they would not use Germany's powerlessness to exploit Germany if the resistance movement should be successful in its attempt to overthrow Hitler's Government. A further demand was an Allied guarantee that the conditions of Versailles would not be reimposed in the chaotic aftermath of a successful coup. The willingness of the German resistance to act was underlined, but the practical and constitutional obstacles were honestly presented as well. Nothing save strong, possibly bloody, action would suffice. There was some discussion of the various techniques which might be employed, and Vatican intercession was considered. Trott agreed with all but minor points of the memorandum, and the two men decided that tactically it would look better if the memo were to be regarded as an initiative of Trott's rather than Scheffer's. Trott took upon himself the task of justifying ex post facto the agreements entered upon as a result of the memo to the group in Berlin, since if accepted by one or all of the Allied governments, it would bind the resistance without their knowledge. Here Trott displayed a typical readiness to act decisively and to take the consequences of his actions.

The document, slightly rewritten, was presented in Washington to George Strausser Messersmith, of the American State Department, who knew Trott from his days in Berlin. Messersmith responded at once and told Trott two days later that high persons in the administration had shown a "lively interest" in its contents and proposals. Trott was then given a list of people whom he was advised to visit. Several of them, however, were less enthusiastic than the men in the State Department. Felix Frankfurter, in those days a professor at the Harvard Law School and an influential adviser of Roosevelt, disapproved strongly. Roosevelt himself, who had at first given tentative approval to the idea, swung around to Frankfurter's position and finally rejected the memorandum entirely. Roosevelt came more and more to take the view that Germany had to be punished and made harmless. Profoundly disillusioned, Trott traveled home in May of 1940, by way of California and Japan. Upon his return he joined the Foreign Office, where he soon acquired an influence and prestige which reached far beyond his relatively minor post in the cultural-affairs section.

During the war Trott and I had had parallel experiences which remained quite incomprehensible to those Germans who had known England and America only during periods of profound peace. In both of those countries, during the war, every German who had not fled or was not in a concentration camp was automatically regarded as a Nazi, without respect to his background, character or convictions. Few opponents of the regime who were not aware of this change in the ideological atmosphere of the Western democracies were able to see in advance what sort of war and what sort of peace were likely to result from this kind of thinking. Trott saw these dangers long before the doctrine of unconditional surrender was first promulgated. The anxieties on this point, which he was alone in feeling, deepened his love for Germany and strengthened his resolve to return home to do what he could. While in New York, he had often been forced to defend his decision to go back after all, being, as he was, a "good" German. He argued forcefully that there were already enough émigrés who might some day serve Germany usefully from their vantage, but that in Germany itself the need for men willing to fight the regime was far greater. Besides, he felt certain that if Germany were ever to return to its place within the community of civilized nations, the leadership would have to be drawn from men who had stayed in Germany during the terror, the war and the humiliation and misery of the inevitable defeat which Hitler would bring on the nation. When his friends objected that he would surely fall prey to the Gestapo, Trott replied calmly that the risk was present but had to be taken. After his return and entrance into the Foreign Office, several of his closest English friends broke off all relations with him. Trott answered:

I have a growing suspicion that a number of my friends identify the evils of Europe with Germany as such and base their continued relationship to me only on the degree to which I happen to fit into their English life. I consider that verdict as profoundly untrue and unjust, and I do not wish to compromise with this kind of acceptance, which I consider both sterile and irresponsible. Yet I see the reason for it happening clearly enough, and we have all been hard pressed to think about it, I imagine. It is the very dilemma which I thought human friendship ought to be able to deal with constructively. . . .

But if psychological warfare was able to smash even personal friendships and render clear thought impossible—even in relation to indubitable facts—how could one hope to establish that necessary modicum of mutual trust and respect which might prevent the futile generation of ever-more-desperate ideological wars? This was a question which Trott often talked over with me. To other members of the opposition who still believed in the ethical stand of the Western democracies, it had not presented itself. Trott felt as I did, that in view of the various public pronouncements of Churchill and Roosevelt and especially after the official adoption of unconditional surrender in 1943, the chance that any distinction would be made between German and German, even after a revolutionary change of government, was as good as nil. He never stopped hoping emotionally that he might be wrong about that. As late as May 1944, when I came to see him, I found him poring over the London *Times* of May 24, 1944, in which Churchill's great speech on the principles of the Atlantic Charter and the meaning of unconditional surrender appeared. As he admitted when I pressed him, he had been trying to read between the lines that there was at least some willingness to distinguish between Nazis and good Germans. What a blessing that Trott never lived to learn of Churchill's comments after the failure of the bomb plot on the 20th of July, or to see the way in which both the English and the Americans threw the opposition into the same pot with the "Vansittart" Germans.

His great disappointment with those from whom he had expected to get understanding and sympathy may have led to his puzzling and much-debated attitude toward the Soviet Union.

He once remarked to Allen Dulles: "If you and yours won't help, well, we'll just have to try our luck with the other side." It was certainly not pique, but his vivid awareness of Germany's geographical and cultural middle position, which moved him to think in terms of the avenues of approach to Russia. He considered himself a specialist in Western affairs. I recall once having a long talk with him during which he expatiated on the necessity, the possibilities and the techniques at hand, for arriving at a *modus vivendi* with the West. When I objected that we would surely have to negotiate with both sides at once, he agreed, but remarked with a laugh: "I'm afraid you'll have to talk to my brother on that. His area is the East." This is not to say that Trott intended any sort of artificial division of labor. I knew few men in Germany who thought so completely in global terms or who had such an active interest in Asia as Adam von Trott. It seems to me that he was merely doing his utmost to prepare for the vital confrontation, which he expected would follow upon the defeat of Hitler, with those countries which he knew so well and to which he was bound by ties of friendship and even blood. Trott preferred Count Schulenburg to von Hassell as prospective foreign minister of a post-Hitler Government, because he recognized that Schulenburg's great experience in the Soviet Union, and greater ability to think unemotionally about Communism, would be vital in postwar Germany. At Stauffenberg's request, Trott prepared a foreign-policy memorandum called "Germany Between East and West," which has been lost. This is especially unfortunate, since it was first joint effort to stem from the intense friendship which grew between the two men after Julius Leber had brought them together.

The quotations cited earlier about the discussions between the older and younger men reveal Trott as the most passionate and eloquent of the Kreisau Circle. I have met few human beings so widely cultured and well read and so intensely interested in life around them. There were no "Iron Curtains" in his thoughts. Hölderlin and Karl Marx had rested peacefully next to one another on his student desk. The following is an example of his ability to see things without prejudice. The director of the cultural affairs department, Dr. F. A. Six, had the reputation of being a great Nazi, which finished him as far as many people, including myself, were concerned. Trott knew he was a Nazi, but also saw his other side, his high intelligence, his energy, his managerial abilities. "You ought to meet him," Trott remarked to me once.

My first meeting with Trott took place at the home of a mutual friend, also a former Rhodes scholar, later executed by the Nazis. I began the discussion by complaining about the fact that we on the *Frankfurter Zeitung* only wrote for the older men. Our "letters to the editor" came mainly from company directors, undersecretaries, gentlemen writing from select men's clubs and judges' offices, almost never from young people. Trott joined in enthusiastically, and a vivid and stimulating conversation began on the reasons for the loss of appeal of the old liberal humanistic language for the young, and on the features which a new language to appeal to the young might require. At that time Trott had just read Ernst Jünger's latest book, *Gardens and Streets,* and felt that this was a prime example of what we were looking for. This was only one interest of his many-sided nature. He had strong romantic leanings, balanced by his radiant calm and inner lightheartedness. His subtle instinct for the "feel" of his times led him, for example, to make the astonishing suggestion that Pastor Martin Niemöller be head of the state to be formed after a successful Putsch. Niemöller's genius for saying the right thing at the wrong time was not quite apparent then, as it is today, nor could anyone have suspected the amount of sheer annoyance and irritation which the famous theologian can arouse in others. At that time he was in a concentration camp, where the possibilities of public expression were limited. Perhaps in a "Kreisau" Germany, Niemöller might have found less to get annoyed about and have been less the general irritant which he has become in the Bonn-Adenauer Germany. The idea, which may appear absurd to some, still strikes me as a shrewd one and reveals to me the fine touch which Trott had in such things.

275

In the letter which he wrote before his execution he speaks of his sorrow that he "will now not be able to put the accumulated knowledge and techniques gained from an almost too strict concentration on foreign affairs to Germany's use." This tends to support the general view of Trott as the man of foreign affairs without anything to say on domestic matters. I can only recall a conversation with him which lasted more than two hours during which he outlined his vision of a Germany freed of Hitler. It is clear that he took an active part in the domestic-policy debates of the Kreisau group and doubtless contributed materially to them. He saw, perhaps a bit more clearly than others, that the nature of a new European Germany would be determined, much more than was generally realized, by alien powers. This is the key to two other sentences in his last letter: "It was all an attempt rising from the essence and strength of our country, a deep love for which I owe to my father, to preserve the unchanging right and its profound consequences against the attack of foreign powers and alien beliefs. Therefore I was always driven to return from abroad, to abandon the temptation of the life of an expatriate, and to undertake the duties to which I felt a call."

FATHER ALFRED DELP, S.J.

(Born September 15, 1907, in Mannheim, Baden; executed in Berlin, February 2, 1945)

Father Alfred Delp belonged, together with Trott, to the activist wing among the Kreisauers, and again like Trott, moved ever closer to Stauffenberg in the last years of his life. Although a priest, he was ready to accept the coup and the assassination of Hitler as the only right way. He saw Germany inescapably pinioned between East and West, as did Trott. "From both sides alien and implacable forces intervene in our lives—Russia and America." Delp was not just a priest. He thought politically, without confessional or theological coloring. "What must be done? Three possibilities are open: Proclaim the divine order and expect everything from its recognition; bring men back to order and await the convalescence and return to health of society as a result of the healing of the individual; bring the outer world back to a semblance of order, and hope that the individual will succeed in finding his own salvation under the more favorable conditions. We must, in fact, do all three."

His own special area of activity was, naturally enough, the Catholic Church. He devoted himself to its inward renewal and self-examination, for he was convinced that the Church shared the guilt in the coming into being of mass man, of collectivism and the rise of dictatorial forms of government. "A type of human being has arisen before which even the Lord stands, as it were, helpless, finding no way into its soul. As long as everything is distorted by bourgeois 'security' and hypocrisy, that type will continue to flourish." He continues in the same passage, taken from his book *Man and History* which appeared in 1943.

. . . The type of the bourgeois man still exists. It has not been defeated, because none of the countermovements reject the type as such. They merely strive to exclude or alter one or the other of his special interests. The majority of the modern movements goes to battle to assure the outsiders the chance to live as good a bourgeois life as possible. . . . The Church has done its share to promote the type of the bourgeois man and then to pervert it. The bourgeoisie, once accepted into the bosom of the Church, has not failed to spread out and to plant the ideals of human frailty within the very domain of the Church itself.

This criticism is directed equally sharply at the Church and democratic Socialism and at the totalitarianism of the Right and of the Left. It is surely no coincidence that the Socialist members of the Kreisau Circle no longer advocated the traditional *"laïque"* anticlericalism of their party. It was certainly not their intention to permit "the outsiders to live as good a bourgeois life as possible." The party and the trade unions had, of course, just that as their acknowledged aim. Reichwein, Leber, Mierendorff and Haubach may well have operated within Marxist theory, but consciously or not, they had left historical materialism behind them. They knew that pension plans, wage scales and standards of living ought no longer to play the main role among the workers—a view easier to acknowledge in an era of full employment than in the days of the millions of unemployed of the 1930's. Mierendorff had been arrested in 1933, and had spent five terrible years of beatings and privations in a concentration camp. From this, as he himself confessed, he had emerged stronger than ever, filled with a variety of new insights into what is really of value in human life.

JULIUS LEBER

(Born November 16, 1891, in Biesheim, Upper Alsace; executed in Berlin, January 5, 1945)

Strictly speaking, Julius Leber was one of the older men, but had been deeply scarred emotionally by the First World War through which he had fought as a young man. A son of the Alsatian borderland, he was very alive to the meaning of political realities. The Nazis considered him one of their most dangerous opponents, put him into a concentration camp immediately they gained power, and kept him there for four years. One year was spent in solitary confinement in a darkened cell. During the 1920's, as the controversial boss of the Luebeck Social Democratic party, he had waged a bitter campaign against the party's bureaucracy and mass rule. Parties were "heavy stones on the lifeline of government." He attacked the leadership of organizations and flailed away at the leaden secretariats. The real holders of power, even in the opposition, exercised their influence behind closed doors, in committee rooms, far from either the public's knowledge or its control. As a result, he looked for "fighting personalities" who would be able to educate the public and who would, under certain conditions, be able to act against its wishes.

Leber did not believe in the Marxist theory of the class war. As a Socialist he believed that society could be changed in such a way that "possession was no longer the fundamental consideration in assessing social prestige." He found Goerdeler unbearable, with his endless memoranda and bourgeois plans. Stauffen-

278

berg had the highest regard for Leber's political acumen and qualities of leadership. While Stauffenberg was still a child, Leber had led his troops to the defense of the Republic against the Kapp Putsch, and nearly lost his life at the hands of a kangaroo court of the Putschists. During the 1930's when Stauffenberg, under the influence of Stefan George, was capable of realizing the sins of the Weimar Republic, Leber was a member of the Reichstag, doing what he could to make this system work and to infuse some life and meaning into its sterile parliamentary existence. Stauffenberg, sitting in the officers' mess in Bamberg, began to suspect dimly in 1933 that dark and inscrutable forces had been released which would not easily be stuffed back into the bottle. At the same time Leber wrote from prison: "How little the outside world understands is clear from its reaction to the atrocity propaganda, as if the decisive thing were that Jews, priests and Socialists have been maltreated. The fact that I and hundreds of others sit in jail is in itself nothing, not even for us, the chief sufferers. The one thing which has any significance is the fate of the people and its relationship to freedom and humanity." Even at the last, Stauffenberg was blessed with a quick, clean death at his own battle station in the Bendlerstrasse. Leber was seized and tortured for four nights. They could not extract a word from him until they arrested his wife and children, at which point he confessed, but only in so far as it concerned his own person. By the time he was taken to court, there was little left of the man except an unbreakable spirit which pried a compliment from the lips of the devil's henchman himself. Freisler admitted grudgingly that Leber had been the most impressive personality in the whole trial.

In one sense Leber was still an old-fashioned Socialist. He, like the members of the "Rote Kapelle," put society above the individual and believed in the eventual triumph of reason and progress. It was Haubach among the older Socialists who had moved furthest from the traditional dogmas of Socialism still reflected in both Communist and Socialist circles today. The irrational, dark powers of the soul were very real to him. In his eulogy at the grave of Mierendorff, he said: "Everything in the world is related. The world of daylight and the world of dreams interweave with one another. The invisible order of the spirit sets limits to and conditions the visible. Anyone knowing this knows that the visible transformation which is death never touches the essence of the living. The radiant strength which once adorned our friend and companion and which flowered in this our earthly light has not dissolved into borderless nothing. It is not gone, for it is tied to the procreating and recreating power of love."

ADOLF REICHWEIN

(Born October 3, 1898, in Bad Ems; executed in Berlin, October 20, 1944)

Adolf Reichwein was a Socialist of the youth movement. He had a world-wide perspective "conditioned" by travel. In contrast to Moltke and Trott, with their elegant upper-class university lives, Reichwein had tramped and hitchhiked. He had crossed America in an old Model T Ford. He had been to Japan, China and the Scandinavian countries as a seaman and as an explorer. He had had adventures. He learned to fly and was one of the first men in Germany to fly a sports plane. His field of activity was education and teaching, and for several years he had been personal assistant to the Prussian Minister of Education, working closely with him in the building of the new Prussian Academy of Pedagogy. After the seizure of power by the Nazis, Reichwein was dismissed at once. There were two choices open to him, a professorship at the University of Istanbul or banishment to a one-room school in the Brandenburg Marches. He chose the latter and later demonstrated in his famous book, *The Creative School,* just how much could be done with forty children in a simple school, even under the Nazis.

"From the teaching of history to carpentry, from the self-constructed microscope to the great outings, from the beginnings of real biological research to music, there grew within that tiny

STAUFFENBERG AND HIS CIRCLE

community a life of happy intensity," wrote Hellmut Becker later. "The intellectual, physical, practical and spiritual sides of the children were developed simultaneously." One of Reichwein's original ideas was to hold school in the winter months only and to let the children discover what they could by themselves in the summer.

Leber and Reichwein were the two who made the ill-fated contact with the Communists in the early summer of 1944. Leber did this in the full knowledge of the dangerous aspects of an alliance with the Communists and of the possibility of Communist penetration of the Kreisau movement. Wilhelm Leuschner, the grand old man of the S.P.D., opposed Leber's intention strongly on the grounds that the formation of Communist cells precludes exact knowledge of the individuals included, and that therefore Leber might in effect be inviting Nazi spies already ensconced in the Communist groups into the Kreisau movement. In retrospect, one must say that both were right. Leber was certainly on the right track in his overall conception of an aroused Volk, a state of agitation in the people only to be achieved by complete cooperation of all the resistance groups. Leuschner was unhappily all too prescient of the immediate consequences. In fact a Gestapo agent was present at Leber's meeting with the Communists which led directly to Reichwein's arrest on the 4th of July and Leber's on the 5th. These arrests in their turn forced Stauffenberg's hand. "We need Leber," he cried in desperation to Trott. "I'll get him out. I'll get him out." Again on the 18th of July he sent a brief note to Frau Annedore Leber in the hospital: "We are entirely aware of our duty." Leber was the man whom Stauffenberg secretly intended to place at the head of his new government instead of Goerdeler.

25. STAUFFENBERG AND HIS CIRCLE

WE now come to the man who planted the bomb, Klaus Count Schenk von Stauffenberg. German chroniclers, with the exception of Zeller, generally stop or at best make a wide detour around him at this point: the admirers of Goerdeler because he was the chief antagonist; others because they suspect he was a truer revolutionist; and all shades of Marxists because of the fact that he was an aristocrat, a General Staff officer of considerable distinction and an erstwhile supporter of Hitler. He must be classed with the younger men, but not initially among the members of the Kreisau Circle. His way took him from his Swabian homeland to the Bendlerstrasse over a long and tortuous route. It was at Wehrmacht headquarters that he first made contact with his Prussian cousin Yorck von Wartenburg, and through Yorck with Moltke, Delp and Leber. Through this contact there arose something much deeper than a purely opportunistic alliance. It was a genuine meeting of the souls, not only in the struggle against Hitler but in the struggle for a new Germany, the outlines of which had become clear to them.

On January 30, 1933, the twenty-five-year-old cavalry lieutenant, Klaus Stauffenberg, dressed in full parade uniform, had led a column of excited citizens in a highly unmilitary but very enthusiastic parade through the streets of Bamberg in celebration of Hitler's nomination as Reich Chancellor. Criticism on the part of his fellow officers did not disturb him. "The great soldiers of the war of liberation would have sympathized with such a genuine popular uprising," he replied coolly. Six years later a visitor found Stauffenberg in a mood of black depression. He saw a deadly, unavoidable fate ahead and murmured over and over again, "That fool is going to make war." By that time the attitude of most of the younger officers, as we have noted repeatedly in the statements of the generals, had gone in exactly the opposite direction. They had become enthusiastic supporters of Hitler. Zeller argues that it is misleading to think of Stauffenberg as a supporter of Hitler who underwent some sort of spiritual conversion and thereupon joined the resistance movement:

> The energy field surrounding Hitler stirred him. The revolutionary vehemence unleashed by Hitler turned the seemingly impossible into the

suddenly possible in a world which otherwise seemed fixed and incapable of change. Stauffenberg was fascinated by the inherent possibilities opened by such a convulsion, and with his vivid imagination saw pictures of their future development. He condemned with passion or irony all those who could merely bemoan the fact of Hitler's success without offering anything better in its place. He rejected all those who clung to the past alone or yearned for the *status quo ante*. On the other hand, one begins to find fairly early in his career sober and penetrating remarks which express the revulsion and passionate concern with which he approached the phenomenon of Hitler.

Stauffenberg never thought in simple political categories. "I know no ideas," he once said, "only men." He might have added, "I have a feeling for hidden forces." He instinctively understood the forces of inertia in society and the dynamic powers released by Hitler. It never occurred to him to try to set the immovable or inherently stable parts of society in motion. He wanted to ride the tiger, as it were, by controlling things already on the move.

The geographical and intellectual landscape in which the brothers Berthold and Klaus Stauffenberg grew up was hardly conducive to an active interest in the current events of the day. They were born on an old, by-no-means-wealthy, estate in the Swabian Alb and attended the renowned Eberhard-Ludwig Gymnasium in Stuttgart. The poet Stefan George was a close family friend, and he made the two handsome boys his heirs. As a child Klaus was very frail and sickly, but with time and determination turned himself into a man equal to the most strenuous exertions. He became a passionate and expert rider. He played the cello with such skill and devotion that many in the family thought that the schoolboy would make music his career. His brother Berthold (the more withdrawn and introspective of the two), with whom he was very close, chose an academic career and became an international lawyer. He worked for several years at the International Court at The Hague, wrote articles in French and English, and in his spare time taught himself Russian and Italian. Berthold later became an important source of information for his brother through his contacts in the Foreign Office and in the neutral world, which he had established during his time at The Hague. Klaus decided to become a career officer in the Army. Certainly his physical love of Germany, her wooded hills and her mellow landscapes, played a part in his decision, but it would appear that, with his sure instinct, he had caught a whiff of trouble in the air. It was not obvious, in those days of the Stresemann era and continental relaxation, that the whole of Europe would be convulsed in a crisis a few years hence, but Klaus seems to have felt a certain foreboding. He joined the Army but was something of an oddity. The tone of the officers' mess did not mold or form him. He talked politics, history and literature to his slightly dismayed fellows. The question which worried him most was: How would it be possible to protect the essence of life against the cancerous growth of technical civilization?

People remember Stauffenberg most vividly for his laugh—an infectious, melodic sound. He could curse marvelously in the fruity dialect of South Germany. "He was always smiling when he talked," recalls a friend of those years, "and was never alone. Everywhere he went, in an instant a group of some devoted followers would appear and join him." An artillery officer remembers him well: "Stauffenberg had no magic and exercised no hypnotic attraction, but one somehow felt in him the existence of impalpable, radiant gifts and hidden strengths. One always wanted to see him in charge, running things. This indefinable promise made one feel that it would be fun to work under and with him on a job. The myth that only rude, brutal types can fascinate men was demolished when one looked at Stauffenberg." A regimental comrade describes his method of work:

I never passed Klaus's door without seeing him on the telephone. In front of him were usually great piles of paper, and with his left hand on the receiver and his right holding a pencil, he would work his way through the documents as he talked. As he spoke, lively expressions passed over his face and, depending on the conversation and its theme, he would laugh (without laughter there was no conversation with Klaus)—or curse vigorously (also a not infrequent occurrence). He would give orders or instructions, writing something else at the same time, either in the huge sprawling characters of his signature or in tiny, unexpectedly precise little letters on documents. The stenographer was always opposite him, taking down at whirlwind tempo a mad rush of detail memoranda, notices, announcements, orders or letters. Despite the speed at which all this went on, Klaus never forgot the whole pedantic structure of military form, and in moments of the wildest excitement dictated these details flawlessly, heading, reference, file number, all painfully and completely correct. He was one of those rare human beings whose power of concentration is so great that they can accomplish two things at once, while he possessed in addition a remarkable talent for separating essential from trivial in a report or a memo. His mind sparkled with a great lucidity, and the sharpness of his questions made it occasionally physically uncomfortable to talk to him. Although he spoke with such clarity and decisiveness, he mellowed and subtly adjusted his tone with innate adroitness, and had an incomparable grace in dealing with older and senior officers. In his relations with equals he was free and entirely unrestrained. Klaus's great personality won respect and confidence from others without the slightest hint of effort or conscious will.

His ability to fit into any situation did not, however, prevent him from expressing his opinions in the most emphatic way. In October of 1942, at the headquarters of the Eastern Command in Winnitza, he gave a little talk on German policy in the East, calling it a scandal, self-defeating and productive of nothing but hate and opposition. The agricultural policy was equally wrong. There was an audible sigh of relief among the assembled officers. At long last someone had had the guts to say what they were all thinking, and he was an officer from the Führer's headquarters at that. When Stauffenberg took over as chief of staff to the Home Army on July 1, 1944, he reported to his new superior, General Fromm, and in the course of this, their first talk, declared that he saw no way of winning the war. At best, by straining every nerve, a "draw" might be achieved through political means. He further said that he considered himself morally obliged to inform his commanding officer of his honest opinion before taking a post under the general's command. General Fromm thanked him for his frankness, and still obviously thoughtful, ordered Stauffenberg to take up his job. Kiesel, who

285

never had the pleasure of getting his hands on Stauffenberg, did, however, manage to compose a picture of the man from his questioning of others: "With all his intellectual clarity he was still a firebrand, exercising a fascinating and suggestive power over those around. Most unusual was the yearning which he, an aristocrat, felt for a union between his noble heritage and an ethical Socialism. His tragedy was that the really indispensable support for all revolutions, which he needed to win, was denied him—the people."

Between Beck, the old man, and Stauffenberg, the young man, there was no real conflict. Beck, aging and sick, merely allowed the revolutionary leadership to pass to the younger man. But there was real enmity between Stauffenberg and Goerdeler. During the final months, Goerdeler was less and less capable of holding the centrifugal forces of the resistance together, whereas Stauffenberg was becoming more and more the nucleus of his own "gang of conspirators," tied to him by the strongest bonds, those of affection and loyalty. The core of the group around Stauffenberg was formed by Haeften, Schwerin, Klausning, Corvette Captain Kranzfelder and Klaus's brother Berthold. By this time he had established close connections with the Conservative, Christian and the Socialist wings of the Kreisau movement. For all these reasons Goerdeler's hostility waxed. He called Stauffenberg "an arrogant, stubborn troublemaker." The feeling was quite mutual. The very atmosphere which each created was diametrically opposed to the other. If Stauffenberg was enraged, moved or depressed, he would give vent to his feelings late at night, alone or with his most intimate friends, perhaps quote poetry, but by day and in public he never allowed himself the luxury of the endless lamentations, the repetitive recitations of the atrocities of the Hitler regime which consumed so much time during the meetings of the Goerdeler group. Despite their sensitivity, the brothers Stauffenberg had a remarkable ability to remain cool in the face of the terror of the Nazi regime. Furthermore, they were able to observe the phenomenon of Nazism with a dispassionate attention to facts wholly denied to the Goerdeler group, not because they approved of it any more than the others, but because they recognized in it certain aspects which they intended to utilize in their reconstruction of Germany. Zeller writes: "Stauffenberg rarely thought of himself as a member of a resistance movement, the main aim of which was the destruction of Hitler and the overthrow of the regime, but rather as part of a dynamic movement to reform Germany, using the popular upheaval which the overthrow of the regime would entail to such ends. The state was to be reformed but in an entirely different sense from that of 1918 and 1933."

Stauffenberg's attitude toward Russia has been debated as often as Trott's. It might, therefore, be useful to talk of the entire foreign-policy question at this point. The universal premise shared alike by Conservatives (of all stamps), Socialists and Liberals, was to arrive at some sort of satisfactory arrangement with the West. There was no disagreement on that point. Stauffenberg, the most nationalistic of the younger men, had in fact, rejoiced in the victory of German arms over France, although he added that victory alone was meaningless unless Germany and France could be made to work in unity in some way. One must act with magnanimity toward the defeated nation. As the war rolled on, the hopes and aspirations of the various groups changed. At first, during the Polish campaign and the period of the "phony war," the parties with whom to negotiate were quite clearly England and France. After America's entry into the war in 1941, America became the crucial factor, and especially when the promulgation of the Atlantic Charter demonstrated that America had begun to assume the ideological leadership in the struggle.

Goerdeler was the most consistently optimistic about the chances of gaining recognition of Germany's territorial claims. The more realistic Canaris group calculated that at the time of the Polish campaign the atmosphere had not yet been sufficiently poisoned to admit of no chance of agreement, though they hoped only to retain the Sudetenland, Austria and the Polish Corridor. They recognized the fact that Czechoslovakia would have to be restored to the *status quo ante* and that parts of East Prussia could be usefully ceded to Poland as evidences of German sincerity. Hitler's powers were to be confined to the presidency. Ribbentrop, Himmler and Göring were to be removed and a democracy restored. After the victory in the West, they realized that Hitler's removal was absolutely necessary to the holding of any talks. Here, too, they were prepared to make territorial concessions, ceding Alsace-Lorraine back to France, in order to demonstrate their good intentions. As the military situation worsened, their readiness to make territorial concessions increased correspondingly. First, it was the status of 1938 to which they clung, then that of 1933, and finally they confined themselves to the hope that no Russian troops would enter German territory.

In so far as disagreement existed on the East-West problem, it was never a question of either/or. The disagreement lay between those who thought only in terms of negotiations with the West, and those who, while recognizing the primacy of agreement with the West, considered it vital to make contact with Russia as well. The possibility of a separate agreement with Russia was reserved for the eventuality of complete Western intransigence. The problem became acute only after Germany's invasion of the Soviet Union in 1941. The "Rote Kapelle" members advocated the closest possible cooperation with Russia from the very beginning, but since the "Rote Kapelle" was effectively eliminated after 1942, it is not necessary to consider it further here. Meanwhile, the German military position took a turn for the worse after the setbacks of the winter of 1942–43, and the first real chance for action came when Stalin began to voice his displeasure at the delay in the Second Front with ever greater vehemence. This seemed to offer the resistance its first genuine opportunity to go East.

The older men, with one exception, opposed any sort of overture toward the Russians. For Goerdeler, Beck and Canaris, Bolshevism was the most awful thing they could imagine. Had General von Hammerstein lived longer, their position might have been different. Leber and Leuschner, too, stood with the "old men" on this question, although Leber had two opinions, a domestic-ideological one and a realistic foreign political one. He saw a good deal more clearly than the aristocrats of the Kreisau Circle just how much ground the Communists had won in the ranks of the German workers and was more alert to the threat. It seems definite that there was no contact of any importance between the captured German generals of the Russian-sponsored "National Committee for a Free Germany" and the rest of the German generals. There was a regular coming and going among the ranks. German rankers, under direct orders from the Russians or from the National Committee, slipped across the front lines with relative ease and enabled the K.P.D., whose organization had been entirely smashed between the years 1933 and 1943, to lay the groundwork for a new party.

Trott, who argued on behalf of Leber as well, presented the intense desire of the resistance movement to cooperate with the West in preventing Central Europe from coming under the rule of the Soviets, during his secret meetings in Stockholm and Geneva. In his talks in these neutral countries, he pointed out that the only constructive ideas for the rebuilding of postwar Germany were coming from Russia, while the Western democracies appeared to have slammed all the doors on the resistance. The German Social Democrats pleaded with the Western leaders to do something to fill the vacuum. Stalin's famous words, "Hitlers come and Hitlers go. The German people is eternal," were actively used by the Communist underground to win approval and sympathy. The West offered the Morgenthau Plan. It was against the negation in Western thinking that Stauffenberg, Trott and Leber struggled. Events in the three Allied zones of occupation, from 1945 until the outbreak of the Cold War, showed that they had estimated the trend correctly. They could not, of course, foresee that the Russians would blunder and lose their great chance by the stupidity and greed of their plunder of German industry, by the unimaginative insertion of alien "Moscow" Germans in high positions, and by the crassness of the repressive regime which they installed.

The one exception among the older men was Count Werner von der Schulenburg, who tried his best during 1940 and 1941 to prevent the German invasion of Russia. The whole story of the secret feelers in Stockholm and Tokyo during the war has yet to be told. Peter Kleist describes peace feelers emanating from Moscow, and Kiesel confirms the fact that Schulenburg was actively engaged in an attempt to bring about a separate peace. Schulenburg apparently volunteered to slip through the Russian lines, in order to open negotiations on behalf of the resistance movement, and Fritz Hesse remembers that Schulenburg said that an agreement with the Russians was just around the corner. This was shortly before July 20, 1944. Hassell on his part, because he, as a diplomat, could never close the door on negotiations with anyone, was certainly less negative about the idea of talks with the Russians than his friends. If Schulenburg got the impression, after awhile, that the resistance was not being honest with the Russians and was only trying to hold them at bay until some sort of agreement could be reached with the West, he probably had Hassell and his friends in mind. Stauffenberg, as we have seen, was at that time actively engaged in the organization of Russian prisoners into fighting groups, and was hardly the person to begin talks with the Soviet Union. Karl Michel concludes from this that: "Stauffenberg would never have considered the possibility of any sort of pact between the Germans and the Russians." Michel misses, I think, the crucial point in Stauffenberg's political approach, his complete freedom from any sort of controlling ideology. There is much disagreement on this point. Michel himself admits that Stauffenberg did, in fact, consider an "East solution" in moments of despair. Gisevius says that Stauffenberg came around to a pro-Russian policy during the summer of 1944, and Albert Norden, a Communist, writing in the *Taegliche Rundschau,* even asserts that Stauffenberg actually demanded a pro-Russian action. In this maze of charges and countercharges the remark of Zeller's seems the most plausible— that Leber, Trott, Schulenburg and Stauffenberg were all agreed that "it was impossible to try to deal with America, which showed so little understanding of German affairs, without at the same time, at least, trying to make some contact with Russia which is, after all, a neighbor."

The continued negative response of the Western democracies to all feelers and the failure of a series of attempted assassinations brought about a crisis within the Beck–Goerdeler group, resulting in a sort of exhausted resignation. In that moment, reports Hassell, it was Stauffenberg who overcame the crisis and brought the entire resistance movement back to action. During the African campaign Stauffenberg had been horribly wounded, losing his right hand and eye and being in danger of losing his left eye as well. He had only three fingers remaining on his left hand. During the agonizing weeks after his injury, he lay, shaken with fever, in the twilight between life and death, and seems at this time to have undergone a great inner transformation. With an almost dark energy, he began to concentrate all his immense *élan vital* on getting well. Refusing all drugs to ease the pain, he worked with obsessive energy and haste to learn to use the remaining three fingers of his left hand for writing and other daily activities. When he got better, he thought over the plans on which he intended to work and began to pull all the strings he could muster to get a job in some high position; and the hospital staff could hardly believe its eyes when a steady stream of the highest-ranking officers began to come and go from the room of the young major so dreadfully maimed.

Sauerbruch had planned an operation to make Stauffenberg's twisted limbs function a little better, but as a consequence of the deep crack in the political and military Axis front caused by the Allied capture of Mussolini and the possible collapse of Italy, Stauffenberg simply could not waste the time in a hospital. On September 9, 1943, the day of the Allied landings at Salerno, he hobbled from the hospital and took what was officially listed as three weeks of convalescent leave. In fact, he went directly to his brother's flat in Berlin, where he met von Tresckow to begin the detailed plannings of an uprising. When Tresckow was sent to the front, he continued the work with a group of his closest

291

friends. Through his cousin Peter Yorck von Wartenburg, he made contact with the Kreisau Circle and had preliminary talks with the Socialists. He finally talked the Moltke group of the Kreisau Circle out of its policy of waiting to let Nazism burn itself out, and began the job of tying it to the military conspiracy which he was beginning to form. At the same time he managed to win several influential members of the Goerdeler group over to his point of view.

The most glaring deficiency in the conspiracy was the lack of one proper "gangster" professional enough to have assured the success of the technical side of the Putsch. It is fantastic that among the wide selection of officers and civilians involved in the series of abortive assassination attempts there was not one who knew enough physics or practical chemistry to make a good bomb.

There was simply no talent for devising lightning changes of plans. There was no one except Stauffenberg himself who could improvise. To be able to do that, a man must be in first-class physical and mental condition, and the men who planned the Putsch were certainly not that. For years they had lived on borrowed time. Their nerves were frayed under the constant pressure of life under totalitarian terror and the strain of transforming themselves into clandestine killers. They may have realized this, because with the exception of the actual assassins themselves, the plan required nothing of the individuals involved but a purely mechanical obedience. It was an impersonal plan, depending on careful, thorough staffwork. The problem was that if one tiny part of the gigantic machinery failed to function, the whole ponderous unfolding of the plan, with its detailed time-table, would just disintegrate into its components. Stauffenberg, for his part, proved to have the necessary genius for improvisation which might have won the day. The way he wriggled out of the Wolf's Lair after the explosion of the bomb demonstrates this to one's complete satisfaction. Upon his arrival in Berlin, he discovered to his horror that nothing had really been done and he began a desperate telephone battle to counter Himmler's orders. Throughout he displayed a sovereign self-control, as testified by Gisevius, whose word carries added weight because he was an outspoken opponent of Stauffenberg. Beck was very impressed by Stauffenberg's behavior during the last hours, and Gisevius writes of it, too, in glowing terms. "In reality," he continues, "we were thinking of something else when we watched Stauffenberg—the lamentable failure of the rest of the officers."

Stauffenberg's tragic mistake was to place his confidence in the machinery of command and obedience. We have already seen his rejection of the Churchillian advocacy of partisan warfare on the grounds that armed might must remain in military and therefore in responsible hands. According to this view, there is no place for the initiative of the common soldier, though it is often just that initiative which decides failure or success at the front. The generals were not the only ones who misjudged the feeling among the younger officers. The "colonels' clique" also misjudged the extent of the falling off of enthusiasm for Hitler and the Nazis among the front-line troops. They were not capable of organizing this disordered underground stream of resistance. It was there, nonetheless, and they might have used it. This is of course much more easily said than done. The plan required absolute secrecy for its success, and the most exacting calculation to eliminate any chance of a slip-up. In retrospect it is no longer possible to say whether or not a shock troop could have been formed. We have already noted the difficulties attendant on the formation of the Brandenburg battalion of the Abwehr. It was, however, unquestionably wrong to rely on blind obedience in the execution of Operation Valkyrie. It ought to have been possible to have formed tiny squads of determined young officers who could have carried out the most critical special assignments. The radio had to be seized. The government buildings had to be cordoned off. No great body of men would have been required. A few highly flexible squads of shock troops could have done the job. Yet even the cars and lorries needed for such simple maneuvers were not at hand. Gisevius needed a staff car to get to police headquarters. "The Putsch had

293

not one automobile at its disposal. Fantastic?" he asks. "Anyone who knows the military bureaucracy will recall that not even a commanding general ever has more than one auto at his disposal at a time. If he calls for more than two or three, other branches will become suspicious and start to ask questions and demand that forms be filled in. No one dared to run that risk. The lorries of the mobile troops which were on their way to the Bendlerstrasse had not yet arrived." Lorries and gasoline were in very short supply by midsummer 1944. Had anyone thought of the need for mobility and emergency moves during the first hours of the Putsch, it would surely have been possible to "wangle" something, to get hold of a few private cars or motorcycles. Admittedly, the date set for the assassination had been changed three times during July alone, which meant that to have assembled a pool of motors three times would most certainly have aroused suspicion. Admittedly, events took a course not expected. Yet all of this merely reinforces the criticism that there was no allowance in the plans for the unexpected, the very first exigency of any revolutionary undertaking.

By the time Gisevius demanded an auto, several crucial things had gone wrong. In the first place, Hitler had unforeseeably not been killed by the detonation of the bomb or by flying splinters of furniture. Fate had intervened in the person of a table leg which blocked the initial force of the explosion. This was bad luck. Still, if the other wheels of the operation had been meshed properly, it might have been possible to carry out the operation. Hitler was, after all, three hours away from Berlin in his remote East Prussian bunker. No one could be certain that he was not dead. How well the generals could work when they all pulled together was demonstrated by the flawless success of Operation Valkyrie in Paris, where General Stülpnagel quietly jailed the entire Gestapo and in a matter of hours had scored the first and only victory for the resistance on that day. General Fellgiebel, communications officer at Führer headquarters in East Prussia, realized that the bomb had failed, but maintained the decision to act and immediately cloud all communications. The fatal omission was that the Valkyrie order was not issued immediately. When Stauffenberg arrived in Berlin at 3:50 P.M. and immediately called Fromm, he heard that three precious hours had been lost while he was in the air. During these three hours the entire massed leadership of the coup awaited the arrival of troops from the infantry school in Döbernitz, the panzer school in Krampnitz, and assorted smaller units. The counterrevolution had time to get rolling. The failure to seal off the Wolf's Lair made it possible to sow confusion by issuing counterorders. Stauffenberg repeated over and over again on the telephone to doubtful commanders: "Yes, Hitler is dead," while the staff at the Wolf's Lair desperately broadcast: "The Führer is alive."

During these crucial hours the broadcasting station in the Rundfunk House in Berlin was not seized, government buildings were not sealed off, and appeals to the people were not issued. Berliners had a feeling that something was going on, but they had no idea what. It is just possible that they might have taken to the barricades if properly aroused. One little incident from the hundreds which could be cited may serve to pinpoint the way in which the 20th-of-July plot failed. The tanks from the Panzer school at Potsdam had reached the strategic East-West highway which runs between the Reichskanzlerplatz and the Siegessaeule. Their commander, General Specht, called a halt and drove to the Bendlerstrasse for further instructions. When he learned what was going on, he demanded to see General Fromm, C.I.C. of the Home Army, at once, since he was the superior officer of both Olbricht and Stauffenberg. The conspirators had already had trouble with Fromm, who after ringing up General Keitel had lost his nerve and refused to join the Putsch. Instead of arresting Fromm on the spot, they courteously confined him to his office. The conspirators either did not know or had forgotten that in Fromm's office there was a second door leading to his private rooms. General Specht simply went in by the one door and out by the other, returning to his tank column unhindered. He ordered the reverse march back to Potsdam. This is only one episode of hundreds. The most important one has often been

295

cited: namely, that Major Remer of the Berlin Guard Battalion, whose assignment was to block the government quarter of the city and to arrest Goebbels, was instead handed the phone, by Goebbels, over which Hitler gave the major the broadest possible authority to proceed against the revolt on the Bendlerstrasse.

Despite the string of failures, there were a few amazing successes. Paris went smoothly. Hitler's men were effortlessly arrested and all of France passed into the hands of the rebels. Originally a version of the plan foresaw moving independently in France, where sympathetic officers were most numerous, and making a separate peace with the West as part of a general "Western solution." There was still hope for areas outside Berlin. Stauffenberg worked like a demon, even after it had become clear that Himmler's counterorders were beginning to take effect. An eyewitness recorded fragments of Stauffenberg's conversations:

Stauffenberg here . . . right . . . all orders from the commanding general of the Home Army . . . yes . . . certainly . . . that is correct . . . all orders to be carried out at once. . . . You must occupy all the radio stations and news agencies . . . all resistance must be smashed . . . it is very likely that counterorders will come from the Führer's headquarters. They are not to be believed . . . no . . . the Wehrmacht has assumed all power. Absolutely no one except the commanding officer of the Home Army is entitled to give orders. . . . Yes . . . Do you understand? . . . the Reich is in danger and as always at such moments, the soldier must take over.

Stauffenberg was quite immune to the doubts which plagued the others. Gisevius began to criticize Stauffenberg for not having S.S. Investigating Officer Piffrader shot on the spot. "How can you allow that man to see everything here? What happens later . . . if he ever gets a chance to unload what he has seen here?" Gisevius reports that Stauffenberg was quite bewildered by this, for he simply did not understand thoughts concerned with "later" and "security" in the midst of failure. In the unconditional quality of his behavior lies an adequate answer to all those who have grumbled at him for not giving his life at the time of the assassination itself. There can be no doubt that Stauffenberg did not think of his own safety, either at the moment of the bomb explosion nor later when he must have realized that all was lost.

It it is true that each of us dies his own death, then surely Stauffenberg's was his own. He died in the very way in which he had lived, unmindful of personal safety. Despite the tragedy of the loss, one can almost call it a happy death, saving him from the dreadful "afterwards" of interrogation, torture, trial and execution which awaited his comrades. On the night of July 20, 1944, Stauffenberg, together with Olbricht, Maertz von Quirnheim and Haeften, was shot in the courtyard of the War Office. His last words: "Long Live Our Holy Germany."

26. OATHS AND UNCONDITIONAL OBEDIENCE

THE moral of the story of the German resistance movement has yet to be decided. Different people under different political banners have viewed it in widely divergent ways. None of them are wholly convincing. In the time of Hitler and Roland Freisler, the conclusion was simple and unequivocal: high treason. Abroad at the time and for quite a while afterward, the verdict was: "A Putsch of a reactionary clique of officers." Churchill declared in a speech in the House of Commons on August 2, 1944, that it had been a case of "the highest personalities in the Reich murdering one another." *The New York Times* spoke of it as "an episode from the shadow world of the gangster." During 1945, it would appear that American foreign correspondents were forbidden to print anything whatsoever about the German resistance movement. As late as the summer of 1946, no radio station in the American Zone was permitted a mention of the 20th of July under any circumstances whatsoever.

In Germany itself, in the shock of the total military defeat and

TREASON IN THE TWENTIETH CENTURY

in a natural reaction to the thesis of "collective guilt," the German resistance was abused. It was used to justify the purgative process. Only a few could resist the temptation to paint themselves as sympathizers, if not immediate participants. There was a rush to join the Army, daily growing, of the "inner emigration." When Germany recovered unexpectedly quickly and found itself suddenly a respected member of the Western alliance, a reaction in the other direction began. It was aroused less by those who may have suffered unjustly as part of the de-Nazification program than by the stubborn, unenlightened and unregenerate Messrs. Remer, Kesselring and company. The young lieutenants and captains, who had once believed in Hitler so enthusiastically, from 1943 on, were aware of the terrible mistakes in German strategy, but continued to do their duty in bitter resignation—these men have remained silent up to the present day.

The problem was by no means laid to rest at that point. Defense Minister Theo Blank, for example, faced a tough scramble with the military personnel committee of the Bundestag over the list of officers whom he had selected for the Federal Republic's NATO contingent. One chief bone of contention was the attitude of the prospective officers to the events and personalities of the 20th of July. The hearings took place behind closed doors, so the actual verdict was never revealed.

Let me try to discuss some of the criticisms which are held privately by those who have remained silent. Men who wore the same uniform have criticized Stauffenberg: "If he wanted to do away with Hitler, he had no right to try to outlive his victim. He ought not to have planted the bomb and then tried to return to lead the action and enjoy its fruits." There are, in fact, two objections here—one ethical, one practical. The ethical objection may be paraphrased with the expression, "If thou willst take a life, thou must pay with thine own." The answer is that Stauffenberg was prepared to do so and did. Anyone who has studied the personalities involved at all closely will, I think, agree that Stauffenberg was much too important a wheel in the conspiracy to be allowed to blow himself to smithereens in the Wolf's Lair. The risks were great and the chance of success slim. No one could be spared the luxury of self-immolation.

All previous attempts to kill Hitler had failed, not because the assassins were fools but because Hitler had the sure instinct for danger of a jungle beast. At the last moment he would suddenly call off a planned appearance somewhere or cut short a visit unexpectedly. It was increasingly difficult to predict his movements, and by the summer of 1944, virtually impossible to reach his person. To get into the Wolf's Lair one had to pass three guard posts where everyone was searched, regardless of rank, for concealed weapons. The circle of persons which one saw in Hitler's presence was not likely to be filled with enemies of the regime or light-hearted Putschists. Finally, it was not part of the plan that Stauffenberg was to perpetrate the deed himself. He was to have been in Berlin, at his post, directing the action, but according to Haffner's anecdote, Stauffenberg simply lost patience after the failure of the third or fourth attempt and shouted angrily, "I'll do the goddamned thing alone—with my three fingers."

The second part of criticism goes deeper, and for those who raise it is a genuine question of principle. It involves the whole complex problem of the significance of oaths and the disobedience of orders. When Hitler forced the Wehrmacht to swear an oath to his person, he knotted the two aspects inextricably. The oath read: "I swear by God this holy oath, that I shall give my unconditional obedience to the Führer of the German people and Reich, Adolf Hitler, and that I shall be prepared to sacrifice my life as a brave soldier in keeping this oath." There is a good deal to be said about this oath. Theodor Heuss said, on the tenth anniversary of the 20th of July, that Hitler of all people—he who persecuted the servants of God of all persuasions—was surely the last man on earth entitled to call on God to witness such an oath. The use of "holy" is equally suspect and for the same reasons. Heuss continued: "It is uncanny that Hitler took up the formula 'by God' again, after it had been dropped in the previous oath to the constitution, being reserved to the individual conscience to use it or not. In Hitler's oath it had a purely tactical sense and an entirely blasphemous effect. With this 'by God' Hitler shrewdly built in a crushing subconscious force."

The thought of obligations toward a higher authority could only be relevant for those who thought for themselves and who were prepared to act independently. In this sense, old Lieutenant General Friebe was surely correct when he said at the Remer trial that one must distinguish between the "thinking" soldier who, impressed by the unique events of the 20th of July, came to the conclusion that under certain conditions the military oath must be broken in the interests of conscience, and the "soldiers only" who rejected the assassination on grounds of military obedience alone. It is interesting that Friebe used the word "unique" for those events. The new army of the Federal Republic was just being founded at the time of the trial. Friebe obviously wanted to prevent any further weakening of the already wobbly concept of military allegiance in Germany at the very moment when young men were being asked to swear new oaths of allegiance. On the other hand, this fact itself reveals the weakness of his position in the face of the obdurate mass of the old Wehrmacht. Surely the "when" of such a unique situation is a decision for the individual to make, and that was what the individual German officer had no preparation for: an independent decision. Tresckow's argument in defense of the coup seems to me particularly apposite here. It was not, he said, so much a question of getting rid of Hitler as a person but much more as the recipient of the oath which bound the mass of the Wehrmacht to him. If that magical bond could be broken, the way would be clear. How right he was can be seen in the attitude at the time, and even today for those officers for whom Stauffenberg and his friends were "old" men. In this attempt to fix the attitude of the young officers, I rely on my own interviews and those of Armin Mohler with the handful which came back alive. For the older generation of officers, for whom an intact social order still had some meaning, the oath of obedience was tied to an institution, the monarch, who was less a person than a part of the institutional framework, or the Weimar Constitution. For the young officers who had been between eight and ten years old when Hitler came to power, there was no longer any order in society. Everything seemed to dissolve when one touched it. All values had crumbled. The oath became for them something metaphysical, quite unrelated to anything concrete, the one fixed point in a world of flux, a kind of surrogate for God. The sworn community to which the oath bound them became the only foundation on which they could build.

They, too, had their doubts. Was the military direction correct? Were the atrocities which many (but by no means all) actually saw, permitted by law? They tended to think in concrete terms of an eye for an eye, and ideas of the dignity of man or freedom were not very meaningful. They could not imagine violating an oath for such vague, ethereal unrealities. Their rejection of Stauffenberg's "horse trade," by which he stayed alive instead of blowing himself up, arose from that curious combination of the practical and the mystical so commonly found in the younger generation of officers. Their ideal of proper soldierly conduct in the face of adversity was the German general in Italy who received orders which he considered wrong. He made dispositions which were contrary, and then, with his hand still resting on the telephone, pulled his pistol from its holster and put a bullet through his brain. This attitude divides the young men, not only from the men of the 20th of July, but also from the pure militarists of the stamp of Manstein, Rundstedt and Kesselring for whom military oaths were inviolable at all times under all circumstances.

There was at one time in the past a genuine German tradition of military disobedience, which had been unhappily forgotten during the course of the nineteenth and twentieth centuries. The Prussian General von der Marwitz had refused to plunder Schloss Bruehl and had consequently resigned. The Prussian General Yorck von Wartenburg had refused to follow his king's orders by joining Napoleon's troops in the retreat from Moscow and had instead concluded a separate peace with the Tsar at Tauroggen. The Prussian officer's son, Heinrich von Kleist, made the

301

conflict between conscience and discipline the subject of his great tragedy, *The Prince of Homburg*. Curiously enough, Adolf Hitler approved of this very tradition in principle in his *Mein Kampf*. "If a nation," argued Hitler, "sees itself being led to certain destruction, it has not only the right but indeed the duty to rebel. Human law breaks civil law." This very same Hitler, however, introduced the concept of unconditional obedience, not only in the oath, but added an aura of fervid participation which for a long time fused obedience and trust into a single unity and raised those who obeyed to a consciousness of jointly accomplished deeds for the fatherland. Success also plays its role, for men are easily led to believe in the illusion that the proportion of success to failure in life must have some significance. This was true even before the war. General Halder correctly pointed to the overpowering effect which the Munich agreement had had on the people and particularly on the Army, which was spared a war against Czechoslovakia. "From that time on," wrote Halder, "the word of the day was: The Führer will do it somehow, just as at Munich." That he no longer "did it" in the summer of 1939 was forgotten in the glamor of the easy victory in Poland. The way in which he led the Wehrmacht to victory in the West was the final uncontestable proof. It is therefore misleading to judge the behavior of the younger officers solely in terms of atrocities, the scorched-earth policy and the final calamity. The oath had something which the Weimar oath never had. Obedience to Hitler's oath under the greatest of trials was a deep, personal affair. The Weimar oath never drew the unflinching personal loyalty and emotional allegiance given to Hitler's.

But when one enters, as here, upon discussion dealing with the soul, one's evidence is nebulous. There is another side which is decidedly not nebulous, the whole question of "automatic obedience" upon which, for example, Stauffenberg's entire plan was based. He assumed that Operation Valkyrie would necessarily work, because of the habit of obedience deeply ingrained in the German soldier. An episode from the 20th of July seems to me to exemplify this phenomenon beautifully. Field Marshal Kluge was generally acknowledged to be in sympathy with the plot, and it was accordingly assumed that he could be counted on to act. How he would have acted had Hitler actually been killed is a different question, as it is in the case of Fromm and several others. When Kluge learned that Hitler was still alive, he began to vacillate and make excuses, asking for time to think things over. He remained undecided, even after General Stülpnagl reported that Paris had been taken over by the conspirators quite effortlessly. Beck called him and begged him as commander in chief of the Army Group West to join the good cause. Kluge did not say no definitely, but it was clear to all that his attitude meant no. On this day Kluge acted only once, and that was not because of the entreaties of his friends or his own conviction that it was urgent to end Hitler and the war. He acted when the first order from General Witzleben arrived. It had all the accustomed features, heading, reference, proper style and salutation. *Ergo* it was valid. The reaction was automatic obedience. Kluge immediately summoned his chief of staff to begin consultation about measures to be taken to arrange an armistice on the Western Front. It was not very long before an equally correct order arrived from the Führer's headquarters, countermanding the first. An equally automatic reaction followed.

Treason is closely tied to the question of oaths. Apart from the survivors of the men in the resistance movement who have the full right to think differently, only people who wish to cloud the issues can deny that some of the deeds of the resistance were treason in the technical sense of the word. It is no good for those who approve the aim of the men of the 20th of July to shrink from calling things by their right names. The participants never fooled themselves nor should we, for in the long run it is healthier to see what was really involved in the meaning of the German resistance. Earlier in the Nazi era, when Brauchitsch was presented with the documents covering the secret negotiations for an armistice which had been carried on through the intermediary activity of the Vatican, he grew excited and cried that the whole thing was "treason of the most blatant sort." He demanded that the whole file be turned over to "responsible authority" at once and that the courier who had carried the documents be arrested. "If anyone has to be arrested," said General Halder, "please arrest me." Brauchitsch was stunned. He simply could not jump the hurdle of traditional legality. Nor could Lord Vansittart, who, having learned from Goerdeler the names of the various German generals involved in the resistance, replied gruffly that all such talk was treasonable. An American Congressman re-acted to the story of one of the men of the 20th of July with the same words: "But surely the man was a traitor." Raymond Aron answers the question of whether or not the men of the 20th of July were traitors in this way: "In reference to National Social-ism, certainly; in reference to the classical concept of patria, per-haps. The problem is that the concept itself has become ques-tionable in the era of the contemporary secular religions."

During the Remer trial, both the accused and his counsel emphasized the difference between treason within the state (*Hoch-verrat*) and treason in combination with the external enemies of the state (*Landesverrat*). Tyrannicide is, it was argued, permissi-ble under certain conditions, and there are even cases where *Hochverrat* might be a trespass, but *Landesverrat*— that is, be-trayal of one's country to its enemies—is always and under all conditions despicable. Canaris, too, felt the distinction strongly and rejected any plans which involved betrayal of military secrets to the enemy. On the other hand, he protected Oster, when he knew quite well that Oster was actually engaged in *Landesverrat*. Canaris was never quite up to resolving the contradictions in his own position. As his biographer puts it: "He could never jump over his own shadow. That shadow was not merely the tradition of his calling but also the demands of his very nature, which shunned all extremes. He was well aware that much of his daily activity was unquestionably *Hochverrat,* but he could never take the step to, let us say, technical *Landesverrat*."

The "outer" circle of the "Rote Kapelle" practiced *Landes-verrat* without any reservations. Some defend Oster's *Landes-*

304

verrat by attributing to it motives essentially national in character, that is, at no time was Oster in the service of a foreign power. Opinions of those who welcomed the 20th of July diverge on the morality of Oster's acts. In the view of Weizsäcker and Kordt, it was permissible to warn a neutral state of an impending attack, providing that the warning was given early enough to permit of effective political counteractions. If, on the other hand, the invasion was immediately to be expected and a warning would do nothing but endanger the lives of German soldiers, while no time remained for political action, the warning ought not to be given. Schlabrendorff defends the warning which Oster gave the Dutch on May 9, 1940, and the Norwegians on April 8th of the same year as "heroic acts," because "he showed thereby that Germany was not in sympathy with these unprovoked acts of aggression which covered the fatherland with shame for generations to come." Disagreeing with Weizsäcker, he continues: "I consider that the honor of Germany is worth more than the possible death of German soldiers which might have been caused, but in fact did not take place [because the Dutch and Norwegians failed to act on the warnings]."

If it is hard to draw distinctions in the relatively clear area of military operations, it is impossible to do so in diplomacy. How is one to judge the countless diplomatic contacts during the war? Freisler extended treason to include "the failure to report defeatist remarks of men like Moltke." At his trial Remer said that it was treasonable to maintain any contact with the enemy in time of war. Transmission of news, as carried on by the "Rote Kapelle," was for him treachery of the highest order. Otto John, at that time the highly regarded chief of the Federal Bureau for Defense of the Constitution (Bundesamt für Verfassungsschutz), objected. "Every day that the war dragged on worsened Germany's position." Remer replied coolly, "Every contact with the enemy strengthened him morally." The man who calls the talks which Hassell, Goerdeler, Trott, Bonhoeffer, Schönfeld, Mueller, Gisevius and Witzleben held with representatives of enemy or neutral powers treason must logically be prepared to call the utterances of any dissatisfied German during the war treason as well. It is true that Germans, on the whole, were exceedingly loose in their talk during the war. Lord Vansittart remarked in 1939: "England hardly needs a secret service these days. The Germans come to us in droves and tell us all." The fact that most of what they described, the imminent collapse of the German economy, the shortage of oil—which meant that the war could not last more than four weeks—munitions mix-ups and so on, was false and dangerously misleading, is beside the point.

In contrast to the general rule, Trott writes that Zeller "always observed with great care the borders of military secrecy in his talks in London, New York, Stockholm or Geneva." He spoke not as a defeatist or pessimist but as a man trying to save his country from a dangerous situation. It is true, as Rothfels points out, that although Trott's efforts in Washington were unsuccessful, the information he gave was very useful to the American Government. It is also true that Allen Dulles was not acting in the capacity of angel of mercy when he met members of the resistance in Geneva. The information which he gathered from Beck through Gisevius and Waetjen could have been very useful, if Washington had listened to him. All of this must be admitted, but on the other hand, it is equally clear that the West did not require the moral support of a handful of German nationals which claimed to know of the existence of "another Germany." In the long run their actions may have a different, namely an historical significance, but as far as the conduct of the war was concerned, these contacts were quite meaningless. Had their message "arrived," it could have done nothing but good. The fact that Rothfels can wonder which wastepaper baskets in the Foreign Office and the State Department were the final resting places for the proposals received from the resistance is indicative of the insignificance of the affair militarily.

I have so far purposely chosen to answer the objections of those who accuse the resistance movement of treason on the same level on which the accusations are raised, that is, the technical question of the treason of the resistance movement. One cannot answer serious objections of this sort without being willing to consider the arguments of the opponents at their face value. There is of course a deeper level, much closer to the core of the matter, on which the argument can be continued. On this level, too, one meets a great deal of partisan thinking, emotionalism and special pleading. Essentially the argument runs as follows: the Hitler regime is a special case, for it was an unusual state, the authority of which cannot be regarded in the same light as normal legal authority. It represented "naked force with no constitutional basis" (Schlabrendorff at the Remer trial). Therefore, since the very state was criminal, there can be no question of treason to it. (Statement of Marion, Countess Yorck von Wartenburg, widow of Yorck, and herself a judge). The difficulty with this argument is the problem of stating the exact point in time at which the Nazi regime lost any semblance of constitutionality, for it must be remembered that Hitler came to power through normal and entirely constitutional means. When did disobedience cease to be treason? Where is the borderline of constitutionality?

There are a great many answers to these questions. Prosecutor Bauer, at the Remer trial, and the majority of the surviving Weimar Social Democrats, place the borderline at the time of the Ermächtigungsgesetz (Enabling Act) of May 1933, which gave Hitler more than constitutional powers and which he used to ban first the Communist party and then the other parties. Theodor Heuss, postwar President of the German Republic, who in 1934 had voted for the Ermächtigungsgesetz, put it after June 30, 1934, the Night of the Long Knives. In his speech on July 20, 1954, in commemorating the tenth anniversary of the bomb plot, he said:

Injustice and brutality began to reign immediately after the coming to power of the Nazis, but it was still clothed in the garments of traditional legal authority. The decisive moment in the history of the Nazi state took place a little over twenty years ago in July of 1934. A German Minister of Justice was forced to yield to his overlords and introduce a Bill to legalize mass murder in the interest of an internecine party struggle. A German Minister of War accepted the murder of the Generals von Schleicher and von Bredow without a murmur, as if such acts were no longer within the realm of punishable crimes. The Wehrmacht, which was at that time still a deciding factor in the state, did nothing.

Other Germans, members of that same Wehrmacht, with perhaps less sensitivity to academic legality and more feeling for political power, watched the events of June 30, 1934, with genuine relief, particularly the suppression of the extralegal military organizations of the S.A. For them the purge of the S.A. represented a necessary, if unfortunately brutal, step on the road back to legality—the end of the sway of the rowdies, perverts and beer-hall toughs. Still others saw the real change in the fusion of the offices of chancellor and president, which followed upon Hindenburg's death, and the creation of the "Führer," whose new personal oath was forced on them. The prosecution at the Remer trial made use of this argument as well by suggesting that the Hitler oath was not legally binding because the Weimar oath had never been formally abrogated. By contrast, the Kaiser had released all his subjects from their oath to him at the time of his abdication. Still others, including Popitz, several members of the Goerdeler group and others of that circle, saw the turning point in the Sudeten crisis. Others saw it after Prague or the Hitler-Stalin Pact or the outbreak of war or the aggression against neutral states or the atrocities. The fact, however, that the Vatican concluded a concordat with the Nazi state still valid today, that the Western democracies suffered all of Hitler's treaty violations, that thousands of foreigners streamed enthusiastically to the 1936 Olympics, that others thought the Nuremberg Party Days rather fun, contributed to the creation of a nimbus around Hitler and the blurring of all serious distinctions. The outside world seemed distressingly prepared to accept Hitler's state.

The disagreement over the point at which the Nazi regime became illegal in the formal sense has not been resolved. Was it illegal to hold talks in Stockholm with agents of the potential enemy one year and legal the next? Refugees today face the same problem. Often the treatment of those who flee from the Soviet satellite states depends on whether they began to resist the Communist rule before a certain point in time. There is not much to be learned in this line of investigation. For our investigation there are no norms which can be based on borderline cases. The best thing we can do is to turn to the final argument used by the prosecutor in the trial of Remer, which seems likeliest to achieve a measure of general acceptance. Bauer argued that the men of the resistance were not traitors, because the intention to harm their country was not present in their acts. Such intent to endanger the Reich was the prerequisite for a finding of treason under the criminal code obtaining in Germany even in 1944. A comparison of this argument with that used in the trial of Quisling, where the accused's intentions were of no import, shows how much we in Germany suffer by comparison with the stability of a land like Norway from a complete lack of agreed principles. This is as true today as in Hitler's time. Everything is somehow a borderline case, and each man is free to be persuaded or not as he sees fit.

No one wants to see the problem for what it is, but, as in a situation which is ignored in public but has the effect of a subterranean malady, occasionally breaking to the surface. Walter Dirks has tried to find a formula that would allow a sort of co-existence between the opposing points of view. He wrote in the *Frankfurter Hefte:* "In a state ruled by a dictatorship and in its wars both the decision to obey and the decision to resist may be personally honorable. Citizens and soldiers have called upon the law to support them in both types of action and have done so respectably." Both attitudes, says Dirks, in so far as they are deeply felt, have given a tragic worth to the actors. Dirks makes it clear that he does not consider both attitudes equally acceptable. He is an outspoken partisan of the resistance, but in justifying it he leaves the sphere of politics and enters that of religion. In the same way, Count Schwerin, when asked after his arrest how he and his friends justified participation in an assassination in the light of their professed adherence to Christianity, replied: "We discussed the question thoroughly and decided that it was not murder but judgment." These words are those of a lonely believer in a secular world and take us into the sphere of theology which is outside the competence of this book. However, they must be mentioned in this context, because a road from the landscape of twilight, of undefined borderlines of treason, will only be found when men all over the world can begin to agree in beliefs that transcend the exigencies of politics.

PART V

Espionage

27. THE SECRET AGENT

WHERE there is mutual confidence, treason cannot arise. It is the peculiar evil of our times to have blurred the line between confidence and treachery so completely that they have become almost inseparable. An external symptom is the use of the word "confidence" in the term *vertrauens-mann,* which means secret agent. "How is one supposed to trust such men?" asks Rolf Schroers in a recent article in the *Frankfurter Allgemeine.* Can one have confidence in their love, ideals or gratitude? Because one has something on them? Because one offers them better terms than the competition? Because there is always some telling threat at hand with which they can be kept in line? Does one, in effect, speculate on their variable greediness? Obviously all these factors may be present. The interesting thing seems to me to be that just such men are selected to serve as *vertrauens-manner,* men of trust or confidence.

In the half-light veiling this whole area of activity, conviction mixes with veniality, courage and anxiety, pursuit with the pursued, concealment with discovery, and truth with lies. There is the simple case, the double motivation and the complex motivation. There are men moved by ideological considerations, nationalism, collaboration, resistance, dissatisfaction. One thing which they hold in common is the determination to camouflage their real aims and methods. As a result, it is not easy to separate the rogue from the idealist or the patriot from the swindler. Indeed, in the flurry of accusations and deliberate prevarication, it is often impossible to say with any accuracy exactly what happened in any specific case. For the observer, the sources of error and confusion seem almost overwhelming, so that one is forced to assume in a simple-minded way, that never-denied stories are true, although one knows that secret services often prefer to

313

permit the falsehoods to gain currency, with a view to later use.

The transition from "classical" espionage to the all-embracing activity of the contemporary Secret Services and counterintelligence agencies was a slow one. It followed the transition from the absolute monarchy to the variety of forms of sovereignty which we know today. What one may call "classical" espionage was essentially a wartime activity which consisted of bringing home enemy secrets, most often military ones. Today, in what we choose to call peacetime, espionage goes on in every aspect of life—cultural, political, intellectual and military—and in the camps of any and all potential or actual enemies and even of one's allies. It has active aims which were entirely missing in classical espionage, the sowing of confusion among enemy public opinion and the undermining of the enemy's way of life. The natural consequence of the development of active, political espionage was the gradual formation of counterespionage services and agents, of whom Napoleon's police commissioner, Joseph Fouché, may well have been the first modern example. It is again relevant to our theme to see that Fouché first became important when the former regime began to work from within to overthrow its successor.

Espionage and treason overlap at this point, since these new tasks cannot be performed by foreigners. Use of local people, not just as paid spies, and therefore only conditionally reliable agents, but as convinced followers of the foreign government or its ideology, belongs among the special features invented in the modern era. This is the second major difference between modern and classical espionage. Spying goes on in peacetime, and the spies are now natives of the countries in which they work. The day of the dark figure in a cape, speaking with a slight foreign accent, is over. Today's espionage has something of the civil war about it. The "Fifth Column," "the fellow travelers" or the plain disaffected are all important. This is why espionage has a rightful place in a book on treason in the twentieth century.

The amount of money spent by governments on these projects is almost beyond belief. Since the budgets for espionage activity are "top secret," one can only estimate their size from occasional clues. The American press reported some years ago on a bill tabled in Congress to provide funds for the recruitment of 10,000 agents, the cost of which must have been very great. The press itself was exceedingly circumspect in its coverage of the incident, but Congressman Dewey Short of Missouri was less so in a speech on the floor. "Let us be perfectly honest about all this. The great majority of the agents will be recruited in Slavic countries. Let us face the fact that this is dirty business. In addition to purely pecuniary incentives, the chance to emigrate to the United States and to become American citizens was dangled before prospective candidates, all of whom were to be between the ages of eighteen and thirty-five and unmarried. In other words, the bill offered a new loyalty relationship to replace that one which would necessarily be undermined by their service as spies for the Americans. Recruiting of agents is carried out by both sides in pretty much the same way. One side is always on the alert for "sympathizers" and "fellow travelers" who might, under proper treatment, take the final step to service in the Soviet cause. The other side keeps an eye on Soviet or satellite diplomats, civil servants, officers or academics who, for personal or ideological reasons, might be ready to switch allegiances. Testing, review and supervision are very strict. Espionage is, after all, quite a dangerous game. The more one knows about a man, the more one can find out about his personal life, past sins, present peculiarities or perversions, the easier one can control him. The area in which all this goes on widens daily, and with the expansion of espionage into every nook and cranny of social life and in which natives of the same country work against each other, becomes more frequent. The resulting tangle of loyalty and disloyalty constantly grows more impenetrable. The outside observer has no idea what is going on.

Berlin is a perfect laboratory specimen of treachery and countertreachery. It is supposed to be the showplace for both competing world ideologies, and naturally enough has become the arena for the competing secret services as well. Infiltration and kidnapping are daily occurrences. In general, the professional spies work directly for one of the four occupying powers, while the amateurs work for a variety of shady information offices, though their role has diminished in the last few years. The variety of work undertaken by amateur spies after the war was quite unbelievable. I knew a Prussian officer who, upon his release from a Russian prison camp, immediately went to work for the Americans, while at the same time his wife combed wastepaper baskets in the American agency in which she worked, looking for information useful to the Russians. Both found it all rather fun and prattled away with evident glee about their activities to anyone whom they met. These halcyon days of amateur spying passed quickly. What took its place is much more serious. Wolfgang Weinert, the Berlin correspondent of the *Welt,* has followed this development very closely over the past years and is certainly one of the best authorities on the situation in contemporary Berlin. He maintains that leading West Berlin politicians consider the entire counterintelligence apparatus obsolete. West Berlin espionage will continue to be bungled as long as there are so many people who know how to turn it into a profitable business. An imaginary prosecuting magistrate in Leipzig, for example, who has for years—and with perfect impunity —been sending his political opponents off to jail, collides with the system one day and flees to West Berlin. If he cannot find a suitable job at once, he merely rents himself an office and unpacks the carefully assembled assortment of official East German documents, letterheads, stamps and protocols which he prudently smuggled out. In business, he open up shop as a "news" agency, a committee, an espionage service or a librarian institute. There are countless examples of just this sort of thing. Hard-bitten careerists of the S.E.D. regime become passionate anti-Communists within twenty-four hours of their arrival. These shady figures busy themselves by the hundreds in various unsavory dodges all over West Berlin. In their adept hands, a trade and commerce in news has grown up and flourishes. Petty spies eventually creep into these nests and (occasionally even literally)

316

blow the little espionage shops sky high. The gap is soon filled by new dealers in information. It is all quite unscrupulous and unburdened by any sort of organized professional supervision whatsoever. There is no problem of morality in this busy little market, and it is in this rather unusual bourse that roughly 80 percent of the informants who fatten on the payrolls of the Western powers serve their apprenticeships. No wonder the budgets are so high.

In Berlin North, the methods of one of these agencies are so unbelievably primitive and extortionate that one shudders at such incompetence. The official, state-supported "Landesamt fuer Verfassungsschutz" has one flat tire after another. The famous "Kampfgruppe gegen die Unmenschlichkeit" (Fighting Group against Inhumanity) which in its early days earned just praise, ought to have been dissolved a long time ago, not least because of the megalomania of its present director. There are no less than forty-two secret services in West Berlin. Of these about one-third are so completely permeated with Soviet and East German spies that one would do better to think of them as West Berlin subsidiaries and affiliates of the Soviet Zone Security Service.

The Hoover Commission, working under a mandate from the American Congress, had quite different criticisms to make of the conduct and effectiveness of the American Secret Service. Its views were strongly colored by the opinions of one of its leading members, General Mark Clark, himself not a novice in the field of espionage. Clark had been dispatched on an almost melo-dramatic mission in 1942, when he had been landed on the darkened Algerian Coast to make the undercover preparations for the Allied landings. Later, as commandant of the American sector of Vienna, he had had ample opportunity to gather information on the techniques of spying in the Cold War. His conclusion was that American efforts in this direction were being seriously hampered by "diplomatic timidity." The chiefs of missions avoided and discouraged anything "which might involve them in embarrassing situations." Initiative was being "smothered" in the Soviet Union and the satellite states. Clark recommended a "daring" policy in the Eastern bloc, a policy prepared to run the risk of occasional diplomatic complications.

The technique for which Clark pleaded was originally introduced by the Soviet Union itself, the first visible manifestation of which was the case of the Soviet representative in Berlin in 1919. At the Friedrichstrasse Station, his attaché case burst rather inopportunely, since it contained an absolute mountain of secret documents and propaganda material which began to blow merrily about the platform. The practice of using diplomatic centers as headquarters for espionage, though never officially recognized by any of the governments practicing it, has by now become a commonplace of contemporary international relations. Diplomatic immunity is widely abused to foment and support espionage activities. Of course none of this has ever been admitted. Denials are loudest when some member of a foreign mission is proven to be connected with a secret agent from his own country.

The few examples cited so far show that we have moved into a very different area of treachery than that in which we found ourselves hitherto. In the case both of the collaborationists and the resistance fighters, the genuine or presumed treachery always served some specific goal and remained a more or less unfortunate by-product of political dealings. Individuals acted on their own authority or that of a group. In espionage, treason comes first and is used to serve ends with which the individual involved may be only remotely concerned; indeed he may not even know what they are. In place of action by individuals, there is the machine. In place of meaningful undertakings, there is a chain of movements and separate deeds, the connection among which is known only to the remote and shadowy chiefs of the secret service itself. The human actor loses his identity and his deed its import. The secret service agent is much more the petty functionary in a large bureaucracy than the self-conscious traitor. His reward is the unconditional protection guaranteed by his organization. As an ironical consequence of this fact, we shall now have to do with living men, or at worst, men who died of natural causes, for the secret service agent stays alive. It is one of his prime capacities. No more shall we see the sombre names and dates of the executed, nor shall we read farewell letters. The men who appear in this section never stand before firing squads. They do from time to time land in jails, but when that happens there is such an attendant fog of denunciation, charge and counter-charge, that the individuals quite often escape. For a good many of these people the years 1944–45 merely represented a change of scene. They continue their work under the same or reverse banners.

Since both the occupation and personality of secret service men lie in the shadows, it is difficult to see where free choice ends and coercion begins. We could formerly say that this or that act was committed of his own free will by the individual in question. William Joyce went to Germany on his own. Ezra Pound chose to live in Italy and serve Fascism. Quisling acted freely in those fateful days of April 1940. The men in Belgium and France had of course the opposite problem, but their situations were equally clear. Pétain, Laval, Darlan and King Leopold had to act, because they were already actors at the time of the invasion. This is not to say that they acted either rightly or wrongly, but not to act would have had consequences equally as great as any action. There were the thousands of homeless refugees, the disordered streams of men from the defeated armies, the collapse of the administration, and the enemies in the land. The man in office had no choice whatsoever. He had to act, which may well be one of the reasons that the problem of "dirty hands" has so exercised the French intellectuals since 1945. Simone de Beauvoir, in *Les Bouches Inutiles,* has asked whether it is possible to keep one's hands clean in our society, a question which is hard to answer positively. The reader should note, however, this important difference between the whole class of traitors discussed so far and the secret agents to follow. Each man so far discussed faced a specific situation. The observer can say fairly definitely how much free choice and how much compulsion seem to have been involved in each case. Some clearly elected to do what they did; others, equally clearly, were forced to decide as they did. The observer can make no such definite assessment in examining undercover agents.

Silence, inaction and nonparticipation are inadequate modes of behavior in a society which repeatedly presents the individual with differing sorts of guilt as the only option. It is often quite impossible to decide upon the least of several evils. An example is the dilemma of Vichy Minister of the Interior Pucheu, who had managed to extract an amnesty for three of six hostages about to be shot by the Germans. When he learned that one of the three was the father of three children, he tried to save this man too. But this would have suspended the pardon of the other three; either one or six were the alternatives. Pucheu's decision was for the number, not for the case. Robert Aron remarked: "This shows the inhumanity of a civilization which forces such a choice between the salvation of the soul and physical survival."

The events in the German resistance were more opaque; everything had to be done under cover and there was generally a contradiction between official thinking and verbal instructions. This was clearly demonstrated by the prosecution at the Nürnburg trials in the case against State Secretary Weizsäcker, an almost classical example of the interaction of effective opposition and guilty collaboration. Compulsion in the cases of men like Weizsäcker, Canaris and Stauffenberg, who work within the Leviathan against the Leviathan, is still keyed to a kind of free choice, while members of a secret service become more and more bound, from year to year, from mission to mission. It is true that all men who resist a totalitarian regime must be on guard against eager listeners, must learn to be silent, to make detours, to distinguish between their official words and acts and their private thinking. Yet even in this kind of camouflaged existence, life can be led truthfully and responsibly without losing oneself in all the necessary compromises.

However, if sleight of hand and deception become a sort of

320

perverse fun, the whole attitude changes. The great majority of the men of the 20th of July found the elaborate game of concealment merely an irksome concomitant of their situations and retained a clear sense that this was just a temporary contrivance. Adam von Trott once got a letter asking for help from Count Soltikow, who was facing what appeared to be certain death in a trial before the People's Court. His only salvation lay in the testimony of a certain Colonel de la Porte, who had been threatened with loss of position and pension if he dared to testify on Soltikow's behalf. Trott's reply was characteristic of the straightforward approach to life which he and a few others of the resistance managed to preserve in the midst of all the creeping and dissembling in a totalitarian state: "How would it be, if you suddenly rose in court and described the threats to Colonel de la Porte, asking permission at the same time of the representatives of the Reichsführer S.S. to allow the witness to speak without constraint? Every once in a while, one has to grab the bull by the horns. I have a hunch that at a show trial where the whole crowd from the other ministries is present they won't have much choice but to let the witness speak up." Soltikow was just desperate enough to follow Trott's seemingly naive advice, and to the general amazement, it worked like a charm. Soltikow was acquitted in a case in which the death sentence had seemed an absolutely sure thing. "Grabbing the bull by the horns" is the very last thing which would occur to a *Vertrauens-Mann,* but typical for the forthright behavior of Trott and his friends, in spite of their abilities for underground work.

On July 20, 1944, Otto John was no less a member of the resistance than his brother Hans or his friends, Klaus and Dieter Bonhoeffer. John's entanglement began with his relationship to the British Secret Service, a contact which saved his life. The British Secret Service would not have bothered to save John from the mighty tentacles of the Leviathan in Spain and Portugal, if it had not been certain of his willingness to take the decisive step from resistance to "treason." It is questionable whether John realized that he had, in fact, taken any such step, for the distinction between fighting the totalitarian state from within and fighting it from without, in the "enemy's" wake, is a debatable and subtle one.

A good deal of confusion arose from the switches in policy of the great powers as well. Torpedo-boat Commander Per Evard Danielsen, the son of the chief of the Norwegian Navy, became a legend during the war because of his daring attacks on German coastal shipping from hidden Soviet naval bases in the Baltic. Adventure was his métier, and the return to orderly civilian existence proved hard for him. In 1951, he was arrested for slipping secrets to the Soviet naval attaché in Oslo. His feeling of solidarity with his former comrades and boredom with routine existence had turned him into a traitor. The forty-year-old American, John Sydney Peterson, had been in the National Security Agency for thirteen years at the time of his arrest for, among other things, informing the Dutch that their allies, the Americans had deciphered their secret codes. He gave as his reasons for his action a deep friendship struck up with a Dutch general during the war and the conviction that "it was not right to put allies upon whom we rely in embarrassing situations."

28. RUDOLF RÖSSLER—
THE STATELESS ONE

RUDOLF RÖSSLER was a man driven from two countries, a wanderer without a country, but still a Bohemian patriot to the end of his life. He is most remarkable because, contrary to the common run of secret agents, he was not used by the complicated and highly efficient apparatus of a great power, but he, a single man, without the benefit of an apparatus, was in a mysterious way able to use the treasonable work of many men who have remained unknown until this day. There are even two versions of his origin. One would have him the son of a Bavarian civil servant, born in Kaufbeuren, educated in Augsburg, who, having fought in the First World War, ended up in Berlin, where he became a journalist and eventually head of the German actors' guild. This is the official Swiss version, entered in the court record at his two trials. According to *Der Spiegel*, which devoted a series of articles to Rössler, the weight of evidence gathered by the various international secret services indicates that Rössler is not even his real name. The second version has it that he was one of the young General Staff officers in the Imperial Austro-Hungarian Army who found themselves jobless and on the streets in 1918. In 1919, the Soviet Republic of Hungary under Bela Kun launched an attack on the newly created Czech Republic which soon became a life-and-death struggle. Together with several of his unemployed comrades, Rössler (or whatever he was called in those days) offered his services to the hard-pressed Czechs, who accepted gratefully. He fought, this version says, with great distinction and contributed in many ways to the defeat of the Red Army of Hungary. After the victory, the German-speaking Bohemian was unceremoniously dismissed and joined the Sudeten resistance movement. His way led him to Berlin from which point the two versions coincide in that both claim that he served as a journalist and head of the actors' guild.

One of the facts which speaks for the authenticity of the second version was that this improbable little man with thick spectacles and limpid brown eyes happens to be one of the greatest military experts in Europe. At the same time he was an active and belligerent pacifist. He waged his intellectual war against war by means of his publishing company, Vita Nova, in Lucerne, Switzerland, whither he wandered after the Nazis came to power. Books published by the Vita Nova were on the Nazi black list in all countries under German hegemony. A variety of distinguished works were published under his imprint—Berdyayev, Paul Claudel's *Concentration and Ideas,* Schubart's *Europe and the Spirit of the East,* Jacques Maritain's *Society and Freedom,* and Karl Löwith's *Jacob Burckhardt.* Among the authors whom Rössler published were Emmanuel Mounier, the publisher and moving force behind the Left-Wing Catholic periodical *L'Esprit;* Helene

Isvolski, the daughter of the former Tsarist Ambassador in Paris, who wrote unique accounts of the survival of Russian Orthodoxy under Stalin, Chiang Kai-shek during his anti-Japanese phase, Stanley Baldwin and Friedrich Wilhelm Foerster. The common elements would appear to be Catholic thought, interest in revolution and the Slavic world. This strange-seeming collection of intellectual doctrines happens to fit the intellectual climate of Bohemia exactly and is a further argument in support of the second version of Rössler's past. Ever since the days of Jan Hus, Catholicism in Bohemia has had a highly eccentric sectarian quality to it, a taste of the revolutionary, a bit of anti-Vatican feeling and a large sprinkling of the Old-Catholic Church which denies the dogma of the Pope's infallibility.

Rössler founded his publishing company through the good offices of his wealthy young Swiss friend, Dr. Xavier Schnieper. Rössler was perpetually in financial difficulties, but Vita Nova managed to keep its head above water because of Schnieper. He had studied Slavic literature in Königsberg, after which he spent time in Berlin, where he met and grew to be an admirer of Rössler's. After the completion in Vienna of his doctoral dissertation on Rilke, he returned to his native town of Lucerne, where he took up a past in the Cantonal library and began to publish a Left-Wing Catholic weekly, *Decision*. The very sensitive spirit of the young Swiss was seriously shaken by the shock of the Nazi accession to power. Having seen the brown columns marching in Berlin during the early 1930's, he was terrified for the future of Switzerland in a world where, as he put it, "the idea of democracy had been debased." He became preoccupied with the task of winning the Swiss working class to firmer adherence to the principles of the Federal Democracy of Switzerland, which drove him ever further Left. He joined a series of Socialist parties, only to leave them again, dissatisfied. He worked for *Vorwärts* until that paper fell too patently under Communist influence. After that he joined the editorial staff of the Socialist weekly *Volksrecht*, which proved equally unsatisfactory.

Schnieper never took root anywhere. Confronted with Rös-

sler's vision of "the new man in our time," Schnieper thought that
at last he had found the long sought for ideal around which to
center his energies. At the same time, he was a practical, calculating Swiss. Schnieper held the rank of sergeant-major in the
citizen army, which brought him into contact with Major Hausmann's "Operation Pilate." Hausmann had the Herculean task
of building a Swiss secret service literally from scratch. Schnieper
first met him at the home of Dr. Oprecht, the famous Zurich
publisher, and spent a time at the Villa Steig near Lucerne where
Hausmann had begun to set up the new secret service agency.
By this time, even before the outbreak of the Second World War,
Rössler had become the Swiss Liddell Hart, and his opinions
were generally highly regarded. Alexander Foote, the British-
born Soviet spy with whom Rössler later worked, as we shall see,
once remarked that Rössler's articles for the Swiss press were
the final word on any military topic. Nothing lay closer to hand
or was more naturally arranged than Schnieper's introduction of
Rössler to Major Hausmann.

The Swiss, of course, were aware that any day the same thing
might happen to them that had happened to Denmark and
Holland. Knowledge of Hitler's war plans was a matter of life
and death for them. Rudolf Rössler delivered this information.
From whom he got his information and how remains today one
of the great mysteries in the annals of the secret services of the
world. It is, as it were, the "perfect crime" in the field of espionage. The Zurich *Tat* once listed the various offices, departments and agencies in which Rössler must have somehow had an
informant. The list reads like the organizational plan of Germany's war administration: Wehrmacht High Command, High
Command Army, High Command Luftwaffe, Commander in
Chief of the Reserve Army, Foreign Office, Army Ordnance Office, Office of Strategic Planning. A part of his information
would seem to have come by courier and a part by radio. Orders from Führer's Headquarters, Hitler himself, or Oberkom-
mando Wehrmacht, were in his hands within twenty-four hours
with astonishing regularity.

TREASON IN THE TWENTIETH CENTURY

Rössler was originally connected with the "Rote Kapelle." The weird part is that after the "Rote Kapelle" was liquidated, Rössler continued to get information of precisely the same reliability and quality as before. He has often been associated with certain men of the 20th of July, and the Lucerne pastor who testified at his second trial stated that Rössler had close contact with the Ecumenical Council in Geneva and through it with Admiral Canaris. Yet even after the wave of arrests and liquidations consequent upon the smashing of the plot, Rössler assured Foote that he was entirely prepared to continue the regular delivery of news as before. By that time Foote was himself unable to pass on any information received from Rössler, because his own network had been broken. In one of his reports Foote suggested that the only possible explanation was that Rössler had a source at the very top of the Nazi hierarchy, someone in the inner circle around Martin Bormann or Himmler himself. One of Foote's contact men owed his alias, Pakbo, to the claim that he got his material directly from Bormann's party chancellery. These allegations belong to the complex of questions relating to the possible treachery of Himmler, which have not yet been tackled by the historians.

Something of Rössler's remarkable services to Switzerland came out in the second trial, which took place before a civil court. It appeared that Rössler had worked for another secret agency in Switzerland, in addition to Major Hausmann's, an agency called "Viking," under the direction of Colonel Waibel. The Viking reports, mentioned in the diary of Colonel Barbey, Chief of Staff to General Guisan, which contained the complete record of all the German deliberations on the advisability of invading Switzerland, were probably supplied by Rössler. As vague as the testimony about his accomplishments was kept, the information which Rössler, under the cover name of Lucy, delivered to the "Rado-Foote" group of the Communist network for transmission to the Soviets was equally exact. Two assignments made by the "director" in Moscow offer some idea of the content and extent of the information delivered:

Radioed from the Soviet Union on January 30, 1943—Pass urgent query to Lucy: Do Infantry Divisions, Numbers 327, 334, 347, 343, and 366, exist in the Wehrmacht? Where present location? Are Infantry Divisions 196 and 199 still in Norway?—DIRECTOR.

February 6, 1943—Give Lucy orders to find out, if possible, how High Command plans to man new defense line. By using retreating troops or newly organized units brought from behind the lines? Tell Lucy that all conversations and debates with General Staff and High Command of interest, not just final decision.—DIRECTOR.

Alexander Foote, the English Communist who, according to his own testimony, worked for the Red Army in Switzerland, but according to some experts, also delivered information to his own compatriots, did not know who "Lucy" was during the course of the operation.

Foote's account of the beginning of Rossler's activity for Moscow is:

Rössler offered his services to one of Rado's coworkers in the beginning of 1941, on the condition that complete anonymity be preserved. As far as I know, this was the only occasion on which Moscow accepted such a condition and received information from an anonymous source. In this case, unorthodoxy bore rich fruits, for Rudolf Rössler, if this was his real name, turned out to be not German but Czech, As a reward for his work, he had received permission to remain in Switzerland, where, until the end of Czechoslovakia, he worked for the Czech General Staff.

The two dates are interesting. First, "until the end of Czechoslovakia" would mean that until March 1939, the Sudeten German and Bohemian patriot, who had once served his native land so well, was apparently still serving it. The second, "the beginning of 1941," was the time at which Rössler made his offer to aid the Soviet spy in gathering information about German troops in the East. By the beginning of 1941, the sources from which Rössler got his information knew of the impending German invasion of Russia. The situation then made it obvious that the Soviets were the only force which could free Czechoslovakia from the National Socialists. Benes himself, head of the Czech Government in Exile in London, concluded a treaty with the Soviet

327

Union. We thus have a straight line from 1919 through 1938–1939–1947, when Rössler resumed intelligence work for a group of Benes' Czechs.

During the years in which Czechoslovakia, as a state, did exist, there was living in Lucerne an energetic and rather curious Czech. We don't know whether Rössler knew him, but Schnieper undoubtedly did. "Uncle Tom," as he was called, was supposedly a Canadian relative of Major Hausmann's wife and seemed to have carte blanche everywhere in the Villa Steig, where Major Hausmann's "Operation Pilate" was concealed. Schnieper noticed that Uncle Tom would very often hurry off to Berne when Rösssler's report, the contents of which could have nothing more than academic interest for the Swiss, had arrived. Uncle Tom had in fact been sent by the Anglo-American Secret Services to act as liaison officer to Operation Pilate. Schnieper's statements on this subject evoke a very complex picture of the subtle interplay of motives and allegiance in the secret services operating in Swiss territory. Schnieper and his defending counsel counsel repeatedly cited cases of information being passed to the English and Americans by members of the Swiss Secret Service. It is entirely possible that Rössler merely wanted to help the Russians to their fair share of the fruits of Allied espionage and to right the balance between information going West and information going East. Rössler, in practice, passed on to the Russians everything he knew, which was a great deal, for he was not only a superb spy but also one of the best military analysts and interpreters of published information in the world. If this assumption is correct, the Rössler's activity would be in many respects like that of Klaus Fuchs's who also felt it morally unjustifiable that the Russians be frozen out of the secrets of the development of the atomic bomb. Roosevelt's attitude of open cooperation with the Russians was generally praised in those days, and certainly helped to create an atmosphere in which aiding the Russians in a slightly extralegal way did not and could not seem terribly reprehensible.

The case of Rössler illustrates the confusion created by the interaction of the pressure of secrecy, the system of double agency, and the practice of feeding wrong material to the opposite. At the same time it allows a glimpse into the mentality of one of the greatest managers of treason the world has ever known. Foote states that the Soviets accepted Rössler without prior investigation. Yet for years they had suspected Foote of being a double agent: a British spy. Their distrust of the unknown "Lucy" was conderably greater, for the most excellent of his reports were ignored for long periods of time, or evaluated as Nazi plants. Among the ignored communications was that reporting that Germany would attack Russia on June 22, 1949. Today we know that Stalin received warnings of Hitler's intentions from at least four sources: directly from Churchill; officially from Sir Stafford Cripps, British Ambassador to Moscow; secretly from Richard Sorge in Tokyo; and from "Lucy" in Switzerland. Thanks to the revelations of Krushchev, we also know that Stalin ignored all warnings. The great psychological question is: Was he motivated by reliance on his friendship with Hitler or by distrust of the British as well as of the Secret Service of the Red Army, which obviously knew how to keep itself reasonably free of GPU influences and remained objective even in times of the worst despotism?

In 1947, Xavier Schnieper was astounded by the visit of Uncle Tom, whom he had not seen since the days of Operation Pilate in the Villa Steig. Uncle Tom blandly revealed that his real name was Sedlacek and that he had just been appointed Czech Military Attaché in Berne. The object of his visit, Sedlacek continued, was to find out whether Rössler would be willing to put his priceless gifts at the disposal of the Benes Government. From that point on, Schnieper began to play the middle-man between Rössler and a succession of Czech secret agents and military attachés. When confronted with this fact at the trial, Schnieper countered by arguing that somehow he had to keep Rössler's head above water and try to save the most important element in the Swiss Secret Service which, he charged, had been allowed to rust and crumble in an outrageous way. Schnieper believed, as did so many in those days, that the Third World War was, at the most, three years away, but at the worst might break out at any time. He said: "It was then, and remains today, a complete mystery to me how our secret news service could have dropped Rössler. If I, as a sergeant major, permit rust to form on my machine gun, I am justly hauled before a court-martial. Yet the Army allowed an infinitely more valuable weapon to go to the Devil, and no one batted an eyelash."

Rössler had been accused in the meantime, in a second case, of having violated Article 301 of the Swiss Criminal Code, which serves to punish all those who infringe the strictly defined neutrality of Switzerland. The article demands imprisonment or a heavy fine for anyone "who carries on a news service for the benefit of one foreign state and to the detriment of another foreign state anywhere within the territory of the Federal Republic of Switzerland, or who recruits for such services or who assists them in any way." In the charges the prosecution listed the United States, Great Britain, France, West Germany and Denmark as the states harmed by Rössler's activities. The case soon developed into an attempt to define the legal nature of the material delivered. Rössler's defense argued stoutly and surprisingly well that these were merely "analyses," based on published articles and reports available to anyone. The defense asserted and the court confirmed that Rössler had developed an archive of remarkable scope and variety and an extraordinary interpretive technique for processing the material. "In military affairs, even in regard to details, a good deal is published about things which one would suppose are top secret." This was the court's opinion. Any journalist can confirm it. An isolated reference in a general report will have no meaning to the general reader, but to the trained journalist who has patiently built up an archive on the topic, a sentence or phrase suddenly springs out of the text, and then another, and here perhaps a third. Soon a picture can be formed, from the distillation of these illuminating references, about something which in one or several capitals is spoken of only in hushed tones. In America there was great dismay when an obscure Japanese technical journal published an account in some detail of a new and hitherto secret airplane type. It soon turned out that the Japanese article was not the result of a brilliant espionage coup or treachery in high places, but simply the result of painstaking assembly of bits and published pieces here and there, combined by imaginative, well-trained specialists.

Rössler described his method in these words: "I collected every sort of material available, that is, information about military, economic, political or organizational facts or events. The raw material was then processed. Each piece was systematically compared and cross-referenced. Contradictions and correspondences were investigated and evaluated in larger terms. Quite often it was possible to arrive at conclusions which threw the correct light on some matter, little known, misunderstood or kept secret." Most of the material was not used for his secret service work but organized for publication in any one of the many journals and papers for which he wrote. The editor of one of those Lucerne dailies described several incidents which occurred as a result of the acuteness of Rössler's analyses. After the paper had printed, unsigned, an article by Rössler on developments in Russian atomic research, the editor had a visit from an American air attaché from Berne who wished to get in contact with the author of an article on Russian atomic research, on the assumption that the information in the article came from behind the Iron Curtain. The harassed editor was visited several times by a man from the German section of the State Department. Rössler's identity was not revealed.

The prosecution rejected the arguments of the defense and pointed out that the prevailing attitude of Swiss courts in the past had been to regard the passing on of newspaper articles "which had been entirely forgotten or known only to a small circle" as traffic in news. The prosecuting attorney continued by introducing two especially damaging admissions by the defendant: that he received regular messages from friends who related various "events in Germany of a personal, intellectual or political nature"; that twice a month an acquaintance from Germany "who played a role in public life" would visit him in Lucerne, in fact, often came to Switzerland just to see Rössler. They knew nothing of his work for the Czech Secret Service.

Thus the puzzle repeats itself. The "Rote Kapelle" is dead. The men of the 20th of July are dead. The men who held high office in 1945 have been removed. A new group, deriving either from the survivors of Weimar or from the new postwar generation, holds the reins in Bonn. Yet the émigré of 1933 still manages to find out everything he wants to know.

The prosecution also cited the high sums which Rössler received. Between 1947 and 1953, he submitted 150 reports and received in payment 33,000 Swiss francs, of which Schnieper got 20 to 30 percent. The defense stuck to its assertion that these were merely military analyses and pointed out that the per-line rate of 1.20 Swiss francs was hardly very high for the quality of the work (i.e., roughly 30¢).

Rössler was finally caught. The proof that he had been sending actual military secrets had been found in a tin of honey containing a microfilm which the Swiss authorities had intercepted in 1953. The film contained figures and facts about the air bases and headquarters of the R.A.F. in Germany, the results of the maneuvers of the 5th Corps of the U.S. Army, the support bases of the U.S. Air Force in Jutland, the nature of the military emplacements in Rhineland-Pfalz, and the numerical strength of the French land forces in Germany. By this time, Benes and Masaryk, who had tried vainly to preserve some independence for their country, had long been dead, and the film was only too obviously valuable on delivery to Moscow. An intriguing question remains. The Czechs had proven themselves the cleverest, and therefore the most effective opponents of the National Socialist regime. They united an apparent will to cooperate and a collective adaptation to circumstances with a remarkably well-concealed resistance. It is just possible that even today, after the 100-percent Communization of the country, the Czech Secret

Service might still hold a few cards of its own and still maintain one or two tiny independent tentacles.

From the legal point of view, the Swiss court ought to have been entirely indifferent to the identity of the power which Rössler served, but today even legal ethics cannot help being overcome by the universal supremacy of political necessity. Rössler appealed to the court to judge his acts in the same spirit in which they would have judged him if he had delivered news from the East to the West, instead of the other way around. The Swiss court had long abandoned the stage at which it could regard both forms of espionage with equal severity. Rössler's words had an almost grotesque naïveté about them. One of the witnesses had testified that Rössler's idealism had been "naive" and "unreal," although he admitted that both the naïveté and the otherworldliness were rooted in deeply sincere Christian principles. The defense used three points in its appeal to the court: first, it pointed to the financial difficulties of the Vita Nova press, which had forced Rössler to accept the Czech offer; secondly, the defense argued that the things done by Swiss officers during the war on behalf of the Americans went far beyond anything ever done by Rössler; thirdly, the defense asserted, and the Swiss press agreed "convincingly," that, in contrast to his wartime espionage for the "Director" in Moscow, he had not carried out each and every assignment given him by the Czechs but had selected only those which he could reconcile with his conscience. The most important testimony concerned the third question—that is, Rössler's motivation. Upon the witness stand, he had testified with evident feeling that his experiences in both the First and Second World wars had made him a foe of war and one who believed that a third world war must be prevented at all costs. He had, to his sorrow, been forced to recognize that American policy aimed at a revision of the Potsdam decisions. The Germans were to be urged to reject the Oder-Neisse line. Since the death of Roosevelt, America had tried relentlessly to rule the world with its money and power. He wanted to make clear that he was not an enemy of the United States, but of its policy "to mobilize the historical bearers of imperialism and militarism." Czechoslovakia was a small, harmless state, threatening no one, which had been forced to turn to the East by the failure of the West in 1938.

Before the trial, all Switzerland had been aroused against him. The Zurich *Tat* published in great detail all the evidence presented, and the general feeling was that long imprisonment, followed by banishment, was the very least which ought to be demanded. Rössler himself changed the attitude entirely by the simplicity and earnestness of his appearance. He impressed the court sufficiently for the prosecution submission to be dismissed, and the stateless Bohemian was permitted to remain in the country. Even the respected *Neue Zuricher Zeitung,* itself hardly a haven for fellow travelers, found it perfectly acceptable that Rössler's work for the Czech Secret Service and his basic anti-Nazi feelings were consistent and that he might well have worked for the Czech espionage without himself having been a Communist.

29. OTTO JOHN—THE DIVIDED LAND

"MAY you never become a prisoner of the Secret Service and never drink from the 'III f.' cup. This poison is fatal." These words were contained in a letter to Otto John by his onetime rival, Friedrich Wilhelm Heinz. Heinz knew what he was talking about. Under Hitler he had been a close collaborator of Canaris and Oster, and was to have arrested Hitler in 1938, had the coup planned by the generals during the Sudeten crisis come off. After Berlin and Prussia had been occupied by the Soviets he seems to have collaborated with the Russians to a certain extent, but he left their occupation zone in 1946, later became information chief in the newly formed West German Army, and in 1954 was kidnapped by the Russians in East Berlin from where he managed to extricate himself once again. At the time he wrote his letter John was secure in a high office of the Federal Republic and the "Spiegel" remarked: "John has so far survived the drink."

A mere eight months later Jens Daniel wrote in the same magazine that whereas ten years ago it was "morally imperative" to rise against the state, today every uprooted, neurotic border dweller was calling on the same principles to justify his wandering back and forth between East and West. As long as there were two Germanys, the 20th of July would be misused to cloak every change of front. Otto John was an example. First an English agent, and then suddenly chief of the German counter-intelligence. That was a little too much. The moral convictions of a people do not form or change as quickly as those of its orators.

Much can be said for the view that Otto John, as a phenomenon, was too much for the German people, but one must add, in all fairness, that Germany and the times were also too much for Otto John. Can one blame him? An enormous amount has been written about him, about the motives for his actions and about his psychology. The comments contained in a letter of the widow of one of the Kreisau counts, written after she met Otto John for the first time in 1953, are, I think, very revealing: "I was startled. John gave me the impression of being somehow undefined, insecure, and yet curiously sympathetic. I had the strange feeling that he was terribly 'harmless,' although I know that he certainly cannot be that." The word "harmless" is perhaps a clue to the riddle of Otto John. He had the sort of German "harmlessness" which is so often paired with high intelligence.

John was one of those people whose world is determined by the idea of "one." "One does this." "One does not do that." He was obsessed by the ideal of the gentleman and was irresistibly drawn to those circles in which "the better" people are to be found. As a young man, he was attracted by the glamor of the Foreign Office, but did not get in. John said that his distaste for the Nazis was too evident during the interviews, but it is entirely

335

conceivable that the choosy and capricious personnel policy of the Foreign Office was to blame. The Lufthansa was a bit less stuffy. It counted among its staff many high-sounding old names, a number of former officers, and several World War I flying aces. These were men who had been around, who had the manners of men of the world. His close friend Prince Louis Ferdinand, whom John visited on the day before his dramatic disappearance to East Berlin in 1954, was a perfect example of the way in which the ancient traditions of the Hohenzollerns could be combined with the behavior of a modern democratic citizen. The Nazis, on the other hand, were quite obviously products of the gutter, whereas the circle which formed itself around Canaris was a social elite, a group in which John could feel at home. He had been introduced by Klaus Bonhoeffer, the chief attorney of the Lufthansa, and soon found himself spiritually very close to Klaus's brother Dieter, to Dohnanyi and others. In addition, he had several contacts in the Goerdeler-Beck group and had been friendly with the sons of General Hammerstein.

As agent of the Canaris group, he worked in Madrid, mainly with the English and the Americans, with whom he had long and intimate contact, according to John Wheeler Bennett. In the last few weeks before the 20th of July, his task had been to prepare the ground for a "feeler" to the Americans. On July 19 he arrived in Berlin and went directly to the Bendlerstrasse, where he expected to receive his final instructions for the arrangements for a meeting between Eisenhower and Colonel Hansen, Canaris' deputy. As he was leaving the War Office on the afternoon of the 20th, Haffner stopped him in the door and said, "Ring me up tomorrow morning at eight. By that time, we shall have done the job or been hanged." At midnight, John got word that the Putsch had failed, and he decided to fly to Lisbon at once. In Portugal, a neutral country, he became the prize in a massive struggle between the British and German Secret Services, the reason for which is still unclear. The fact is that the British won and that they must have had reasons for making such a great effort. This would permit the conclusion that John went further in his conversation with the British than the men described in the section on the resistance. He probably did not reveal any military secrets, but gave more of himself, which is typical of many Germans confronting foreigners whom they consider to be "better" people.

We have already mentioned John's activity as an English agent after the collapse in 1945. He felt fine in the British uniform and wore it with real pleasure during the months of chaos which followed the end of the "Thousand-Year Reich." When things began to settle down a bit, he tried again to get into the new German Foreign Office and again failed. After his appointment as chief of the Federal Bureau for the Defense of the Constitution (Bundesamt für Verfassungsschutz), he enjoyed a period of high regard and prestige. Manfred George, publisher of the New York German language newspaper, *Der Aufbau,* described John in the New York *Herald Tribune* as "a quiet, sober and determined man" with an "innate sense of justice," who is "admirably equipped for the post which he now holds, thanks to his political integrity and specialized experience." His friend Sefton Delmer stuck by him, even after his sensational disappearance in East Berlin. Don Cook, Bonn correspondent of the *Herald Tribune,* in a thoughtful article after his flight to East Germany, said of him:

There were deep cleavages and mental struggles in the man—at one moment a charming, warm humor and the next moment a deep, reflective, almost depressing state of mind. As with many thinking Germans, he often showed how torn he was between what he—as a sophisticated and worldly man with an understanding of other countries and peoples—knew Germany could be and what it is; what the past has done to Germany and the dangers that the future holds. Dr. John was not by nature a depressed personality, but he was reflective, he felt deeply, and he had lived dangerously and emotionally. He was perhaps mentally drained and exhausted by facts and by problems and by events which no one can know. He knew well the sinister side and the megalomania of his country, and could talk of it lucidly and with candor.

John fairly obviously constructed a political ideal against which to measure the nation, just as he had his personal ideal against which to measure himself. One imagines that this national ideal would have had strong Anglo-Saxon features, a liberal, Western democratic state, against which the various real Germanys in which he found himself at the moment—whether the Germany of Hitler, of Adenauer or of Ulbricht—would always be painfully deficient. In this sense John never betrayed Germany to Russia or England, but rather sacrificed the real for the sake of an ideal.

In a way John visualized an ideal Germany, which, like William Joyce's vision of England, did not exist. The difference was that John lived long enough to follow the story to its bitter end, for from 1944 on he had lent his voice to the power which won the war and was allowed, under aegis, to return to the fatherland. At first an avenger, he soon switched to the role of reformer, trying to force his ideal of the nation on a woeful and guilt-ridden people. He could assume that many, perhaps the majority, agreed with him in his judgment of the Third Reich. His dissatisfaction with the Federal Republic was also not without justification. In an article for the *Frankfurter Allgemeine*, the C.D.U. member of the Bundestagk, August Dresbach, described the change in social values in Bonn which so upset John and others. The common question of the 1950's was: Well, why wasn't X a member of the Party? The burden of proof shifted to the anti-Nazi, to show that he was not an oddity. "Applications to firms, trade associations and official agencies in which the prospective candidate emphasizes that he was not a member of the Nazi party do not have the effect which they had immediately after the war. Sometimes they produce the very opposite effect and lose the applicant his chance."

These are surely some of the "facts, problems and events" to which Don Cook was indirectly referring in his article. However, Dresbach pointed out in his article, "The Exaggerations of Herr John," that all these things must be kept in proper perspective;

John's objections and reservations have substance, but they are too extreme; he was more right than wrong, but his point of view was oblique and his vision distorted. He repeatedly failed to maintain a balance in his relations with the world around him. It is important, furthermore, to recall that John's views were not the expression of organic development in his own thought, but had been taken over bodily from people whom he respected. As a result, his judgments were always a shade awry. Dresbach points to one of these when he writes that: "John was as incapable as were the High Commissioners of perceiving the difference between the Nazis and the soldiers in the Army." For John, all generals were bad per se. When we recall the opinions of several leading members of the resistance, we see that here, too, John was in good company.

His ideas about National Socialism were even more rigid. He worked out an article on the re-Nazification of Germany. The Foreign Office chose to ignore it, which could only have strengthened John's browing sense of isolation. Then there was the affair of Heinz. For a man of John's taste and attitudes, Heinz must have been particularly repellent, for John hated the Nazi "type" as much, if not more, than he hated the ideology. Heinz was precisely that "type." Here again, John stood together with the "good" Germans.

If one examines John's famous statement at his East Berlin press conference and strips it of the standard Soviet-Zone phraseology, one arrives at a hard core, which consists of opposition to the policy of rearming Germany, to NATO and to the Adenauer regime. John felt that all chance of reunification had been destroyed by the sellout of the cause of Germany in exchange for junior partnership in the Western alliance. There is nothing especially unusual about these views. West German politicians of all political persuasions, Left-Wing Social Democrat Herbert Wehner, Liberal Thomas Dehler, Conservatives Paul Sethe and Karl Silex, have publically professed them. The difference between the West German politicians just named and Otto John is, as it always was, one of degree. Most members of the resistance did not become British agents. Most opponents of Adenauer-American policy for Germany did not feel it necessary to flee to the East, but preferred to stand up for their opinions in Western Germany, which necessitates a certain amount of courage.

Hans Zehrer said that just before his disappearance John had reached "a state of disintegration and collapse." Most of the reasons cited for his flight—the fear that his job was no longer safe because the new minister of interior was critical of him, the anxiety that his entire organization might be absorbed by General Gehlen's new military secret service, all the various temporal and practical aspects of his life—seem to me very insignificant when I consider the psychological state of mind in which John found himself. It is not really very important whether or not he was abducted in an unconscious state by Dr. Wohlgemuth. It is entirely conceivable that John, in his inner turmoil, agreed to pay a visit to East Berlin in the company of Dr. Wohlgemuth. After all, he used to fly back and forth to Madrid for talks in the same way. As Heinz declared, John could easily have been talked into staying. We know that he was aware of the dangers to which he might be exposed, because he took care before he left to remove from his pockets all papers, notes or keys which might in any way have interested the Russians.

John did show himself to have the integrity attributed to him by Manfred George and Don Cook, for not one *v-mann* of the bureau was uncovered or endangered because of his flight. The work of the bureau continued uninterrupted, and the West German authorities, as well as the Western Allies, admitted that he harmed no one but himself. He refused to make a joint appearance with Field Marshal Paulus (the commander of the German VIth Army at Stalingrad, who, after his capture, cooperated with the Russians). It is typical of Germany today that each considered the other a traitor. His utterances were on the whole noncommittal and went only a little way beyond what opponents of the Bonn Government's policies were saying in West Germany at the time. Minister of the Interior Schröder, in his report to the Bundestag in September 1954, took the view that John had not, in fact, committed treason. There was no hint of such an accusation in the entire report. Schröder confined himself to criticism of John's failure to impress his personality on the bureau under his care. The case continued to cause uneasiness in Germany. It is a striking coincidence that John returned to the West at the very moment when the government had been driven into a corner. The committee of the Bundestag investigating the John case had just begun to clamor publicly for the right to examine the files of the Federal Bureau for the Defense of the Constitution, which would very likely have thrown light on several other affairs of an embarrassing sort. The case was, in one way, an "all-German" affair. Literally everybody who had a word to say about the conduct of affairs in the divided Germany of the 1950's —the Adenauer Government, the Ulbricht Government, the Russians, the Americans, the British, and not least, the West German Social Democrats, who had made a terrific fuss in 1950 about John's failure to get a job in the Foreign Office, which they attributed to the presence of "Old Guard" elements in high places —all of these groups were heartily embarrassed by the case.

Someone compared John's disappearance with Rudolf Hess's flight to England, and there is a certain aptness in the comparison. Both men tried to build a bridge over the abyss of hate, and in trying proved themselves to be rare political dunces. The crucial difference lies in the "type" of war. Hess escaped to an enemy country. On July 20, 1954, Otto John simply traveled from one part of a city to another. His case is a symptom of the schizophrenia under which Germany labors today, a psychosis of which he must have been aware. His reaction to the case of Dr. Wilhelm Scheidt, who had been official war historian at the Führer's headquarters, suggests that John was only too well aware of the German mentality. In 1953, as an employee of the Federal Press Office, Scheidt wrote an article in a neutralist West German newspaper in which he attacked the Bonn Government's policy of rearming Germany. As a press officer of that very government, he was presumably active eight hours a day in the propagation of a policy which he publicly condemned. John said that Scheidt was obviously sincere, but equally obviously a case of the national schizophrenia of which he often spoke. On the day before he disappeared in East Berlin, John and his close friend Wolfgang Hoeffer had talked at length about the gloomy aspects of the Scheidt case. Hoeffer, who had been a school friend of John's, had been forced to flee during the Nazi era because he was half Jewish, and had returned in 1945 as an American agent. Hoeffer asked for the meeting to beg John to help him find a job somewhere in industry, because his situation in the C.I.C. had become intolerable. He had just been informed by his superiors that he was to be transferred from Berlin to Bonn with the specific assignment of spying on John. One can imagine how unpleasant this bit of news must have been for John, the man in charge of the West German Secret Service, presumably one of the most trusted men in Bonn. Later that night John was horrified to learn that his friend Hoeffer had committed suicide immediately after leaving him. One can only guess at the thoughts revolving in John's mind on that gloomy evening before July 20, 1954, thoughts of all the dead of ten years ago, his own brother to whom he had been very close, shock at Hoeffer's suicide, and dismay at the news which Hoeffer brought, a sense of failure, a general depression. His mood must have been one of absolute hopelessness.

Otto John was once an unhappy but respected man, standing in his person for the division in the spirit of his nation under Adolf Hitler. Today he stands for an even graver split in a country already divided by occupying powers. No one knows how widespread the divided consciousness which so vexed Otto John is in West Germany nor how many potential Otto Johns there are in Bonn. The Bonn correspondent of the London *Times* expressed more clearly than the German press the fact that the case had a much greater significance than that attending the person of Otto John:

Not only in the talking with the man himself, but also in the strength of feeling one can sense behind the public interest. In less than a year and a half he has called attention to his misgivings with the state of democratic life in West Germany as well as to the impossibility of furthering the cause of reunification from East Germany. Reunification and democracy are both issues affecting him emotionally if not logically. In his varied personal protests, involving at least one flight and probably two, he may well have dramatized the inarticulate sentiments of a large number of Germans, neither in the position nor with the desire to make so sensational a contribution to public affairs. If a trial is held, it will be of outstanding significance to many Germans, and not least to observers of the state of German political mentality.

PART VI

The Revolt Against The Middle Class

THE REVOLT AGAINST THE
MIDDLE CLASS

To THIS point the purpose of this work has simply been to report facts and opinions as to whether and in which cases the noose of treason can justifiably be tightened. The reader can only come to a proper conclusion after the completion of the projected second part of this inquiry, which is to deal with treason on behalf of, or in the struggle against, Communism since the Second World War.

Yet there is a generalization which can be drawn from the facts presented in this volume. The question to be answered is: Have we here had to do with random individual phenomena or has there been a common element? What is it which brings Ezra Pound and Count Stauffenberg between the covers of the same book? Have they anything in common? Indeed, at first glance it would appear that Pétain and Rudolf Rössler, Moltke and Quisling and Julius Leber could not have less to do with one another. The startling fact, however, is that when one examines their aims, their deeds and their ideas in terms of the society which they faced, there is a remarkable degree of similarity. This is the more striking since the individuals herein described did not act in concert—were even unaware of one another's existence. The farmer notices these spots in the field he has sown with a single species of seed; unexpected varieties may have come on the wind from far away.

The principal prerequisite for the development of the contemporary "Landscape of Treason" was the metamorphosis of the European world caused by the French Revolution and its spreading the philosophy of the Enlightenment. It identified the people as the state, fostered the development of nationalism, and under-

347

mined the unifying force of religion. It had been a religious principle which was the focus of loyalty. The tidal wave which crashed over Europe in the years after 1789 flooded every nook and cranny of European life and consciousness. In one place it simply washed away established institutions. In another it seeped into cellars and rotted the walls until the institutions fell of their own weight. Crowns toppled. The clanging of the fall was loudest where the regimes had been stiffest. When the Habsburg and Ottoman empires sank under the burden of their own decay at the end of the First World War, the last supranational structures based on personal loyalty disappeared. With them, the wave had washed to the eastern border of Europe.

Domestic dissolution of old forms was followed by social leveling and technical simplification. In Europe, the replacement of the human foot by the objective-scientific metric system and the abolition of hereditary orders and distinctions were expressions of this change. One no longer wore the habit of one's trade or calling. Healthy common sense was now to be the arbiter of society and politics, and each person was assumed to be capable of exercising his reason, assuming proper environment and education, which reason was thought to be uniform and divisible. The man of the middle would achieve perfect interchangeability and society would hum with the smooth perfection of a functioning, frictionless machine. These tendencies under the Holy Trinity of capitalism, bourgeoisie and natural science are well known. Aldous Huxley's *Brave New World* was a prophecy of developments in the sign of science—confirmed in the three decades since his book was published. Stalin's system, partly also that of National Socialism, accelerated the democratic-totalitarian process, and was described in Orwell's *1984*.

During its course, this development produced an offshoot which arose from the insight, soon gained, that the initial assault on the remnants of the medieval order and privileges had not produced the bourgeois unitary man. Another class lurked beneath the surface of bourgeois life. It contained the mass of men without collars, the men without heritages and often without independent existences. The scientific, technical and sociological developments began to merge, about the turn of the century, with a different stream: the rationalist, automatic, pragmatism of American capitalism. Specialization in activity, direction from impersonal authority, and compression in great urban beehives produced a phenomenon known as the atomization of society, long before the atom itself was split. Nothing reflects the atomized modern consciousness more accurately, and is in consequence more hated, than modern painting.

With a few exceptions such as Tokyo Rose, who belongs to the new relationship between America and Asia, most of the accused studied in this book belonged to this large countertendency which manifests itself in single uncoordinated waves. Goerdeler is one of the exceptions. His national conservatism has its roots in the Enlightenment. Some of the members of the "Rote Kapelle" do not belong to our counterwave. They are examples of the transition from the national French Revolution to the international Marxist revolution, and as a consequence also of the transition from national to abstract ideology. Old as the wave of progress and of development may be, the counterwave has been there from the beginning. However, its adherents always had more difficulty in expressing their ideals, for they were always in danger of either becoming reactionary themselves, or being misused by the reactionaries. As long as the wave was confined to pure thinking, was called enlightenment, and was preparing the rule of pure reason, the countermovement was represented by Johann Gottfried Herder and his adherents in the Sturm-und-Drang movement. It is no mere chance that it was possible to show a kinship in the works of Ezra Pound with those of Herder. After the revolution, the Romantic Movement took up the resistance. In our century of materialism it was centered in what Hugo von Hofmannsthal called the "conservative revolution"—a movement which does not try to return to what was of value in the past, but ever to renew the forces of what remains essential at all times.

What were the points upon which most of the men studied in this book would seem to have agreed? All opposed the prevailing

349

TREASON IN THE TWENTIETH CENTURY

forms of rule developed by the middle class in the nineteenth and twentieth centuries. They did not believe in "progress" and the absolute sovereignty of reason. They hated the power of money in daily life and the suppression of individuality involved in the average factory or office existence. However, they split sharply on what to do about these things. Some sought to return to the *ancien régime,* while others forged ahead, in varying degrees conscious of the fact that they would have to pass a zone of nihilism before reaching their targets. Age alone was not the determinant. Among the younger men were many who looked solely to the past, while several of the older men were pushers and strugglers. Others were divided in their wishes: their hearts drew them into the past; their reason drove them into the future.

The degree of agreement is surprising. Both Marshal Pétain and General Beck declared that the word "revolution" did not have a place in their vocabularies. Beck spoke at the very time when he was assuming the leadership of an underground movement, the success of which would most certainly have unleashed a revolution, though perhaps of restoration. Pétain made his remarks during the dog days of 1940, just before he came to power under the banner "Révolution Nationale." Leber hoped to abolish property as the basis for all social valuations, while Father Delp collided with the Social Democrats whom he charged with perpetuating thinly veiled bourgeois ends. Rössler and Schnieper were against the role of money in the contemporary economic system. Heinz mocked his fellows "scrambling for pennies around their troughs." Ezra Pound worked out monetary theories to do away with capitalism. In their youth, many of the Vichy officers had been disciples of Marshal Lyautey, who had demanded that soldiers become independent of the power of money.

There were other parallels in their attitudes toward parliamentary democracy. Quisling wanted to abolish it. Joyce despised it. The Kreisau Circle was determined to prevent its return, at least in the Weimar form. Stauffenberg rejected the "egalitarian fallacy." Leber struggled against the bureaucracy of

350

his party, which stifled all personal iniative. Laval resigned from the Social Democratic Party and, in doing so, declared that the only deputies who were worth anything at all were those who remained true to their constituencies regardless of how many times they might, as a result, have to switch political labels. Laval is, however, an excellent example of how discordant and diverse the opposition to the bourgeois world is. Despite his contempt for the bourgeois standards of value, Laval was emotionally tied to them; he only wished to put order and sense into their worship forms, and praised the Revolution's famous maxim "Enrichessez-vous." In so far as his will was directed toward the future, it was sheer opportunism. Leopold of Belgium bound the past to the present, too, but in a different way. He sought ways to adapt the inherited forms of sovereign responsibility to fit the time of the industrial proletariat in which he lived.

The parallels can be multiplied endlessly. They are all, it seems to me, signs of an uncoordinated stream which breaks into the open at certain points only. It bears atheists, Marxists, Christians and agnostics on its currents, but somehow does not always bear them sufficiently far from their points of origin to free them entirely from all traces of their original convictions. That is the reason why they have difficulties in recognizing each other by ignoring the remaining differences. One fights against the depersonalizing force of the technical world, another against corruption, the third against the dictatorship of what seems to be the free reign of public opinion or against the division between the paragraphs of law and life as it is lived.

Another parallel is that between Vichy and the German resistance, in respect to the distinction between the old and the young. In the immediate circle around Pétain were several outspoken reactionaries: the Monarchist Weygand, who called the government of the Third Republic "ephemeral"; the prime mover of the new order under Pétain, Alibert, of whom the then Minister of the Interior Peyrouton remarked: "That was a man of another age. . . . He thought, spoke and lived in the style of the ordinances of the Monarchy." The body of thought which formed the basis of the Vichy regime had two origins. One, the older, dated back to the era before the First World War in the group about the "Action Française," consisting mainly of Charles Maurras, Jacques Bainville, Leon Daudet and Henri Massis. The group distinguished a *"pays réal"* which they intended to restore, and a *"pays légal,"* that is, the Third Republic, which they wanted to destroy. The "true country" was to have a hereditary leadership which would be independent of political party and private interest. The "natural communities" would achieve their just share in the Commonwealth through a radical decentralization of the state power. The provinces were to regain their autonomy, and the professional orders and estates were to be restored. In this way all Frenchmen, instead of the "irresponsible parliamentarians," would themselves preserve their own freedoms. The second source which appeared between the wars was called "personalism." It had no central focus and cannot be discribed in an entirely systematic way. It included Left-Wing Catholics of the stamp of Emmanuel Mounier, publisher of the magazine *l'Esprit,* and Right-Wing radicals like Thierry Maulnier. Regardless of whether they stood on the Right or the Left, they wanted to dismantle the large party organizations, and demanded, as Georges Izard expressed it in 1932 in *Nouvelle Revue Française,* that "power be near the human being who is ruled, that servitude to a center be abolished, that the essential part of politics be confined to the homes and places which people love, and that citizens be asked to decide only on those questions about which they know more than the others."

The relationship between these ideas and those of the Kreisau Circle is clear. The question, so hotly and excitedly debated in France, as to whether the "Révolution Nationale" was a purely French or a Nazi-inspired movement, is really quite beside the point. It is best to say that as a movement it belongs somewhere in the larger context of the various revolts and protests against the rule and domination of the middle class. There is no profit in trying to classify too sharply streams of thought so shapeless and fed by so many springs. As a result, the multi-

352

plicity of the forms of treason in our age tend to defy classification. The forces which drove the actors are not always clear. Some appear radically new and yet lie within the long shadow of the past. The tragedy of the fanatical old man, Charles Maurras, was that he hated the Third Republic and the Germans with equal passion. He lived through a "divine surprise" when the victory of the detested foreign enemy made possible the defeat of his domestic ones. By that time, old and deaf, he could no longer see how high the price had been for his *pays réal* and what damage the Germans were doing to it.

Among the forward-looking younger groups there is scarcely one which is not more or less Socialist in outlook. Origins, backgrounds and common elements differed enormously. In the Löwenberg work camp, where Count Moltke, Reichwein and von Trotha first met, there were rival groups of the Youth Movement, Marxists, Liberals, Conservatives, students, workers, professional people and aristocrats. Their thought deviated as much from the Second and Third Internationals as it did from the traditional textbook formulations of liberalism. They rejected the class war but accepted the necessity for the complete nationalization of the basic industries. Even on this point they were less concerned about the actual physical possession of the means of production than they were about limiting the power of private industry and the uncontrolled application of capital. The teacher and close friend of the men of Kreisau, Rosenstock-Huessy, investigated the variations in collective structures involved in the theories of dualism and pluralism. Living together in groups made humanist cooperation possible between the center and the periphery, and between the generations.

The younger men were far more acutely aware of the collapse of the European claim to absolute superiority than were the older men, to whom this was a sacrosanct premise of all social thought. In their search for new ways of life, for a new picture of man, they went in different directions. But almost all try to reach the "Ur," the elementary forces that lie at the root of all historical materializations. Knut Hamsun, older than the oldest reaction-

353

ary, embodied the "Urmensch" in his very person. D. H. Lawrence's entire work is nothing but the obsessive drive to return to some assumed basic forces of nature. Restlessly moving into communities only to destroy them by his departure, wandering the face of the globe, Lawrence paradoxically sought the new in that which was oldest, in the primitive confrontation between man and the sun, between man and woman, and between man and myth. On the exact other wing were the French "technocrats," T. E. Lawrence and Ernst Jünger, who believed that through working on and with machines man might liberate himself from the anarchy of Liberal freedom, with its purposelessness, and create a new community. This vision of a fusion of nature and construction, of the organic and the mechanical world, was nullified as soon as it became clear what could happen when the mechanism was forced into the service of an antihuman totalitarianism. But Jünger and T. E. Lawrence had other ideas as well. During his long years in the desert, Lawrence had learned how very much it meant to the Bedouins that England was ruled by a king. "It reassured them to know that the highest place in my country was neither the prize of service nor the goal of ambition." In his *Der Arbeiter,* Jünger played with "the natural relation to poverty," which is given to soldiers, priests, scholars and artists. Pain became for Jünger a recognizable point of human existence from which fruitfulness springs. Poverty, rank and heredity have absolute worth in his terms, forgotten in an age which saw competition as the only necessary and sufficient cause for human activity. It was irrelevant whether the competition had taken the Western form—that is, for profit —or the Eastern form of struggle for fulfillment of goals within the planned economy. In a world where performance is the only thing that counts, the "man without characteristics" has the best chance of success. These groups wanted to regain access to the buried sources of creativity.

Under the prevailing conditions, the only way out could be to revolt against the dominance of reason. Yet that very revolt makes it hard for the student to understand it, because the individuals concerned placed all their faith in unsystematic a priori insights which they chose to explain, at best, in symbols. The verbal expressions are pitifully insufficient in most cases, and if we think that they are serious, we have no choice but to wander around the world of image and design which they have constructed, hoping now and again to find a clue.

The word "love" cropped up unexpectedly in the sentences quoted from Izard a little earlier. Izard meant love, and not loyalty, patriotism or national discipline. The use of the word in political discussion is itself new and suggests that the door to theology has been set ajar. In the beginning of our century it was old-fashioned to believe in God; by the middle of it, it has become old-fashioned not to. From Nietzsche to Heidegger, the old cry, "God is dead," rang out. Nietzsche drew a line under a completed intellectual balance, while Heidegger begins at that point his search for a new relation to the transcendental. This is incidentally another of those points at which the various groups suddenly come together, though the differences and contradictions remain great. Of course there were those who had never lost their God, and among them the older men for whom he was the prop and stay of the *ancien régime*. But men like the Kreisauers had found a transformed concept of God in their inherited Christian tradition. The theologian Dieter Bonhoeffer, one of the men of the 20th of July and one of its casualties, wrote that: "In the secular world of today, man will have to come of age in his relations with God." On the other side there is the group which only came to the conclusion that God is a necessity on the force of their own experience and long thought. Ernst Jünger, who accompanied all these movements, changes and defeats as an observer and chronicler, is one of them. Instead of the egalitarian ideal of the French Revolution, with its interchangeable Everyman, he pleads for equality before a higher principle when he demands to differentiate between the people and the state:

We face the task of filling the old word '*Volk*' with new meaning. The past cannot relieve us of it, although the way in which our work-a-day

355

world has progressed has made the job oddly easier than in the uncontested reign of individualism in the nineteenth century. Without theological help, however, it won't be solved. Through theology alone can man recognize his neighbor, his truly free, genuinely equal companion. Through theology alone can he find release from the bondage of his awful isolation from which the smoking pyres and torture chambers of our century have grown.

The horrors of our times, concentration camps with their unimaginable sufferings, the dreadful dullness of endless years of misery, fear and privation, became for a few the settings for the rediscovery of God. In some cases He had shed his Christian garb and was no longer even a purely personal God. But there is one thing they all have in common, even an old man like Pétain, and that is a belief which contradicts the claim that happiness is one of the fundamental rights of man. They are convinced that suffering brings merit and that sacrifice, even if it seems meaningless at the moment, is never offered in vain. In their acceptance of insecurity especially, the younger ones found an unexpected source of strength and an unsecular kind of security which may be interpreted with different expressions: confidence in providence; belief in fate; or awareness of heavenly guidance.

In her brilliant book, *The Meaning of Treason,* Rebecca West develops the idea that in two thousand years of our visible history we have completed a circle. At the time of Christ, the economic needs and desires of man were expressed in theological terms simple enough to be grasped by the simplest of men and capable of participation by the whole community. Two thousand years later, just the reverse is true. Religious needs and desires are discussed as if they were economic or social. Men rarely realize when they are fighting about theology. The movement, in which a good many of the accused described in this book had a part, may represent what is just the beginning of an attempt to release from his entanglement in economic and political categories of thought, man, secularized, but still far from reasonable after two thousand years of history. Because men are different today

356

from what they were in the Middle Ages, and because they are beginning to charge away from the so-called Modern Era, the way to the rediscovery of their souls and subconscious have changed. Realist politicians like Laval, activists like Schulze-Boysen, idealists like Harnack, were hardly aware of these changes. Eccentrics like Joyce and Quisling saw them through veils of romanticism. But Anne Morrow Lindbergh's *The Wave of the Future* was alive in all those who had already realized some "wholeness" in their own person. For them politics was but one part of a larger entirety, not something to be spurned or despised, but just part of a bigger job.

This stream of thought, hardly definable, succeeded nowhere. It cannot justly be called a movement although it appeared here and there in shoots, in missed opportunities and in falsifications of its real meaning. It is hard to catch, and impossible to judge. We, of course, stand in its very midst and have some difficulty in seeing it. The future may well decide that one or two of the traitors in this book were actually voices crying in the wilderness, precursors of a great bend in the flow of history. The heretics were burned and anathematized by their contemporaries, yet for us they are the heralds of a new era in European history. Even after the short lapse of time since they were tried, it is apparent that they were not isolated figures, but had ties and bonds to one another, ties of which they themselves were most often unaware.

There is much to indicate that the "heretics" described in this book may themselves be the heralds of another great historical swing of the pendulum; that they may be in the vanguard of a reaction against the great heresies of the sixteenth and seventeenth centuries. There is good reason to be cautious before passing judgment on the people described in this book. Before we do that, we ourselves have much to think about.

BIBLIOGRAPHY

THE theme "treason" is not easily included in the traditional scientific divisions to which we are accustomed. It concerns several different disciplines: history, political science, constitutional law, sociology, depth psychology and others. In the present work, which is the first attempt to study the phenomenon in its entirety, several aspects have only been touched on briefly—the legal aspect, for example. Unfortunately the same treatment has been necessary in respect to psychology. It is particularly important that treason and the deepest motives of the actors be examined by competent psychiatrists and psychologists. I have merely pointed to interesting possibilities here and there.

The major part of the material discussed in this volume has never been assembled in book form. Most of it has been collected by assiduous study of German and foreign newspapers, magazines, periodicals and pamphlets. What is available is listed below.

GENERAL WORKS

ABRAHAMSEN, DAVID: *Men, Mind and Power.* Columbia University Press, 1945.

CAMUS, ALBERT: *Actuelles, Chroniques. 1944–1948, 1948–1953.* Paris, 1950 and 1953.

GUARDINI, ROMANO: *Das Ende der Neuzeit.* Hess, Basle, 1950.

HEUSS, THEODOR: *20 Juli 1944. Ansprache am 19. Juli 1954 in der Freien Universität Berlin.* Privatdruck.

KUTEMEYER, WILHELM: *Die Krankheit Europas. Beiträge zu einer Morphologie.* Suhrkamp, Frankfurt, 1951.

NAUMANN, HANS, *Zur Soziologie des Verrats. Nacht-Studiosendung.* Freier Sender, Berlin, 1. VII, 1955.

ROSENSTOCK-HUESSY, EUGEN: *Die Europäischen Revolutionen und der Charakter der Nationen.* Kohlhammer, Stuttgart, 1951.

SCHNEIDER, REINHOLD: *Verhüllter Tag.* Cologne 1954.

THERIVE, ANDRE, *Essai sur les trahisons; Préface de* RAYMOND ARON. Calman-Levy, Paris 1951. Essays on the topic by RAYMOND ARON and THERIVE in *"La Table Ronde," "Écrits de Paris," "Confluentes."*

WEIZSACKER, VIKTOR VON, *Begegnungen und Entscheidungen.* Köhler. Stuttgart, 1949.

WEST, REBECCA, *The Meaning of Treason.* Macmillan. London, 1952.

WEYL, NATHANIEL, *The Battle Against Disloyalty.* Crowell. New York, 1951.

COLLABORATION

ARON, ROBERT, *Histoire de Vichy. 1940–1941.* Arthème Fayard. Paris, 1954.

BARADUC, JACQUES, *Tout ce qu'on vous a caché.* L'Elan, Paris, 1949.

CHURCHILL, WINSTON, *The Second World War.* Cassell. London, 1948–1954.

FABRE-LUCE, ALFRED, *Une tragédie royale. L'affaire Léopold III.* Flammarion. Paris, 1948.

————, *Le mystère du Maréchal. Le procès Pétain.* Paris, 1945.

DE GAULLE, CHARLES, *Mémoires de guerre. I: L'appel. 1940–1942.* Collins, 1955.

HUBATSCH, WALTHER, *Die deutsche Besetzung von Dänemark und Norwegen.* Muster-Schmidt. Göttingen, 1952.

JAFFRE, YVES-FREDERIC, *Les Derniers propos de P. Laval. Recueillis par son avocat.* André Bonne. Paris, 1953.

LAVAL parlé. Editions du Cheval Ailés et de la Librairie Charles Béranger. Paris, 1948.

LEAHY, WILLIAM, *I Was There.* McGraw-Hill. New York, 1950.

MICHEL, PAUL LOUIS, *Le Procès Pétain.* Paris, 1945.

NOACK, ULRICH, *Norwegen zwischen Friedensvermittlung und Fremdherrschaft.* Verlag Aufbau der Mitte. Krefeld, 1952.

PUCHEU, PIERRE, *Ma vie.* Amiot Dumont. Paris, 1948.

REYNAUD, PAUL, *Au coeur de la mêlée.* Flammarion. Paris, 1951.

SCHMIDT, PAUL, *Statist auf diplomatischer Bühne 1923–1945.* Athenäum-Verlag, Bonn, 1949.

SCHWOB, ANDRE, *L'affaire Pétain. Faits et documents.* Deux Rives. Paris, 1944.

SPEARS, SIR EDWARD, *Assignment to Catastrophe. II. The Fall of France.* Heinemann. London, 1955.

VOGT, BENJAMIN, *Quisling. The Man and the Criminal.* The American-Scandinavian Review. XXXV. 3. 1947.

WEYGAND, GENERAL, *Rappelé au service.* Flammarion. Paris, 1950.

PROPAGANDA

GRODZINS, MORTON, *Americans Betrayed. Politics and the Japanese Evacuation.* University of Chicago Press. 1949.

HAMSUN, KNUT, *Auf überwachsenen Pfaden.* List. Munich, 1950.

————, MARIE, *Der Regenbogen.* List. Munich, 1954.

————, TORE, *Mein Vater.* List. Leipzig, 1944.

DE MENDELSSOHN, PETER, *Der Geist in der Despotie.* Herbig. Berlin, 1953.

POUND, EZRA, *The Pisan Cantos.* New Directions Books. 1948.

RESISTANCE

ABSHAGEN, K. H., *Canaris, Patriot und Weltbürger.* Stuttgart, 1949.

BECK, LUDWIG, *Studien.* Stuttgart, 1955.

BIBLIOGRAPHY

BERNSTORFF, ALBRECHT, *In Memoria.* Private edition, Helmut Küpper.

BONHOEFFER, DIETRICH, *Widerstand und Ergebung.* Munich, 1951.

DULLES, ALLEN W., *Germany's Underground.* New York, 1947.

FLICKE, W. F., *Spionagegruppe Rote Kapelle.* Kruezlingen, 1954. (This book ought not to be regarded as a reliable source work. The names in it are coded, e.g. Müller-Boyd for Schulze-Boysen, Grauhoff of Kuckhoff, and much has been treated with considerable poetic lincense. It does, however, give the reader an exact insight into working procedures, coding and decoding methods of the various information and espionage services.)

FOERTSCH, HERMANN, *Schuld und Verhäangnis.* Stuttgart, 1954.

GISEVIUS, HANS BERND, *Bis zum bitteren Ende.* Zurich, 1946.

GOLLWITZER, KUHN AND SCHNEIDER, *Du hast mich heimgesucht bei Nacht* (You Pursued Me by Night). Munich, 1954.

HAFFNFR, SEBASTIAN, *Beinahe.* A History of the 20th of July, 1954, in *Neue Auslese,* Jahrgang 2, Heft 8.

HARNACK, AXEL VON, *Arvid und Mildred Harnack.* Appeared in *Die Gegenwart,* 2 Jahrgang, Heft 1/2.

HASSEL, ULRICH VON, *Vom anderen Deutschland.* Zurich, 1946.

HEUSS, THEODOR, *The 20th of July, 1944.* An address delivered at the Free University of Berlin, on July 19, 1954. Privately printed.

KIESELMANNSEGG, GRAF, *Der Fritsch-Prozess* 1938. Hamburg, 1949.

KIESEL, GEORG. The SS Report on the 20th of July, appeared in *Nordwestdeutsche Hefte.* 1947, 1/2.

LEBER, ANNEDORE, *Das Gewissen Steht Auf.* Berlin, 1954.

————, JULIUS, *Ein Mann Geht seinen Weg.* Berlin, 1952.

Lettere di condannati a morte della Resistenza Europea. Milan, 1954.

MICHEL, KARL, *Ost und West, Der Ruf Stauffenbergs.* Zurich, 1947.

MOLTKE, HELMUTH, J., COUNT VON, *Letzet Briefe.* Berlin, 1951.

The Parliament, Bonn, Special Number of 20th of July. 1952.

PECHEL, RUDOLF, *Deutscher Widerstand.* Zurich, 1947.

POELCHAU, HAROLD, *Die letzten Stunden.* Berlin, 1949.

REICHWEIN, ADOLF, *Blitzlicht über fernem Land.* Berlin.

RITTER, GERHARD, *Carl Goerdeler und die deutsche Widerstandsbewegung.* Stuttgart, 1954.

ROTHFELS, HANS, *The German Opposition against Hitler.* Hinsdale, 1948.

SCHLABRENDORFF, FABIAN VON, *Offiziere gegen Hitler.* Zurich, 1946 and 1951.

WEISENBRON, GUNTHER, *Der lautlose Aufstand,* Hamburg, 1953.

WHEELER-BENNETT, J. W., *The Nemesis of Power.* London, 1953.

ZELLER, EBERHARD, *Geist der Freiheit. The 20th of July.* Munich, 1954.

ESPIONAGE

The literature on the 20th of July, 1944, contains many references to the theory and practice of espionage, to which the following should be added:

DIELS, RUDOLF, *Der Fall Otto John,* Göttingen, 1954.

FLICKE, W. F., *Agenten Funken Nach Moskau.* Kreuzlingen, 1954. (*Cf.* the comments made in the section above about Flicke's book on the "Rote Kapelle.")

FOOTE, ALEXANDER, *Handbuch für Spione.* Darmstadt, 1954.

JOHN, OTTO, *Ich wählte Deutschland.* Berlin, 1954.

THE UNCOORDINATED STREAM

See the works under the heading "General" in the first part of the bibliography, to which the following may be added:

BERGGRAV, EIVIND, *Der Staat und der Mensch.* Hamburg (no year).

JUNGER, ERNST, *Rivarol,* Frankfurt, 1956.

MOHLER, ARMIN, *Die konservative Revolution in Deutschland,* 1918, bis 1932. Stuttgart, 1950.

ROSENSTOCK-HUESSY, EUGEN, *Der unbezahlbare Mensch.* Berlin, 1955.

INDEX